SAYYID QUTB AND THE ORIGINS
OF RADICAL ISLAMISM

JOHN CALVERT

Sayyid Qutb and the Origins of Radical Islamism

Columbia University Press
New York

Columbia University Press
Publishers Since 1893
New York   Chichester, West Sussex
Copyright © John Calvert, 2010
All rights reserved
Printed in India

Library of Congress Cataloging-in-Publication Data

Calvert, John.
    p. cm.
ISBN 978-0-231-70104-4 (alk. paper)
1. Qutb, Sayyid, 1906-1966. 2. Islamic fundamentalism—Egypt.
3. Jam'iyat al-Ikhwan al-Muslimin (Egypt) 4. Islam and state—Egypt.
I. Title.

BP80.Q86C35 2010
320.5'57092—dc22

                    2009051954

∞

Columbia University Press books are printed on permanent and durable acid-free paper. This book is printed on paper with recycled content.
Printed in India

c 10 9 8 7 6 5 4 3 2 1

CONTENTS

A NOTE ON TRANSLITERAT

For the most part, I have used a simplified version
transliteration adopted by the *International Journa*
Studies. I use the diacritic (') for the Arabic consonar
or *'ulama*, and (') for *hamza*, the character that repre
stop, as in *Shi'r* . I have not employed the subscript dia
I assimilated the *l* of the definitive article *al-* to the f
nant. *Ta marbuta*, signifying feminine singular endings,
a terminal "a"; the adjectival *-ya* followed by *ta marb*
-iyya. I have generally transcribed proper names acc
system of transliteration, the primary exception being '
which follows the relatively established rendering o
English. I provide initial references to Arabic books in
and English translation. Thereafter, I use the English tra

PREFACE

My first "encounter" with Sayyid Qutb occurred, appropriately enough, in Egypt, where I studied Arabic at the American University in Cairo in the late 1980s. I had arrived in Cairo as an aspiring mediaevalist, intent on investigating the history and culture of the Mamluks. Soon enough, however, the pulse of contemporary history took hold of me, nudging the mediaeval dynasties to the periphery of my academic interest. In those days, trouble was brewing in Egypt. Seven years after the Jihad Group assassinated Egyptian President Anwar Sadat, militant Islamist organizations were again on the prowl, especially in the middle and southern regions of the country, and Sayyid Qutb's name was in the air. At that point, I did not know much about Qutb or his influence on the modern *jihadi* trend. It was only after I began talking with knowledgeable people, poked around the sprawl of Cairo's bookstalls, and read Gilles Kepel's *The Prophet and the Pharaoh*—a pioneering work on Egyptian Islamism—that the importance of the man came home to me. I thought that here is somebody worth studying—a man who drew upon the hallowed corpus of the Islamic heritage in order to craft a vision of life and governance ostensibly different from that currently in place.

I did not know it at the time, but that initial spark of interest marked my transition from mediaevalist to student of modern history, and signalled years spent in the company of Sayyid Qutb's written work. This book, then, is the fruit of my efforts to understand the evolution of the thought of one of the most significant figures of radical Islamism. But beyond Qutb's influence on Islamism, what was it about him that intrigued me? I came to the subject prior to 9/11, so I was not motivated to study him in the light of bin Laden and al-Zawahiri, as so many have been. Looking back, I think I was fascinated, and unnerved, by Qutb's ideological certainty—his conviction that there is in the universe an objective truth holding answers to all of life's quandaries, which people are obliged to realize in the here and now, forcefully if necessary. As someone possessed of a liberal and questioning attitude, at least on most matters, I was interested in discerning the circumstances and motivations that might lead a person, such as Qutb, to struggle and sacrifice at the altar of an abstract, encompassing idea.

Certainly, Qutb was not alone in espousing ideological certainty. From the nineteenth century to our own time, numerous leaders and followers—adherents of Anarchism, Communism, Nationalism, and Imperialism—have laid claim to truth in attempts to realize utopian dreams or manifest destinies, usually with harmful consequences. In the 1950s, as the Cold War unfurled, Eric Hoffer famously referred to such people as "true believers"—individuals who "plunge headlong into an undertaking of vast change". Qutb was not quite the impetuous fanatic that Hoffer had in mind. His staunch morality propelled but also mollified his ardour, to the extent that many Muslims who are in no way attracted to radical causes—in other words, the vast majority of Muslims in the world—will read aspects of his works for benefit. Yet there is no denying the fact that Qutb, gripped by the design of the universe, was driven by the belief that he was defending God's absolute truth against the apparent barbarism of the modern world. Ultimately, then, I wanted to know how, why, and to what effect, Qutb transformed the ritualistic and latitudinarian faith that he had inherited from his father into a political discourse of opposition.

Because this project has evolved over a long period of time, I have many people and institutions to thank. I have benefited from various forms of support provided by Creighton University, including a Summer Faculty Research Fellowship that allowed me to return to Egypt to consult journals and archival materials. I owe a debt to Creighton's Reinert-Memorial Alumni Library, especially to Lynn Schneiderman, its inter-library loan specialist. I owe special debts to a number of scholars whose influence, either direct or indirect, permeates this work. Issa J. Boullata, Emeritus Professor of Islamic Studies at McGill University, guided my first excursions into the thought-world of Sayyid Qutb. I am grateful to him for his expert advice on textual sources and interpretive schemes. One could not ask for a better mentor. From Adnan Musallam I gained an understanding of the pre-Islamist phases of Sayyid Qutb's career. William Shepard, the doyen of Qutb scholars, aided me in making sense of the transitions in Qutb's Islamist thought, and was always quick to respond to my queries. I thank both of these scholars for paving my way. Over the years, Joel Gordon has been willing to share with me his deep knowledge of modern Egyptian history and culture and to offer feedback on some of my articles relating to Qutb; for all of that I am most grateful. I benefited immensely from the helpful insights and pointers of Thomas Hegghammer who read and commented on the manuscript. This study is all the stronger for his sage advice. Rasheed El Enany, Leon Carl Brown and Ahmed al-Mansoori shared with me articles, insights and documents relevant to the topic. I thank them for their generosity. I have also benefited from the assistance of Musa al-Hindi, Selwa Nasser, Mohammed Hagona, and Nasser Alsharif, especially in matters pertaining to Arabic. I thank Syracuse University Press for allowing me to incorporate into this study passages from Sayyid Qutb's *A Child from the Village*, which I translated, edited and introduced with William Shepard. I am most grateful to Michael Dwyer of Hurst & Co. for his unflagging interest in the project and his gentle yet persistent goads for me to get the manuscript done. Many thanks, also, to Jonathan Derrick and Daisy Leitch at Hurst, for their careful readings of the text. Needless to say none of the above is responsible in any way for errors and shortcomings in the book that may remain.

My most profound thanks are due to my family, which has supported my rather arcane academic interests and endeavours over the years. My parents, Jack and Jean Calvert, encouraged me at an early age to follow my muse. Ultimately, this book springs from their good parenting. My wife Im and my son Sean were bulwarks of support over the writing of the manuscript, even when I disappeared for long periods to write at my basement desk, or stared into space at the dinner table, contemplating this or that aspect of Sayyid Qutb and his cultural milieu. Clearly, Im and Sean put up with a lot. It is to them that I dedicate this book.

INTRODUCTION

Who was Sayyid Qutb?

This is a book about Sayyid Qutb (1906–66), the influential Egyptian ideologue of Islamism. It traces the development of Qutb's worldview from his village childhood up to his execution at the hands of Egypt's 'Abd al-Nasser regime. In so doing, it pays attention to the gamut of influences—cultural, political, social and economic—that shaped his discourse on the role of Islam in the state and society.[1]

Scholars, journalists and other observers generally credit Sayyid Qub with formulating the theoretical bases of Islamism in the post-colonial Sunni Muslim World. The judgment is valid. No other Islamist ideologue, with the possible exception of the South Asian Abu l-A'la Mawdudi (1903–79), exerted a comparable influence on the phenomenon, both in his own day and in the generations that followed. Before Qutb, Islamists such as Hasan al-Banna (1906–49), founder of Egypt's Muslim Brotherhood, had devoted the greater part of their attention to combating threats to Islam that came from outside the Abode of Islam—European imperialism, Zionism, and the Western cultural invasion. Qutb shifted the emphasis. Although he followed al-Banna's lead in condemning the West's hegemony over Muslim lands, he urged Muslims to confront what he regarded as the corrupt cultural and political foundations of their own countries. Muslims must strive, he said, to replace secular governance with God's judgment as manifested in the Shari'a. He urged Muslims in Egypt and around the world to unite around this goal.

In fact, wrote Qutb, the materialist ethos of the West had so deeply penetrated Muslims in countries like Egypt that they were no longer truly Islamic in character. Rulers had usurped the legislative prerogative that belongs to God and had thereby precipitated a condition of *jahiliyya*—"ignorance" of the divine mandate—that coursed through

1

the whole society. Nowhere in the world, Qutb intoned, did a genuine Islamic society exist. Yet, although he despaired, Qutb was not without hope. He believed that by the efforts of a "righteous remnant", a vanguard of true believers, the sovereignty of God over the earth could be restored, first among Muslims and then more expansively. Men who gave themselves wholly to the triumph of the creed should comprise the vanguard. It should begin by waging a "struggle by word of mouth, by propagation, by exposition, by refuting the false and baseless with a statement of truth proclaimed by Islam." Once the ground was prepared, the men of the vanguard should then lead others in forcefully striking at the "obstacles" in their path.[2] Only when the "idolatrous tyranny" (taghut) was overthrown would people be free to reconnect with God's universal order. As Qutb wrote in his Qur'an commentary, Fi Zilal al-Qur'an (In the Shade of the Qur'an), "Disbelief is a thick curtain. When it is dropped, nature establishes its links with the creator."[3] Qutb was under no illusions as to the difficulty of the task ahead. The struggle, he said, would be long and difficult. The vanguard would have to deal with Islam's traditional Christian and Jewish enemies, but also the legions of deceivers and hypocrites from within, the faux Muslims who fed from the troughs of Western-inspired barbarism. As the forces of the Egyptian state closed in on him, Qutb became convinced that he would not live to see the Islamic revolution and so prepared for martyrdom. In fact, Egypt's Nasser regime executed him and two of his closest companions in 1966. Today, Islamist circles revere him as an exemplary individual who sacrificed his life for the truth of God's sovereignty.

Qutb's quest for a clear alternative to the hegemonic social and political order, in combination with his call to resist the powers-that-be in the pursuit of change, qualifies him as a radical. In contrast to the reformist trend within Islamism, which has sought to implement change gradually through a campaign of hearts and minds, Qutb's writings targeted the state, insisting that the elite either conform to the precepts of Islam or step down. Yet he was late in coming to this position. During the first part of his Islamist career he was a moderate, a dyed-in-the-wool Muslim Brother who looked to politics as the appropriate means for Islamists to attain power. Only in the mid-1950s, largely in response to the Egyptian state's determined suppression of the Muslim Brotherhood, did he switch to radicalism. Consequently, Qutb's body of Islamist work spans the spectrum of Islamist positions, from reformism to revolution.

It should come as no surprise, then, that Islamists of various stripes have been attracted to different aspects of Sayyid Qutb's thought. All have found his basic position, that Muslims have an obligation to build a community based on the divinely mandated principles of compassion and respect for others, compelling. Thus, Abdallah Benkirane of Morocco's neo-conservative party al-Tawhid wa al-Islah (Unity and Reform) remembers how he was "overwhelmed" by reading Qutb's seminal tractate *Ma'alim fi al-Tariq* (*Milestones*): "Thanks to him I began to understand things. He completely changed my life."[4] In the late 1980s and early 1990s 'Ali Belhadj ('Ali Ibn Hajj), the firebrand preacher of Algeria's Islamic Salvation Front (French acronym FIS), adopted Qutb's teachings on the imperative of divine governance in condemning the state's party apparatchiks and "usurping" generals.[5] The Persian translator of Qutb's first Islamist book, *Al-'Adala al-Ijtima'iyya fi al-Islam* (*Social Justice in Islam*), published in 1949, explained his widespread appeal as due to his ability "to offer to the world Islamic issues in the style of today", as against "communism, imperialism, socialism and capitalism."[6] Rashid Ghannouchi of Tunisia's Islamist al-Nahda (Renaissance) Party recalls how after turning to Islamism in the 1960s he availed himself of the writings of its most important thinkers, especially Sayyid Qutb.[7] Shaykh Salamat Hashim (d. 2002), the leader and ideologue of the Moro Islamic Liberation Front (MILF), testified that Qutb inspired him to plant the seeds of Islamic revolution in the Bangsamoro homeland in the Philippines.[8] Jamal Khalifa, a Saudi, was a student when he first started reading Sayyid Qutb: "In '76, '77 we used to read [Qutb's books] Milestones and In the Shade of the Koran [*sic*]. So Sayyid Qutb was concentrating on the meaning of Islam that it's the way of life. It influenced every Muslim in that period of time."[9] In 1984, the Shi'i Islamic Republic of Iran honoured Qutb's commitment to Islamist revolution by issuing a postage stamp showing him behind bars at the 1966 trial during which he was sentenced to death.[10]

Qutb's popularity among Islamists is such that translators have rendered his most important works from the original Arabic into a great number of languages, including, in addition to Persian, Turkish, Malay, Urdu, English, French and German. Reflecting Islamism's current presence in cyberspace, numerous web pages and blogs reproduce his writings and proffer commentary on them.[11] These blogs are interesting as they offer insight into how young Muslims, from around the world, interact with the ideas of Sayyid Qutb. Many of Qutb's books are available for purchase through on-line vendors.

It is easy to understand the reasons for Qutb's popularity. More systematically than others before him, he established Islam as a culturally authentic, programmatic ideology at odds with the various political orders dominating the Muslim world. Against the modern-era Western hegemony, he upheld Islam not in terms of privatized religion but as a comprehensive ideological system (*nizam*) covering politics, society and the economy, which finds its form as an Islamic state. His was an ethical vision that connected Muslims to God's truth against the contingency and dross of the material world. It was also one intimately connected to the question of worldly power. According to Qutb, once Qur'anic principles are implemented in their entirety, Muslim societies will find their God-given potential and slough off the defeatism that has plagued them for the past two centuries or more. Strengthened thus, Muslims will defeat their enemies and lead humankind to a new future of prosperity, peace, and deep spiritual satisfaction.

Given Qutb's advocacy of systemic change, his influence has been strongest among Islamist militants who adopt the methods of "direct action" to bring about a theocratic state. By stressing the imperfection of man-made systems of governance, and through his advocacy of an activist approach, Qutb provided Islamist militants the justification for forcefully, even violently confronting the secular bureaucratic-authoritarian regimes of the Muslim world—what Islamists since the early 1980s have called the "Near Enemy", in contrast to the "Far Enemy", the Western foes. So for example, in the 1970s Marwan Hadid and his Syrian Muslim Brother colleagues drew upon the writings of Sayyid Qutb in launching their *jihad* against the 'Alawi–dominated Ba'thist regime in Damascus.[12] In the late 1980s and first half of the 1990s, Qutb's ideas inspired the vociferous and violent cadre of Egypt's Islamic groups (al-Jama'at al-Jihad) in their attacks on personnel and institutions connected to the Husni Mubarak government.[13] These and other Islamist revolutionaries may have taken Qutb's radical thought further in the direction of violent resistance than he would have counselled. Yet whether faithful to his strategic purpose or not, they followed the master in insisting that legitimate sovereignty belonged to God rather than to man. Given the influence that Qutb exerted over these and other Islamist activists, it is understandable that the political and religious establishments in many Muslim-majority countries regard his ideas with suspicion, loathing and fear.

Critical scholarship has been quick to recognize Sayyid Qutb's contributions to the Islamist cause. Already in 1951, three years or so after Qutb had hitched his wagon to Islamism, the American Council of Learned Societies' Near Eastern Translation Program placed his book *Al-'Adala al-Ijtima'iyya fi al-Islam* (*Social Justice in Islam*) near the top of its list of "the most significant modern works" in Arabic that should be translated.[14] Especially in the 1980s and 1990s, studies appeared that examined, in some detail, the contours of his thought and, to a lesser extent, the political and social circumstances that gave it shape. Gilles Kepel's *Le Prophète et Pharaon* (*The Prophet and the Pharaoh*, 1984), and Olivier Carré's *Mystique et politique: lecture révolutionnaire du Coran par Sayyid Qutb, frère musulman radical* (*Mysticism and Politics: A Critical Reading of the Qur'an by Sayyid Qutb, Radical Muslim Brother*, 1984), were two of the earliest of these studies. Composed in the wake of the Jihad Group's assassination of the Egyptian President Anwar Sadat, they carefully unpacked Qutb's key concepts, and in so doing paved the way for the studies that followed. These latter included books and articles by William Shepard, Youssef Choueri, Ibrahim Abu-Rabi, Ahmad Moussalli, Leonard Binder, Shahrough Akhavi, Yvonne Haddad, Muhammad Hafiz Diyab, Hilmi al-Namnan, Muhammad Tawfiq Barakat, Roxanne Euben and Emmanuel Sivan. More recently, Adnan Musallam and Sayed Khateb have produced volumes concerned with the evolution of Qutb's thought.[15] Collectively, these studies have significantly advanced our understanding of Qutb's position within the spectrum of Islamist thinkers and movements.

One of the most reliable sources on the objective aspects of Qutb's life and career comes from the pen of a strong supporter of Islamism, 'Abd al-Fattah al-Khalidi. A Palestinian who teaches the Fundamentals of Religion (*Usul al-Din*) at Jordan's al-Balqa Applied University, al-Khalidi obtained postgraduate degrees at the Imam Muhammad Ibn Sa'ud Islamic University in Riyadh, on the basis of a thesis on Qutb's life and thought; this work was published in 1991 as *Sayyid Qutb: Min al-Milad ila al-Istihhad* (*Sayyid Qutb: From Birth to Martyrdom*).[16] Despite al-Khalidi's strong partisan bias, his biography of Qutb is notable for its detail and pertinent excerpts from Qutb's vast *oeuvre*. Muhammad Qutb, Sayyid's younger brother, regards al-Khalidi's biography as "authoritative".[17] Muhammad Qutb's endorsement is perhaps not surprising given that al-Khalidi consulted him closely as he researched his topic. Indeed, his thesis gained him the congratulations of Muhammad Qutb, whom the university had engaged as a discussant for the thesis defence. Al-Khalidi says, "Muhammad Qutb's praise for my thesis made me blush."[18]

The appropriation of Sayyid Qutb

If at first Qutb was a relatively obscure figure known principally to Islamists and handfuls of scholars, things changed following the September 11, 2001 attacks on New York City and Washington. Those attacks put Qutb on the map because of the supposed sway his ideas had over the hijackers. In the aftermath of the 9/11 atrocity, commentators scrambled to piece together Al Qaeda's ideological genealogy. Leading the way in the search for origins were investigative journalists—the chroniclers of contemporary history. Often supported by major media organizations, they roamed the earth interviewing personalities connected to the story. Perhaps not surprisingly, Middle East and Islamic Studies scholars were a little to the rear. As Thomas Hegghammer explains, many of these scholars "had long shunned the study of Islamic militancy for fear of promoting Islamophobia and of being associated with a pro-Israeli political agenda."[19] Quite soon, out of the confluence of journalistic and academic efforts emerged a bevy of studies that highlighted the contributions of four key players in the unfolding of the Al Qaeda saga: Usama bin Laden, his "lieutenant" Ayman al-Zawahiri, 'Abdullah 'Azzam, who in the 1980s mobilized Muslim volunteers against the Soviet Red Army in Afghanistan, and Sayyid Qutb. Sometimes the *silsila* ("chain") extends to include Hasan al-Banna and even mediaeval figures such as the Hanbali jurist Ibn Taymiyya (d. 1328). Generally, in these studies, Qutb stands at the fore in the genealogical trail. A consensus has emerged that the "road to 9/11" traces back to him.[20] Some go so far as to conflate Qutb's identity and moral purpose directly with bin Laden and the Al Qaeda network. The popular media, especially, often portray Qutb sensationally as a "terrorist", an "Islamo-Fascist", or an advocate of murder.

Of course, not only journalists and critical scholars note Qutb's pivotal role in the formation of Al Qaeda ideology. The ideologues of Al Qaeda also explicitly recognize him as an important progenitor of the global *jihadi* cause. In his book *Fursan Taht Rayah al-Nabi* (*Knights under the Prophet's Banner*), composed in Afghanistan in the immediate wake of the 9/11 attacks, Ayman al-Zawahiri was concise in spelling out Qutb's importance: "Qutb's message was and still is to believe in the oneness of God and the supremacy of the divine path. The message fanned the fire of Islamic revolution against the enemies of Islam at home and abroad. The chapters of the revolution are renewing one day after another."[21]

Another Islamist who finds affinity between Qutb's ideas and those of bin Laden is the above-mentioned Salah 'Abd al-Fattah al-Khalidi, Qutb's Arabic biographer. In the introduction to his 2003 update of his anthology of Qutb's writings relating to the United States, al-Khalidi portrays Qutb as a prognosticator of America's current "war on Islam", including, most notably, the conflicts in Iraq and Afghanistan. According to al-Khalidi, long before bin Laden was a twinkle in the eye of Islamists, Qutb had predicted that America would bait Islam into entering in a "war of civilizations", during which it would attempt to stifle the Islamic resurgence and exploit for its benefit the petroleum resources of the Arabian Peninsula. On the scantiest evidence, al-Khalidi supposes that Qutb would have aligned with bin Laden and welcomed the 9/11 attacks on America.[22]

One cannot deny Qutb's contribution to the contemporary tide of global *jihad*. His practice of sharply distinguishing between those who uphold a true and authentic understanding of Islam and iniquitous "others", no less than his view of *jihad* as the obligatory means to eliminate obedience to anyone but God, anticipate aspects of the Al Qaeda discourse. Yet, if the Al Qaeda threat has made Qutb a household name, it has also monopolized and distorted our understanding of his real contribution to contemporary Islamism. In the search for Al Qaeda's origins, even well intentioned observers tend to focus on points of similarity between Qutb's thought and that of Al Qaeda at the expense of significant anomalies between the two. Some have even suggested that the global *jihad* has remote origins in Qutb's uncomfortable experience at a church social in the conservative town of Greeley, Colorado in the late 1940s.[23] Read backwards from the event of 9/11, these accounts enfold Qutb in the Al Qaeda mantle in an attempt to make the variegated history of the Islamic movement into a cohesive narrative. If some students of the *jihad* are careful to situate Qutb correctly in relation to Al Qaeda, still they often consign him to the position of opening act. Rarely do observers of the scene address Qutb's singularity.

Yet in resorting to short cuts, we pass over a history that is as nuanced as any other. We run the danger of succumbing to a "neo-Orientalist" trope that subordinates particulars to an essential and enduring identity, and ignores complexity in favor of simplicity. Just as it makes no sense to confuse the outlook of Hamas, an organization focused on redeeming land lost to Israel, with the pan-Islamism of Al Qaeda, so too is it unwise to assume a direct link between Sayyid Qutb and Usama bin Laden. Researchers need to study each on its own terms with reference to its distinctive environment and concerns.

This book aims to rescue Qutb from obfuscation by examining the development of his thought on its own terms and within the multiple contexts of his time. It covers much the same terrain as previous studies of Qutb but pays more attention than these to biography, social and political structures, political events and the role of culture in articulating patterns of protest and dissent. In treating these areas of concern, it attempts to understand the evolution and meaning of Qutb's ideology in the myriad details of his life. It is a study of an individual and of his times; of objective circumstance and subjective experience, and of how each influenced the other.

At the heart of the narrative is the struggle between what the Egyptian historian Tariq al-Bishri termed *al-wafid* and *al-mawruth*, that is, the imported Western values favoured by Egypt's political elite, and elements that are indigenous to Egyptian-Islamic culture.[24] The conflict engaged the literate and politically aware sectors of Egyptian society and Qutb was a key player in the drama. In following Qutb's career, this study looks at his motives for drawing upon the rich resources of the Islamic heritage and how he formulated and repackaged these in order to fashion an antagonistic discourse in relation to the political establishment. As someone who straddled the dichotomous worlds of tradition and modernity, Qutb articulated an understanding of Islam that addressed the concerns of contemporary Muslims. Adopting language, doctrines and symbols resonating primordial truths, he eventually presented Islam as a revolutionary vision geared towards restoring God's justice on earth.

'Passionate politics'

We cannot properly understand Sayyid Qutb unless we plumb the depths of his religious imagination and take seriously his ethical and moral concerns. All too often in studies of Islamism, the Islamist subjects are caricatures, treated casually as responding variously to anomie or to an ill defined quest for "cultural authenticity". As Roxanne Euben notes, scholars often understand Islamism with reference to its efficacy as a channel for material discontent, or else in terms of rational choice theory, which holds that most, if not all, forms of human activity are goal-oriented and organized around sets of hierarchically ordered preferences.There is a great deal of merit in these functionalist approaches and the present study draws upon some of them for explanatory effect. Yet, Euben continues, scholarly treatments of the phenomenon rarely acknowledge the religious motivations that drive many, if not most Islamists.[25]

It is true that some Islamists consciously manipulate religion for political ends and others, consumed with envy, are inspired to humiliate the strong. It is also true that Islamists, especially those in the ultra-radical Al Qaeda mould, are nihilists or anarchists in the style made famous by Dostoevsky. For nihilists, ends typically justify means, with conventional morality giving way to merciless purpose.[26]

Not for Qutb. For him, as for other Islamists, God is very real and very dear. In his view, humans must heed the ethical and moral demands God has placed upon them. For in submitting to God's will, people realize their potential and fulfil their destiny. Qutb wrote, "My study of the Qur'an has led me to the firm conviction that humanity will see no tranquility or accord, nor can peace, progress or material and spiritual advances be made, without total recourse to God."[27]

Qutb believed the divine message to the core of his being. Throughout his life, he was possessed of a mystical temper. It is true that he never joined the *dhikr* circles of the Sufi brotherhoods, something that Hasan al-Banna, a man of similar deep faith, was prone to do. Nevertheless, he displayed a Sufi–like disposition. In his Qur'an commentary, he repeatedly makes the point that the Qur'an speaks to the heart and the emotion rather than to the intellect. Occasionally, he says, God will reward the believer with great insight, as when, on a day of great inner temptation, he "lived for an instant in the company of the Prophet" in a "voyage of ecstasy".[28] Qutb wrote, "Beyond the visible world lies an unseen dimension which encompasses this life and the Hereafter. Man's origins extend back into the dim and distant past, and death is not the end of our perennial journey but a passing phase of a long journey that stretches to infinity."[29] Sayyid Qutb revered the Prophet Muhammad, and in the minutiae of his life he discerned the Godly template of human existence. His primary contribution to Islamic thought lay in his ability to harness this deeply felt spirituality for purposes of worldly transformation. Acutely attuned to the needs, fears and passions of the people, he worked to restore a sense of religious meaning to an immoral and disenchanted colonial world. Olivier Carré is on the mark when he says that Qutb's Islamism was born of a confluence of "mysticism and politics".[30]

Not only do we need to enter into Qutb's world of mysticism, we must also tap his emotional state, especially his simmering discontent, which often spilled over into anger. Some of his irritation was undoubtedly a product of his personality—namely, his sense of intellectual superiority and inability to suffer fools gladly. On the other hand, objective factors also spurred his annoyance, specifically, the economic injustice, political corruption, cultural degradation and domination by foreigners that were characteristic of his time and place. As we shall see, the Qur'an's deep message of social equilibrium, justice and fair dealings in human relationships organized and energized Qutb's emotions, transforming them into a plan of action. In paying heed to the affecting aspect of Qutb's discourse, we recognize the contributions of social historians and anthropologists who have emphasized the importance of emotional perception as a form of social practice with effects in the world.[31]

All of this requires that we adopt an attitude of empathy toward Sayyid Qutb—empathy, not necessarily sympathy. In opening up to Qutb's universe of thought and emotion, by affording him a degree of compassion, we become privy to the textures, feelings and imaginings that contributed to the production of his Islamism. To be sure, there is much in Qutb's thought that many, if not most, people will find disagreeable. Against a liberal view that encourages openness, mutuality and communication across group boundary lines, Qutb spoke of cultures as monolithic and static—a hard "us" vs. "them" vision of the world that encouraged the worst kind of stereotyping. Yet if the goal is to understand him, an empathetic attitude allows the researcher to penetrate the discursive wall; it encourages him or her to discern textual nuance and ambiguity and to touch on the intimate aspects of the subject's life, such as family relationships, reading habits and styles of dress, all of which can reveal much about an ideology. It enables us to enter into dialogue with the subject, to hear his voice, rather than regard his thought simply, and uncritically, as a modern pathology.

Contours of a life

Qutb's career lends itself easily to the type of contextualization here suggested. His life unfolded against the backdrop of one of the most colourful and eventful periods in modern Egyptian history, years that witnessed the full flush of the British tutelary regime, the advent of Egyptian nationalism, and the political hegemony of 'Abd al-Nasser and the Free Officers. Over the course of his adult life, Qutb rubbed shoulders with influential and interesting figures, men like Taha Husayn, Naguib Mahfouz, and Gamal 'Abd al-Nasser himself. He was a brooding, introspective man who suffered inwardly from the type of melancholia common to intellectuals living in troubled times. He fancied himself a literary type. Constantly writing, he drove himself relentlessly, taxing his feeble body to the limit. He had few close friends—his younger brother Muhammad was his only true confidant. Yet, within literate Egyptian society, many knew him. His name popped up frequently in Cairo's lively press.

Qutb did not conceive his Islamism in full form. Rather, it evolved from interests that initially had very little to do with religion. In his formative years, he was representative of the cohort of nationalist intelligentsia that emerged in Egypt in the wake of the 1919 popular uprising against the British occupation. Like his mentor, the literary figure 'Abbas Mahmud al-'Aqqad, he was originally a man of the Wafd, the mass-based nationalist party that dominated the politics of Egypt until the Free Officers' 1952 coup d'état. However, in the mid- and late 1930s Qutb became increasingly critical of the political regime, chiefly in response to its inability to resolve Egypt's problematic relationship with Britain, diminish the growing gap between rich and poor Egyptians, and effectively support the Arabs of neighbouring Palestine against the influx of Zionist settlers. In voicing his displeasure, he was typical of a generation of Egyptians who were disappointed at the failure of the nationalist movement to bear fruit. In common with other writers of the period, he directed and subsumed the chronic discontent into a coherent theory of the Egyptian nation's unique identity and relationship with other Eastern lands.

All the while, he wrote literary criticism and imaginative works. Compared with the literary luminaries of the day, his creative writing was erratic and uncertain. But he had a passion for poetry, and through it he tapped into a secondary world that existed apart from the travails of mundane society. Throughout Qutb's career, the aesthetic realm propelled him, providing teasing glimpses of a truth that lurked beyond the dross of everyday existence. His delight in art paid dividends. He was the first critic to put forward the thesis that the Qur'an's stylistic genius resided in its method of artistic representation.

Two competing tendencies, both fiercely critical of the traditional culture and each drawn from a different source, beset Egypt during Qutb's formative years. On the one hand was the Western cultural and material achievement, on the other, the pure and uncorrupted values of the nation, rooted in the traditions of the people and expressed perfectly in terms of Islam. Thus, there emerged in the 1930s and 1940s the opposition between the Westernizers and the Islamists. The struggle was similar to other cultural-political conflicts that took place in the nineteenth and early twentieth centuries, for example, that between Slavophiles and Westernizers in Czarist Russia. Whereas the Islamists believed that the revival of purified religious virtues could redeem Egypt and serve as an example to the world, the Westernizers desired to transform Egypt in the image of Europe. The contest was not absolute: Islamists conceded freely that they had much to learn from the West, especially in the realms of technological and organizational expertise; and the Westernizers were interested in maintaining the core features of Egypt's distinctive personality in relation to the Western and other nations of the world. Within each camp, also, there were numerous sub-positions and tendencies, either traditional or radical. Sayyid Qutb moved easily among these circles and debated the great issues of the day with their representatives. He held fast to his point of view, but at this stage he believed in open dialogue.

Increasingly, however, Qutb turned to the language and symbols of Islamism to voice his discontent. This change, which took place in the late 1940s, marks the second stage in the development of his thought. The transition from a scheme of freedom and fulfilment conceived in nationalist terms to one centred on Islam was easy for him; his definition of Islam as a self-contained system of ideas and practice was grafted easily onto his earlier concerns with organic romantic nationalism. In emphasizing the unique requirements of an Islamic order, he freed the nationalist discourse from its moorings in Western political concepts, which he now regarded as synonymous with European colonial domination. Additionally, his Islamism grew out of and complemented his spiritual disposition. As a "spiritually enlightened" person, Qutb believed that he saw through "the Grand Illusion" to the heart of God's truth.[32]

Qutb knew the Qur'an well, having memorized it in his youth. He had studied the Arab-Islamic heritage at Dar al-'Ulum (Teachers' Training College) and was familiar with the classics of mediaeval Islamic learning. But he had no training at a *madrasa* or other formal institution of Islamic learning. In this respect he was typical of most other Islamist thinkers, including al-Banna and those who came after him, for example, 'Abbassi Madani (b. 1931), one of the former leaders of Algeria's Front Islamique du Salut (FIS), who studied for a PhD in Britain before returning to Algiers to teach the sociology of education. Qutb's lack of Islamic scholarly credentials earned him the censure of many *'ulama* (religious scholars) who believed that his interpretations of the Qur'an broke with tradition.

Recourse to Egypt's Islamic identity allowed Qutb effectively to distinguish Islamic civilization from the colonizing "other", thus allowing Muslims a sense of being different from it. At the same time, Islam elicited in him a burgeoning religiosity rooted in sentiments of cultural pride and authenticity. Whereas the peoples of the West were de-Christianized and materialistic, the Muslims of Egypt and the Islamic East were spiritual and holistically connected to the divine order. A sojourn of almost two years in the United States on behalf of the Egyptian Ministry of Education hardened his negative views of Western civilization. However, his American study mission was not the turning point in his career that some have supposed. It reinforced, rather than initiated, his Islamist predilections.

From the mid-1930s to the early 1950s, Egypt was a country awash in ideologically articulated discontent. By then, traditional forms of protest and rebellion, organized around Sufi *turuq* (orders) and millenarian expectation, had given way to an eclectic variety of social movements, voluntary associations, freelance guerrilla groups and secret societies, which reflected the interests of new social classes caught up in radically altered political, economic and cultural circumstances. Several displayed a distinct corporatist bent in their calls for the integration of all social classes into an organically whole community. Chief among these was the Muslim Brotherhood (Jama'at al-Ikhwan al-Muslimun), the Arab world's first true Islamist organization. Amid a continuum of political assassinations, workers' strikes and street brawls, Qutb began openly to call for the creation in Egypt of an

Islamic order (al-nizam al-Islami). In spirit, he was a liberator who moved from the contemplation of the idea to dynamic activism.

At first, Qutb was an independent Islamist thinker without institutional affiliation. Only in 1953, following the Free Officers' *coup d'état*, did he join the Muslim Brotherhood; in the confused period following the fall of the Old Regime, he understood the necessity of channelling all energies into the one organization capable of realizing the creation of an Islamic state. Recognizing Qutb's talents, the Brotherhood's leadership chose him to head its Propagation of the Call Department (*Qism Nashr al-Da'wa*). In common with other Muslim Brothers, Qutb hoped, and perhaps expected, that the military men would join the historic cause of Islam's revival. When it became clear that the Free Officers did not intend to fully implement the Shari'a, relations between them and the Muslim Brothers soured. In 1954, as tensions between the two mounted, 'Abd al-Nasser proscribed the Muslim Brotherhood and imprisoned hundreds of its members, including Sayyid Qutb. Qutb's imprisonment, which lasted about a decade, was by any standards a harrowing experience. If we seek a true turning point in his life, the moment when his ideology crystallized, it was during the period of his incarceration when he suffered terrible deprivation and ill-treatment.

Qutb spent his time in prison reflecting on the events that had transpired. Prison officials granted him the opportunity to write and he spent much of his time elaborating his Islamist doctrine in light of the changed circumstances. In a spate of forcefully written "prison works", he reacted to the Free Officers' "betrayal" of the Islamist cause by equating their rule, and the global secular culture that they emulated, with the disbelief of the pre-Islamic era: just as in the pre-Islamic era, *jahiliyya* enveloped the contemporary world. In Qutb's view, however much 'Abd al-Nasser and other government heads might claim to represent their populations, their refusal to fashion a polity based solely on Qur'anic principles qualified them as usurpers of God's sovereignty. In privileging the concept of the supra-denominational nation-state, Nasserism and Arab nationalism generally were mere avatars of European discourses that put the "people" ahead of God.

For Qutb, this period was one of intense reflection during which he hardened the lines between *Hizb Allah* ("the party of God") and *Hizb al-Shaytan* ("the party of Satan"). It represents the third and most radical phase of his intellectual career. No longer did he talk about competing nations, regions or civilizations. He now preached a total and uncompromising struggle between Islam and its conceptual opposite, which must end in total victory for Islam. If there is a connection between Qutb's mature Islamism and the Al Qaeda ideology, it is here, in this existential understanding of global combat.

Released from prison in 1964, ostensibly for reasons of ill health, Qutb was shortly afterwards implicated in events—an alleged conspiracy against the government—that lead to his execution in 1966. However, his ideas lived on to inspire a younger generation of Islamist radicals. During the 1980s and 1990s, Qutb's ideological heirs attempted to topple the state regimes in Egypt, Algeria, Syria and elsewhere. In most cases the thinking of these militants, which they exposed both in writings and actions, was extreme and strayed wildly from the stated ideas of their mentor. For one thing, Qutb never would have sanctioned the killing of civilians, which several of the militant groups committed. For another, the militants went further than Qutb in casting aspersions on the fidelity of rulers and, in some cases, of general Muslim populations to Islam. Although Qutb condemned the general culture of the age as "ignorant", he avoided branding individuals *kuffar* ("unbelievers"), something that many of the radicals of the 1980s and 1990s were willing to do without compunction.

However, the efforts of these organizations to instigate revolution were unsuccessful. These failures eventually prompted one of their members, Ayman al-Zawahiri, to conceive the idea of striking the "puppet master" that sustained the "wayward" Arab regimes: none other than the United States. Such an attack, he figured, would inspire Muslims around the world and put the *jihad* on a new footing. Al-Zawahiri's bloody war against the "Far Enemy" took radical Islamism to a place that Qutb had never imagined.

Nation, revolution, and Islamism

As will become clear, Qutb's Islamism, in both its mainstream and radical incarnations, is modern and revolutionary in ways that take it well beyond the framework of a backward-looking utopia. It supplements the symbolic repertoire and rhetorical devices that were the common patrimony of pre-modern Islamic societies with styles of conceptualization appropriate for the generation of political action in a radically transformed social environment. Consequently, Qutb's Islamist ideas have as much in common with processes of systems-oriented "imagining" and "planning", characteristic of twentieth century revolutionary nationalist ventures, as with the restorative visions of premodern Muslim activists such as the Fulani Usman dan Fodio (d. 1817) or Muhammad Ahmad (d. 1885), the Sudanese Mahdi—two of the better known nineteenth century Islamic revivalists. Beneath the Qur'anic veneer of Qutb's Islamist writings resides a structural resonance with modern-era ideological currents. That is to say, Qutb imbibed and repackaged in Islamic form the Jacobin characteristics of the European revolutionary tradition.

This is nowhere more evident than in Qutb's emphasis on the relationship between ideas and practical life. In a manner reminiscent of the Young Hegelians, Qutb sought to overcome the inhumanity of the world order by merging the "Islamic conception" (*tasawwur*) into the synthesizing practice of life. In common with the ideologues of the European Left, he eschewed the validity and worth of idealist and rationalist philosophies—the inert, exclusively cerebral contemplation of ideas—in favour of the active reshaping of society. Furthermore, he believed that a new moral and material world could only come into existence through the efforts of an elite cadre of revolutionaries. In espousing this idea, he resembled the nineteenth century Russian revolutionary Chernyshevsky and, later, Lenin. Like the professional revolutionaries of the nineteenth and twentieth centuries, he was prepared to forego all enfeebling compromises in pursuance of the revolutionary idea, in his case even to the point of martyrdom.

Qutb absorbed the revolutionary discourse through osmosis. By his day, Western theories of collective assertion and national transformation were spreading through the Afro-Asian and Latin American worlds in a kind of global chain reaction against the "new imperialism"[33] of the predatory Western powers. Theories of this kind had taken hold in Old Regime Egypt. Revolution had become part of the global landscape, offering colonized and post-colonial African, Asian, and Latin American peoples new visions of their future and of community belonging.

The first two decades of the twentieth century were pivotal in this regard. In 1905, the revolutionary impulse in the Romanov realm crossed the Caucasus into Iran where it inspired an alliance of *'ulama* and reformist intelligentsia in a common effort to mobilize the popular classes against the Qajar Shah. In Mexico, a coalition of peasants and constitutionalists arose in 1910 to undermine the entrenched powers of the *latifundistas*. In 1911, Sun Yat-Sen and the Chinese "self-strengtheners" moved to overthrow the divine authority of the Manchu Son of Heaven. In the Middle East, the most significant instance of nationalist revolutionary endeavour was that undertaken by Mustafa Kemal, after 1935 known as Atatürk, whose decisive actions and daring vision succeeded by 1923 in establishing an independent Turkish nation-state. Later, in the following decade, the Indonesian Tan Malaka (d. 1949), the Indian Manabendra Nath Roy (d. 1954), Vietnam's Ho Chi Minh (d. 1969) and the Tartar Mir Said Sultangaliev (d. 1940) all adapted the powerful Bolshevik model, at least in theory, to the regional and cultural specificities of their respective countries.

Certainly, there is an overlap between Qutb's Islamist project and the revolutionary nationalist tradition. Given Qutb's involvement in Egyptian nationalism during the first part of his life, one would expect as much. As an Islamist, he discerned in the Qur'an a paradigm of action and belief, relevant to all times and places, which mirrored the nationalists' opposition to the existing colonial order. Further, he infused his Islamism with nostalgia for an earlier age of social integration and moral absolutes, in this way maintaining the nationalist endeavour to awaken community members to moral and political regeneration.

But there is also a fundamental difference between Qutb's nationalism and his mature Islamist position. Whereas, in common with nationalists everywhere, he had originally conceived the community in terms that separated law and citizenship from religion, later he was forthright in affirming the metaphysical over all aspects of worldly existence. As an Islamist, Qutb did not believe that the Islamic community (*umma*) was limited by territory, nor that it was sovereign. Rather, following the Classical Islamic jurists, he defined the "homeland" of Muslims as a "theological space"—one that was given over to the practice of Islamic life in the world. It embraced all Muslims everywhere, and should eventually include all of humanity. Instead of taking cues from the sovereign will of the people and its political representatives, Muslims were beholden to the Shari'a, the assemblage of laws, regulations and advice that guides them in their affairs, and which exists prior to and independently of them. In Qutb's mature view, all the ideologies of the West, whether they championed ethno-linguistic autonomy or, as in the case of Marxism, secular trans-nationalism, were "ignorant" and misguided in their dismissal of divine truths. Qutb's Islamism may have emerged from the matrix of Egyptian nationalism, but following a period of transition, it transcended the horizons of the nation-state to conceive Muslims as self-governing agents beholden to God's will. Seen in this light, Qutb, the Islamist, was much more than a cultural or a religious nationalist. He was at the forefront in conceiving a new moral framework for politics, one that in the present moment continues to inspire Muslim insurgents of various kinds.[34]

Even so, we must keep in mind the point already made—that Qutb shaped his Islamism in relation to contemporary realities. Thus, if Qutb conceived his prison writings as constituting a radical rupture, he deployed that claim, by default, within an existing symbolic field occupied by the nation-state. For when Qutb castigated the world order in terms suggesting rebellion against God's divine plan, he in effect defined his hoped-for new global order in relation to what had gone before. In this sense, the form of the Egyptian nation-state structured and limited Qutb's Islamist discourse, even as Qutb invented—the better to destroy—an image of the state wholly alien to the ideals he propagated.

Source material and chapter contents

Researchers are often surprised at the amount of material that exists for their projects. This was certainly my reaction as I waded into the ocean of Qutb's written work. For much of his life, Qutb was a part-time journalist, someone who could knock off a reasonably polished review piece in an afternoon. His articles, poems and essays, scattered in numerous journals, number many dozens. In addition to articles, he wrote books, including his multi-volume Qur'an commentary, *Fi Zilal al-Qur'an* (*In the Shade of the Qur'an*). In writing this book, I have drawn on as many of Qutb's writings as possible, focusing on those that are representative of his thought during the various stages of his career. English translations of several of Qutb's better-known works exist, and I have availed myself of many of these, taking care, where appropriate, to reference the Arabic originals. Adil Salahi's and A.A. Shamis's stylish English translation of Qutb's Qur'an commentary has been especially useful to me.

I have also drawn on articles and books by Sayyid Qutb's contemporaries, people like the Muslim activist Zaynab al-Ghazali, Qutb's

18

sister Hamida, and fellow Islamists like 'Ali 'Ashmawi, in addition to others who knew Qutb personally, sometimes shared his experiences, and had opinions about him. These materials have proven invaluable in fleshing out the details of Qutb's life and in illuminating aspects of his personality. Throughout I have used the Qur'an translation of Taqi-ud-Din Hilali and Muhammad Muhsin Khan (*The Noble Qur'an*, Riyadh: Darussalam, 1996), except in cases where Qur'anic quotes appear within excerpts from translations of Qutb's works.

The United States—a country about which Qutb had generally negative feelings—is home to a particularly interesting source of information relating to Qutb's career. In the summer of 1999 my friend and colleague Joel Gordon and I travelled by car across the hot prairie of Nebraska to Greeley, Colorado where Qutb had studied at the Colorado College of Education (the present University of Northern Colorado) in 1949–50. Aided by the university's librarian and Registrar, we unearthed the small cache of documents that has since become famous, at least among people interested in Islamist history. In addition to Qutb's college transcript, we found photos of him as a student there and an essay that he had written, in English, for the college's literary magazine. I have made use of these materials in reconstructing Qutb's American sojourn.

Finally, in order to gauge the social, cultural, economic and political forces that shaped Qutb's discourse, I have tapped both the vast corpus of scholarship pertaining to Egypt in the nineteenth and twentieth centuries, and select documents housed at the National Library and Archives of Egypt (Dar al-Kutub), the British Foreign Office and the US State Department. In drawing on all of these materials, I have tried to keep the focus on Qutb the person. To be sure, I discuss his ideas, but always in relation to the unfolding of his life.

The chapters that follow trace Qutb's journey to radical Islamism through the shoals and eddies of early and mid-twentieth-century Egyptian politics and culture. Chapter 1 treats Qutb's rural upbringing and his awakening to a wider world beyond the village. Here we examine the dialectic of the British-dominated Egyptian nation-state and the traditional peasant culture, which resulted in the intrusion of modernity into a world of divine order and the appearance at the local level of new forces of ideological cohesion.

Chapter 2 deals with Qutb's emergence as a literary figure and examines his early forays into the cultural politics of the 1930s. It covers his education at Cairo's Teachers' Training College (Dar al-'Ulum), his relationship with a network of Romantic poets, among them al-'Aqqad, and his growing disenchantment with the political regime and the Westernizing culture that sustained it. The chapter demonstrates that Qutb was typical of the cohort of nationalist intellectuals that emerged on the scene following the 1919 popular uprising against the British occupation.

Chapter 3 focuses on Qutb's activities over the 1940s. During this period Qutb continued his literary endeavours, including important studies of the Qur'an's literary effect, and also became a stronger advocate than before of Egyptian nationalism. The chapter goes on to discuss the reasons for Qutb's turn to Islamism in 1947–48 and analyzes his first true Islamist writing, *Social Justice in Islam*.

Chapter 4 follows Qutb as he made his way across the United States to study American curricula on behalf of the Egyptian Ministry of Education. Qutb recorded his impressions of America in letters and articles that were published in Egyptian periodicals, and the chapter draws on these to show how Qutb distinguished Islamic values from what he perceived as American materialism and atheism. The chapter makes the point that Qutb's American experience reinforced, rather than provoked, the development of his Islamist sentiment.

Chapter 5 traces the further development of Qutb's Islamist thought within the context of the political developments of the early 1950s, both within and beyond Egypt, including anti–colonial struggles for independence throughout Africa and Asia. It examines Qutb's early involvement with the Muslim Brotherhood and his troubled relationship with the Egyptian Free Officers. The chapter concludes with Qutb's arrest and imprisonment following the Free Officers' round-up of the Brothers in 1954.

Chapter 6 deals with Qutb's experience in prison and the effect it had on the development of his Islamism. Focusing on Qutb's "prison works", the chapter explains how Qutb sharpened the edges of his thought, emphasizing the chasm that existed, in his mind, between Islam and its opposite. It explores his conception of the much-contested Islamic concept of *jihad*, and examines his call for a vanguard of "true Muslims" to restore God's sovereignty on earth.

Chapter 7 covers the last years of Qutb's life, during which some of his followers established a clandestine organization aimed at reestablishing the Islamist movement in Egypt. The chapter explains how

Qutb became part of this secret organization following his release from prison, and goes on to recount his role in an alleged anti–regime conspiracy. The chapter concludes with Qutb's execution and his elevation to the status of martyr.

The book concludes with a short examination of how subsequent Egyptian Islamists took up Qutb's ideas, often giving them far more radical interpretations than Qutb would have allowed.

1

SON OF THE COUNTRY

'A world aflame with revolution'

During the months of April and May 1947, the Cairo newspaper *al-Hawadith* serialized the diary of one 'Abd al-Fattah 'Inayat, a convicted assassin recently released from prison.[1] In the first instalment of the series 'Inayat explained to his readers how, in the months following the 1919 anti–British uprising in Egypt, his eyes were "opened to a world aflame with revolution." In January 1922, "the year in which the late Saad Zaghloul Pasha [sic] was exiled," he attended a secret meeting at Cairo's Qasr al-Nil Gardens with four other youths, three secondary school students and a labourer. They intended to form an underground nationalist society. As 'Inayat tells it, the group quickly decided in favour of a direct method "in which the angel of death" would be their leader. The society would not have a leader; all members would be equally subordinate in their goal of liberating Egypt from the clutches of British imperialism. Eventually, the group comprised some twenty-five individuals organized into cells of five members each.[2]

In subsequent issues, 'Inayat related how the members would stalk unsuspecting British officials through Cairo's busy streets, awaiting opportune moments to strike. One of the first victims was the British controller of the Ministry of Education, a man infamous in nationalist circles for his autocratic style and haughty attitude towards Egyptian bureaucrats. "On a day in which the sun was at its full glory, and the light of independence invaded the darkness of occupation," the assassins struck, shooting the Englishman dead as he left his office.

Other assassinations soon followed, including an attack upon the Acting Commandant of the Cairo City Police. 'Inayat had been "astounded by this intrusive foreigner" who used to appear "in the streets of the capital riding a horse, as though he were an Emperor of the Roman Empire." After shadowing him for several days, the assassins fired five bullets into him as he returned to his Garden City apartment for his midday meal. This episode had a great effect upon the population of Cairo:

The situation was now changed and Englishmen were now afraid of Egyptians. The entire British community was talking about the danger which threatened their lives in Egypt and did not realize that, in spite of the various countries and races which have reigned over Egypt, Egyptians still remembered the past glories of the pharaohs. They have always hated oppression and will fight by every means to achieve a national and independent life.

Two years later, in November 1924, 'Inayat and his youthful colleagues assassinated the British Sirdar (Commander-in-Chief) Sir Lee Stack, an event that led to their arrest and elicited the wrath of the British government upon the entire Egyptian nationalist movement.

'Inayat passed his prison sentence in full knowledge that his efforts had come to naught. Throughout the 1930s and 1940s the British continued, as they had since the late nineteenth century, to interfere politically in Egypt's national life. Yet he did not regret taking up the gun. As a youth, he had "read the works of the heroic Moustafa Kamel Pasha [sic] and his idea that 'reputation is an additional age for man'." In the dankness of his cell, he came to understand that his revolutionary activities had gained him this "additional age". Within a socially stratified colonial context that offered limited opportunities for personal fulfilment and public recognition, 'Inayat had made his mark.

'Inayat's reminiscence points to the presence within Egypt of modern revolutionary discourse. He and his youthful colleagues are shown as men whose minds are aflame with the promise of national freedom and fulfilment. Like Prometheus, the mythical model of the social revolutionaries of nineteenth century Europe, they deliver the fire of freedom to their countrymen by means of direct action. Freedom will take root and triumph over the darkness and humiliation of foreign occupation only by their concerted effort in the material realm. Explicit in the vision of 'Inayat's society is a new world rising from the ashes of the battle its members intend to precipitate.

From his early years, Sayyid Qutb dwelt in the "dream life" of collective assertion, focusing on features common to the Jacobin traditions of the modern period. These included the enumeration of grievances based on sentiments of victimization, humiliation and oppression; the presentation of reality in terms of binary opposites— good vs. evil; the articulation of an alternative vision for the future; and the demand for action to realize this vision. All of these elements would feature prominently in Qutb's Islamism, whose remote origins go back to his boyhood in the Egyptian countryside. It is to this background that we now turn.

Musha

Sayyid Qutb Ibrahim Husayn Shadhili was born in 1906 in a village called Musha. Administratively, Musha fell within the orbit of Egypt's Asyut province (*Mudiriyyat Asyut*). Geographically, it was part of the Sa'id, the narrow strip of cultivated land, bounded by desert plateaux, which follows the course of the Nile from Aswan to near the base of the Delta. Dominating a spot on the west bank of the Nile, Musha was within a day's walk of the small city of Asyut. Until the late nineteenth century, Asyut was famous as the terminus of an ancient caravan route called the *Darb al-Arba'in* ("the Road of Forty Days") that led up from Dar Fur in the Sudan, whose chief article of trade was slaves.[3] In Qutb's day the city was a bustling centre that served the commercial and administrative needs of the surrounding districts.[4] For the inhabitants of Musha and other nearby villages, Asyut was a window on the world beyond.

There was little to distinguish Musha from the hundreds of other villages and small towns that crowded the flood plain of the Sa'id. Like these settlements, it was a community of agrarian producers although it also included a number of traders and petty merchants, many of whom were also farmers. Comprising brick and adobe dwellings of two, three and sometimes four storey, it was a relatively prosperous place. According to Qutb, each family owned a house, "whether large or small". The land, Musha's most precious commodity, was divided evenly among the principal residents, and even the poorest of the village's inhabitants enjoyed a weekly meal of meat, which still today is considered a luxury in the Egyptian countryside. Yet, the village was not uniformly comfortable. On its fringes lived an assortment of individuals who lived from hand to mouth.[5]

The essential ingredient of identity among the villagers was religion, both Islamic and Christian. The village stood near a Coptic monastery that had been prominent enough in its mediaeval heyday to merit a mention in the great topographical survey of the fifteenth century Egyptian historian Taqi al-Din al-Maqrizi (d. 1442).[6] For Qutb and other Muslims living in the area, the monastery was a tangible reminder that even after centuries of indigenous conversion and Arab-Muslim settlement, Christians continued to comprise a significant proportion of southern Egypt's population.

Musha's Muslims expressed their communal identity in the weekly congregational prayers and on feast days and, above all, in devotional activities associated with the tomb of its Muslim saint (*wali*), Shaykh 'Abd al-Fattah.[7] The tomb was a simple square structure, capped by a dome, which served as the focus of prayers for the saint's intercession with God for favours and blessings. Once a year Musha came alive in raucous celebration of the *mawlid*, the commemoration of the saint's passing from the earthly realm.

In Qutb's day, the livelihood of the region's inhabitants still largely depended on the annual inundation of the Nile, which deposited a layer of rich black earth on the surrounding fields over the late summer. The crops matured in the muted sunshine of winter until, after the harvest, the ground cracked in anticipation of the next flood.[8] The Egyptologist Barry Kemp's comments on the situation in ancient times are applicable to the period in which Qutb lived: "It was an ideal natural cycle, but one that human ingenuity could still do much to improve. Earthen banks could be raised to enclose large basins where the farmer could allow the waters to remain for a period before releasing them back to the river. Water could be raised mechanically to irrigate areas above the normal reach of the flood, or in summer, when the river was at its lowest, to irrigate fields for a second crop or to maintain kitchen gardens throughout the year."[9] The tombs and burial grounds that dot the cliff faces and barren plains of the Nile valley bear mute testimony to the myriad farming communities that have taken advantage of this fecundity since Neolithic times. Seen from the dun-hued sand and gravel of the surrounding desert, the green landscape of the Nile valley appears as a realm of life, defining the world in stark, uncompromising categories.

Qutb's father, al-Hajj Qutb Ibrahim, was a medium landowner who kept a close watch on the yield of his fields.[10] Originally the family had been well-to-do, gaining a measure of social prestige in relation to the big families that dominated the village; these latter included the Bayt-

'Abdin from amongst whom Musha's headmen ('*umad*, sg. '*umda*) were chosen.[11] However, by the time of Sayyid Qutb's birth the family's wealth had diminished, owing mainly to the splitting up of the inheritance and the financial responsibilities that devolved upon the father as the central figure within the extended family, such as the hosting of celebratory occasions and the bestowal of favours upon clients.[12] In addition, Qutb's maternal uncles had squandered portions of the family's landholdings by living beyond their means.

Qutb's father was an honourable man whose sense of obligation and magnanimity were anchored in a quiet, dignified religiosity.[13] He married twice and by his second wife, Fatima, fathered three daughters, Nafisa, Amina and Hamida, and two sons, Sayyid and Muhammad.[14] A third son died soon after birth. The earlier marriage had produced yet another son, Qutb's half brother. Anecdotal evidence scattered in Qutb's published writings suggests that while his dealings with his father were mostly formal, his relationships with his mother and siblings were close.[15]

Patrilineal kinship ties, which defined family units in relation to larger social collectivities, such as neighbourhood and village, also determined group identity. In face of strong family ties, it is not surprising that inclusion in administrative units such as Asyut province or the much larger entity of the Egyptian nation-state did not normally register in the consciousness of the villagers as meaningful or significant. If the villagers identified in supra-village terms at all, it was only vaguely and then as members of the *umma*, the worldwide community of Muslims.[16] It took an extraordinary circumstance such as the 1919 countrywide anti–British uprising to prompt even limited numbers of villagers to think in terms of their membership within the nation.

The limited availability of resources sometimes led to inter-family contention. A challenge from within the village community to a family's social standing could, and often did, lead to the outbreak of feuding (*tha'r*), which normally ended with the shedding of blood or the payment of a compensatory fee by the offending party. Qutb's extended family did not escape involvement in this form of retributive justice. In his childhood autobiography, discussed below, he recalls how assailants took their revenge on one of his uncles by poisoning and mutilating his cattle.[17] Even today, southern Egypt has a reputation among Egyptians for its relatively high incidence of vendetta killings. Yet then, as now, the demanding material conditions of village life required that the inhabitants of Musha establish ties of social solidarity. As Father Aryout remarked in his 1933 study *The Egyptian Peasant:* "When the vital interests of a village are threatened, everyone feels deeply that he is one of the community: Men, women, children all grouped together in a single force."[18] Even regarding Musha's thieves there was an ethic that looked to the wellbeing of the community. According to Qutb, thieves who robbed the weak were despised and those who robbed the rich and powerful were admired. The village mainstream delighted in the "adventures" of the thieves, viewing them as a way of restoring the social balance that the rich, through their alleged avarice, were believed to have upset.[19]

Corporate identity, especially at the level of the extended family, was reinforced by a deeply ingrained sense of natural honour, the moral code that determined a social group's "feeling of self-worth and the public, social acknowledgement of that worth."[20] Individuals who acted in defiance of the prevailing cultural standards of village Egypt invited shame, not only on themselves but also upon the group of which they were a part. Communities thus downplayed individuality in favour of social conformity. As Andrea Rugh points out, Islam played an important role in defining public morality in villages such as Musha by detailing family roles and responsibilities, and by providing a "widely accepted irrefutable authority for continuing the practices that support connection between kin."[21] Sayyid Qutb's parents strove hard to inculcate in their children the high standards of decorum and moral behaviour that were necessary to negotiate successfully the village's web of social relationships. These efforts paid dividends. Throughout his life, Qutb lived in self-conscious accordance with the ethical standards that his parents had impressed upon him in childhood. This deeply ingrained traditional morality informed the ideological writings of his adulthood.

'All has changed'

Local concerns and inherited customs dominated the life of Musha. Yet the village was not a wholly "traditional" society, at least not in the way the sociological school inspired by Weber and Tonnies understands the term. According to that line of thought, "tradition" denotes a static, ideal type of society unaffected by change and the complex, universalistic patterns of modernity.[22] While it is true that during the period of Qutb's childhood a significant dimension of Egyptian rural life remained unchanged from previous eras, by the time he was born much of this life was in a state of transition and flux as forces incorporated Egypt into an international order of trade, politics and culture. Two basic processes were at work that radically changed the ways in which Egyptians like Qutb lived and thought about their destiny. One of these related to the changes in Egypt's society and economy initiated by Muhammad 'Ali Pasha (r. 1811–49) and his grandson Isma'il (r. 1863–79), the two most important figures in the ethnically-Turkish line of dynastic rule that governed Egypt until the Free Officers' seizure of power in 1952. The other development had to do with the imposition over Egypt of European economic and political controls, exemplified in the British occupation, which commenced in 1882 and lasted in its pure form until 1922. These processes interacted and provided the context out of which emerged the dissenting politics and social movements of the early and mid-twentieth-century.

Changes in Egypt's productive life go back to the efforts of Muhammad 'Ali and his successors to enhance the power of the Egyptian state.[23] During the mediaeval period Egypt's governing Mamluk households (*buyut*) had been limited by the means at their disposal to the periodic extraction of the country's surplus. The Muhammad 'Ali dynasty took on the additional responsibilities of its production and management. Its members reasoned that a strong centralized state would enable them both to impose their authority decisively over the country and to obtain a significant degree of political autonomy from the Ottoman Sultan-Caliph on whose behalf they governed Egypt. To this end, Muhammad 'Ali abolished the economically wasteful system of tax farming and in its place established a deep reaching provincial administration organized so as to access the maximum amount of agricultural surplus and direct it to the centre. He divided the country into a descending order of provinces, departments, districts, sub-districts and villages, all of which he placed under the authority of a general inspectorate. In the central administration, he set up a system of specialized ministries under the control of the *dhawat*, the primarily Turco-Circassian administrative aristocrats who had arrived in Egypt during the early years of his reign.

The Pasha increased the overall level of revenue by encouraging, and often forcing, the peasant cultivators to grow lucrative cash crops such as rice, indigo, sugar cane and especially long-staple cotton, all of which found ready markets within the system of *laissez-faire* capitalism favoured by Britain and other core manufacturing countries of the world economy. The "cotton famine" experienced by European countries in the 1860s, due to the naval blockade of the cotton-exporting Confederate ports by the Union during the American Civil War, further enhanced the value of cotton and prompted Isma'il dramatically to expand its cultivation. Roger Owen is succinct about the consequences: "When the period began some half a million canters were being grown on perhaps 250,000 *faddans*; five years later the harvest had increased four times in size, the area by five, and from then on cotton became once and for all the crop which absorbed the major portion of Egyptian energies and the overwhelming share of its export earnings."[24]

The turn to cash crop cultivation was not without victims. The peasants, in particular, suffered from the state's insatiable thirst for revenue. Lady Duff Gordon, an aristocratic Scotswoman who travelled to Egypt "for her health", describes acidly in her memoir how Isma'il turned Egypt into "one vast plantation where the master works his slaves without feeding them."[25]

The introduction of cash crops required that the ruling elite replace traditional basin irrigation with a complex perennial system capable of holding the waters of the Nile over the dry summer months. In order to ship the crops to Europe, Egypt's rulers constructed an elaborate network of canals, railways and port facilities. The greatest expansion took place during the boom years of Isma'il's khedivate, during which 112 canals, some 12,000 km long, were constructed. By the end of his reign he had expanded telegraph links, built bridges, enlarged and improved port facilities at Alexandria, and established a string of sugar factories in Middle Egypt and the Fayyum Oasis. "Thus Egypt", wrote Charles Issawi, "whose total inhabited area is only 35,000 square kilometers, had built up an internal system of transport and communications comparable to that of many European countries at a much higher level of development."[26]

Eager to expand the cultivatable area and secure the loyalty of state functionaries, the Muhammad 'Ali dynasts made gifts of state lands to members of the Turco-Circassian aristocracy. Between 1863 and 1865 Isma'il granted 77,628 *faddans* (one *faddan* = 1.038 acres) to *dhawat* officials and a further 132,941 *faddans* to himself and to members of his family.[27] In the following decades the rulers gifted tracts of land to Egyptian notables (*a'yan*) and to village headmen; the latter were responsible for collecting the agricultural taxes. Further, the dynasty consolidated the landholdings of both of these groups, *dhawat* and *a'yan*, by a series of laws issued between 1858 and 1871 that transformed land from a usufruct into a commodity that could be bought and sold on the open market. Economically empowered, many landowners proceeded to turn their estates into formidable agricultural enterprises that encompassed, in some instances, well over one thousand *faddan*s.[28] The accumulation of capital by indigenous landowners provided opportunities for the most wealthy among them to marry into the Turco-Circassian ruling caste, thus augmenting their social status and allowing them to advance within the bureaucracy. By the time of Isma'il's reign many had been elevated to the post of provincial governor (*wakil al-mudiriyya*) and, in several cases, to the ranks of the central administration. New wealth also enabled many native landowners to migrate to the principal urban centres of Cairo and Alexandria, or to major provincial towns like Tanta, the hub of the profitable cotton-growing region of the Delta, where they built elaborate villas.

Below these few tremendously wealthy landowners stood the much larger group of medium landowners whose holdings varied from five to fifty *faddan*s. Sayyid Qutb's family appears originally to have belonged in this category. Unlike many of the large landowners who gravitated to the cities, the medium and middle class cultivators tended to remain on their lands where they exercised traditional forms of paternalistic authority over wage-earning peasants.[29] These peasants were for the most part sharecroppers who eked out a meagre existence on plots of land leased to them in return for their labour, or else itinerant labourers mainly from the impoverished districts of Upper Egypt. Although private landholding constituted the engine of economic growth for the Egyptian state, it also led to the emergence of an extremely inegalitarian land regime, a situation that by the 1940s would arouse the attention of Qutb and critics of Egypt's socioeconomic order.

The construction of the modern Egyptian state gave rise to developments in areas of life ancillary to the economy, such as law. In the view of the country's modernizing elite, Egypt's integrity as an administrative realm was contingent upon the introduction of standardized legal codes capable of uniformly addressing issues that fell outside the purview of the Shari'a,[30] for example, issues associated with commercial and diplomatic dealings but also civil and criminal affairs. By 1883 these areas had come to be covered by a comprehensive system of Western-inspired National (*Ahli*) courts. Although scholars such as the influential Muhammad 'Abduh (1849–1905) attempted to stem the tide of legal Westernization by laying the foundations of a reformed Shari'a, the surge of secular law proved too great. As a result, by the turn of the century, the judicial competence of Shari'a courts was limited to matters of domestic relations and personal status, such as marriage, divorce, inheritance, and charitable endowments (*awqaf*).[31] As we shall see, Sayyid Qutb and other Islamists would attempt to reverse the secular trend in the law.

Dramatic changes also occurred in education, considered by the modernizing elite to be the fundamental method of sustaining Egypt's economic and social development.[32] Muhammad 'Ali established the first modern institutions of learning, but these schools were limited to military related subjects for the training of officers. Isma'il moved beyond this narrow focus by establishing a centralized network of European-style primary and secondary government schools for the general population. He also set up higher education for civilians at Cairo's Darb al-Jamamiz palace complex. At the same time foreign entrepreneurs, mostly French and American missionaries, created a stream of private education that catered to Egypt's religious minorities, especially the Copts. Overall, the new education propelled Egypt's native sons, especially those from economically advantaged backgrounds, into the ranks of the civil service and the professions. The new schools did not replace the traditional Qur'an schools (*kuttabs*) or the more advanced *madrasa*s but rather existed alongside them. The result was a dual system of education—one part modelled on Western prototypes, the other Islamic and focused on the Qur'an and exegetical sciences.

The rapidity of Egypt's social and economic transformation surprised even those at the helm of the state building enterprise. 'Ali Mubarak Pasha (1823–93),[33] a native Egyptian who had a chequered career as a teacher and engineering inspector before becoming Director of Education and Public Works, expressed the view of many when he wrote: "All has changed. Anyone who saw Egypt fifty years ago and who now sees it again today will find nothing he knew from former times...He will realize that it has experienced an upheaval (*inqilab*) and that it has become similar to a region of Europe."[34]

Mubarak's statement may have been hyperbolic. Yet it communicates the energy and optimism of the state technocrats. Adopting a scientific posture, Mubarak measured the degree of the transformations in his principal work, the twenty-volume *Khitat al-Tawfiqiyya al-Jadida* (*The New Tawfiqian Survey*, 1886–89). Modelled on the great survey of al-Maqrizi, the *Khitat* examined and classified the economic conditions and topographical history of 1,155 of Egypt's villages, towns, and cities.[35] The inventorial nature of the work belied its principal purpose. Looking down from his administrative mountain, Mubarak imposed visibility on the land of Egypt that enabled the state elite more effectively to plan the course of its development. In the *Khitat*, knowledge combined with power in a relationship geared towards objectification and control.

However, Mubarak's effort had another effect. It allowed educated Egyptians concretely to envision Egypt's ancient nexus of towns and regions as comprising a historical and administrative unity—in other words, a nation. Although it would be an exaggeration to regard the processes of state monitoring as approximating Weber's horror image "of a society impregnated with the bureaucratic values of order and stability as its sole ideal...",[36] they did establish Egypt as a more definitely defined territorial entity, one worthy of patriotic feeling and pride. The fact that by the late nineteenth century a growing number of Egyptians were able to conceive their land in these terms set the stage for the emergence of a variety of articulations of collective identity based on the nation-state.

The intrusion into Egypt of outside agencies heightened patriotic sentiments. From the mid-nineteenth-century well into the twentieth, foreigners, not native Egyptians, dominated Egypt's commercial economy. These took advantage of the economic opportunities made available to them by Egypt's open markets.[37] European companies seeking investment opportunities in banking, land reclamation, shipping, and utilities employed many of the foreigners. Others belonged to an incipient Syrian and Jewish bourgeoisie, which dominated internal commerce and overseas trade. Numbers reflected the dominance of foreigners in the economy, rising from some 3,000 in 1836 to 68,000 in 1878.[38] Small native merchants, unable to compete against the influx of Western goods and services, suffered from the commercial invasion.

From the 1880s onwards, foreign economic interests enjoyed the protection of the Mixed Tribunals. Established by Isma'il's energetic foreign minister Boghos Nubar Pasha, these applied a unified system of French civil and commercial law to cases that involved a "foreign interest". The expansive field of European commercial endeavour meant that the Mixed Courts asserted the right to try almost every important case in the country.[39] In so doing, the courts provided foreign business interests with the opportunity freely to pursue profits.

Foreign political control over the apparatus of state matched the unrestricted foreign control of Egypt's internal economy. Britain attained a dominant position in Egypt owing to the European loans contracted by the Khedives Sa'id and Isma'il to fund their public works projects.[40] By the early 1870s, the usurious terms of these loans plunged Egypt into an abyss of indebtedness. Eager to secure repayment, Britain and France placed Egypt's finances under an International Debt Commission, which they dominated. Shortly thereafter, these same powers pressured the Ottoman Sultan to replace the discredited Isma'il with his son Tawfiq. The erosion of Egypt's sovereignty by foreigners prompted a loose coalition of indigenous notables and military men led by Army Colonel Ahmad 'Urabi to overthrow the "puppet" government of Tawfiq and establish in its place a completely independent regime under their control. However, the rebel government of Ahmad 'Urabi did not last for long. Afraid both for its financial interests and for the security of the Suez Canal, Britain invaded Egypt and defeated 'Urabi's army at the battle of Tal al-Kabir in 1882.[41]

Upon assuming control in Cairo, Britain's stated goal was to put the Egyptian house in order. Although Egypt's rulers had accomplished much in the way of state building, it was clear to the British that the legal rational forms of Egypt's state apparatus fell far short of matching the requirements of the Anglo-Saxon ideal type. Steven Cave, a British government official sent to Egypt at the peak of its financial crisis in the 1870s, attributed the country's condition of fiscal insolvency and political instability to the fact that the country was in a "transition state". According to Cave, it suffered from "the defects of the system out of which she is passing as well as from those of the system into which she is attempting to enter." Government, he wrote, maintained a capricious authoritarian streak "after the manner of the East", and public office, far from being the impersonal embodiment of a public function, continued in the old way as a private property exploited by its holder.[42] Developing the theme of Oriental incompetence, Lord Cromer, Britain's iron willed Consul General in Egypt

(1883–1907), likened the Egyptian state to a flawed piece of machinery in need of an overhaul. In his view, it was in Britain's enlightened self-interest to propel "the machinery of government into motion".[43] In much the same way as the policy planners of US President Kennedy's "Development Decade" of the 1960s, the British believed that they could serve the interests of empire best by stemming, through reform, the threat of dissidence and rebellion in countries essential to their geo-strategic security, such as Egypt. For Cromer, it was important that Britain's mission in Egypt should be limited in terms of duration and purpose; once the British had shored up Egypt's finances and established a responsible pro-British government, they should withdraw. The fact that Britain maintained a presence in Egypt until 1955 is indicative of the magnitude of the reformist task and the ongoing importance of Egypt to Britain's imperial designs.

The model for the British enterprise was the Raj in India, the great incubator of colonial policy. There, in the wake of the 1857 Mutiny, the British had replaced radical measures of Benthamite social engineering with a strategy of indirect administration and remunerative public works. They now applied the same strategy to Egypt. The British controlled the choice of Egyptian government ministers and placed a shadow bureaucracy of British advisers behind the native personnel of the key government departments of Finance, Public Works, Interior, Justice, Public Health, and Education.[44] "By World War I the British had established a dominant position in every ministry and government department except those relating to the religious life of the country such as the Ministry of Waqfs."[45] Indigenous political expression was limited to the Legislative Council, an appointed Assembly established in 1883, which functioned primarily as a rubber stamp for decisions made by the British. Behind the British advisers stood the British military, a 5,000–strong occupation army, commanded by the Sirdar. Equipped thus, the British were in a position to interfere forcefully in Egypt's affairs if ever they felt their interests to be threatened. Egyptians felt chagrined and humiliated by Britain's easy takeover of their country.

Britain strove hard to expand Egypt's agricultural capacity, even while it allowed the country's educational system to stagnate. Working through the Department of Public Works, Anglo-Egyptian hydraulic engineers recruited from the Raj continued the transition from basin to perennial irrigation. Taking over from the British, Egyptian engineers completed the process only in 1965, one year prior to Qutb's execution.

Significantly, the British included Upper Egypt in their development schemes. In the pre-occupation era, the Sa'id had received less in the way of development funding than the rich cotton-producing Delta. The British built the first Aswan dam (1898–1902), which facilitated the cultivation of cotton in the southern provinces. In 1889, the British linked Asyut to Cairo by telegraph as part of the effort to bind peripheral regions to the political centre.[46] These efforts resulted in the marked increase in the population of Asyut and other southern cities and towns. By the time Qutb was born, the population of Asyut City had grown to over 40,000, putting it in the same league as the cities of the Delta and Canal Zone, such as Port Sa'id, Damanhur, Tanta, and Mansura.[47]

The social, economic, and political processes at work in the nineteenth century gave rise to a basic contradiction that beset the Egypt well into the following century. Although the country's modernizing elite made tremendous strides in transforming the country's infrastructure and economic base, this same development rendered Egypt increasingly dependent on the linkages of the world economy. By the turn of the century this foreign domination would prompt Egyptians, especially those attached to an incipient middle class recently emerged from the countryside, to fashion discourses aimed at political and economic independence. In so doing, they would perceive the land of Egypt in terms of its historical destiny and links with past ages of glory.

Memory and desire

Qutb left an account of his childhood encounter with the forces of change in a retrospective autobiography entitled *A Child from the Village* (Arabic, *Tifl min al-Qarya*),[48] published in Cairo in 1946 when Qutb was forty years old. Composed only two years before his turn to Islamism, it is a classic *Bildungsroman* that treats his formation as a boy from the provinces. Befitting a man who considered himself a littérateur, the book's prose style is sophisticated and its vocabulary rich and evocative. In places, particularly in its description of Musha's cultural beliefs and practices, the book's tone is almost anthropological, evidence of the degree to which Qutb as an adult had distanced himself from the parochial outlook of his village background. Throughout the work, Qutb reinforces this sense of cultural estrangement by referring to himself in the third person, thus allowing the reader easily to distinguish between the author's adult worldview and that of his child protagonist. He treats his life between roughly the ages of six and fifteen. But his narrative lacks a distinct chronological thread. Rather, he presents his material in a series of thematic episodes. Taken together, these vignettes document what Qutb perceived to be his "awakening" from the unreflective slumber of customary rural life to a new kind of existence lived within the problematic context of the modernizing nation-state.[49] In relating his story, Qutb knows that he is addressing other "sons of the country" (*abna al-balad*) who had made similar journeys from rural villages to Cairo in order to partake of that city's larger and more complex social reality.

Qutb's work was one of a number of autobiographical works written by Egyptian authors in the early and middle decades of the twentieth century. Within this cluster of works, pride of place belongs to *al-Ayyam* (Volume I, 1929, Volume II, 1939, Volume III, 1973) by Taha Husayn (1889–1973),[50] which relates the author's formative years in a rural community in Upper Egypt and his efforts to transcend the limitations of village life by means of modern education. *Al-Ayyam's* significance derives, in large part, from its status as the first truly modern autobiography in Arabic. Especially in the first volume, Taha Husayn casts a critical eye on features of Egypt's social and intellectual life that he believed hindered Egypt's transition to modernity, including the folk beliefs of the villagers and the spiritual and social authority held by the tradition-minded men of religion. Implicit in Husayn's autobiography is the idea that Egyptians must jettison these and other manifestations of tradition if Egypt is to take its place among the progressive nations of the world.

Al-Ayyam's prominence encouraged several writers, including Qutb, to choose autobiography as a vehicle for recounting their often similar encounters with the forces of change. Like *al-Ayyam*, Qutb's autobiography documents its youthful protagonist's acquisition of new knowledge and perspectives. In fact, Qutb explicitly acknowledged his debt to Taha Husayn in the dedicatory inscription at the beginning of *A Child from the Village*. However, despite the similarity, the purposes of the two authors are somewhat different. Whereas Taha Husyan's experiences led him to embrace the civilization of the West, Sayyid Qutb's response was to seek a modernized and reformed version of the Egyptian national community, which, throughout his career as a writer, he identified with Eastern, Islamic civilization. Writing years after the events he described, Qutb looked back and viewed his village as a cultural site that encoded in the myriad details of its community life an ideology of national exceptionality. Other writers who took cues from *al-Ayyam* include Ibrahim al-Mazini (*Qissat Haya* 1943), Salama Musa (*Tarbiyyat Salama Musa* 1947), Ahmad Amin (*Hayati* 1950, revised 1952), Ibrahim 'Abd al-Halim (*Ayyam al-Tufula*), and Qutb's friend Tawfiq al-Hakim (*Sijn al-'Umr* 1964). Although each of the autobiographical works brings to bear its particular perspective, all tend to treat their subjects as moving from early states of gullibility and ignorance to higher levels of critical social and personal awareness. In documenting such individual journeys, these books are in large degree concerned with Egypt's effort to create itself as a modern nation.

A Child from the Village situates the young Qub within the framework of Egyptian village traditions, the social milieu in which he and many of his readers attained their foundational outlook on the world. Nostalgia infuses the book's vignettes. Qutb describes the enduring rhythms of the agricultural cycle, explaining how the busy time of the harvest followed the season of "wet planting" when migrant workers from less privileged villages and provinces arrived in the village.[51] He writes how the yearly flood transformed the village into a series of islands, and remembers how he and his boyhood companions would playfully jump into the waters from the rooftop of their school.[52] He tells also of birth ceremonies and of rejoicing during Ramadan. "The secret of this rejoicing is, in the first place, the light—the light that shines from the many houses that are hosting parties at night, where doors are opened to visitors and the Qur'an is recited throughout the month."[53]

Amid a population that was largely illiterate[54] Qutb was eager to tap into the knowledge and social power that came with the study of Islam's scholarly tradition. Role models of scholarly achievement existed within his extended family. Two of Qutb's maternal uncles had attended al-Azhar, the great mosque-university in Cairo, as young men. Their studies had transformed them into figures of local prestige.[55] Qutb relates how he attempted to broaden his own understanding of Islamic doctrine by attending the lessons in Qur'anic interpretation (*tafsir*) provided by students of al-Azhar who visited villages like

Musha on holidays as a service to provincial Egyptians.[56] The lessons were related in the difficult, elevated discourse of formal literary Arabic (al-fusha), which differed on points of grammar and vocabulary from the earthy dialect of everyday conversation. As Qutb became aware, the purpose of these scholars was simply to present the work of the original author, not to amplify or explain its content. Consequently, their method consisted of a word-by-word recounting of the text under review.[57] Qutb relates that during a session on the Qur'an commentary of the twenlth century exegete Zamakhshari he broke with etiquette by questioning the Azhari on an obtuse point of grammar. The problem turned out to have a simple solution. However, his insolence earned him a mild rebuke from the scholar. It also reflected a precocious intellectual ability that set him apart from the other children in the village. Throughout his life, Qutb would evince intellectual airs.

The lessons imparted by these scholars introduced Qutb to what the anthropologist Robert Redfield termed the "Great Tradition" of literary texts and legal and theological schools, which differed from the "Little Tradition" of the mostly non-literate or semi–literate rural population.[58] This background would enable Qutb to enter the school system in Cairo with an enthusiastic appreciation for the classical texts of Islam.

Qutb notes that despite the villagers' interest in Qur'an studies, the realm of folk belief had the greatest hold on them. He relates how within every villager's mind, including his own, there existed an unshakeable belief in a parallel reality of unseen, mainly malign, forces. These were the 'afarit and jinn, which hovered over the lives of people like ominous clouds. "Everything in the village," Qutb writes, "inspired belief in the 'afarit…The naïve village imagination explained phenomena and events in terms of deeply rooted images and phantoms, frightening and mysterious in the dark gloom."[59] According to Qutb, these apparitions could appear anywhere and at any time and in a variety of forms. When Qutb's baby brother died of tetanus seven days after birth, as a result of the midwife's infected surgical knife, the family was quick to blame the death on the mischievous wiles of the baby's invisible "twin" (qarina), the ghostly companion that villagers believed haunted the presence of each child and adult.[60] Qutb explains that people could manage these intrusive elements only by evoking the saints (al-awliya) or reciting a Qur'anic verse. He mentions in passing how the women of the village would sometimes conduct zar ceremonies, exorcisms aimed at eradicating demonic possession, which were characterized by trance-like music and dancing.[61] He tells us that after his baby brother's death his parents gave him an amulet inscribed with a depiction of the Prophet Solomon to wear as protection against Iblis and his progeny.[62]

At the very beginning of his autobiography, Qutb introduces us to the fearsome figure of the "God possessed" *Magzub*, a dervish whose dishevelled appearance and unconventional behaviour were considered by the adults of the village as signs of divine favour.[63] Villagers familiar with and tolerant of the tradition of "holy foolery" actively sought contact with the *Magzub* in the hope that he might bestow blessings upon them—they believed that such individuals had the ear of God. However, in the perspective of Qutb and his young friends, the *Magzub* was a terrifying figure whom one should avoid. "They would swallow their saliva to relieve the dryness of their throats while their eyes stared at this fearsome and terrifying man."[64] When Qutb suffered a neck injury while playing with his friends, one of the villagers suggested that he spend a night in the company of the *Magzub* to be healed. Qutb writes of his relief when his mother vetoed the idea, preferring to leave the matter of his injury to the "knowledge and power of God" rather than to the alleged powers of the holy man.

Qutb's concerns about the *Magzub* did not prevent him from tapping into the mysteries of the spiritual world. He possessed two books on astrology and magic, which he purchased on condition that he did not use the occult knowledge contained within to ill effect. Every village had its "sorcerer" (*al-sahir*) whose magic spells were thought to counteract the evil eye, secure the affections of a marriage prospect, or ensure the birth of a healthy child, and Qutb's possession of these books made him a contender for such a role. Young women, especially, consulted him. They confessed to him their secrets and desires in the hope that the books might indicate an appropriate course of action, particularly with regard to affairs of the heart.[65] Qutb says that as a ten-year-old he was still too young to feel embarrassment at these visits, since "sexual impulses had not yet begun to stir in him." He admits, however, that contact with these women aroused in him "a wonderful and obscure pleasure" (*ladhdha ghamia ʿajiba*), for even at this early age, he says, "his sensitivity to living beauty was keen."[66]

Qutb tells his readers that in a short time he came to dismiss the *jinn* and *ʿafarit* as figments of the popular imagination.[67] He cites the important influence on him of one of his teachers at the state school, a young *effendi* who tried hard to prove to his students that the phenomena they attributed to occult forces had natural explanations. Qutb goes on to say, however, that although his belief in supernatural phenomena dissipated over time, they "were more deeply embedded in is soul than education and that the *'afarit* of his childhood and youth continued to inhabit his adult imagination" as the imprint of his rural upbringing.[68] Here Qutb touches on a theme found throughout the body of his writings: that Egyptians such as himself had an inherent spiritual disposition that distinguished them from the essentially materialistic outlook of the West. As Qutb came to appreciate in the years following the publication of his autobiography, the divinely ordained principles of the Qur'an expressed perfectly this spiritual outlook that was manifested vulgarly in village beliefs. In this view, Musha's customs and folk beliefs, "backward" as some of them appeared in relation to modernity, nevertheless constituted markers of the authentic roots of Egypt's collective identity in the contemporary era. Later, during the mature Islamist phase of his career, Qutb would validate his childhood belief in "unseen worlds" with reference to the Qur'anic teaching on *jinn* and angels. More so than is commonly recognized by scholars, adherence to Islamist ideology can be grafted easily onto the predisposition to believe in a supernatural realm.

The lure of the modern

Qutb mingles his reminiscence of rural tradition with an account of the forces of change and development that affected the village. In common with other rural Egyptians, Musha's inhabitants tended to fear and distrust individuals and institutions associated with the state, the principal agent of this change, which they viewed as intrusive, exploitative, and intent upon eroding the relative autonomy of village communities.[69] Although the rapacious appetite of Egypt's ruling elite for taxes and corvée labour had diminished by the early 1900s, owing mainly to the reformist interventions of the British, peasant distrust remained strong in face of other, more insidious methods of elite control. For one thing, the British-dominated Egyptian government now made sure that it imposed new structures of criminal law and investigation on local village affairs. The government also further rationalized the administration of farming. As Nathan Brown explains, "Decisions about agricultural production and irrigation that had previously been made locally now became matters of state policy to be enforced by agricultural and irrigation inspectors who reported them to ministries in Cairo."[70] State power, traditionally perceived as something external and remote, now influenced the daily affairs of the villages in ways that were unprecedented.

Most contacts with outside officialdom occurred without incident. However, a single hostile encounter was often sufficient to confirm the villagers' suspicions of the state's hegemonic purposes. Qutb provides a harrowing account of a government operation, probably soon after World War I,[71] to disarm the villagers of Asyut Province as a condition for its more thorough integration into the structure of the state. He describes how soldiers, having surrounded Musha, brutally interrogated the peasants, at one point firing bullets over the heads of the village elders. "Every child, woman and man" was "horrified" at the abrupt and violent intrusion of these outsiders into the affairs of the community, and stunned by the seeming ease with which the government could impose its will on the countryside.[72] At the end of the day, the soldiers stood before piles of arms: guns, revolvers, large knives, axes and spears. Qutb writes, "The great officer surveyed the scene contentedly, puffed up like a rooster at his decisive victory over the 'accused villagers.'" When he wrote these words in 1946, Qutb had no way of knowing that one day he, too, would be a victim of the interventionist state.

Yet the forces of transformation were as capable of seduction as they were of coercion. Throughout the work, Qutb identifies the agencies and subtle influences that encouraged his young protagonist to identify with the encroaching new order rather than regard it simply as an object of opprobrium. One of these was what Benedict Anderson, in relation to the European experience, has called "print capitalism", the commodified production of newspapers, journals and books that was part of the overall commercialization of the Egyptian economy in the nineteenth and twentieth centuries.[73] As Reinhard Schulze notes, the first commercial press in Egypt was set up at Bulaq, just to the north of Cairo, in 1862, and supplied the Egyptian market with editions of classical Islamic texts in addition to a wide range of books translated from European languages.[74] Later other publishing houses were established.

Qutb took advantage of the dramatic increase in the availability of book titles. Over time he assembled a collection of twenty-five books that he purchased from an itinerant book peddler with allowance money. Qutb describes the peddler's eclectic mix of titles.[75] They included standards such as the folk epic of the Banu Hilal, based on the tenth century migration of a Bedouin tribe from Arabia to North Africa, and the *Qasidat al-Burda*, a mediaeval devotional poem in praise of the Prophet, in addition to "low brow" detective novels and thrillers, including Arabic translations of Sherlock Holmes. But the peddler also made available to "select customers", like Qutb, "dangerous books" such as the risqué *A Thousand and One Nights* and works on magic, divination and astrology; the sale of these was "carried out in the same manner as the most weighty pacts and secret agreements."[76] In Qutb's estimation, the only important book he lacked was al-Bukhari's collection of "sound" (*al-sahih*) *hadith*, which many desired to possess on account of its supposed value in the taking of oaths. Qutb kept his books in a specially made tin box that protected them from the destructive effects of dust and insects.[77] The books whetted the young Qutb's intellectual appetite and stirred his imagination. He was one of many thousands of beneficiaries of a revolution in book production in Egypt that was instrumental in creating an incipient national reading public to which he, as a writer, would one day appeal.

More significant for the development of Qutb's outlook was the influence of Musha's state-run primary school. Qutb joined the school in 1912 at his mother's behest at the age of six. His mother hoped that a modern education would enable her son eventually to enter the ranks of the *effendiyya*, the rapidly growing, modernizing social stratum that had emerged a generation earlier in conjunction with the processes of socio-economic development.[78] As a salaried *effendi* employed in the civil service or as a schoolteacher, he would be in a position to rescue the family from its precarious economic situation. We learn in *A Child from the Village* that in the years leading up to the outbreak of World War I, Qutb's father had been forced to sell portions of the family's already-diminished estate in order to cover his debts. The sale of the family home, in particular, had a deep psychological impact on the family. Qutb informs his readers that the family lived in fear of financial ruin and the possibility that it might have to join the growing throngs of destitute peasants.[79]

In common with state schools elsewhere in Egypt, the Western-inspired methods and curricula introduced by Egypt's educational reformers in the last decades of the nineteenth century provided the model for Musha's primary school. The state schools subjected students to a more precise system of ranking and taught them "practical" subjects such as reading, writing, arithmetic, and physical education. In addition, they monitored attendance and classroom behaviour, to a greater or lesser extent.[80] As Timothy Mitchell explains, the purpose of the new subjects and disciplinary habits was to create motivated and literate citizens capable of contributing to the county's productive life.[81] To be sure, modes of discipline based upon "shared norms of personal cultivation" had a long history throughout the Islamic world. Sufism, the emulation of the prophetic *sunna*, and the princely tradition were each interested in the development of moral character through the internalization of specific norms and values.[82] However, the new methods of educational activity differed from these in that their final object was not self-mastery but utility, the maximization of economy, efficiency, and organization.[83] Together with the more tangible products of economic and administrative development, these qualities were considered by their proponents to be prerequisites for the attainment of "civilization", a concept that originally connoted a transitive activity and not, as was now the case, an achieved state of being.

Qutb admits that his school fell short of the disciplinary and administrative ideals set by Egypt's technocrats.[84] The school did not have enough qualified staff and, out of necessity, had to recruit teachers incapable of adequately taking charge of the curriculum.[85] It drew some from the traditional Qur'an schools. However, gym instruction fell into the hands of a retired soldier who was notorious for his harsh and domineering methods; Qutb remembers how the gym instructor would bark Turkish military commands at the pupils as he led them through callisthenic exercises. Moreover, the school was irregular in its system of placement of pupils. According to Qutb, the school granted his father the "privilege" of enrolling his son in the school's fourth grade rather than in the kindergarten, where the boy properly belonged, because of the family's high honour rating within the village.[86] Qutb might well have foundered had the school's headmaster not intervened to convince the father to enroll his son in the appropriate level of instruction. Yet, despite the irregularities, Qutb accommodated to the ways of the school and settled into the routine of classroom instruction. Attired in a *tarboush* (fez) and smart *quftan* (cloak), he worked hard at his studies and stood out among the other pupils because of his excellent work.

In his second year at the school, his father abruptly forced him to withdraw and to enrol instead in the local Qur'an school (*kuttab*). In contrast to the relatively expansive curriculum of the state schools, the normal method of instruction in the *kuttab*s was to inculcate in the colloquial-speaking pupils extensive passages of the classical Arabic of the Qur'an. As Qutb tells the story, his father took the action in response to a rumour that the Ministry of Education was plotting to phase Qur'anic instruction out of the state school curriculum. The rumour, which "spread like wildfire", had its effect on the villagers, many of whom withdrew their children from the school and enrolled them at the *kuttab*. Qutb's father was "too sensible" to be taken in by the claim, which in fact was fabricated by the shaykh responsible for Qur'anic instruction at the state school; the school had dismissed him and he saw the story as a way of sabotaging the reputation of his former employer.[87] Nevertheless, out of deference to the shaykh, Qutb's father placed his son in the *kuttab*.

Qutb tells how unhappy he was with the change of schools. The lack of discipline and "dirty habits" of the *kuttab* teacher and the pupils filled him with repugnance. Gone were the playground, desks, chairs, and blackboard of the state school. Qutb now sat on the ground in a study circle and etched his lessons on a tin board, which the pupils would clean in a "filthy" way by spitting on it and wiping it with the edge of their garments. The pupils did not raise their hands, as they did at the state school, but waved, snapped their fingers and called out.[88]

Qutb recalls his relief when the headmaster of the state school intervened to convince his father to change his mind. "From that time on," Qutb writes, "the school became for him a holy place, like a *mihrab* for prayer. Everything and everyone associated with it rose several degrees in his eyes."[89] In Qutb's view, the ways of the *kuttab*, like so much else in the village that was habitual and customary, appeared disorderly and chaotic when measured against the orderly methods of the new schooling. In order to prove the irrelevancy of the *kuttab*, and thereby destroy its purpose, Qutb joined other pupils to memorize the Qur'an on his own, an effort that kept him awake far into the nights. His dedication to the task paid off. Within months, he was on his way to attaining the honoured status of *hafiz*, or "keeper" of the holy text. Soon he and his companions at the state school were regularly defeating the *kuttab* boys in contests of Qur'an recitation.[90] Secure in his beloved school, Qutb came to admire the "cleanly dressed" *effendi*s who were his teachers and harboured "a feeling that almost amounted to worship". He longed to be their age and attend the teaching college in the great and distant city of Cairo. For him, the *effendi*s lived a "special kind of life whose true nature he could no more understand than he could that of ghosts and spirits."[91] Everything about them—their outlook, appearance, and life experiences—seemed connected to an exciting new world of change, movement, and intellectual liberation. The *effendi*s represented a world that he yearned to be a part of and that made his "imagination swim".

Qutb's schooling unfolded against the backdrop of growing nationalist agitation, and this also influenced his maturing worldview. By the time he had reached school age demands for the end of the British occupation were commonplace among the politically articulate sectors of Egypt's population. Although many in the governing elite were reconciled to Britain's presence in Egypt, most Egyptians looked forward to the day when the foreigners would relinquish their hold on the state. Resentment was particularly rife among the emergent class of young professionals who stood at the apex of the *effendiyya* stratum. These men had profited by the schools established by Isma'il. Yet, because British officials monopolized the top administrative posts, they had not advanced in their careers to levels commensurate with their talents and ambitions. Bitter at the blockage, they brought to the foreground other issues of discontent, such as Britain's control of the Sudan, which Egyptians considered to have been unjustly excised from the jurisdiction of the Egyptian Khedivate, and Britain's unwillingness to expand education beyond levels set by the Khedives in the nineteenth century. A strong sense of cultural pride and national honour underpinned these grievances. The challenge facing the nationalists was to convince other sectors of the Egyptian population, including the urban proletariat, the well-to-do peasantry, and especially the up-and-coming cohort of students from the state schools, of the need to eject the British from the country.

Egypt's nationalists found a strong advocate in the charismatic Mustafa Kamil, founder in 1907 of the Hizb al-Watani (Nationalist Party). Mustafa Kamil came into public view in 1906 when he mobilized the Egyptian public following the outrage of the Dinshaway Affair, in which a British military tribunal sentenced four peasants to hanging and others to flogging for their alleged role in the death of a British officer.[92] Adopting a hard line, Mustafa Kamil demanded the total and unconditional withdrawal of all British military and government personnel from the length of the Nile Valley. The party's maximalist attitude encouraged radicalism and some Watanists went so far as to form secret terrorist cells, one of which, the Mutual Brotherhood Society, assassinated Prime Minister Butrus Ghali in 1910 for his pro-British sympathies.[93] Thus sounded an ominous chord of violence in the name of the general will. The Watanists were at heart Egyptian territorial nationalists, but they also emphasized Egypt's cultural and political links with the Ottoman Empire. In so doing, they aimed to tap the sentiments of Muslim identity held by the majority of Egyptians and turn them against the foreign occupier.

Nationalist feeling was inflamed during World War I, chiefly because of the economic privations and national indignities endured by the population, for which it held the British responsible. All sectors of the population felt aggrieved for one reason or another. The *effendiyya*, already smarting under a tutelary regime that cramped its free development, resented Britain's declaration in 1914 of a protectorate over Egypt, which excised the country officially from the Ottoman Empire. *Effendis* were outraged at Britain's exile of the popular Khedive 'Abbas Hilmi II on account of his pro-Ottoman sympathies. Large and medium landowners shared this grievance and resented also that Britain chose to exploit the wartime situation by purchasing Egypt's cotton crop at prices well below the market value. The unemployment, inflation, and food shortages that accompanied the war aroused the anger of the urban poor who made up nearly half the population of Cairo. Finally, the conscription of peasants into the ranks of the Labour and Transport Corps of Britain's Egyptian Expeditionary Force fanned the primordial anti–state sentiments of the peasants. In the peasants' view it appeared as though the bad old days of Muhammad 'Ali and Isma'il had returned. Faced with these hardships and humiliations, most Egyptians supported, if only passively, the Ottoman Sultan-Caliph against the British, hoping that a British defeat in the war would spell the end of the protectorate and allow Egypt to reestablish itself as a politically autonomous component of the Ottoman Empire.[94]

The Watanists' advocacy moulded the nationalist vision of Qutb's father, an educated provincial landowner who was, in fact, a member of the party's local committee. Qutb remembers how over the course of the war his father regularly invited the handful of committed patriots who lived in the village to the family home for political meetings and discussions; one of those invited was the young headmaster of Qutb's school. Because of Britain's wartime crackdown on nationalist activities the meetings took place in secret. Qutb remembered how he heard the men discuss, in hushed tones, the venerated figures of Egyptian-Ottoman resistance to Britain and her allies. These included the exiled Khedive 'Abbas Hilmi II, known popularly as "Our Effendi", the Young Turk leader Tal'at Bey, who directed the Ottoman war effort from Istanbul, and 'Abd al-'Aziz Jawish and Muhammad Farid, who succeeded Mustafa Kamil in 1908 as leaders of the Nationalist Party. Like 'Abbas Hilmi, they had been exiled from Egypt before the start of the War. Also mentioned was the Ottoman commander "Ra'uf and his ship the Hamidiyya, which caused the Allies pain and about which legendary stories were told." Qutb writes, "The feelings of the entire village were on the side of Turkey, the State of the Islamic Caliphate, and against the Allies who represented the 'unbelievers' and were fighting Islam." Eventually, Qutb's father allowed him to participate in some of the meetings and even to assume the task of reading the nationalist press to the group's members, many of whom were probably illiterate or semi–literate.[95]

The young Qutb found an outlet for his emergent nationalism in the celebrated anti–British uprising of 1919. Although the uprising was rooted in the cumulative effects of foreign domination, its immediate spark was the failed attempt by a group of Egyptian lawyers and absentee landowners, called the "Wafd" (delegation), to lobby British officials in 1918 for permission to represent Egypt's case for independence at the Paris Peace Conference. Led by the son of an 'umda from al-Gharbiyya province named Sa'd Zaghlul, the Wafd filled the void created by the wartime hiatus of the Hizb al-Watani. When, after unsuccessful deliberations, Sa'd Zaghlul was arrested by the British and exiled to Malta, the Egyptian people erupted in open rebellion.[96]

The unexpected spontaneity and early success of the uprising prompted the Wafd quickly to develop an infrastructure that could channel and sustain the energies of the population for a countrywide independence movement under its leadership. At the cadre level, the Wafd functioned as a coalition between the middle strata of Egyptian society, represented by lawyers and other professionals, literati, students and civil servants, and the nascent class of proletarians. Within days of the uprising's outbreak on 9 March 1919, the Wafdist Central Committee set about collecting funds, mobilizing students for street demonstrations, and forging links with striking rail and tram workers from the Cairo neighbourhoods of Bulaq and Muski.[97] In Cairo's old city, the lower *'ulama* organized neighbourhoods in civil disobedience. A significant feature of the uprising, much emphasized in subsequent Egyptian nationalist historiography, was the unprecedented display of unity among the various sectors of Egyptian society. A Coptic priest mounted the *minbar* of al-Azhar to demand national independence.[98] The entwined image of the cross and crescent was upheld as the uprising's symbol. In the course of eight weeks of demonstrations, British troops shot dead scores of students and workers. Spurred to action by local officials and activist *effendi*s, peasants severed rail links in order to safeguard rural localities from British troops and engaged in other acts of sabotage.[99] In several provincial towns, landlord-*effendi* collusion resulted in the formation of local governing committees, most notably in Zifta in Gharbiyya Province, which excised itself from the jurisdiction of the state to form a short-lived, self-governing commune.[100]

Qutb writes that he learned of the uprising and the "new sacred name" of Sa'd Zaghlul from his school headmaster, who after delivering a fiery patriotic speech announced to the class that the school would close indefinitely. He and his *effendi* colleagues were off to "work for the "revolution". It was, the headmaster said, the duty of all. Brimming with "enthusiasm" (*hamas*), the thirteen-year-old Qutb mimicked the headmaster's example by composing his own patriotic speech, which he delivered "at meeting halls and mosques, where the spirit of the sacred revolution was breathed into all."[101] Qutb was not aware of the secular, Wilsonian discourse of national rights put forward by the Wafdist leadership in its deliberations with the British. At this stage, the name "Zaghlul" was for him, as it was perhaps for most Egyptians, simply a rallying symbol of anti–foreign agitation. Rather, the young Qutb appears to have followed the nationalist mainstream in interpreting the Wafd's call for independence in terms of Egypt's loyalty to the civilization of Islam and the institution of the caliphate. As Gershoni and Jankowski point out, Ottomanist and Islamic sentiment remained strong among the Egyptian public, both during and after the uprising, until Mustafa Kemal, on establishing the new Turkish Republic, abolished the Caliphate in 1924.[102]

Although the 1919 uprising does not qualify in terms set by contemporary social science as a true revolution, an upheaval in which "rapid basic transformations of a society's state and class structure" are effected,[103] in the minds of its participants it presaged the advent of a new era in Egypt. A quarter of a century later, Qutb would evoke the heroic examples of Mustafa Kamil and the events of 1919 as goads to energize a new generation of young Egyptian nationalists.

'The sorrows of the countryside'

Qutb infuses his personalized account of tradition and modernization in a rural community with a strong social justice message. Despite its tone of nostalgia, *A Child from the Village* paints a picture of Egypt's rural districts that is not entirely happy. Social and economic issues were of concern to Qutb and other public intellectuals in the 1940s. It is therefore not surprising that one of Qutb's stated purposes in his autobiography was to educate city dwellers about actual conditions in the countryside.[104]

The spectre of peasant indebtedness and loss of land haunts the pages of the autobiography, as do disease caused by unhygienic conditions and the peasants' recourse to folk remedies and barber surgeons rather than to scientifically trained physicians. Throughout the work, Qutb juxtaposes the joys of Ramadan nights, birth ceremonies and other special occasions to death, tragedy, and the laments of women who patiently endure their hard lives. Captives of poverty and ignorance, the peasants of Qutb's autobiography toil endlessly in their fields with little expectation that their lives will improve. They are the victims of the few large landowners and politicians who control Egypt's wealth. According to Tetz Rooke who examined a wide range of Arabic childhood autobiographies, the critical portrayal of rural life found in *A Child from the Village* represents a "break with the tendency towards pastoral idealization which dominated much of the first Egyptian creative writing concerned with country life." It is thus a "precursor of the later Egyptian novel that embraces the subject of the village with a true-to-life, descriptive intent such as *al-Ard* [*The Earth*, 1953] by 'Abd al-Rahman al-Sharqawi (1920–1987)."[105]

Qutb recalls the moment when the "sorrows of the countryside" awakened his conscience. Each year gangs of itinerant seasonal labourers, mostly from the more southerly regions of Qena and Aswan, came to Musha to help with the harvest. According to Qutb, the villagers treated these men with airs of contempt and paid them wages as little as one piastre per day. Treated as outsiders, the labourers formed a caste apart. Qutb remembers how he developed a powerful affinity for the men who worked his family's land. He admired their stoicism in the face of adversity and loved their heart-rending songs sung in the rustic dialect of their regions. He befriended them and, because they were illiterate, wrote their letters and arranged for their remittances to be sent to their home villages. Qutb writes of the effect that this new awareness of suffering and deprivation had on his conscience. Clearly, in his view, his relatively privileged family was complicit in the structural conditions of social-class division that existed at the national level:

He learned many things, whose harsh impact on his feelings have only become evident as he now reflects on them from time to time, and feels shame in the depth of his soul and contempt for himself and his people. He is a robber. He has robbed these "foreigners" and many millions like them who create the wealth of the Nile Valley yet go hungry. He is a robber! If there were a just law in the valley it would send him to prison before those multitudes who the law counts robbers and criminals. This was the feeling that always kept coming over him whenever he sat down to eat rich food or sweet fruit or luxurious sweets or whenever he enjoyed the simple pleasures of life amidst the millions of deprived.[106]

Implicitly and sometimes explicitly in his autobiography, Qutb advocates reform and appropriate strategies of modernization to be applied to Egypt's villages. He believed that the introduction of modern schooling in villages like Musha was a step in the right direction but also thought that there was need for many more improvements, especially in the areas of land redistribution and health care. In his view, the state was the obvious agent to undertake the necessary reforms, but it too often imposed its ameliorative efforts with a heavy hand or else conceived them badly. Throughout his autobiography, he documents the unwelcome and often inexpert interventions of various government officials in the affairs of the community. He introduces us to medical officials, coroners, judges and others, all of whom attempt to manage the countryside in ways that make sense to the state but not to the villagers. In the same way as Tawfiq al-Hakim's *Diary of a Country Prosecutor*, Qutb's reminiscence documents the gulf in understanding that existed between urban officialdom and the dwellers of the countryside, the difference being that Qutb's book provides the reader with the perspective of the peasants rather than that of a government official. Qutb appears to argue in his autobiography that for modernization in the Egyptian countryside to be effective, the state technocrats must take into account the cultural sensibilities and social and economic realities of its inhabitants.

All autobiographies, especially those dealing with childhood, bear the impress of ideas and feelings held by their authors at the time of writing. The stories and anecdotes scattered throughout Qutb's work echo the desire of the mid-twentieth-century Egyptian middle class for a modern Egyptian national community anchored in the "authentic" spirit of Muslim-Egyptian civilization. Drawn from the personal experiences of his boyhood, these stories meld the Enlightenment view of history as a trajectory of progress with fragments drawn from a memory of cultural belonging. Thus, while *A Child from the Village* documents its protagonist's growing awareness of the new opportunities that were afoot in the village as it was pulled into the orbit of the modernizing state, at the same time it touches on the issues of collective identity and reform, the two sides of the nationalist coin.

Two years after the publication of *A Child from the Village* Qutb adopted the Islamist position upon which his fame rests. We will examine Qutb's motives for making this ideological change in a later chapter. What we need to emphasize here is that Qutb's early Islamist writings display many of the same concerns for social justice and national community that figure in his *A Child from the Village*. To this extent, *A Child from the Village* illuminates an important aspect of the context out of which Qutb's Islamism emerged.

2

THE MAKING OF AN EGYPTIAN NATIONALIST

'A prodigiously crowded city'

The 1919 uprising delayed Qutb's departure to Cairo by two years. The disturbances in the rural districts had disrupted transport and the country was in an unsettled state. When Qutb finally did bid farewell to his family sometime in 1921, he did so with a sense of destiny and "mission" (*muhimma*).[1] In the perspective of his parents and siblings, the trip to Cairo, with its promise of higher education and economic gain, was an opportunity for the eldest son to restore the fortunes of the family. As Qutb wrote, "Cairo, in the mind of the villagers, was always associated with great happiness and a radical change in condition."[2] Although Qutb never lost sight of his responsibility to his family, the journey held the deeply personal promise of growth and fulfilment.

Qutb's arrival in Cairo coincided with the onset of political negotiations between Britain and the Egyptian government over the issue of Egypt's independence. Unnerved by what they saw as the "Bolshevik" tendencies of the 1919 uprising, particularly the involvement of the peasants in the countryside,[3] and pressured by a wave of terrorist assassinations, the British saw fit to recognize Egypt unilaterally on 28 February 1922 as a sovereign state. However, the terms of the settlement fell short of the call for full sovereignty that demonstrators had raised above the rooftops of Egypt's villages and cities during the uprising. Britain reserved for itself the right to secure the imperial lifeline of the Suez Canal, protect foreign interests and communities in Egypt, defend Egypt against foreign aggression, and maintain its controlling interest in the Sudan, which the Anglo-Egyptian Condominium had governed since 1899. According to the British, these points would hold until it became possible "by free discussion and friendly accommodation on both sides to conclude agreements in regard thereto."[4]

Without the participation of the Wafd, in 1923 this partial independence was codified in a constitution that stipulated a two-chamber parliament comprising deputies elected by universal male suffrage and an upper-house Senate, made up predominately of notables appointed directly by the sovereign, who was now given the title "king". True to the liberal spirit, the constitution guaranteed individual civil and political rights, including the right to form associations and the freedoms of belief, opinion, and the press. Although authority was officially vested in the people, actual power within the parliament was weighted heavily in favour of the king, who possessed the executive privilege of dismissing legitimately elected cabinets by royal fiat and of rejecting legislation promulgated by the Chamber of Deputies. The Wafd was pleased with the general tenor of the constitution but highly critical of the wide powers it gave the monarch. Nevertheless, the Wafd's overriding desire to engage in politics and thus determine the course of Egyptian politics prompted its leadership to reorganize as a political party, the Hizb al-Wafd, and participate in Egypt's first elections, which were held in January 1924.

The Wafd's main competition was two political organizations, the reconstituted Nationalist Party and the Liberal Constitutional Party (Hizb al-Ahrar al-Dusturiyyun), the latter founded in 1923 by a clique of large landowners. The bond forged between the Wafdist cadre and the Egyptian people during the 1919 uprising proved decisive, allowing the Wafd to secure 179 of the 211 seats in the Chamber of Deputies. With its hands on the levers of power, the Wafd prepared to wrest Egypt's unfettered independence from the British through sustained and reasoned negotiation. In the view of Sa'd Zaghlul and the party hierarchy, the Wafd was uniquely qualified among Egyptian political organizations to undertake the task of governance. Not only had it played a key role in the uprising, its leadership consisted of men of property, education, and professional talent.

Standing above the population of Egyptians, the Wafd and its party competitors professed to know the cure for Egypt's many ills. However, in assuming the mandate, Egypt's political elite took a course that would alienate it from the people. In a way recalling contemporary European political elites, the liberalism of the parties evoked a divided world in which rational and responsible agents were to exercise politi-

cal authority over "irrational" and dependent masses of poor, ignorant, and traditionally educated Egyptians. It suggested not only the
superior knowledge of the patriarchal father but also forms of tutelage
and control displayed, for instance, by European colonialists who in
like manner set aside participatory principles in contexts requiring, in
their view, guided development. The elitism inherent in Egypt's new
political system would be manifested forcefully in the decades to come,
prompting the *effendiyya* and other segments of the population to
withdraw their support for it. For the moment, however, the new leadership united the country under the promise of national fulfilment.

Qutb does not record his initial impressions of Cairo and its turbulent political atmosphere. However, it is likely that the sights, sounds,
and bustling activity of the city confirmed the image of vibrant urban
life and open possibilities that he had nurtured as a boy growing up
in Musha. By the standards of the time Cairo was "a prodigiously
crowded city"[5] numbering just over a million inhabitants. Much of the
city's growth was recent and was the result of increased immigration
from the rural districts where landlessness was on the rise. Then, as
now, Cairo was a microcosm of Egypt. This was so in terms of the
regional origins of the inhabitants, but also as regards the divisions
between old and new, rich and poor, and political elite and masses,
which were increasingly characteristic of the country as a whole. As
with other "dual cities" of the high imperial age, for example Rabat in
French Morocco,[6] these juxtapositions were ideological as well as
social and economic and bespoke, through a plethora of spatial and
architectural signs, institutionalized relationships premised upon the
unequal distribution of political and economic power.

The European-style portions of Cairo planned by 'Ali Mubarak
Pasha, Isma'il's master technocrat, claimed the wide open spaces of the
city's hitherto underdeveloped western flank.[7] Like France's Napoleon
III, Isma'il had aimed to fashion a capital worthy of a great dynasty,
one that boasted modem amenities and was open to modern commerce
and vehicular traffic. Following the example of Baron Hausmann, 'Ali
Mubarak laid out a network of straight-arrow streets that flowed into
traffic *étoiles* and public squares and in the process levelled many
established neighbourhoods. In a few short decades, smart *fin de siècle*
apartment buildings and large commercial establishments, such as the
Sednaoui, Chernla, and Cicurel department stores and the highly
regarded Groppi confectioner, lined the new streets. As Magda Baraka

states, "Urban historians and specialists generally agree that the great era of expansion for Cairo was between 1895 and 1907 when construction activities in the town intensified and there was a high influx of foreigners who constituted 16 per cent of the city's population in 1907."[8] The influx of foreign capital facilitated the construction of luxury hotels like the Semiramis, the Continental Savoy, and the more famous Shepheard's, which served the growing number of European tourists who used Cairo as a jumping off point for visits to the antiquities in Egypt's southern provinces.

New Cairo was very much the city of Egypt's elite class, both foreigners and native Egyptians. Appropriately, the new city hosted the institutions of imperial domination. Running down from Midan Ismail'iyya to the bank of the Nile and to the nearby Gezira Sporting Club and Anglican Cathedral were the British Residency and army barracks. To the east of Shari' Qasr at-'Aini were located the buildings of the Egyptian government ministry complex, and a little beyond, the Abidin Palace. Downtown, on the centrally located Midan Sualyman Pasha, Cairo's British colonial officials and other Europeans could be "fitted up in the English style" at the Mohammed Ali Club.[9] In the evening, Cairo's well-to-do returned home to the villas that graced the tree-lined streets of Garden City and the residential island of Zamalek. Although Egyptians of humble background lived and worked in Cairo's newer districts, they tended to be the employees of the Egyptian politicians and cotton *basha*s, British controllers, industrial entrepreneurs, land brokers, and well-heeled Greek, Italian, Syrian, and Sephardic Jewish merchants for whose economic benefit the new city functioned. The wealthy Egyptian and Levantine inhabitants of the new city tended to converse among themselves in their native Arabic, but most were equally comfortable speaking French and often English, which they had learned at private schools or else abroad. In keeping with European custom, the wives and daughters of the native elite "traveled freely, drove motorcars, dressed in sleeveless clothes and high heels, and wore make up, fancy hairdos and no veil."[10] The winner of the 1954 Miss World Contest, the Egyptian Antigone Constanda, emerged from this relatively liberal environment.

These exclusive areas of the city contrasted sharply with Cairo's historical districts whose origins dated to the Fatimid era. Here was the rich architectural legacy of Egypt's mediaeval Mamluk and Ottoman periods—great mosques and religious schools standing next to merchant residences, many of which were still graced with *mashribiy-yat*, the decorative wooden screens that shielded the women of the household from the scrutiny of the street. Here too were vibrant but decaying neighbourhoods like al-Darb al-Ahmar, al-Husayniyya, and al-Gamaliyya, the settings for several of Naguib Mahfouz's short stories and novels written in the 1940s and 1950s. Scattered throughout the area were mediaeval shrines that commemorated the great saints, figures such as Sayyida Zaynab, Sayyida Nafisa, and Sayyid Husayn, which the faithful visited in search of miracles and blessings. The household heads in these neighbourhoods naturally varied in terms of occupation but for the most part made their living as bazaar merchants, artisans, and minor civil servants. In contrast to the European-ized areas, Arabic was the dominant language of communication. Rather than dress in the jackets and trousers that were common on the other side of the city, the residents of Cairo's mediaeval core dressed in robes (*al-ghalibiyyat*) and turbans or sometimes donned a combination of European and traditional clothes. As Andre Raymond comments, "This old city had been sacrificed to the European city, as early as the time of Isma'il, and this abandonment only worsened subsequently. The road system was neglected, there was insufficient rubbish collection, sewers were poor or non-existent, the water supply was incomplete."[11]

To the northwest and northeast of the city there the were newer, lower class neighbourhoods of Bulaq, Shubra and Matariyya, which grew in tandem with the new city but did not enjoy its wealth and privilege. These tended to comprise neighbourhoods of *effendi*s and other upwardly mobile Egyptians recently arrived from the countryside.

The Egyptian and European elite regarded these less-developed sectors of Cairo, the old Fatimid city especially, as spaces of relative backwardness and, potentially, as breeding grounds of uncontrolled popular upheaval. Egypt's political leaders faced the challenge of melding the various sectors of Cairo into a prosperous integrated unit, just as they faced the larger challenge of forging social progress and national unity in the country as a whole. That Egypt's semi–independent political establishment failed to meet this challenge does much to explain the widespread popular disaffection towards the ruling regime that emerged in the 1930s and 1940s. Magda Baraka quotes the writer Ahmad Amin, "It was in these underdeveloped areas in tenements with minimum sanitation, safety and comfort" that "the future bureaucrats and nationalists, revolutionaries and intellectuals, dictators, and emigrants to Canada and the Arab countries were born."[12]

Soft landing at Dar al-'Ulum

Like many of the rural migrants then spilling into Cairo, Qutb had a family member who preceded him and who now provided him with bearings and a base of support. This was his maternal uncle, Ahmad-Husayn 'Uthman, with whom he lived for four years in the working-class suburb of Zaytun. Under 'Uthman's guidance, Qutb began a course of studies designed to fulfil his boyhood ambition of becoming an *effendi*. He spent the first three years of his studies enrolled at a state secondary school (Madrasa 'Abd al-'Aziz), and from there progressed to Tajhiziyya Dar al-'Ulum, created in 1920 to prepare students for entry into Cairo's Dar al-'Ulum, the teacher's training college. The curriculum at the Tajhiziyya was similar in many respects to that of a regular secondary school. In addition to courses in the religious sciences, Qutb studied calligraphy, biology, and government. Upon graduating in 1929, he was admitted into Dar al-'Ulum.[13]

Dar al-'Ulum was an institution of significance in Old Regime Egypt. Founded in 1872 at the behest of the Khedive Isma'il, the college aimed to bridge the gap between the traditional *madrasa* instruction, centred on al-Azhar, and the new system of modern, state-directed primary and secondary education.[14] As Donald Reid writes, its primary purpose was "to provide what al-Azhar and the professional schools could not: men who could teach the humanities in Arabic with at least some reference to western scholarship."[15] The college's transitional nature was reflected in its course offerings, which combined instruction in the traditional religious sciences, such as jurisprudence (*fiqh*) and Qur'anic exegesis (*tafsir*), with "scientifically-oriented" subjects, such as history, economics, and politics. Overall, Dar al-'Ulum was of a conservative bent. One of the first salvos aimed at Taha Husayn's controversial 1926 book *Fi Shi'r Jalili* (*On Jahiliyya Poetry*), which upset conservative opinion by questioning the veracity of the traditional account of Ibrahim and Isma'il, was delivered by Muhammad 'Abd al-Muttalib, a professor at Dar al-'Ulum.

From the start, Dar al-'Ulum put itself forward as an institution dedicated to high educational standards. The instructors expected the incoming students, mostly from modest backgrounds, to recite the Qur'an from memory and to have a thorough knowledge of the thousand-verse grammatical poem *Alifiyya*,[16] composed by the Damascene scholar Ibn Malik (d. 1274). For centuries, this work had primed students for the advanced study of the Arabic language. Once enrolled, students were exposed to the teaching methods and disciplinary practices associated with the new educational order. Students were obliged to appear in class smartly attired in trousers, jacket and a tarboush rather than the customary robe and turban. They were also required to sit for regularly scheduled mid-term and final examinations.[17] The college screened its applicants and provided modest monthly stipends to those who were needy or exceptionally qualified. Students earning a diploma from Dar al-'Ulum were almost always guaranteed employment. As a result, graduates of the college came to comprise the largest contingent of teachers and administrators in the state school system.

Not surprisingly, the rectors of al-Azhar deeply resented Dar al-'Ulum, regarding it as a challenge to the venerable *madrasa*'s long established monopoly over Arabic and Islamic studies. In 1929, al-Azhar won a small victory against Dar al-'Ulum when its rector, Muhammad al-Ahmadi al-Zawahiri, great-uncle of the Al Qaeda second in command Ayman al-Zawahiri, successfully pressured the Wafdist-Liberal coalition government of the day to close down Tajhiziyya Dar al-'Ulum. Prospective Arabic instructors could now also be recruited from al-Azhar.[18] Qutb, one of the last students to graduate from the Tajhiziyya, was fortunate to have enrolled when he did.

Dar al-'Ulum's hybrid character provided Qutb and other would-be *effendi*s a soft entry into the modernizing world of Cairo. Hasan al-Banna, founder of the Muslim Brotherhood, graduated from Dar al-'Ulum in 1927. He wrote that the college was a place that allowed youths of rural origin to disengage from their peasant backgrounds with a minimum of psychological discomfort.[19] At Dar al-'Ulum Qutb cultivated new intellectual interests, in an environment that honoured traditional virtues and the scholarly traditions of Islam. He honed his skills in literary Arabic, enhanced his knowledge of the exegetical sciences, studied mathematics, geography and history, and participated in at least one literary debate, which the college's faculty and student body attended. Qutb's engagement with his peers in the classroom led to a number of friendships, several of which endured long after he graduated. Dar al-'Ulum's location in Munira on the edge of the government ministry complex allowed Qutb and his student colleagues to observe at first hand the city's ferment of politics and ideas. Cairo's politicians and intellectuals were a talkative bunch and the cafes and modest restaurants dotting the neighbourhood were alive with their conversation. Dar al-'Ulum's proximity to Cairo's "public sphere" led to encounters that encouraged Qutb to make his mark in public life.

Within a year of graduating from Dar al-'Ulum, Qutb joined two of his close friends, Sa'd al-Labban and Muhammad Ibrahim Jabr, to found the journal *Sahifat Dar-al-'Ulum*. According to Lois Aroian, the journal's articles "emphasized helping teachers by introducing them to the latest educational, social and linguistic theories. Some articles translated foreign language materials or considered ideas of foreign education, e.g., 'Abd al-Hamid Hasan's series on DeCroley's method of educating mentally retarded children or on the Montessori method."[20] By including articles of this kind, Qutb and his friends sought to uplift Dar al-'Ulum's students and alumni intellectually and thus enhance the college's reputation against two very different competitors, al-Azhar and the Egyptian University. Although Qutb was on the ground floor of this enterprise, other commitments prevented him from contributing more than a few articles and poems to the journal. Consequently, Sa'd al-Labban assumed the editorship of *Sahifat Dar al-'Ulum* and retained this position until it ceased publication in 1947.[21]

Qutb thrived at Dar al-'Ulum. Yet his views of the college were not uniformly positive. He complained that Dar al-'Ulum was deficient in foreign language instruction, particularly in English, knowledge of which was necessary for an understanding of the wider world. Years after graduating, Qutb recalled that, as he studied, his mind would sometimes wander across the Nile to the Egyptian University whose Faculty of Arts offered instruction not only in English but also in Hebrew and even Syriac. Qutb was jealous at the apparently more progressive and inclusive curriculum of the university, and he hankered to join its student body. However, these yearnings dissipated somewhat after he came to appreciate the positive value of Dar al-'Ulum's commitment to the Arabic-Islamic Classics, which the university, with its French-European cultural orientation, tended to ignore.[22] As Qutb later wrote, "I admit that the curriculum of Dar al-'Ulum is loaded with old, difficult, exhausting and sometimes dry subjects, but a firm grasp of the Arabic language is important."[23]

Qutb lived with the consequences of Dar al-'Ulum's deficit in foreign-language instruction. Although he developed into an excellent Arabic prose stylist and was a published poet and literary critic, it was not until his two-year visit to the United States between 1948 and 1950 that he attained limited proficiency in the English language.[24] Until then, he was wholly dependent for his knowledge of Western society and thought on Arabic translations of European works. In the late 1930s, when his younger brother Muhammad was ready to begin studies at the university, Qutb urged him to take advantage of the English language studies offered there. He did not want monolingualism to hamper his brother's intellectual development.[25]

Qutb graduated from Dar al-'Ulum in 1933 with a diploma in Arabic language and literature. That same year his father died. As the eldest son, Qutb might have felt obliged to return to Musha to take charge of the family's affairs. It was common in Egyptian society for older sons "to accept full responsibility for their younger siblings, even to the extent of sacrificing their own welfare."[26] However, Qutb believed that he could best advance the interests of the family by remaining on his career path. Immediately upon graduating he accepted from Taha Husayn, then supervisor of Elementary Education, a position at the Ministry of Education, and for seven years he taught elementary school, first in Cairo and then in the provinces. The first of these postings was in Dumyat in the eastern Delta, which Qutb took up in September 1935. Qutb found the cold and damp of the Mediterranean winter to be irritating and hard on his health. He was therefore glad when, towards the end of the year, the ministry transferred him to the climatically more agreeable town of Bani Suwayf, some 250 km south of Cairo. In 1936 the ministry transferred him again, this time to Hulwan, a leafy suburban town located on Cairo's southern fringe. There he settled down.[27]

Qutb did well to put down his roots in Hulwan. Created in 1874 by the Khedive Isma'il, it had thermal springs and a tranquil atmosphere that attracted the attention of Cairo's wealthier inhabitants who constructed elaborate villas in the vicinity of its spa. The town was compact and boasted a khedival palace, several sanatoria, the Kabritage Grande Hotel, and an assortment of modest pensions that served the steady stream of European and Egyptian visitors who arrived each winter season, hoping to benefit from the spring's reputed medicinal properties.[28] As Ralph Coury notes, "Friday concerts were provided by the khedival band in one of the palace's gardens, and there was regular steamship service on the Nile. The new homes were stately, many of them having been built with fine quality tiles and gypsum."[29] Although Hulwan's social exclusivity had diminished by the 1930s, largely as the result of the influx of Egyptians of modest means such as Qutb, it remained nevertheless an address of distinction.

Qutb felt at home amid the town's graceful residences and tree-lined streets. The "remarkably pure and dustless atmosphere"[30] agreed with his constitution and he purchased a house on one of the town's main thoroughfares. At some point in the late 1930s, his mother and siblings, discomfited by the combined effects of the Great Depression and the death of the family patriarch, joined him.

It was at his desk in Hulwan that Qutb composed many of the writings associated with the nationalist and early Islamist phases of his career. In both his work and his mode of living, he was every inch an *effendi*. Like others of his social class, he drew a modest salary. In public, he wore a European suit and tie, although in the comfort of his home he would slip into a *jallabiyya*. However, even at home he would eat with a knife and fork at a table rather than with his fingers from a large tray of food, as was the custom in the villages. It was about this time that he began to sport his signature toothbrush moustache. In contrast to the styled "Kaiser" moustache favoured, for instance, by Egypt's King Fu'ad and the aristocratic class, Qutb's sparse facial hair signified values of middle class thrift and expediency. Having attained his goal of employment with the state, he now worked towards fulfilling his true calling, that of a poet and man of letters.

Freedom and expression

At Dar al-'Ulum, Qutb entered into a long-lasting intellectual relationship with 'Abbas Mahmud al-'Aqqad (1889–1964), one of Old Regime Egypt's most important literary figures.[31] Qutb's uncle Ahmad 'Uthman, the Azhar graduate with whom he lived, introduced al-'Aqqad to him. 'Ahmad 'Uthman was a schoolteacher whose interests in journalism and cultural affairs had put him in touch with figures like al-'Aqqad. In the company of his uncle, Qutb visited al-'Aqqad at his home in Heliopolis, a fashionable upper-class suburb near Zaytun. Al-'Aqqad allowed the impressionable teenager to borrow books from his well-stocked library. Both he and 'Uthman were supporters of the Wafd and it was through these men that Qutb's own enthusiasm for the party strengthened. Al-'Aqqad awed Qutb with his commanding presence and prominence as a man of letters.[32] The fact that al-'Aqqad hailed from a similar background constituted an additional point of attraction for Qutb. Born and raised in Aswan, al-'Aqqad shared with Qutb the swarthy complextion of Upper Egypt. Like Qutb he had journeyed to Cairo as a youth to forge a career and a life of the mind. It is difficult to know how much contact Qutb had with al-'Aqqad at this early stage. What is clear is that in him Qutb found a mentor whose life encapsulated everything that he aspired to be. Qutb's relationship with al-'Aqqad was to be one of the most significant of his life. His example not only determined the direction of Qutb's thought, it also set the artistic standards against which Qutb would for many years measure his own literary output.

Al-'Aqqad stood at the cusp of Egypt's national awakening. According to Israel Gershoni and James Jankowski, an important component "of the Egyptian intellectual climate of the 1920s was the belief of Egypt's intellectuals that the Revolution of 1919 must and would be a cultural as well as a political phenomenon. According to this concept the Revolution had to be extended from politics to the economy, the society, and above all to the realm of culture."[33] Whereas the Khedives and their advisers had focused on economic development, the post-independence literary intellectuals celebrated values of national freedom and expression. Many of the intelligentsia made serious attempts in their writings to accommodate selected elements of the heritage, yet they did so in a way that contrasted sharply with the formalism of the inherited culture. Taking cues from the European literary tradition, they expressed their yearnings for cultural regeneration by turning to new literary styles, and genres, such as the novel, the short story, and the drama, which until then had not been part of Arabic literature's generic repertoire.

The social backgrounds and career paths of Egypt's literary intellectuals were remarkably similar. Most were born into medium land-holding families over the last two decades of the nineteenth century. All had benefited from the limited educational opportunities available to Egyptians under the British "Veiled Protectorate". As adults, they earned the income they needed to support their families and literary activities by taking up careers in the professions or in the government ministries. Taha Husayn (1889–1973), the doyen of twentieth-century Egyptian letters, made his name principally as a literary historian, although he also composed novels and some poetry. Muhammad Husayn Haykal (1888–1956), a protégé of the influential Lutfi al-Sayyid, also engaged in literary criticism, and composed what many regard as the first true novel in Arabic, *Zaynab* (1913). Salama Musa (1887–1958), in many ways the most daring of the patriotic literati, advocated the use of the vernacular (*al-ammiyya*) for literary purposes, thus breaking completely with the prevailing literary standards. Ahmad

Amin's (1886–1954) fame rested primarily on his historical works, which proffered modern, critical accounts of Islam's glorious past. The junior member of the cohort, Tawfiq al-Hakim (1902–88), made his mark as a novelist and playwright. Other notable figures included Isma'il Mazhar (1891–1962) and 'Abd al-Qadir Hamza (1880–1956) who were important primarily as journalists commenting on the literary scene.[34] Although the party allegiances of these men varied, and despite their often acrimonious disagreement on points of literary theory, all were nationalists committed to the independence, secular modernization, and cultural renaissance of the Egyptian nation-state. The Western underpinnings of their thought meant that they were often at odds with the conservative-Islamic trend in Egyptian letters.

Al-'Aqqad began his writing career in 1907 as a contributor to the nationalist organs *al-Dustur* and *al-Liwa* and the more literary-oriented journals *al-Bayan* and *Ukaz*. During this early stage he developed a passionate interest in romantic poetry, one of the most important manifestations of the Egyptian literary efflorescence of the 1920s and 1930s. According to M.M. Badawi, Egyptian romanticism, like its European exemplar, "was the literature of revolt", "the product of a society which is at odds with itself and in which the individual questions the relevance of traditional values."[35] This is not to suggest that al-'Aqqad and his literary colleagues yearned for comprehensive rebellion. In many ways they were decidedly conservative, especially on issues pertaining to Egypt's social hierarchy. Yet Romanticism's appetite for innovation, coupled with its concern for questions of personal identity, fit perfectly with their modernist intention to loosen the formalism of the inherited culture.

Al-'Aqqad and his colleagues Ibrahim 'Abd al-Qadir and al-Mazini (1890–1949) spawned a programme of poetic renewal that they set forth in two volumes of literary criticism entitled *al-Diwan: Kitab fi al-Adab wa al-Naqd*.[36] After those volumes, they referred to their programme as the "Diwan School". Immediately they set about to challenge the established neo-classical trend in poetry, which had emerged in the later part of the nineteenth century. According to S. Somekh, the main thrust of neoclassicism "was to go back to an old, venerable model, and to relive the glorious experience of the ancient poets."[37] The neoclassicists were especially interested in the great Arabic poets of the pre-Islamic and early Islamic periods and of the Abbasid age, figures such as Abu Tamman, Abu Nuwwas, Bashshar Ibn Burd, and al-

Mutannabi, acknowledged masters of the *qasida*, the old Arabic ode. The neoclassical poets consciously imitated the thematic types (*aghrad*), metrical structures and imagery of their classical-era mentors.[38]

Leading the charge, al-'Aqqad heaped scorn upon what he considered to be neoclassicism's out-of-date rhetorical style and impersonal subject matter. Inspired by the English romantics Coleridge and Hazlitt, he called for a new kind of poetry that looked not to the past but to the wellsprings of individual feeling and emotion. In al-'Aqqad's opinion, artifice and the imitation of the "ancients" were to be sacrificed to the realm of the authentic, which alone possessed the power to "interpret the soul" and to unite the disparate parts of the poem into an organic, seamless whole of unmediated meaning.[39] In order to make his point al-'Aqqad famously subjected the poetry of the venerable Ahmad Shawqi (1868–1932), neoclassicism's most accomplished practitioner, to withering attack. Claiming that Shawqi's poetry lacked unity and coherency, al-'Aqqad arbitrarily rearranged the verses of Shawqi's panegyric of Mustafa Kamil and challenged readers to discern the difference between the altered version and the original.

Polemic often dominated al-'Aqqad's energies. Yet he never lost sight of the larger purpose of his efforts. For him, romantic poetry possessed the unique ability to touch and transform the sensibilities not only of the individual reader, but also of nations. In contrast to the artistic imitation of the ancients, which fostered a slavish attitude supportive of political authoritarianism, the "poetry of nature" motivated in its audience attitudes of freedom, a quality which al-'Aqqad considered necessary for the establishment of a more politically open and progressive society. Al-'Aqqad wrote, "Give us a poet who composes a poem in which he makes the Egyptians love the flower and I guarantee [that it will give us] the greatest national benefit and the truest renaissance."[40]

Qutb was immediately attracted to the freshness and novelty of al-'Aqqad's literary approach. In it he saw a model capable of accommodating and structuring the artistic aspect of his personality. As a youth, he had displayed a fascination with the conventional poets of the time, snippets of whose verse had infiltrated the village from the world beyond.[41] Now, living in Cairo, he was face to face with the urban sources of a literary trend contrasting sharply with the "old fashioned" culture, which, he came to understand, clouded the worldview and social praxes of traditional Egyptian life. As Qutb saw it, literary modernism marked him off culturally from his parent's generation and opened the door to a new kind of life lived within the modernizing nation-state.

Qutb may have been attracted to the new literary orientation for another reason. Al-'Aqqad's romantic outlook spoke directly to the condition of personal alienation that he experienced during and immediately following his years at Dar al-'Ulum. Cut off from the nurturing and stable social environment of Musha, Qutb, like many new arrivals in Cairo, learned quickly that the sweeping reorientation of one's life came at the price of social estrangement. We get a sense of the "Durkheimian" state of "normlessness" that Qutb experienced in a book entitled *al-Atyaf al-Arba'a* (*The Four Phantoms*), which he wrote with his brother Muhammad and his sisters Amina and Hamida in 1945, years after these feelings had initially set in. In the book, Qutb recalls how he and his siblings had felt like "strangers" (*ghuraba*) in their new home in Hulwan. The unexpected death in 1940 of their mother, who while she lived had instilled in the family a sense of continuity with the past and the traditions of the countryside, magnified this feeling. Qutb pointedly wrote, "We are exiles; we are the small branches whose roots have withered after their estrangement from their native soil. And how far are the branches from establishing themselves in the foreign soil!"[42] Al-'Aqqad's poetic romanticism, with its emphasis on subjective feeling, provided Qutb with the artistic means to recover his authentic self in a social world that for him had lost many of its certainties.

Qutb was not alone in experiencing disillusionment and existential anxiety. According to the literary critic Badawi, the decade of the 1930s was replete with like-minded poets "driven to escape from social and political reality into a solipsistic inner world of private sorrows and vague longings, and into excessive preoccupation with depopulated nature."[43] These men were of roughly the same age as Qutb, and like him took cues from the pioneering efforts of the literary luminaries. Of particular note were the young poets attached to Ahmad Zaki Abu Shadi's short-lived Apollo Society (*Jam'iyyat Abullu*) founded in 1932, which included Muhammad 'Abd al-Mu'ti al-Hamshari (1908–38), Ibrahim Naji (1893–1953), and 'Ali Mahmud Taha (1902–49).[44] Like Qutb, the Apollonians were sensitive men who expressed through the medium of poetry highly personalized responses to their environment.

As a teenager, Qutb cut his literary teeth in a number of smallish, naively written articles that he contributed to journals and organs of the Cairo press. The literary magazine *al-Balagh* published the first of these, in 1922, in which he addressed the issue of pedagogy in the state schools.[45] His first substantial work of criticism was a book entitled *Muhimmat al-Sha'ir fi al-Haya wa Shi'r al-Jil al-Hadir (The Mission of the Poet in Life and the Poetry of the Present Generation)*. The work found a publisher in 1932 when Qutb was twenty-five and in his final year at Dar al-'Ulum. In it, he gave explicit support to the "new" (*al-jadid*) direction in Arabic poetry.[46] Based on a lecture he delivered to Dar al-'Ulum's faculty and student body, it echoed al-'Aqqad's belief that "true poetry" built upon the poet's authentic feelings. The real poet, Qutb wrote, is "a strong personality"[47] whose artistic "taste" (*dhuq*) and "feelings" are uncommonly acute.[48] Armed with insight, he has a responsibility to interact emotionally with the world and to communicate his observations to those whose sensitivities are not as highly developed. In so doing, the poet provides readers with an intuitive account of the issues and concerns of the contemporary age.[49] At the same time, he elevates them to higher levels of perception. As Qutb put it, the poet's mission was "to mediate between what is and what should be." The goal was "to get closer to high ideals, which life's realities hinder."[50]

Qutb took a thinly veiled swipe at the neoclassical poets by mocking the respected poetic canon of the *jahiliyya*. The term "*jahiliyya*" is a Qur'anic reference to the period of "ignorance" that preceded Islam in the Arabian Peninsula, and the poetry of the period was one of the sources of inspiration for the neoclassicists.[51] According to Qutb, *jahiliyya* era poems were flawed. They were divided internally into discrete, disconnected units, a trait that had originated in the Arabs' "childlike" and fragmented view of the world. It was telling of the neoclassicists' conservative tendencies that they continued to emulate this poetic tradition even though it worked against the creative foundations of the modern spirit.

Qutb's negative assessment of the neoclassicists endeared him to the modernists. Most Egyptians, however, continued to admire the neoclassicists. Muhammad Mahdi 'Alam, one of Qutb's professors at Dar al-'Ulum, wrote in his otherwise supportive introduction *The Mission of the Poet* that its author was perhaps too harsh on the neoclassicists, especially Shawqi who had contributed so much to modern Egyptian

67

letters. According to 'Alam, "If [Qutb] had taken objective stock of Shawqi's achievements, he would have seen that his accomplishments far outweigh his shortcomings."[52]

Qutb set forth his yearnings in poems published in several of the literary and scientific journals of the time, including the Wafdist periodicals *al-Balagh* and *al-Balagh al-Usbu'i*, edited by 'Abd al-Qadir Hamza, *Sahifat Dar al-'Ulum*, and Ahmad al-Zayyat's *al-Risala*. Many of these poems subsequently appeared in Qutb's anthology of verse, *al-Shati' al-Majhul* (*The Unknown Shore*), which appeared in January 1935 when Qutb was twenty-nine and working as a schoolteacher in the provinces.[53] In keeping with common practice, he took pains to justify his approach to poetry in the anthology's preface. Thus, poetry is the product of "spiritual forces" that reside in the heart and link the poet with the "great cosmic unity" (*al-wahda al-kawmiyya al-kubra*). Poetry transcends the limitations imposed by science and philosophy, reason and conscience. It encompasses "unknown worlds" devoid of divisions between "past, present and future, self and other". Although reason is necessary for the maintenance of everyday life, it cannot connect the individual with higher truths.[54]

All of this is common stock. However, Qutb did strike new ground in comparing poetry to the artistry of painting. Just as the painter evokes an aesthetic response in the observer, so the poet fashions mental images that reflect his emotions. Qutb explains that almost all of the poems in his collection "possess the element of depiction (*taswir*)". Later on, Qutb would further develop the notion of "depiction" and apply it creatively to the literary appreciation of the Qur'an.

So the collection's feature poem portrays Qutb as a spiritual wayfarer, distrustful of "waking consciousness", who eventually finds repose on an "unknown shore".[55] *'Awda ila al-Rif* ("Return to the Countryside"), which he wrote upon returning to Musha, probably because of his father's death, evokes the physical and emotional landscapes of his past. "Oh, countryside, cradle of my hopes and dreams...I lost you in my childhood, without appreciating what I had...."[56] Other poems are more political in nature, decrying the "dark age" of colonial oppression through which Egypt was then passing. Qutb sums up the overall tenor of the collection in *Gharib!* (Stranger!), in which he is cast as a stranger, not only to his family and friends but also to himself (*gharib bi–nafsi*).[57] These, and the other poems in the collection, underscore Qutb's introspective character, mystical temper and social unease as he attempted to find his way in the big city.

Cairo's watchful critics commented on the effusive quality of Qutb's poetry. The columnist Mahmud Khafif commented on the "other-worldly" quality of the collection. He complained that the wording in many of the poems "was so ambiguous as to render the meaning unclear." Qutb, he said, was typical of many younger poets in his undisciplined use of metaphor and simile and in his careless choice of words. According to Khafif, "weird mental images" and an overwhelming "sense of melancholy" burdened most of the poems. They lacked a clear moral vision and philosophical outlook. In addition, Khafif admitted to being troubled by the praise Qutb heaped upon himself in the anthology's introduction, which was "excessive" even by the standards of Egypt's literary culture, in which self-glorification was the norm.[58] Khafif approached Qutb's collection with a certain bias against the "modernist" poets. Yet Qutb perhaps deserved the harsh critique. He was at this stage a sophomore when it came to poetry, still too intoxicated with words and emotions to apply systematically the artistic principles drawn from al-'Aqqad's more measured example. Qutb would have done well to heed his mentor's advice, that the poet was obliged to capture a vision of reality, not give free rein to his emotions.

Yet what attracts notice in these poems is Qutb's apparent alienation from the world around him. He comes across very much as the outsider, a young man at odds with the banality of existence, who reaches for and sometimes catches a glimpse of a higher spiritual truth. He is of a type well represented in European Romantic and Existentialist literature. As we noted, that literature, communicated to him indirectly by means of al-'Aqqad, served as one of his inspirations. However, there were other influences at work. By casting himself as a wandering ascetic seeking after higher truth, Qutb was close to a narrative tradition long honoured in Islam, particularly among the Sufis. Having grown up in an environment in which people took occult forces for granted, he was predisposed to a belief in "other worlds". Yet, in an obvious departure from that tradition, Qutb finds his profession not in a dogmatic conception of God or even magic, but in subjective consciousness, like the Romantics.

The basic structure of Qutb's thought would remain constant over the decades. In his condition of alienation, we may discern the seeds of his mature Islamist belief in a radical disjuncture between God's transcendental truth and the lies and deceit that were, in his view, characteristic of his age, which were the consequence of man's separation from the divine truth. Famously, Qutb would apply the term "*jahiliyya*" to the barbarism that he believed dominated modern life, excising the term from its original temporal context. Egyptians and other modern peoples, he would say, were "ignorant" of God's will, in the same way that the pre-Islamic Arabs had been. Just as the poet had a mission to see beyond the dross of the 'disenchanted world', so too was there need for a vanguard of spiritually enlightened believers to carry forward the ennobling message of the Qur'an. Throughout his career, first as a poet and then as an Islamist ideologue, Qutb believed in the possibility of illuminating ordinary existence through recourse to truths culled from the spiritual realm.

Qutb's strong views on the merits of the new literature led to his involvement in the disputes that marked the literary scene in the interwar era. By his own admission, Qutb loved nothing better than a good scrap between authors. "From the start I exalted in literary battles (*al-ma'arika al-adabiyya*)...I preferred the clamour of the [literary] storm to the silence of tranquility."[59] Qutb's style in these debates was hostile. He called opponents "flies" and "worms". On one occasion, he questioned a literary rival's humanity. It is tempting to view this verbal violence as reaching back to the mediaeval Arabic thematic of the *hija*, the literary defamation of rivals and enemies. Carefully crafted lampoons, often modelled on mediaeval prototypes, made their way into modern Arabic literature.[60] Indeed, Qutb once accused a literary rival of resorting to *hija* in his literary argument with al-'Aqqad.[61] However, the constancy of Qutb's angry style suggests that it was less the function of literary device and more the expression of an ambitious personality seeking to prove his mettle in the competitive field of Egyptian letters.

Qutb joined the fray in defending al-'Aqqad against fellow Romantics in the Apollo Group. Relations between al-'Aqqad and the Apollonians had deteriorated after al-'Aqqad suggested that they replace "the Greek 'Apollo' by 'Utarid, who had been the God of writers to both the Chaldeans and the Arabs."[62] Al-'Aqqad followed this snipe by alleging that Abu Shadi, the Apollo Group's founder, was closely tied to the unpopular political regime of Isma'il Sidqi, which had come to power in 1930. The Apollo poets returned the slander by deriding al-'Aqqad for his "overbearing pride". They compared him unfavourably to their patron, the Lebanese Khalil Mutran (1872–1949), one of the original proponents of poetic Romanticism. Abu Shadi went on to disparage al-'Aqqad's 1933 Diwan, *Wahy al-Arba'in* (Inspiration in the Fortieth Year), which al-'Aqqad considered his best work to that date.[63]

Qutb answered the attacks upon his mentor, explaining the Apollo Group's calumny as the product of jealousy.[64] In Qutb's opinion, their adulation of Mutran was undeserved. It was simply a roundabout way of snubbing al-'Aqqad.[65] Qutb dubbed the Apollo Group "mawaqib al-'ajazah" (*The Procession of the Handicapped*) because, in his view, the major reason for their grouping together was a feeling of individual handicap and weakness despite their pretensions to maturity and health.[66]

Qutb was more vociferous in his support of al-'Aqqad against Mustafa Sadiq al-Rafi'i. Of Syrian descent, al-Rafi'i was a staunch defender of conservative values in literature and religion, and believed that these were under siege by the secular, iconoclastic agenda of the literary modernists.[67] As a self-proclaimed defender of the "Qur'an, its language and its eloquence",[68] he accused the modernists of wreaking havoc upon the style and pronunciation of the Arabic language, especially by introducing foreign words into its lexicon. Confident of his abilities and the justness of his cause, he sparred with some of the most talented representatives of the new trend. In 1924 he entered into a feud with Salama Musa over Musa's declared intention to develop the colloquial into a literary vehicle. According to al-Rafi'i, such an undertaking was blasphemous because it diminished the importance of the Qur'an-based literary language. That same year he penned a series of articles aimed at Taha Husayn's *Fi al-Shi'ir al-Jahili* (*On Pre-Islamic Poetry*), a book whose critical methods questioned the authenticity of the pre-Islamic poetic canon and the factual basis of certain events mentioned in the Qur'an, most notably the narrative of Abraham and his son Isma'il.[69] In Husayn's view, one should not regard such accounts as history but as literary devices designed to make certain points about morality and religious identity. For al-Rafi'i, however, the book was an assault on the Islamic-Arabic heritage.

Al-Rafi'i's conservatism made him a tempting target for modernists like al-'Aqqad. Al-'Aqqad ripped into al-Rafi'i's works, especially Part II of his *Ta'rikh Adab al-Arab* (*The History of Arabic Literature*), which dealt with the rhetorical and stylistic genius of the Qur'an (*al-*

71

i'jaz), a topic that Qutb would later address.[70] Al-Rafi'i countered by accusing al-'Aqqad of plagiarism.

Al-Rafi'i's died in 1937. But his followers (the "Rafi'iyyun") took up the battle against the modernists. It was after they launched fresh attacks against al-'Aqqad that Qutb rushed to his mentor's defence. Qutb decried the torrent of unfair criticism levelled at al-'Aqqad. He denied the Rafi'iyyun's claim that al-'Aqqad's stature as "first writer of the Wafd" rested on his political connections to that party. According to Qutb, al-'Aqqad was widely hailed as "the colossal writer" (*al-katib al-jabbar*) of the generation even after he left the Wafd Party in 1937, proof that his fame was not dependent upon political patronage.[71] In Qutb's opinion it was fitting that, in 1934, al-'Aqqad should have received from Taha Husayn, Ahmad Shawqi's venerated title "Prince of Poets" (*Amir al-Shu'ara*).[72] In Qutb's view, al-'Aqqad was the "imam of the new school",[73] a man whose "psychological capacity" (*taqat al-'Aqqad al-nafsiyya*) and sweep of artistic vision surpassed al-Rafi'i's limited and purely "intellectual" (*dhiniyya*) propensities.[74]

Viewed decades after the events, Qutb's squabbles with the Rafi'iyyun and other literary opponents appear petty and insignificant, driven more by ego than by any substantive issue. Qutb admitted as much when he confessed that most of the motivations behind the literary fights were "ignoble". Indeed, said Qutb, future generations would surely look upon them with "disgust".[75] Yet what is significant is Qutb's view of the role of religion in the debate. According to Qutb, al-Rafi'i's supporters sought advantage by appealing to people's religious sensibilities, turning the question of "the new and the old" in poetry into one of "religion or irreligion", the "people of paradise" against the "people of the fire". In Qutb's mind, the reference to the Islamic religion was a smokescreen: "Religion, religion.... This is the battle cry (*saiha*) of the feeble and the weak person who defends himself with it whenever the current threatens to sweep him away (*jarafahu al-tayyar*)." Following al-'Aqqad, Qutb asserted that religion should be limited to "the performance of the good and the reform of the individual soul for the sake of society, and to the preparation of this society for the life of the individual. At times this is accomplished through advice, sometimes through admonition, and at other times through legislation." According to Qutb, religion has nothing to do with the arts (*al-funun*), for whereas religion is "based upon the conviction of emotional sensibility and upon intellectual investigation," art is "the translation of the human soul and of its sentiments and hopes. These are not religious tendencies except in areas which concern the reform of the individual within the context of society."[76]

Qutb is here a long way from his eventual Islamist position, in which he would insist that all aspects of life and human endeavour, including the literary and the artistic, must be grounded in and reflect the divine mandate. At this stage of his career, he was prepared to challenge the representatives of Islamic orthodoxy on the basis of an avowed literary progressivism whose roots lay in Europe.[77] Although he was by nature "fascinated with the spirit and everything related to it",[78] doctrinaire understandings of Islam had no appeal for him.

The malaise of the effendiyya

Qutb's involvement in progressive literary trends matched his strong interest in social and political issues, especially questions related to Egypt's independence and national identity. These issues were important topics of concern and debate among the Egyptian intelligentsia in the post-World War I era. Many things in Qutb's background made him receptive to the nationalist current. His father's support of the Nationalist Party, coupled with Musha's involvement in the 1919 anti–British uprising, encouraged him at a young age to look beyond the traditional solidarity networks of kinship and village to the larger conceptual community of the nation. Cairo's educational institutions, where Qutb forged bonds with other literate and politically aware *effendi*s, furthered his ability to "imagine" Egypt. In addition, Cairo's prolific publishing houses disseminated dozens of periodical journals, magazines and books, which put him in touch with thinkers and ideas from around the country, thus enhancing his apprehension of the national community. Qutb found in all of these sources a template of meaning. He discovered in the professed cross-sectional solidarity of the Egyptian nationalist movement a surrogate for the primordial village community that he had left behind. Such identification was a balm that went a long way in soothing his general malaise, which, we have noted, he expressed in his poetry.

Qutb and his fellow *effendi*s applauded many aspects of the developmental impulse that had touched even rural Egyptians by the first decades of the twentieth century, including changes in the structure of the state and the advent of new technologies. However, the enthusiasm of these young men for state building and national advancement did not generally extend to the cultural Westernization that occurred in tandem with modernization. On this issue, they disagreed with the relatively small group of Westernizing intellectuals like Taha Husayn and Salama Musa who believed that Egyptians should emulate the cultural patterns of Europe rather than those of the Muslim East.

One reason for this distaste related to the lingering hold upon these "sons of the country" of the primordial ties of religion and custom, ascribed identities that cut close to the bone. Scattered references in Qutb's published works suggest that beneath his jacket and tie stood a man anchored in the cultural universe of village Egypt. We have already noted the presence in Qutb's adult imagination of the *jinn* and *afarit*, which, despite his professed modernity, he was unable to shake off. Another example is Qutb's attitude towards women. As we shall see, he was uncomfortable with the relatively liberal gender relations that were a feature of the time; in his view, cultural Westernization diminished the traditional female virtues of modesty and domesticity.[79] Given this enduring framework of identity, it was natural that Qutb and men of similar background should have been hesitant in accepting uncritically the full range of social and economic transformations, especially those that eroded the "cultural givens" of the customary society.

But another, perhaps more decisive factor related to the political and economic failures of the 1930s and 1940s, which had the effect of heightening awareness among the *effendiyya* of the political implications of culture. These troubles prompted Egyptians such as Qutb to associate Egypt's malaise with the cultural Westernization that found favour among the intellectuals, politicians and businessmen who were attached to Egypt's elite stratum. In an effort to give voice to their concerns, they transformed their everyday sense of cultural belonging into a passionate patriotism that distinguished strongly between the national Self and the foreign Other. The unfolding of this process, common to modernizing societies subjected to colonialism, lends historical legitimacy to the contention that it is above all in times of collective strife that communities invest emotional attachment in the symbols of the collective community.[80] That is to say, the focus of the Egyptian *effendi* nationalists on the indigenous and culturally authentic rather than the foreign created a classic boundary mechanism, which marked off politically disenfranchised and economically distressed Egyptians from the Westernized political culture of the dominant order. It provided their quest for political empowerment with a "cultural affect" grounded in the validating sentiment of national pride.

The seeds of political trouble followed upon Egypt's attainment of its truncated independence. Although the Wafd continued to put itself forward as the legitimate "conscience of the nation", the unwillingness of either the Palace or the British residency to allow it and other parties to function on their own terms cut short its goal of forging a fully independent state.[81] Threatened by a political force that aimed to diminish its divinely sanctioned authority, the King did what he could to shore up his position against the Wafd. To this end, he forged alliances with al-Azhar, which felt threatened by the secularizing tendencies of the liberal forces, and made a claim to the caliphate, which Mustafa Kemal Atatürk had abolished in 1924.

The monarchy's strongest card, however, resided in its ability to "short circuit" the parliamentary process by means of its constitutional prerogative. The tone of royal intervention was set in 1925 when King Fu'ad (reigned 1917–36) dismissed parliament on the day of its opening and installed in its place a new government comprising loyal courtiers who organized themselves as the pro-Palace Union Party (*al-Hizb al-Ittihad*). The pattern was repeated when, with palace support, Isma'il Sidqi assumed the premiership and replaced the constitution with one that increased the monarch's veto powers to cover all parliament-enacted legislation. For five years Egypt was subjected to a Palace dictatorship while the Wafd, which from 1927 was under the helm of Zaghlul's successor Mustafa al-Nahhas, stood by in impotent disarray.

The British tended quietly to support the Palace in its efforts to curb the ambitions of the Wafd. They were also prepared to apply direct force when, in their view, the situation demanded it. Thus, in response to the 1924 nationalist assassination of Sir Lee Stack, the British issued an ultimatum to the Wafd government, insisting that Egypt pay a cash indemnity, withdraw its troops from the Sudan, and issue a public apology. Outraged, Zaghlul resigned rather than give in to the demands. Two years later, in 1926, the British High Commissioner, Lord Lloyd, brought a gunboat into play, an action that prompted the Wafd to step down from power after having recently attained its second overwhelming electoral victory.

Only in 1935 did Britain soften its anti–Wafd stance by insisting that the Palace put an end to the unpopular Sidqi dictatorship and bring the party of Zaghlul back to power. But even here British self-interest prevailed. Wary of Italy's African ambitions, Britain deemed it important that Egypt cooperate with it in the event of war with the fascists. Such cooperation, the British understood, could only come about on the heels of a new treaty arrangement, which only the Wafd, on account of its political legitimacy, would be in a position to negotiate.

Britain's gambit paid off. Once restored to office after new elections, the Wafd signed the Anglo-Egyptian Treaty of 1936, which modified the previous arrangements by limiting the British military presence chiefly to the Suez Canal Zone and by instituting provisions to terminate the Capitulations and Mixed Courts.[82] In acknowledgment of these changes, the British High Commissioner in Egypt was re-designated Ambassador. Some Egyptian intellectuals and politicians heralded the treaty as a meaningful moment in the struggle for full independence. Many others, including Qutb, regarded its provisions as meagre and inadequate. In the view of the Egyptian mainstream, the treaty was a betrayal of the popular demand for unfettered sovereignty.

*Effendi*s were also angered that Egypt's economy continued to operate according to terms dictated from abroad. Egypt's position as a producer of commodities in the European-directed world market economy limited the expansion of local manufacturing. Such manufacturing as did exist was owned by Europeans, for instance, the French-owned Société Générale des Sucreries et la Raffinerie d'Egypte, located north of Cairo, and the Belgian-owned Société Anonyme des Ciments d'Égypte, near Hulwan.[83] According to the historian Marius Deeb, the preponderant foreign elements tended to perpetuate their dominance by employing local foreigners, and rarely employing Egyptians: "Egyptians," therefore, "had little chance of being employed in business houses."[84] The unprecedented numbers of graduates of the expanded education system attempting to enter the job market in the 1930s aggravated the situation. As Gershoni and Jankowski remark, "Between 1925–6 and 1935–6, enrollment in state secondary schools nearly tripled and enrollment at the Egyptian University more than doubled…"[85] Yet rather than slip into jobs, many recent graduates found themselves unemployed. The onset of the worldwide Great Depression in the 1930s made matters worse.

The condition of Egypt's mass base was even more desperate. In the effort to hamper the emergence of an independent working class movement, Egypt's political establishment tightened controls over the emerging trade union movement. As a result, the normal conditions of these urban workers remained "unsafe, unhealthy and personally degrading",[86] In the countryside peasants found themselves living in conditions of financial uncertainty and poverty unknown since the rapacious days of the khedives. A sharp decline in cotton prices led to indebtedness for those who had to meet mortgage payments or other financial obligations. During the period, per capita national income declined by ten per cent.

The political regime's relationship with Bank Misr illustrates its hold on economic power. Founded in 1920 by the upper-class nationalist Tal'at Harb, the bank aimed to fund a native controlled capitalist sector capable of challenging foreign enterprise. Until its collapse in 1939, "the bank was highly successful, having created companies that included the largest textile firm in the Middle East, transportation, cotton ginning and insurance companies, Egypt's first national airline and a host of smaller companies."[87] Yet, as in other areas of elite activity, nationalist principles took a back seat to self-interest and expediency. Although geared towards national empowerment, Bank Misr in fact ended up providing indigenous landowners the means by which to diversify the wealth. Pressured by the cotton pashas, the bank compromised its opposition to foreign capital and entered into a number of joint ventures with European corporations, hence securing for itself junior partner status within the world capitalist economy.[88]

Bank Misr's capitulation was perhaps inevitable. In most cases, Egypt lacked the economic capacity to initiate advanced commercial and industrial projects on its own. Regardless, in the final analysis the Misr Group did not differ substantially from the economic activities of comprador capitalists such as Muhammad Ahmad 'Abbud, who in open partnership with British investors amassed a personal fortune in the 1930s and 1940s.[89]

It was galling to the *effendiyya* that Egypt's political elite had done so little to advance the economic condition of the people and the cause of Egypt's national sovereignty. As the generation that emerged after World War I came slowly to understand, the pashas were far too jealous of their privileged access to state and economic power to desire quick and far-reaching modifications to the status quo. In the view of the *effendi*s, careers, livelihoods, and national dignity were shortchanged by a system mired in the governing class' material self-interest and excessive preoccupation with the attainment of political office. In place of pride and self-worth, the young men of the inter-war period felt deep humiliation. Gradually the upbeat tone of the 1920s gave way to a mood of malaise and increasing anger. Many younger Egyptians abandoned the Wafd and other establishment parties for alternative organizations and modes of national expression. Even al-'Aqqad, once a stalwart supporter of the Wafd, distanced himself from the party. Bitterly angry at the terms of the 1936 Anglo-Egyptian Treaty and weary of Nahhas Pasha's domineering ways, he joined the newly formed, rival Sa'dist Party (Hizb al-Sa'diyyin), named after Sa'd Zaghlul, in 1937. A few years later, Sayyid Qutb would follow suit.

'Wake up, Egyptian youth!'

The currents of discontent travelled the social pathways of Cairo's civil and educational institutions. Writing from his student perch at Dar al-'Ulum, Qutb captured the simmering mood of discontent in this passage from his 1932 work *The Mission of the Poet*:

Why do our poets not compose happy and cheerful melodies? Why do our arts not depict an atmosphere of strength and energy? Have we fought and won a battle against our enemies? Have we opened a new era for the world? Have we gained our independence? Can we breathe freely? Have we made any industrial breakthrough that we can be proud of? Have we made any scientific advances that we can brag about?

One can protest and agonize. A nation that does not complain about a situation like this is senseless and is certainly doomed to be destroyed. Those who are ecstatic and exhilarated belong to one of two groups. Either they are selfish and do not care about the nation [...] or lack emotional ardor (*wijdan*), have no dignity, and live like animals and germs.[90]

Several of Qutb's poems of the period played on the brooding disillusionment. In one of these, he shamed the youth of the nation by contrasting their "ignorant, slack" attitude with the willingness of the young men of the Sudan's nationalist White Flag League to sacrifice their lives in pursuit of a Nile Valley united under the Egyptian Crown. Drawing upon the rhetoric of national rebirth, he accused Egyptians of having fallen into slumber, indolence and lassitude. Egyptians, Qutb intoned, should follow the heroic example of these energetic Sudanese. He put it plainly, "Wake up, Egyptian youth!"[91] He believed that the educated young men of Egypt had a moral responsibility to prod the politicians to respond vociferously to the political and economic challenges of the time.

The coronation of the sixteen–year-old King Faruq was a bright spot in this atmosphere of gloom. There was wide consensus that Faruq's father, the late King Fu'ad, had fallen short of popular nationalist hopes and expectations. With other Egyptians, Qutb heralded the 1937 coronation of Faruq as signalling a new era in the country's history. He was confident that the boy-king would apply his executive powers in ways beneficial to the wellbeing of ordinary Egyptians, thus reversing Fu'ad's inept policies. He was not alone in his expectation. The "popular periodical *Akhir Sa'a* published a special 'coronation edition' ('*adad at-tatwij*) for Faruq that featured on its cover a cartoon of the king—sitting on his throne in a dignified manner and dressed in full military regalia—being given a lavishly bedizened crown by al-Masri Effendi, a popular caricature character from the period."[92] Replicating the gushing praise accorded the new monarch by the press, Qutb wrote, "It is a celebration of the unity of God and the people...We are a nation that appreciates the good deeds of a virtuous man."[93]

However, in this case too Egyptians would be disappointed. Stories of Faruq's alleged personal excesses, including his enormous appetite for women and food, gradually diminished his standing in the eyes of the people. Over the following years, Qutb and others looked on in dismay as Faruq slid inexorably into what appeared as moral decline. Within a decade of his coronation, Faruq was an embarrassment to the Egyptian people rather than a source of pride and hope.

Qutb was teaching in the Delta town of Dumyat when in 1935 student demonstrations broke out in Cairo demanding the full restoration of the constitution, which Sidqi had abrogated five years earlier. Qutb, no doubt, was pleased upon hearing of the throngs of young men, most of them students, who took to the streets in what was the largest political manifestation Egypt had seen since the 1919 uprising. He would have read in the press how British-officered Egyptian police met the demonstrators and opened fire on the crowd at the 'Abbas Bridge, killing one and wounding another. He would have felt strong emotion, too, at hearing how the martyred student's large funeral procession turned into an occasion of national solidarity.[94]

Among the student demonstrators was the seventeen–year-old Gamal 'Abd al-Nasser, Qutb's future nemesis. Although important differences eventually set these two at odds, at this stage they shared a common orientation toward the future and the need for change.

Qutb viewed Egypt's predicament from the vantage point of a man of letters. Sensitive to the role of culture in the formation of identity, he understood that foreign domination over Egypt extended beyond the political and economic spheres to those practices and beliefs by which Egyptians made sense of their lives. It was bad enough that Egyptians were victims of economic exploitation and ineffectual government. That they were also in danger of losing their souls to the corroding effects of Western culture was, in his view, of equal or greater concern. Qutb regarded the European residents of Egypt as the primary sponsors of this cultural invasion. But he understood that acculturated elements within Egypt's political and business elite were also to blame. He discerned that the Westernized legal and educational institutions facilitated the spread of foreign values and habits. These were institutions concerned with the most basic and intimate realms of the country's social existence.

Qutb challenged the cultural foundations of the dominant order by drawing upon aspects of the ethical, religious and Arabic traditions of Egypt's collective heritage (*turath*). In his view, only by wedding cultural traditions with political agency would Egyptians be in a position to challenge imperialism and the legitimacy of the British-sanctioned political establishment. In less contentious circumstances, Qutb might have been content to relegate the vast portion of this ancestral tradition to the background of his consciousness. However, the social and political environment of the time encouraged him to regard tradition as a powerful and available indicator of national difference. As Partha Chatterjee succinctly states in his study of the subaltern nationalisms of nineteenth century Bengal, "The most powerful as well as the most creative results of the nationalist imagination in Asia and Africa are posited not on identity but rather on a difference with the 'modular' forms of the national society propagated by the modern west."[95]

Sayyid Qutb was not alone in holding such a view. He was part of a large *effendi*-driven effort to fill the spaces of the modernizing Egyptian state with culturally authentic content. Two of the most forceful manifestations of this trend were the Society of the Muslim Brothers (*Jama'at al–Ikhwan al-Muslimun*)—the organization that Qutb would later join—and Young Egypt (*Misr al-Fatat*), founded in 1928 and 1933 respectively. Both were true grassroots organizations that emerged independently of the political establishment. Their self-identity was not of any specific social group or economic class, but of the ennobling traditions of the people against the political, economic, and cultural power of the elite.[96] Yet, despite the similarities, the Muslim Brotherhood and Young Egypt differed in one important respect. Whereas Young Egypt was secular and focused on the unity and independence of the Nile valley, the Muslim Brotherhood sought to regulate the conduct of Egyptians in terms of *Usul al-Din* ("The Principles of Religion") and, at least theoretically, privileged the *umma* over the territorially defined Egyptian nation-state.

The Muslim Brotherhood was founded in 1928 the Canal Zone city of Isma'iliyya by Hasan al-Banna (1906–49), a twenty-two–year-old schoolteacher who like Qutb had left his native village to pursue higher education in Cairo.[97] Al-Banna's father had been the prayer leader and teacher at the local mosque, and from him he gained a deep appreciation for Islam's moral foundations. His burgeoning religiosity found an outlet in the Hasafiyya Sufi order, in whose *dhikr*s, devotional exercises for "remembering" the divine Reality, he joined; al-Banna had been initiated into the order by the son of its founder, Hasanayn al-Hasafi.[98] At the same time, he strengthened his ethical framework by reading the works of the mediaeval theologian and Sufi Abu Hamid al-Ghazali. In 1923, he travelled to Cairo to enrol in Dar al-'Ulum, the same school that Qutb would later join. During this formative period in his life al-Banna, the pious young man from the provinces, became alarmed at the moral condition of the country, which he blamed on Western influences. He writes in his memoirs, "After the First World War and during my stay in Cairo, a tide of atheism and lewdness overtook Egypt. In the name of individual and intellectual freedom, it devastated religion and morality. Nothing could stop the storm. Circumstances made it still more dangerous."[99]

It is telling of al-Banna's motivations that he founded the Muslim Brotherhood in Isma'iliyya, where after his graduation in 1927 the Education Ministry recruited him to teach Arabic. No other city in Egypt bore as many traces of Egypt's subservient position within the international order. As he settled into his modest accommodation, al-Banna took note of the luxurious homes of the European Suez Canal employees and compared them with the "miserable dwellings" of the Egyptian workers. Such was the degree of foreign power in the Canal Zone that even the street signs were printed in European languages, not in Arabic. Just beyond the city were the military bases of the British, a visible and humbling reminder of Egypt's subordination to a foreign power.

Other indignities and threats to Islam's well-being bothered al-Banna. He decried the presence of Christian and Bahai missionaries who, in his view, conspired to separate Egyptians from the Islamic source of their moral strength. He was perturbed at the prevalence in elite circles of Theosophy, the mystical philosophy founded by the Russian Madame Blavatsky in 1873, and was "very much pained" at the progress of secularism.[100] The Egyptian University, which he saw as a main purveyor of atheism, was on the same low level as the nightclubs that dotted Cairo's entertainment districts. Finally, the muted response of the religious scholars of al-Azhar to the "harsh Western invasion" disillusioned al-Banna.[101] In his view, the *'ulama's* inaction stood in the way of Islamic renaissance.

On the other hand, al-Banna expressed deep respect for the common people. In order to reach them and awaken the faith that lay "dormant" (*na'im*) in their souls,[102] he preached in Isma'iliyya's coffee houses, rather than the mosque, the traditional site of Islamic sermonizing. Standing on a chair, he used "everyday language" to remind his listeners, made up mostly of workers and minor civil servants, of the divinely mandated principles of the Qur'an and the normative precepts of the Prophet's *sunna*, which together provided guidance for the effective and just ordering of society.[103] According to al-Banna, one day six of the men who had been attending the lectures approached him. They bore the pain that was in their souls, a pain that he shared:

You see that the Arabs and Muslims have no dignified place in this country. They are no more than servants belonging to the foreigners. We have nothing to offer except the blood running in our veins, our lives, our faith, our honor, and these coins that we cut from our family expenses. You know better than we do how best to serve Islam, the Muslim *umma*, and our country.[104]

The account is highly dramatized, but as Richard Mitchell remarked, it effectively communicates the "inspiration and spirit of the movement".[105] In fact, it was in response to these men's appeal that al-Banna established the Society of the Muslim Brothers. The Brothers held their first meetings in a rented room on top of a local library. Al-Banna was concerned mainly with his followers' moral education, and their ability to spread the revivalist message to the "wayward" Muslims of the nation and beyond. To this end he had them study *hadith*, Qur'anic recitation and the biographies of the Prophet and companions, and encouraged them to excel in public speaking in preparation for the Brotherhood's missionary activity. The training was practical and focused not on advanced theological arguments but on the basics of the creed.

There was a distinct mystical flavour to the Brotherhood's outlook, especially in its formative stages. Drawing upon forms of piety that were familiar and meaningful to him, al-Banna incorporated Sufi practices into the Brotherhood's religious devotions. According to Brynjar Lia, the imprint of Sufism was especially evident in the Brotherhood's gatherings for song recitals and *dhikr*, in its processions, complete with flags and banners, which were characteristic of the Sufi orders (*turuq*), and in its hosting of night vigils. The Sufi influence was also apparent in al-Banna's stipulation that he must receive an "oath of allegiance" (*bay'a*) from the Brothers, in the same manner as Sufi *shaykhs* who demanded obedience from their disciples.[106]

However, these Sufi practices diminished by the late 1930s. As Lia explains, by that time Salafi influences, stemming mostly from the reform tradition of Rashid Rida (d. 1935) and the Wahhabis of Saudi Arabia, encouraged al-Banna to distance the Brotherhood from the Sufi tradition. It was thus that "the green banner and the Sufi hymns of the Muslim Brothers in Ismailia were abandoned and a new banner adopted (the legendary two swords cradling a Qur'an), as well as a new official hymn."[107] Even so, aspects of the mystical tradition remained strong among the Muslim Brothers. Al-Banna never abandoned the Sufi–oriented quests of moral purification and transcendence. Throughout his career, he continued to regard the bond that existed between him and his followers in spiritual terms.[108] As an inward-looking aesthete, Sayyid Qutb would come to appreciate the Muslim Brotherhood's underlying mystical temper. Indeed, the Brotherhood's strong emphasis on religion's experiential dimension was one of the factors that encouraged him to join it in 1953.

In 1932 al-Banna moved the Brotherhood's headquarters from Isma'iliyya to Cairo. In order to attract people to the organization he resorted to "methods of propaganda" (*wasa'il al-da'iyya*) similar to those employed by the Wafd and other nationalist organizations. The Brotherhood had its own "publications, journals, newspapers, articles, plays, film, radio broadcasting". In al-Banna's words, these publications "made it easy to influence the minds of mankind, women as well as men, in their homes, places of business, factories and fields."[109] In the mid-1930s, at a time when nationalist youth groups were forming around the world, the Brotherhood established Rover Scout units

(*Jawwala*) whose goal was to instil in young Muslim males the ethos of *futuwwa* (noble manliness, chivalry, bravery, courage and persever-ance). According to al-Banna, cultural development and grassroots mobilization constituted the necessary groundwork for the Brother-hood's goal of returning Muslims to their faith. He was explicit that ideological "acquaintance" (*ta'rif*) and organizational "formation" (*takwin*) should precede the "execution" (*tanfidh*) of the organization's reformist vision.[110]

The strategy bore fruit. By 1938 the Brotherhood had spread beyond its initial bases in the Canal Zone, the eastern Delta and Cairo to mid-dle and southern Egypt. Although its membership numbered at this time only in the thousands, its popularity was growing. By the mid-1940s, the Brotherhood was reputed to have half a million members and supporters throughout Egypt. Most of the adherents were *effen-di*s of rural origin, although some religious shaykhs also joined. The Society's growing success allowed al-Banna to appreciate, as never before, Islam's power to meld the disparate interests of Egyptians into a common front of purposeful action. "Brethren...you are a new spirit making its way into the heart of the nation and revivifying it though the Qur'an."[111] He saw that, once strengthened by a true understand-ing of Islam, Egyptians would be in a position effectively to resist for-eign political and cultural encroachment. Slowly and without precise design, al-Banna had transformed what had originated as an Islamic benevolent society with strong Sufi overtones into a burgeoning social movement.

In these circumstances, it was natural that al-Banna and the Brothers conceived the possibility of establishing an Islamic political order (*nizam*), to be set up first in Egypt and then in other countries. After all, was not Islam a comprehensive system of belief and social practice that touched every important aspect of individual and community con-cern? Beginning in 1933, al-Banna directed a number of *rasa'il* ("mes-sages") to the Palace, the most notable being a 1938 letter addressed to King Faruq, entitled *Nahwa al-Nur* (Toward the Light), enjoining the monarch to stand behind the Brotherhood's reformist programme:

Your Excellency,

Peace be with you, and God's mercy and blessings! To proceed: All that impels us to submit this message to Your Excellency is a keen desire to guide the nation, whose leadership God has placed in your care and whose affairs He has delegated to you during its modern era, in a benevolent manner which will set it on the most excellent of paths.... Be the first to come forward in the name of God's Apostle (May God bless and save him!) bearing the vial of Qur'anic healing, to save the tormented, sick world![112]

The tone of these messages is respectful and deferential. By gracefully pulling the Palace into its orbit, the Brotherhood hoped to supplant the British as the power behind the throne. The Palace tended to encourage the Brotherhood's forays into street politics, regarding the organization as a valuable counterweight to the Wafd. Interestingly, the political authority was tolerant towards the Brotherhood and other *da'wa* (missionary) groups that began to take shape at this time. This was because instead of preaching political change, to all appearances they confined themselves to discussing issues of moral development.

Nonetheless, eventually the Brotherhood did enter the political arena. Having originated as a missionary movement, it took the next step of using the political institutions as a vehicle for the Islamization of society. In the campaign leading up to the 1941 elections, al-Banna ran for a seat in the district of Isma'iliyya but was persuaded by Prime Minister Nahhas to withdraw in return for specific social reforms, including the prohibition of alcohol and prostitution.[113] Brotherhood candidates likewise participated in the 1945 elections but lost in an electoral process "believed to have been the most obviously dishonest held in Egypt".[114] The inability to gain political influence through legal channels would contribute to the turn taken by some Brotherhood members to political violence and other forms of extra-constitutional action in the late 1940s.

Yet for all his contributions to the Islamist cause, al-Banna was not an innovative thinker. Rather than engage in novel and fresh understandings of the Qur'an, as had the modernist Muhammad 'Abduh (d. 1905), he tended to emphasize the revival of traditional virtues, especially those related to *jihad*, spiritual strengthening, and group solidarity. In the words of Richard Mitchell, this "preference for 'deed' over 'idea' was demonstrated in preference for the word 'programme' (*minhaj*) as against 'ideology' (*fikra*) to describe what the Society believed...It was no accident, perhaps, that, with minor exceptions, neither Banna [sic] nor the movement produced any work remotely identifiable as theology or philosophy."[115] In common with other fundamentalisms, including those of the Christian and Jewish traditions, the Islamist discourse of the Muslim Brotherhood served "as a bulwark against the encroachment of outsiders" threatening "to draw the believers into a syncretistic, areligious, or irreligious milieu."[116]

A lawyer named Ahmad Husayn (1911–82) founded Young Egypt. Like al-Banna, he was also concerned with the issue of moral rearmament.[117] However, unlike the Muslim Brotherhood, Young Egypt did not strive to implement Qur'anic principles but rather energized the Egyptian nation by pointing to examples of national assertiveness in Egypt's long history; these included the glory days of the Pharaohs, the mediaeval dynasties, and the more recent Muhammad 'Ali period. In the estimation of Ahmad Husayn, these were eras in which the social fabric of the Egyptian nation was intact and its people capable of great accomplishments. In addition, Ahmad Husayn looked to models of discipline and organization present among the Fascists in Italy, the Nazis in Germany and the Falangists in Spain. He was not alone doing so. In the Middle East, Antun Sa'ada's Syrian Socialist Nationalist Party, Pierre Jumayyil's Lebanese Maronite Phalange and the Revisionist Zionist Betar youth movement of British Mandate Palestine were similarly inspired by the extreme forms of nationalism then current in Europe. To this list, we could add the Muslim Brotherhood's Rovers. All of these movements shared the premise of community regeneration through solidarity and struggle.

Young Egypt was originally respectful of Egypt's parliamentary system but in the late 1930s began to denounce it. At the same time, the organization began to exhibit a thuggish posture characterized by "attacks on taverns, prostitution and Jews",[118] the latter receiving attention on the supposition that they supported Zionist activities in Palestine. Spearheading the new assertive attitude was the movement's special section of paramilitary Green Shirts. In a nod to cultural authenticity, Ahmad Husayn enjoined the organization's 1,800 or so members not "to speak in any language but Arabic" and to avoid illicit pleasures and the cinema. "Go," he told his followers, "everywhere in full confidence as an Egyptian."[119]

A corresponding shift in discourse accompanied the growing militancy of Young Egypt. In reaction to the greater popularity of Muslim Brotherhood, Young Egypt made a tactical decision to stress the nation's Islamic dimension over other aspects of its historical identity. In 1940, the party changed its name to the Islamic Nationalist Party (al-Hizb al-Watani al-Islami). By co-opting aspects of the Islamic discourse, Young Egypt hoped to win over those effendis who might otherwise look to Hasan al-Banna for leadership.[120] The purely cosmetic nature of its application reflected the opportunistic nature of the change. The organization's leaders did very little to implement Qur'anic principles within its ranks. Young Egypt remained a fascistic organization lacking any clear programme of action. Like the Muslim Brotherhood with which it was sometimes allied, its discourse and practices changed in accordance with the requirements of the factional political struggle.

A genuine national culture

Qutb shared these organizations' basic dislike of the cultural sources of Western power in Egypt. However, he was not attracted to their strictly defined ideologies and emphasis on group discipline. Rather, he favoured a generic, less ideological form of cultural nationalism that did not yet withdraw support for establishment politics. The trend was secular and infused with an openness and creative edge lacking in the strident discourses of the Muslim Brothers and Young Egypt. It included several prominent literary intellectuals of the previous generation, in addition to many more belonging to Qutb's cohort. Like Qutb, these intellectuals perceived symmetry between the effort of literary self-expression and the struggle to forge a genuine national culture. For each, the prime effort was towards rupture, renewal and the apprehension of authentic meanings. As a group, they resembled the "organic intelligentsia" described by Antonio Gramsci, in as much as they functioned as organizers, critics, and articulators of the popular current of ideas.[121]

One of these, Qutb's mentor al-'Aqqad, supplemented his poetry with biographies (*tarajim*) of influential Muslims, which included studies of the Rashidun Caliphs, Khatib Ibn al-Walid, the commander of the first Muslim army, and venerated members of the Prophet's family. He hoped that by capturing in literary form the energy and volition of these individuals, he might spur his countrymen to heroic activity.[122] Tawfiq al-Hakim infused his writings with a didactic message that drew attention to the enduring aspects of Egypt's history. His novel *'Awdat al-Ruh (The Return of the Spirit,* 1933) evoked a regenerative ethos inspired by the Pharaonic past. Muhammad Lutfi Jum'a also called attention to the collective heritage in his book, *Hay al-Sharq (The Life of the East,* 1932).

Qutb articulated his thoughts on Egypt's cultural identity in articles prepared for the literary-political journals *al-Thaqafa (Culture), Sahifat*

Dar al-Ulum (*Dar al-'Ulum Journal*), *Majallat al-Shu'un al-Ijtim'iyya* (*The Journal of Social Affairs*) and *al-Risala* (*The Message*). These served as forums in which writers concerned with the issue of cultural nationalism could editorialize and give voice to their concerns. The contents of the periodicals were diverse and represented the spectrum of views present among the dissenting *effendiyya*, ranging from progressive critiques of the old Arabic literary tradition to conservative assessments of the emergent literary culture. *Al-Risala*, for instance, simultaneously reviewed the works of the iconoclastic Apollo poets and published articles by the neoclassicist Mustafa Sadiq al-Rafi'i, the conservative writer whose work had so infuriated Qutb. Even Ahmad al-Zayyat, the founder of *al-Risala*, saw no contradiction in simultaneously admiring the French literary theorists Taine and Brunetière and criticizing what he termed "sandwich literature", the "hastily contrived" style of the literary modernists.[123] Despite editorial differences, all of these journals were interested in the creation of a politically and culturally independent Egyptian state. Clearly, for many of the partisans of the heritage, cultural reassertion did not imply the type of "political correctness" that might lead to the cessation of open debate.

Qutb's starting point in these writings, which span approximately the years 1933 to 1941, was his assertion that Egypt possessed an integrity and wholeness in its collective life. Far from existing as a mere political unit, Egypt was a living, organic entity whose individuality unfolded from a central core of meaning. At root, this life took its bearings from the ensemble of moral habits (*akhlaq*), virtues (*fada'il*), and outlooks that were enduring features of civilization in the Nile Valley. These included "manliness" (*muru'a*) and all that it entailed in terms of nobility, honour and generosity, in addition to the distinctly female virtues of modesty, mercy, and sacrifice for the family. They also included ethical traits common both to men and women: purity of conscience (*damir*), moral dealings with others, and concern for the general welfare of society. All of these qualities, Qutb wrote, were evidence that Egyptians, both Muslims and Christians, were heirs to an innate spirituality that contrasted markedly with the materialism and individualism of the West.[124] It was important that Egyptians should step into the ancient current of identity and perception. They should follow their ancestors' example and reach towards all that is sublime and noble.

Qutb believed that the Egyptian ethical sensibility was the product of the social and physical environment. Centuries of human development within the geographical matrix of the Nile Valley had moulded a particular type of person. "The social situation of a people—including its traditions, customs, economy, politics and education—is the product of [a people's] successive responses to their environment, which leaves their traces in the subconscious of individuals."[125] Although Qutb acknowledged the contributions of the Pharaonic era in forging the "deep structure" of Egypt's national character, he paid special attention to the impact on the Egyptian psyche of Islam, which preserved and strengthened the nation's enduring religious orientation.[126] Qutb did not yet advocate the creation of a state regime governed by Qur'anic principles. Theocracy, as advocated by the Muslim Brotherhood, flew in the face of his secular attitude. Yet he honoured the central precepts of the faith. In Qutb's developing view, Islam stood with language, culture and history as an integral, but not sufficient, component of Egypt's national identity.

Qutb lamented that the heavy weight of the imposed Western culture eroded this special life. He was concerned that the French and English languages, each of which found advocates among sectors of the Westernizing elite, were changing the natural rhythms of the national culture. Egyptians, Qutb feared, were abandoning Arabic—the linguistic vehicle of their culture—in favour of languages that were alien to their historical experience. Qutb made a point of channelling the energies of the Dar al-'Ulum Society, of which he was a founder, in defence of Egypt's Arabic language heritage.

The "dizzying speed" and "abruptness" by which Egyptians adopted Western mores and practices of consumption unnerved Qutb. The fast pace of Western style modernity, he writes, caught Egyptians off guard. It threatened to sweep all before it: "This [Western] civilization that is based on science, industry, and materialism operates with crazed speed and is without heart and conscience. Driven by invention and material advancement, it sets forth to destroy all that humanity has produced in the way of spiritual values, human creeds, and noble traditions."[127]

The Western attitude of heedless activity and impulse was colonizing the minds of Egyptians, affecting negatively the time-honoured national characteristics of repose and spiritual reflection. Further, it was corroding the bonds that held the nation together. "We are paying [a tax on progress] at the expense of our psyches, morals, happiness and comfort...and wealth."[128] Qutb believed that Egyptians who succumbed uncritically to the glossy temptations of foreign culture were planting seeds of imbalance and disharmony within the national society. He wrote, "A given society is a system that operates consistently as long as its parts fit. When a component of this system is replaced with a part from a different model, it loses balance and even ceases to function, even if the part is more valuable than the original." This cultural borrowing had transformed Egypt into a "Tower of Babel", a confusing mix of European and Egyptian mentalities and cultures that were not meaningfully connected.[129] Qutb cited the great fourteenth century North African scholar Ibn Khaldun as someone who understood the psychological tendency of defeated peoples to emulate the conquering culture, even when such emulation was against their best interests. Modern Egyptians, in Qutb's view, followed this mimetic tendency at the expense of their honour. They ought to resist further surrender to the domineering culture of the West.[130] Just as it was unseemly for a poet or author to plagiarize, so too was it undesirable for nations to pattern their national lives on the model of another culture. Whether in literature or in national life, originality had a positive value.[131]

Qutb made the point that he was not a Luddite. He understood that progress was an inevitable process in history, and that no country was immune to it. "Our fathers and ancestors were confronted with this tax [of progress]—each generation is bound to have a share of it."[132] Yet, he continues, change did not exhaust Egypt's forefathers as it does the current generation. That is because, unlike today, its pace was slow, deliberate, and easily digested by the people. Because the pace has quickened, Egyptians must learn to regulate modernity in order to maintain cultural authenticity. They must adopt a slower pace of change and hold fast to those spiritual resources of the nation that are the secret of its past greatness. Only when Egyptians attain cultural self-confidence will they be able to defend themselves against the political, economic and cultural onslaught of Europe. The carnage unleashed by the European powers in the Great War of 1914–18, no less than the savage struggle waged by the democracies against Hitler's Germany and the Italian fascists, were sobering reminders that the West did not have a monopoly on the good life.[133] Egyptians must look inward to the essential qualities of their identity, and must understand that the world can learn many things from their example, especially in the area of values.

Qutb was pleased that there were Westerners who shared his assessment of the damaging effects of Western materialism. In a 1941 article published in the *Journal of Social Affairs*, Qutb quotes approvingly from the Arabic translation of the 1935 book *Man the Unknown* by the French-American medical scientist Alexis Carrel (1873–1944).[134] Winner of the 1912 Nobel Prize in medicine, Carrel held research positions in Montreal, Chicago and the Rockefeller Institute in New York City before returning to his native France in 1939. Under the collaborationist Vichy regime, he directed the French Foundation for the Study of Human Problems. In Carrel, Qutb found a fellow traveler. Qutb passed over Carrel's advocacy of eugenics (Carrel called for the medical engineering of a spiritual and technically proficient elite) and instead focused on the scientist's belief that life was analogous to a work of art whose aspects found proper meaning only in relation to the whole. After witnessing the seemingly miraculous cure of a gravely ill woman at Lourdes in 1902, Carrel pushed medical practitioners to examine the relation of man's soul to the mechanical workings of the body. A sceptical medical establishment chided Carrel for his interests in mental telepathy and the healing power of prayer. Unbothered by the criticism, he continued to insist that the spiritual and physical attributes of Man were complementary.

It impressed Qutb that Carrel so strongly indicted the "dehumanizing" impact of modern, materialistic Western culture. Instead of liberating man, as the post-Enlightenment narrative claimed, he believed that Western modernity enmeshed people in spiritually numbing networks of control and discipline, and that rather than build caring communities, it cultivated attitudes of selfish individualism. Qutb regarded Carrel as a rare sort of Western thinker, one who understood that his civilization "depreciated humanity" by honouring the "machine" over the "spirit and soul" (*al-nafs wa al-ruh*).[135] He saw Carrel's critique, coming as it did from within the enemy camp, as providing his discourse with an added measure of legitimacy.

Carrel's work alerted Qutb that he and like-minded Egyptians were not alone in their thinking. In fact, whether he knew it or not, Qutb stood within a spectrum of Romantic-oriented reaction to post-Enlightenment culture and politics. Across Europe and increasingly around the world, a backlash spread in the interwar years against a conception of man that was "utilitarian in its ethical outlook, atomistic in its social philosophy" and "analytic in its science of man".[136] Individuals as diverse as the French writer Drieu la Rochelle (d. 1945), the German "conservative revolutionary" Ernst Junger (d. 1998), the

French philosopher Henri Bergson (d. 1941), the neo-Marxist scholars of the Frankfurt School, and a host of others worked in various ways to restore meaning to the "amoral" and "disenchanted" bourgeois world. Inclined by temperament and experience to the Romantic spirit, Qutb naturally gravitated to figures like al-'Aqqad, but also to Alexis Carrel whose ideas regarding man as an expressive being buttressed his indictment of a shallow and pretentious West.[137] Like many of these critics, Qutb was driven by the utopia of a superior organic community "conceived in terms of an anti–materialist revolt which made the sphere of 'culture' in its widest sense, rather than that of politics, economics or militarism, the primary focus of transformation and renewal."[138] Qutb would almost certainly have concurred with his contemporary T.S. Eliot that Europeans were "Hollow Men" lacking strong convictions or beliefs.

In time, as we shall see, Qutb responded to the empty lures of modernity by drawing upon and further developing Hasan al-Banna's ideology of moral rearmament. All the while, he continued to quote Carrel. However, he would do so in a critical spirit. Although he would remain in basic agreement with Carrel concerning the pathologies of the modern age, they differed over the treatment. Carrel had advocated that people look within themselves for the solution to the human condition. In contrast Qutb, the Islamist, would hold that salvation from the "hideous schizophrenia" that separated Man from the "truth" could only come with recognition of God's objective truth.[139]

Nevertheless, it is an indication of the ground shared by Islamism and the anti–Enlightenment critique that cultural critics like Alexis Carrel should have continued to attract the attention of Islamists. The Tunisian Islamist Rashid al-Ghannushi recalled that, in the 1960s, Islamists employed in criticizing the West Carrel's *Man the Unknown*, Oswald Spengler's *Decline of the West*, and the meta-histories of Arnold Toynbee. "These books," writes al-Ghannushi, "gave credit to the Islamist position."[140]

Qutb's most substantial treatment of national identity was a lengthy review article of Taha Husayn's controversial 1938 treatise *Mustaqbal al-Thaqafa fi Misr* (*The Future of Culture in Egypt*), published in the April 1938 issue of *Sahifat Dar al-'Ulum*.[141] Taha Husayn was an obvious target for Qutb.[142] Although he came from the same sort of rural background as Qutb, his higher education, first at the Egyptian University and then at the French universities of Montpellier and the

Sorbonne, led him to respect Western culture, a trait that earned him the harsh rebuke of all those in Egypt opposed to the importation of an alien spirit. In 1926 he weathered an Azhari–led attack on his study on the pre-Islamic poetic canon. Throughout the early and mid-1930s he continued to draw the fire of cultural nationalists whose disparate voices dominated both the periodical press and the university that employed him. As Donald Reid relates, "On one occasion students burst into Taha's office and denounced him for backing coeducation."[143] Taha Husayn composed *The Future of Culture in Egypt* as a riposte to the "reactionary" forces afoot in Egypt. In his view, these forces included not only the conservative scholars of al-Azhar but also the heritage-minded *effendiyya* of whom Qutb was a representative.

The Future of Culture in Egypt articulates Taha Husayn's vision for Egypt in light of the promise of full sovereignty set by the 1936 Anglo-Egyptian Treaty. How, Husayn asked, should Egyptians proceed now that they have opportunities for independent development? In a manner reminiscent of the Khedive Isma'il's technocrats, Husayn stated boldly that Egyptian modernization should take cues from Europe, the most highly evolved civilization in the world. However, he provided this assertion with an interesting twist. He claimed that Egypt's core identity was based on Hellenic-Mediterranean culture, the same culture that had informed the renaissance of the Western nations. Egyptians thought and felt as did Europeans, even if their immediate Arabic-Islamic culture told them otherwise. Taha Husayn conceived Egypt as an autonomous nation-state existing within the larger Mediterranean-European cultural sphere.

Taha Husayn was not alone in presenting a territorially delimited version of Egyptian identity. The theoretical model of the nation-state had been gaining ground, largely because of the post-World War I demise of the Ottoman Empire, which deprived Egyptians of an important transnational dimension to their identity. Territorial nationalism was especially common among Egypt's Westernized elite who identified it with modernity.[144] By radically circumscribing the cultural parameters of the Egyptian nation, Egypt's elite thinkers and politicians hoped to undermine the identification with Islamic values common among the *effendiyya*. According to Lutfi al-Sayyid, the intellectual father of Egyptian territorial nationalism, "...an Egyptian is one who does not identify himself with any nation but Egypt...Our nationalism directs our desires towards our nation...and our nation alone."[145] In the 1920s the most important expression of the territorial trend was "Pharaonism" (al-fir'awniyya). This was the "belief", in the words of Charles Smith, "that the true 'spiritual heritage' of modern Egyptian culture could be found in the pharaonic era which had sparked the world's first great civilization."[146] The British archaeologist Howard Carter's discovery in 1922 of the intact tomb of Tutankhamun, which harkened to a past of which Egyptians could be proud, provided an important impetus to the development of this trend.

Husayn believed that Egyptian education should follow the European model. As an educator, he was aware that many examples of modern schooling could be found in Egypt. Yet, in Husayn's view, these schools were not of equal value. While he waxed eloquent about the potential of his own university to bring about the necessary changes in national life, he demeaned the contributions made by Dar al-'Ulum, Qutb's alma mater. Husayn writes, "I must admit in all candor that Dar al-'Ulum...has made an utterly insignificant and disappointing contribution to the modern renaissance of our Arabic language and literature...." He continued, "The alumni of the school simply cannot compare" with the graduates of the modern schools. "It is no wonder then that they feel embittered and frustrated."[147] In Husayn's view, national progress depended on unambiguous commitment to modern science and European culture, not adherence to the outmoded scholastic methods and texts that formed a significant part of the Dar al-'Ulum curriculum.

There is no doubt that Husayn's dim view of Dar al-'Ulum stung Qutb. It was probably the reason he chose Sahifat Dar al-'Ulum over other journals as his vehicle of refutation. Nevertheless, Qutb's rejoinder was informed by a tone of respect that contrasted markedly with his exchanges with al-Rafi'i's supporters. Such deference reflected Qutb's recognition that Husayn was the towering figure of Egyptian intellectual life, a man whose opinions, even if one disagreed with them, one must treat with respect. As an up-and-coming writer, Qutb trod carefully around those who stood at the forefront of the literary culture.

Despite his basic disagreement over the issue of Dar al-'Ulum, Qutb agreed with Husayn on other points. For example, he supported Husayn's suggestion that administrative superiors should improve the pay of schoolteachers and should grant them more respect. Only in this way could the ministry alleviate their malaise and bitterness.[148] He also supported Husayn's argument that the state should consolidate its supervisory role over all forms of education, most especially al-Azhar. The only exception should be university instruction, which it must leave independent within the limits of public law. For Qutb, as for Husyan, it was important for the state to deny al-Azhar the privilege of placing its graduates in the state schools as Arabic instructors until its Faculty of Arabic came under state control. In Husayn's view as in Qutb's, the state must unify Egypt's educational system in order to ensure the conditions of national solidarity and progress.[149] To exempt al-Azhar and other religious schools, such as the private schools of the Copts, would undermine the state's efforts to unify the nation.[150] In expressing his opinions, Qutb indicated not only his belief in a strong state, but his feeling that the government should not grant the religious institution special privileges.

Qutb agreed with Husayn on educational matters. However, he questioned the writer's contention that historically, Egypt was a component of Hellenic-based Mediterranean civilization. According to Qutb, this thesis obscured the fact that history in general and the Qur'an in particular had stamped Egyptians with ethics and values distinct from the Hellenic heritage upon which the Western nations drew. In fact, Qutb claimed, despite Egypt's distinctiveness, its overall outlook placed it firmly in the orbit of Eastern, rather than Western civilization. Egypt, Qutb said, had much more in common with its Arabic-speaking neighbours, and even with countries such as India and Persia, than it did with the nations of Europe. Whereas Westerners attempt to explain the workings of the mind in strictly physiological terms, Egyptians and other peoples of the East emphasize the immaterial realms of intuition, spiritual insight, and deep feeling. This innate spirituality has affected their individual and collective outlooks.[151] Qutb explained that the advent of the Qur'an provided "Eastern spirituality" with an important practical direction. As evidence, he pointed to the sustained influence on ethical life of Islam's myriad rules, regulations and moral injunctions. In its focus on the practical application of ideals, Islam differed from Christianity, the heir of Hellenism, which was limited to the mere preaching of spiritual and moral precepts.[152]

But what of Taha Husayn's contention that, in the past, Egyptians cooperated with their "Western" Greek mentors against fellow "Easterners", such as the Persians? Does not this history of cooperation belie cultural affinity? No, Qutb answered. Although collusion between Greeks and Egyptians did take place on certain occasions, it took place for the practical purpose of defending the homeland against the aggression of an invading Persian army, which, despite its Eastern identity, was bent on conquest. Wars, Qutb writes, often break out between nations of the same civilization. Indeed, the Chinese of his own time were resisting the onslaught in Manchuria of fellow Asians, the Japanese.

Qutb was adamant on the point of Egypt's Eastern identity. However, he did not believe that Egypt's Eastern affinity should prevent it from adopting the superior aspects of Western civilization. Western nations might be deficient in the area of values, but they had mastered modern technology and the applied sciences, areas of knowledge in which Eastern nations like Egypt were lacking. Qutb noted that Japan was a country that had succeeded in maintaining its distinctive culture while selectively adopting the technical features of Western culture. In Qutb's opinion, Egyptians should likewise keep in mind the fundamental distinction between culture (al-thaqafa) and material civilization (al-madaniyya).[153] For Qutb, civilizations were not discrete, indivisible entities, but rather internally variegated assemblages of culture that possessed the capacity to interact fruitfully with cultural "others" while holding fast to their core identity. This was a viewpoint that Qutb would carry with him into his Islamist phases. In his seminal 1964 Islamist tract *Milestones*, Qutb writes:

The Muslim community today is neither capable nor is required to present before mankind great genius in material inventions, such as would make the world bow its head before its supremacy and thus to re-establish once more its world leadership. Europe's creative mind is far ahead in this area, and for a few centuries to come we cannot expect to compete with Europe and attain supremacy over it in these fields.

Hence we must have some other quality, a quality that modern civilization does not possess.

That quality, Qutb goes on to explain, is, "Faith and a way of life that both promotes the benefits of modern science and technology and fulfills basic human needs."[154]

In addition to Qutb, other writers also derided Husayn's Mediterranean thesis. As Gershoni and Jankowski remark, "Critical reviews of The *Future of Culture in Egypt* became something of a growth industry in 1939, as various Eastern-inclined intellectuals joined in denouncing Husayn's westernizing perspective and in defining the validity of the East-West distinction denied by Husayn."[155] The writer Ahmad Amin, for example, composed an article critical of Taha Husayn's stance in which he proffered explicit definitions of materialism and spirituality and their applications to the Western and Eastern nations respectively.[156] Hafiz Mahmud, editor of the periodical *al-Siyasa al-Usbu'iyya*, likewise countered Husayn in emphasizing the presence of ancient spirituality in Egyptian collective life.[157] Although he did not directly refer to Husayn's work, Tawfiq al-Hakim similarly juxtaposed a spiritual East and a materialistic West, most explicitly in his novel *'Usfur min al-Sharq (Bird of the East)*, first published in 1938. As Rasheed El-Enany remarks, "The axial idea in *'Usfur* is that the West is materially powerful but spiritually hollow, whereas the East, materially weak and at the mercy of the West, is the true abode of the spirit and the source of light for humanity since time immemorial."[158]

As Qutb was aware, the Eastern view was popular beyond his circle of secular writers and activists. It especially encompassed writers who were representative of the Islamist trend. Hasan al-Banna encouraged Egypt's Muslims to temper their allegiance to the homeland by recognizing Egypt's place within the larger, transnational communion of believers. To this extent, the Islamists upheld the extra-territorial focus that had been common among Ottoman-minded Egyptians in the pre-World War I period. In al-Banna's view, a Muslim could be a patriot striving for the improvement of his country, provided his ties to blood and soil did not transcend those owed to Islam.[159] It is telling of Easternism's broad appeal that Qutb's critique of Taha Husayn's thesis immediately attracted the notice of the Muslim Brothers. They asked for, and received, permission from *Sahifat Dar al-'Ulum* to reprint it in the 9 June 1939 issue of their weekly organ *al-Nadhir (The Warning)*.[160] Qutb, however, did not follow up this early contact with the Brotherhood.

Some of the men associated with the Eastern trend, for instance, al-'Aqqad, 'Abd al-Qadir al-Mazini, Ahmad Amin, Muhammad Husayn Haykal and Hafiz Mahmud, came to their position after previously favouring cultural accommodation with the West. Charles C. Smith has argued that the shift of these men to Eastern and Islamic themes was, in fact, a device to satisfy the religious and political opposition of the time. Realizing the futility of espousing Western cultural and political values in an environment that was increasingly anti–Western, these writers clothed their liberal ideas in the language of Islam. By so doing, they hoped to remain influential in society. At least in the case of Haykal, Smith provides strong justification for this motivation. Yet, as he explains, the stratagem proved counterproductive and short-lived. Rather than influence the literate public towards a reassertion of liberalism, the writings of these men had the opposite effect of reinforcing reverence for the Arab-Islamic heritage. In acknowledgment of their defeat, in the late 1930s and early 1940s, Taha Husayn, al-'Aqqad and others complemented their Islamic-inspired writings with works that overtly favoured Western-style liberal democracy.[161]

'The Palestine Question'

In Qutb's estimation, Egypt was a component of Eastern, primarily Muslim civilization, but it was no ordinary Eastern country. In line with mainstream *effendiyya* opinion, he believed that Egypt's cultural resources and political influence positioned it uniquely to lead the Arabic-speaking and Muslim countries to their cultural reawakening. This was not empty talk on Qutb's part. Over the course of the Mamluk and Ottoman periods, Egypt had been the leading light of Islamic civilization in the Arab East. In the nineteenth and twentieth centuries, under the aegis of its reforming and modernizing elite, it again possessed the capacity to assert a leadership role in the region. Qutb wanted Egyptians to tap the country's rich resources to propel forward the dream of civilizational unity and renaissance.

As a first step towards this goal, Qutb encouraged Egyptians to foster closer ties with their Arab neighbours. He believed that the best way to accomplish this in the short term was by means of educational missions and cultural exchanges. He applauded efforts already made in this direction, including Dar al-'Ulum's establishment of a student section "for our Eastern brothers". King Faruq's efforts to fund the visits to al-Azhar of 'Eastern mission students' also heartened him.[162] Yet in Qutb's opinion, there was much more that could be done. Like Taha Husayn, he regarded the 1936 Treaty as an opportunity for Egypt to flex its muscles, but in the direction of Eastern rather than European involvement. "Egypt," Qutb wrote, "is no foreigner to the Arab World and is, in fact, its big sister in the eyes of the people. The Arab World follows Egypt's steps, benefits from her experiences, is illuminated by her light, and regards her with love, wonder and expectation."[163] Later, in the mid-1940s, Qutb would champion the creation of the Arab League as an important step in the direction of regional solidarity.

Qutb regarded the mounting struggle between indigenous Arabs and Zionist settlers in British Mandate Palestine as a catalyst that drew Egypt into the affairs of the Arab East. Throughout the 1920s and into the 1930s Egypt's governments demonstrated very little interest in events in Palestine or sympathy for Palestinian Arab concerns. This lack of attention reflected the politicians' exclusivist, territorial understanding of the Egyptian nation-state. Within government circles, the view persisted that a foreign people whose interests did not directly coincide with their own should not concern Egyptians. Egypt's politicians, additionally, were concerned that their meddling in the affairs of British-controlled Palestine might jeopardize the delicate diplomatic relations between Egypt and Britain as the countries edged towards renegotiation of their treaty relationship. Yet another reason for dismissing the issue was the possibility of popular passions boiling over should the Palestine question come to the fore. As the politicians were aware, demonstrations on behalf of Palestine's Arab population could easily turn against Egypt's government.

So, for example, when rioting broke out in Jerusalem in 1929 between Jews and Arabs over the status of the religiously significant Western Wall in Jerusalem, the Liberal Constitutionalist government of the day quickly censored anti–Zionist articles in the Egyptian press in an effort to preempt a potentially disruptive reaction among the Egyptian population. Following the disturbances in Palestine, the government of Isma'il Sidqi expelled from Egypt scores of Palestinian Arabs who had taken refuge there. The extent of the Egyptian governments' indifference to Palestinian Arab interests was reflected in 1933 in Sidqi's allowance for "1,000 Jewish immigrants to land in Port Sa'id on their way to Palestine."[164]

Despite government efforts to play down tensions, the Palestine issue did spark the regional and religious loyalties of common Egyptians. This was especially true during the Palestinian Arab Revolt of 1936–39, aimed at the Yishuv (Jewish community) and the British Mandate authority. The Muslim Brotherhood, still in the mid-1930s a relatively minor organization, played a leading role in mobilizing public support for the Palestinian Arabs by issuing publications and organizing special events. Starting in 1936, Muslim Brothers delivered lectures to "remind Muslims about their duties towards Palestine".

Many of these took place on Ascension Night (27 Rajab), a yearly event that commemorates the Prophet Muhammad's journey from Jerusalem to heaven.[165] Muslim Brothers also initiated fund raising campaigns and distributed pamphlets at the university, and "in shops and coffee houses, among civil servants and in the provinces".[166]

In the view of the Muslim Brothers, the effort to roll back Zionism was a religious duty born of Jerusalem's status as the first *qibla*, or direction of prayer. It was, in their view, the most important step towards the ultimate goal of Islamic unity. Secular organizations, including the Egyptian Women's Union led by the feminist Huda Sha'rawi (1879–1947), followed the Brotherhood's activist example, if not its Islamist message, in demanding that the government apply full diplomatic pressure on behalf of the Arabs in Palestine. Many intellectuals and writers, especially those with "Eastern" inclinations, joined the anti–Zionist chorus. For example, Muhammad Tawfiq al-Diyab, editor of the Wafdist organ *al-Jihad*, stressed that "the Palestine question is not a local one, but is a general Arab Islamic question," developing the theme of an expansionist Zionism that threatened to "spread into all the Arab lands" in order to accommodate continued Jewish immigration.[167] Having lived for decades in the shadow of foreign power, ordinary Egyptians could relate to and sympathize with the struggle of an Arabic-speaking and predominately Muslim people against what they considered was imperialist sponsored settler colonialism.

Faced with mounting pressure from the grassroots, by the late 1930s the Egyptian government modified its policy in favour of Palestine's Arab population, but only a little. Its reasons for doing so were purely pragmatic: Egypt's politicians realized that its non-committal approach played into the hands of the popular movements, not only the Muslim Brotherhood and Young Egypt, but also the Young Men's Muslim Association and other student groups that were at the forefront of the agitation. Not only that, the Egyptian government further understood that if it did not intervene politically in the Palestine impasse, other regimes in the Middle East would, thus diminishing the country's role as an effective and influential regional player.[168] In order that internal and external competitors should not compromise its status, the Egyptian government changed its tune.

Qutb was delighted at the change of government attitude. The Palestinian Arab uprising, he wrote, had succeeded "in gaining the sympathy and attention of every Egyptian." It was a welcome event, which pulled Egypt politically into the affairs of the Arabic-speaking East. He applauded the efforts of the coalition government of Prime Minister Muhammad Mahmud to convene "The World Parliamentary Congress of Arab and Muslim Countries for the defense of Palestine," scheduled for Cairo in October 1938. The delegates at this conference, drawn from a variety of Muslim countries, condemned the Balfour Declaration and called for the immediate cessation of Jewish immigration to Palestine. Qutb wrote, "I know from trusted sources that the Egyptian government has submitted to London a special reminder regarding [this conference], in which it expressed its viewpoint boldly and explicitly."[169] In a poem entitled "Bloody Palestine" (*Filastin al-Damiyya*) Qutb called on the Palestinian Arabs to continue on their path of struggle. Adnan Musallam notes of this poem, Adnan Musallam notes of this poem, Qutb "attacks the savagery of the West for spilling the blood of the East, and assures Palestinians that Egyptians, both old and young, wholeheartedly support them, and attach great importance to their struggle."[170] By evincing support for the Palestinian Arab resistance, Qutb felt that Egyptians, at both the grassroots and governmental levels, recognized more explicitly than ever before the bonds of civilization that linked Egypt with the Arabs of the surrounding countries. Yet it would only be after World War II, when nationalist sentiments in Egypt were at their height and the Zionist project appeared close to fruition, that Qutb would devote sustained attention to the issues of Palestine and of Arab unity in general.

The decade of the 1930s was formative in the development of Qutb's outlook. Having experienced the pains and pleasures of rapid socioeconomic change, he came to share with other *effendi*s a common orientation toward the future. Early on, he desired to make his career in Cairo, the largest city in the Arab world. As a student, and subsequently as an employee at the Ministry of Education, he contributed to the creation of a new and dynamic Egyptian culture, one that was "authentic" and open to modernization. At the same time, he joined a rising chorus of dissenters as he inveighed against the West as a destructive, materialist force in world history. Underlying his literary efforts and political writings was his romantic, spiritual sensibility, which soon would find grounding in the Qur'an.

3

TURN TO ISLAMISM

World War II: a 'silver lining'

As the Second World War loomed, Britain prepared its defences in Egypt. Wary of German and Italian designs in the Mediterranean and the Western Desert, Britain invoked the 1936 Anglo-Egyptian Treaty, which allowed Britain to maintain troops and facilities in the country in time of warfare, in addition to those already there in peacetime. Within two years of the war's start, Cairo and Alexandria swarmed with troops from the British Isles and the Dominions. As during World War I, Egyptians were incensed at what appeared to them as Britain's cavalier treatment of their country. Looking back at this period. Writing in the early 1950s, Qutb recalled the "contempt" of the Allied soldiers who "ran over Egyptians in their cars like dogs..."[1] Britain channelled the country's resources, including the lucrative cotton trade, to the war effort and forced the Egyptian Government to sever its relations with the collaborationist Vichy regime in France. There was a shortage of food in the country and the cost of living almost tripled. Many Egyptians spoke of the transit of Allied troops through the country as a "second occupation" analogous to the deployment of British forces following the defeat of Ahmad 'Urabi in 1882.[2]

In the view of most Egyptians, the war was a European affair that involved Egypt only because of Britain's still-strong position in the country. Most Egyptians were pleased that Egypt's wartime coalition governments managed to secure Egypt's neutrality. Only near the war's end did Prime Minister Ahmad Mahir secure the assent of Parliament to declare war on the Axis. Nevertheless, sympathy for Germany and Italy was strong among the nationalist and Islamist sectors of the population, not because Egyptians were attracted to the Nazi or fascist ideologies, but because many viewed a German victory against Britain as potentially benefiting the cause of Egypt's independence. The British acted decisively against these pro-Axis elements. In early 1940 the British dismissed a leading pro-German military officer, Commander-General 'Aziz al-Masri, after he was caught attempting to contact Axis forces advancing in the Western Desert. At the same time, state authorities radically circumscribed the activities of the Muslim Brotherhood and Young Egypt whose loyalty to the government was suspect. In response to British demands, the Egyptian Education Ministry transferred al-Banna to politically remote Upper Egypt in May 1941.[3]

British mistrust extended to individuals within the official political class. Uncertain of the support of Prime Minister Mahir's pro-Palace coalition government, British Ambassador Sir Miles Lampson ordered tanks to surround the 'Abdin Palace and forced King Faruq to appoint a compliant Wafdist cabinet under Nahhas. This occurred on 4 February 1942. The Wafd's willingness to cooperate with Britain offended nationalists of all stripes, with the result that many who had been loyal to the party turned to other organizations and movements, including the Muslim Brotherhood and the revamped Marxist groups. "This Government," said Dr Ahmad Mahir, "has been formed at the point of British spears."[4] In 1943 another serious blow hit the Wafd when the dissident Wafdist Makram 'Ubayd published his "Black Book", which laid out in excruciating detail the alleged corruption of the party.

Sayyid Qutb shared the outrage of his countrymen. Following al-'Aqqad, he distanced himself from the Wafd Party and began to support the rival Sa'dists, the party of Ahmad Mahir and Nuqrashi Pasha. Like al-'Aqqad, Qutb was attracted to Ahmad Mahir's forceful personality. He believed that Mahir was aware of and sympathetic to the public's concerns. At a time when landlords and businessmen dominated the Wafd, the Sa'dists put themselves forward as the *effendis'* party.[5] Qutb felt at home among these men. Like him, they belonged to the conservative middle class.

Qutb, an avid reader of the press, kept abreast of developments at the battlefront. He was dismayed at the ferocity of the war, which "harmed all of the earth's nations."[6] The actions of the Germans appeared to him as particularly "monstrous". He thought that it was unfortunate that the war should involve small countries, like Egypt, which had done nothing to precipitate it. As in the nineteenth century,

Egypt was a field upon which the Great Powers played out their interests. In the circumstances, Egyptians could do little but hunker down and endure the war's uncertainties and privations.

However, Qutb saw a silver lining. Writing in 1943, he looked ahead to the post-war era and saw an opportunity for Egypt and other small Eastern nations to unite as a bloc, perhaps allied with the Western democracies. Such a union, he speculated, would enable countries such as Egypt to assert their interests on the global stage. Moreover, the formation of an Eastern bloc would benefit the world. Given the wartime collapse of Western civilization there was need for spiritual regeneration of the kind that only the East could provide. Qutb wrote, "It seems that Eastern civilization and its spiritual treasures is the sanctuary for the world in its present crisis."[7] In his proposed union, Egypt would play a leadership role because of its cultural maturity and experience with modernity.

Qutb's vision of an emergent third force in world affairs reflected the fundamental impulse of civilizational rebirth that was common to the Egyptian political and cultural discourse of the time. Politically, it was inspired by the discussions then taking place among Arab state officials on the possibility of inter-Arab cooperation following the war. At the time, the Iraqi Prime Minister Nuri al-Sa'id floated the idea of a union of Fertile Crescent states, including Iraq, Transjordan, Lebanon, Syria and Palestine, while Egypt's Prime Minister Nahhas countered with a plan in which Egypt would have a leadership role. The mooting of Arab unity by the Arab leaders anticipated the creation of organizations such as the Arab League and the Non-Aligned Movement in the decade following the war.

'Unwholesome masculinity'

The troubles created by the war did not hinder Qutb from advancing in his career. In March 1940, the Education Ministry promoted him to its office of General Culture. A month later, the ministry transferred him to its office of Translation and Statistics. In 1944, it briefly demoted him to the rank of school inspector, perhaps in consequence of his increasingly negative attitude to the Wafd; in Old Regime Egypt, political affiliation could impact one's social standing. A full year passed before the ministry allowed Qutb to return to the relatively prestigious General Culture office.[8]

Qutb was a busy man. Each morning of the working week, he rose early to catch the rickety commuter train from his Hulwan home to the ministry complex in central Cairo. The time-consuming journey took him past the Muqqattam Hills and the Tura prison in which he would one day be incarcerated. Arrived at his office, he had to prepare reports or plan visits to the schools he needed to inspect. Over this period, he suffered bouts of illness that confined him to bed. In 1941, sickness prevented him from attending the funeral of 'Abd al-Qadir Hamza, an early mentor with whom he had worked on the Wafdist organ *al-Balagh* in the late 1920s.[9] In 1946, lung problems prompted him to spend time in Alexandria "for its fresh air".[10] It is revealing of Qutb's work ethic that he was able to produce dozens of published essays, articles, and books despite his work schedule and health problems.

The 1940s were a productive period for Egypt's literary men and Qutb busied himself reviewing their works. Leaving behind the harsh words he had applied to the Rafi'iyyun, he wrote thoughtful analyses of al-'Aqqad's *'Abqariyyat Muhammad* (*The Genius of Muhammad*) (1942), Tawfiq al-Hakim's autobiographical *Zahrat al-'Umr* (1944),[11] 'Adil Kamil's *Millim al-Akbar* (1945),[12] and Naguib Mahfouz's historical novels *Kifah Tiba* (*The Struggle of Thebes*) (1944),[13] *Khan al-Khalili* (1945)[14] and *al-Qahira al-Jadida* (*New Cairo*) (1946).[15] He saluted the ethical, religious and nationalist contents of Mahfouz's writing. Writing of *Kifah Tiba*, which treated ancient Egypt's struggle against the Hyksos invaders as an allegory of anti–colonial struggle, he said: "Had it been in my power, I would have put it into the hands of every young man and woman: I would have it printed and distributed in every house for free."[16] Qutb's enthusiasm pleased Mahfouz. Later, he made the point that Qutb was one of two critics (the other was Anwar al-Mu'addawi) responsible for rescuing him from obscurity.[17]

In 1946 Qutb collected many of his reviews and essays in a volume entitled *Kutub wa Shakhsiyyat* (*Books and Personalities*).[18] His hands-on experience with criticism encouraged him to produce a scholarly, critical study under the title *al-Naqd al-Adabi: Usuluhu wa Manahijuhu* (*Literary Criticism: Its Sources and Methods*). In it he called for an "integrative approach" to criticism, one that encompassed the artistic, historical and psychological elements of the literary subject.[19] Qutb dedicated the work to 'Abd al-Qahir al-Jurjani (d. 1078), in his view one of the few mediaeval philologists to have concentrated on meaning and aesthetic value at the expense of form and rhetoric.[20] Presumably, Qutb sought to accomplish something of what al-Jurjani had in his time.

In the mid-1940s, Qutb began to distance himself from the influence of al-'Aqqad. He said that he feared his identity was becoming indistinct from that of his mentor. But it is also clear that Qutb, a published author in his thirties, began to view his mentor as a literary competitor. Consequently, relations between the two men turned cold. Qutb justified the falling-out by claiming that al-'Aqqad's poetry had become excessively "intellectual", going against the *wijdani* ("emotional") approach that al-'Aqqad had helped pioneer. As Qutb put it, "true poetry is free of the burden of the intellect, the glitter of the mind."[21]

The break provided Qutb with new confidence as a writer. In prose works composed in the 1940s, he displayed his independent spirit. We have already noted A Child from the Village, in which Qutb recounted the formative experiences of his rural upbringing. Also noteworthy were two novels, *al-Madina al-Mashura* (*The Enchanted City*, 1946) and *Ashwak* (*Thorns*, 1947).[22] Written as an addendum to the Arabian Nights stories, *The Enchanted City* reflected his ongoing fascination with fantasy and the supernatural. In this short novel, Qutb has Shahrazad spin Shahrayar a story about a prince's love for an elusive girl from the countryside. The story is full of references to caves, magic and wilderness, images that bespeak Qutb's mystical frame of mind.

Ashwak provides insights into Qutb's character. Striking the same sentimental chord as Muhammad Husayn Haykal's pioneering Arabic novel *Zaynab* (first published in 1913), the story concerns the doomed relationship of an engaged couple, Sami and Samira. Qutb constructs Sami as an urban, middle class *effendi*. Although deeply in love, Sami breaks off the engagement when he learns that Samira had a previous romance with a young army officer. Haunted by doubt and suspicion over Samira's moral demeanour, Sami attempts to come to terms with the situation, at one point even arranging for Samira and her former boyfriend to reunite, an effort that comes to nothing. Eventually, Sami ends the relationship altogether. Emotionally wounded, he feels an uneasy emptiness overtake his life, such as "the atheist, who has abandoned his atheism, or the Sufi who has fallen into uncertainty and confusion."[22] He comes too late to realize the inappropriateness of his suspicions and high-handed behaviour. Samira, he realizes at the end, was "the victim of the unwholesome masculinity of the men of this generation" who cast unfair aspersions on the characters of good girls.[24]

Judging from the dedication page, a shattered love affair sometime in the early 1940s inspired Qutb to write *Ashwak*. "To the one who plunged with me into the thorns, bled as I bled, was wretched as I was wretched, then went her way as I went mine: both wounded after the battle," so reads the dedicatory inscription.[25] The novel thus provides insights into Qutb's attitudes toward, women, sexuality, and romantic love at a time when important changes were taking place in gender relationships. New educational opportunities, combined with the example of pioneering feminists such as Malak Hifni Nasif (1886–1918), Huda Sha'rawi, and Duriyya Shafiq (1908–75), encouraged many Muslim and Coptic women to challenge traditional gender roles.[26] During the interwar period, many women from the upper and middle classes adopted European styles of dress and attempted to free themselves from the strictures of the prevailing patriarchy. While a select few women joined the professions, many more joined the workforce as clerks and factory workers, especially during World War II when Egypt's role as a base for the Allied armies made employment opportunities available. The participation of women in the workforce correlated with the state's support for the legal emancipation of women. Minor changes to the Shari'a laws of personal status had already been made in 1920 and 1929, which allowed women to initiate divorce on the basis of non-maintenance and placed restrictions on the husband's right to divorce by pronouncement of *talaq* (repudiation), "making sure that it must be a clear, sober and deliberate decision."[27]

Having grown up in a village affected minimally by these developments, Qutb was unprepared for the more open and diverse gender relationships found among the modernizing sectors of Cairene society. Although, as he writes, he did not want to see Egyptian women revert to their former condition of seclusion, which he considered to be outdated and socially debilitative, he regarded the "current level of freedom" enjoyed by many women as socially deleterious. He writes, "The leap made by the Egyptian woman following the Great War is the reason for the lack of balance in our social system." The free mixing of men and women threatened family life and kinship structures. In Qutb's opinion, unmarried men and women should meet only to choose marriage partners, and then only under the watchful eyes of their parents. Unchecked, women's sexuality had the power to entice men. To follow uncritically the Western example in gender relations and women's freedom was to open the door to social "discord" (*fitna*). Qutb justified this traditional view with reference to recent "scientific" findings at the Egyptian University that claimed to prove women's biological suitability for domestic, rather than public, responsibilities.[28]

Qutb's conservative attitude led him to castigate the entertainment industry. In a period that featured artists like Umm Kulthum and Muhammad 'Abd al-Wahhab, the revered giants of Arabic song, Qutb regarded popular music as weakening the moral constitution of the nation.[29] Noble love, he says, is a fine thing. However, "love" of the kind celebrated by the popular singers debases this nobility by exciting the animal lust that is potentially present in every human.[30] Qutb railed against commercial publishers who for the sake of profit splashed "naked thighs and protruding breasts" across the covers of their magazines. Such images, Qutb editorialized,[31] were damaging not only to the individual, they sapped the energy and will of the nation. In holding this view, Qutb fastened on to the traditional, Islamically sanctioned notion that morality was a public concern, relevant to the wellbeing of the entire community, in this case, the Egyptian national community.[32]

There was another reason for Qutb's attitude. A strong romantic temperament reinforced his moral concerns, and this led him to idealize women. In the novel *Ashwak* he paints a picture of the "girl of his dreams, not to be found in real life: a nymph from Cairo (*al-huriyya al-Qahiriyya*), a girl with a virgin body and heart, dressed in the Cairo way, a sensitive and poetic girl who is kind and pure in his soul."[33] He summarizes his outlook through his alter ego, Sami:

He had grown up in a clean, conservative environment and the solemn attitude he had adopted in the way he went about his life did not allow him to fool around (*'abath*). The love of poetry and things artistic prevented his imagination from being soiled...All these personal circumstances had put a distance between him and women. He felt uneasy and disturbed whenever he came face to face with them, whatever their social class or age.[34]

Qutb writes about the temptations and opportunities for sexual gratification that confronted and flustered his protagonist. He describes how Sami surprised Samira in her room, as she was undressing. Samira's body leaps into sharp focus: "It was the first time he had seen her in her underclothes...It was an awesome moment. His eyes rested on the beautiful visage. The moonlight created a special and seductive atmosphere. Many things made him want to approach her, but many other things prevented him from doing so." Soon, Sami's ingrained sense of "right order" prevails and he beats a hasty retreat, mumbling apologies for his intrusion into the private space of a woman beyond the circle of his family. Similar temptations, no doubt, confronted Qutb in his dealings with the romantic interest behind *Ashwak*.

As it was, Qutb, like his protagonist, was denied the fulfilment of his romantic imagination. Unwilling for ethical reasons to choose a bride from among the "dishonourable" women common to the public sphere, and unable for lack of necessary family connections to meet a woman of sufficient moral purity, Qutb reconciled himself to a life of bachelorhood; he never married, something unusual in Egyptian society and Islamic culture generally.[35] In fact, he probably died without ever having had sexual relations. The succour of women may have tempted Qutb. Yet in his view, it paled beside the prospect of congress with the spiritual realm. It was an attitude that he carried with him all of his life. Qutb would later write, regarding male-females relations, "It is the attraction of the soul that really matters."[36]

At this stage, Qutb regarded moral propriety in gender relations as an aspect of the national personality. Although he may not have phrased it this way, he had internalized the ethical standards promoted by the traditional culture, which upheld women as the bearers of family honour. Only later did he came to terms with the trauma of sexuality by crafting from the Qur'an an ideology that sanctified gender segregation explicitly as an aspect of the divine order. In his book *Social Justice in Islam*, and even more so in his great Qur'an commentary *Fi Zilal al-Qur'an* (*In the Shade of the Qur'an*), Qutb devotes much space in discussing God's rulings regarding male-female relations, including such topics and divorce, polygamy, and sexuality, all of which take their bearings from the family unit. Although, he would write, men and women have the same devotional and creedal obligations, they have unique functions within the family and society. The husband is the patriarch whose primary duty is to maintain the family financially and make decisions relevant to its overall welfare. Conversely, the role of the woman is that of wife and mother who defers to the authority of her husband. In Qutb's view, these roles are complementary in the sense that one fulfils the other to form a complete whole. To step beyond these divinely ordained gender roles is to invite disharmony.

Qutb would write: "The Islamic social order is family-based by virtue of its being a Divinely-ordained system for society that takes full account of the essentials of human nature and its basic requirements."[37]

The aesthetic power of the Qur'an

Qutb was forging his own path. However, one should not suppose that he was in any way on a par with the literary luminaries of the time. Rather, he was a writer "of second rank who followed the approach developed by the intellectual leaders of the age" and who, in turn, diffused "in modified form, the patterns of procedure and belief of the most creative workers in their respective fields."[38] Only when Qutb turned his attention to the literary and aesthetic aspects of the Qur'an, a subject far from the minds of most literary intellectuals of the time, did he show signs of the creative spark that would make him one of the most influential dissident writers of the 1950s and 1960s. Qutb's literary studies of the Qur'an mark the high point of his career as a critic and presage his future commitment to the Islamist cause.

Qutb first approached the subject of the Qur'an's aesthetic properties in articles written for the monthly literary-scientific journal *al-Muqtataf*, published in 1939.[39] However, these were small, modest studies, which did not yet grasp the full import of the approach. It was not until 1944, in a book entitled *al-Taswir al-Fanni fi al-Qur'an* (*Artistic Depiction in the Qur'an*),[40] that he gave the topic comprehensive treatment. In the introduction Qutb relates how, when he was a child, the images that took form in his imagination as he heard the Qur'an recited during the holy month of Ramadan and on other occasions compensated his sketchy and incomplete understanding of the text. Later, he says, this "pleasant" and beautiful" Qur'an was lost amid the "difficult" and "complicated" Qur'an commentary that he was forced to read as a student in Cairo.[41] He states that he turned to the analysis of the Qur'an in order to understand the nature of his early encounters with it. As a literary critic, essayist, and poet, it was natural that he should attempt to find the secret of the Qur'an's affect in the beauty and power of its word and imagery.

Qutb's concern with the Qur'an's aesthetic propensities put him in touch with an old scholarly quest within Islamic studies. Since at least the time of the theologian-grammarian al-Rummani (d. 996) Muslim scholars had set themselves the task of investigating the qualities that

111

set the Qur'an apart from other literature. Central to their concern was the concept of the *i'jaz*, the Qur'an's "inimitability", which the scholars upheld as proof of the divine origin of the revelation. Generally, the scholars identified the *i'jaz* with the Qur'an's style and rhetorical *élan*, although many pointed also to supporting doctrines, such as Muhammad's *ummiyya* or "illiteracy", and the Qur'an's "challenge" to humans to "produce a chapter like it". (2:23; cf. 10:38, 17:88) *I'jaz* studies continued right up to Qutb's own time. His literary nemesis al-Rafi'i published a 1926 study that aimed to validate the Qur'an as a "confirmatory miracle". However, unlike al-Rafi'i, Qutb was not interested in proving the divine origin of the Qur'an; he appears to have taken this for granted. What did concern him were the sources of its artistic genius. Qutb wrote:

We can set aside—temporarily—the religious sanctity of the Qur'an and the intentions of the Islamic call...in order that we may find absolute artistic beauty, a distinct element having an essence unto itself, everlasting in the Qur'an, which expresses art independently of all interests and purposes. This beauty can be enjoyed in and of itself, although its value is enhanced within the context of religious interests.[42]

Qutb argues that "artistic depiction" (*al-taswir al-fanni*) is the major "expressive element" (*qa'ia al-tadbir*) in the Qur'an, and that it provides all portions of the Qur'anic text, excluding those passages dealing with strictly regulatory and legal matters, with their emotive effect.[43] The Qur'an, therefore, possesses a uniform methodology. It has a

single way of expressing all of its purposes, whether these be for preaching or admonition, stories of the past or prognoses of the future, logic to convince or a call to belief, a description of this world or of the world to come, a portrayal of the perceptible or of the tangible, a presentation of the apparent or of the hidden, manifesting what is in the heart or what exits phenomenally.[44]

In expressing this view, Qutb was influenced by al-'Aqqad's teaching that all parts of a poem must be unified within a single aesthetic field.

Qutb is explicit about the novelty of his insight. The early Qur'an commentators, he tells us, were too preoccupied with "wording" and "meaning" and with the internal ordering of the Qur'an to notice the "comprehensive rule" that governed the text's disparate components. Only 'Abd al-Qadir al-Jurjani, and after him al-Zamakshari (d. 1143), came close to "hitting the mark" in their attention to the principles of personification and metaphor in the Qur'anic discourse. Al-Jurjani, in particular, demonstrated an unusual awareness for his time of the inherent aesthetic quality of individual words and passages. But generally, the "ancients" were far too dependent on the limiting methodology of scholasticism ever to have established a general rule that could be applied to the Qur'an as a whole.[45] While some contemporary authors, most notably Taha Husayn, were interested in "sensory depictions", none thought of examining the Qur'an from the perspective of aesthetic appreciation.

How, then, does the Qur'anic depiction affect the individual conscience? Qutb argues that it does so by exciting the imagination with vivid portrayals of "intellectual meanings, mental states, palpable events" and "models of human character". According to Qutb, the Qur'an "takes up the [particular] image that it has drawn and gives it a living personality or a renewed dynamism" which the listener, "as though struck", imagines to be a "spectacle" or actual event presented before him.[46] Rhythm, the sound of words, and the symmetry of images are the methods employed by the Qur'an to implement this effect. In a manner reminiscent of James Joyce's concept of "aesthetic arrest",[47] Qutb explains that the Qur'anic *taswir* implements a radical transformation of belief and sensibility. Just as the artist speaks through forms, which affect emotionally the individual consciousness, so too does God communicate by means of images designed to render absolute value as intuitive.

As evidence of the Qur'an's aesthetic power, Qutb evoked the example of 'Umar Ibn al-Khattab, who "avoided Islam" until his heart "opened up to it" upon hearing the magic of the Qur'an; Qutb supposes that he was first swayed by the beginning of *surat* Ta Ha (Q. 20). 'Umar went on to lead the Muslim community as second Caliph in the line of the Rashidun. Even Walid Ibn Mughira, the arch-enemy of the early Muslims, is said to have been affected by the Qur'an's disarming charm, in his case upon hearing *surat* al-Muzzammil (Q. 73).[48] These and other early Meccan *sura*s summoned people to the faith, and, for Qutb, it was no accident that they were the most powerfully descriptive in the Qur'an.[49] Only with reference to Qur'anic depiction is one able to explain the Arabs' early attraction to Islam, which they diligently upheld even before the entirety of the Qur'anic message had been revealed to them. For the first community of Muslims, belief occurred prior to and independently of religious understanding. Affected by the Qur'an's aesthetic power, the early Muslims understood the Qur'an with an artistic naturalness unencumbered by intellectual meaning.

Qutb applied the concept of "artistic description" in a more directed way in a study called *Mashahid al-Qiyama fi al-Qur'an* (*Scenes of Resurrection in the Qur'an*), published in 1947.[50] In the study, Qutb analyzed the graphic ways in which the Qur'an represents the Day of Resurrection and the Afterlife as perceptible realities. "Muslims," he writes, live with "these scenes in their minds, alternately frightened and comforted by them, but always knowing this Other World well before it arrives." According to Issa J. Boullata, Qutb "points out that the religious purpose of such scenes is to call upon human beings to lead a morally good life in this world knowing that there is a just God who rewards and punishes them according to their faith and deeds in the end. The scenes of the Day of Resurrection and of the Afterlife are constant emotive reminders of this reality."[51] In keeping with his background as a littérateur schooled in the uses of metaphor and simile, Qutb suggests that Paradise and Hell might denote "psychological conditions". As Jane Smith and Yvonne Haddad write, "One does not die so that he can have rest, nor does he live so he can have enjoyment. But he continues suspended to an eternity, the end of which is unknown."[52]

Upon completing *Artistic Depiction in the Qur'an*, Qutb experienced within himself a "rebirth of the Qur'an". Having appreciated its charm, he now perceived in it a "beautiful unity based on a special rule" and "wondrous coordination" he had never thought possible.[53] But *Artistic Depiction* also signalled the faint beginnings of a new stage in Qutb's career as a writer and intellectual. His rediscovery of the Qur'an put him in touch with a dimension of his personality, one anchored in the ancestral religious knowledge of his early life and schooling. Having approached the Qur'an through poetic Romanticism with its emphases upon subjectivity and expressive fulfilment, Qutb came in the following years to see in its imagery a source of power.

Perhaps uniquely among Islamists, Sayyid Qutb explicitly understood the emotional dimension of the Qur'anic message. In his mature Islamist writings, composed in prison between 1956 and 1964, he explained how the catalytic power of the religious imagination, not logical arguments meant to convince Islam's detractors, propelled the Islamic movement. Especially during the Meccan period of the Prophet's career, writes Qutb, the early Muslims acted immediately in accordance with the divine mandate without asking questions. In Qutb's developed view, Islam was not a truth to be analyzed but an ensemble of images that stirred souls and called Muslims to action. What we can say is that Qutb's revolutionary Islamist discourse traces back, in part, to his theory of the Qur'anic aesthetic.

Yet in the mid-1940s, Qutb was still distant from the Islamist position. As 'Abdallah 'Azzam (d. 1989), the great organizer of Arab volunteers in the anti–Soviet *jihad* in Afghanistan in the 1980s, noted in an appreciative essay, Qutb did not begin either the *Depiction* or the *Scenes of Resurrection* with the pietistic phrase, "In the name of God, the Gracious, the Merciful."[54] Islamists know well that that Qutb was a latecomer to the cause.

There is a brief literary portrait of Qutb at this stage in his life, when he was in his late thirties and engaged in his writing career. In his semi–autobiographical book *al-Maraya* (*Mirrors*, 1972), Naguib Mahfouz introduces his readers to a character he calls "'Abd al-Wahhab Isma'il" whom he models on Sayyid Qutb. Mahfouz's "Isma'il" is a self-assured and even-tempered person, a "polite conversationalist" and man-about-town who "never spoke about religion, pretended modernity in his ideas and dress, and adopted European habits in food and going to the cinema."

However, Mahfouz writes that beneath the fastidious *effendi* exterior, there was something vaguely disturbing, even sinister about the man. "Although he always showed me generous fraternity, I was never comfortable with his face or the look in his bulging, serious eyes....I was disturbed by his opportunistic side, doubting his integrity. A permanent revulsion, despite our friendship, settled in my heart." In time, he became aware of the growing influence of religion on "'Abd al-Wahhab Isma'il", even to the point of "fanaticism". But, says Mahfouz, the change was subtle and "'Abd al-Wahhab Isma'il" did little to clarify the matter to his friends. "He had the ability, rare in Egyptians, to keep his secrets."[55] According to Rasheed El-Enany, the barbs that Mahfouz directed at Qutb, a man he otherwise liked, were prompted by the novelist's lifelong aversion to Islamism.[56]

Mahfouz's unease with "'Abd al-Wahhab Isma'il's" emergent bent proved to be well founded. In 1994 a twenty–year-old Islamist, encouraged by a condemnatory *fatwa* issued by the blind Shaykh 'Umar 'Abd al-Rahman, stabbed the aged Mahfouz in the neck, wounding him severely. Shaykh 'Abd al-Rahman had issued the *fatwa* because he had taken exception to Mahfouz's "blasphemous" writings, particularly his novel *Children of Gebelawi* (*Awlad Haritna*, 1959). As spiritual Guide of the radical Islamic Group (al-Jama'a al-Islamiyya), the Shaykh was influenced by the Islamist writings of Sayyid Qutb, the shifty "'Abd al-Wahhab Isma'il" of *Mirrors*. As of this writing, Shaykh 'Umar 'Abd al-Rahman languishes in an American maximum security prison in Colorado for his role in the 1993 conspiracy to blow up New York landmarks.

'Where are you, oh Mustafa Kamil?'

Events in the mid- and late 1940s encouraged Qutb and other dissenting *effendis* to mobilize the resources of the heritage for more explicitly political purposes. The termination of the Second World War created an environment conducive to the emergence of radical responses to Egypt's problems, especially the issues of Anglo-Egyptian relations and socioeconomic underdevelopment. During the War, British censorship had effectively capped nationalist expression of every variety. While the 4 February 1942 incident ensured government compliance with the will of the British Embassy, press censorship and a ban on political meetings kept the agitations of the intelligentsia and the popular movements to a minimum. When the British lifted martial law on 4 October 1945, the pressures that had been building over the previous six years found their release. Yet rather than resume the relatively low-key posture that characterized the pre-war period, opposition parties and movements revived the spirit of revolution of the 1920s, which they saw the Wafd had abandoned.

Two inter-related developments contributed to the radicalization. The first was the postwar mood of self-determination and anti–colonial revolt current in many parts of Africa and Asia following the war. As the old European empires collapsed or were in disarray, everywhere in the colonial world there was movement towards the creation of new, independent states. In 1945 Ho Chi Minh proclaimed the independence of Vietnam; India became two independent states in 1947; and in 1949, the Dutch were compelled to recognize Indonesian independence. At roughly the same time, anti–colonial movements emerged in Kenya, Malaya and Cyprus. One of the most telling indicators of the new mood occurred in Sétif, Algeria, on 8 May 1945, where celebrations of the end of the War in Europe transformed into anti–French demonstrations, which in turn led to a viscous French response that resulted in the deaths of thousands of Algerians.[57] This anti–colonial trend, replete with programmes of wealth redistribution and the reassertion of national cultures, alerted Egyptians to the international dimension of imperialism and encouraged them to step up their own struggle.

The second, related, factor was the acceleration of Zionism following World War II and the resultant Arab-Israeli war of 1948–49. Egyptians and other Arabs were dismayed at the Zionists' attempts to sidestep Britain's 1939 White Paper, which had set limits on Jewish immigration to Palestine, and at the growing diplomatic support that Zionism was gaining from the United States. The growing power of the Zionists at the expense of the Arab Palestinians enhanced further the awareness of many Egyptians of their Arab identity and of the existence of a common Arab struggle.[58]

Qutb joined the mounting chorus of anti–imperialist rhetoric. In a spate of invective, he heaped scorn upon what he saw as the arrogance and self-serving policies of the Western nations. The "history of France in the East", Qutb wrote in 1945, was rooted "in savage barbarism and pools of blood." From Napoleon's invasion of Egypt in 1798 to the ongoing Gallicization of North Africa, France has been intent upon the subjugation of Arab lands.[59] The rule of the Netherlands in the East Indies is likewise to be condemned. Egyptians are well aware of Britain's shameful imperial record, and should not expect British troops to evacuate Egypt any time soon.[60]

Qutb reserved his harshest words for native "collaborators". He expressed dismay at the unwillingness of Egypt's political establishment to take charge of Egypt's political predicament. Speaking as a "man of the people", he accused the Pashas of working with the British and of ignoring the nationalist demands of the larger society.[61] He called Egypt's politicians "dwarfs",[62] and criticized writers and journalists who did not stand with the population as having "sold out" to the political establishment.[63] In Qutb's view, myriad connections, financial, cultural and social, bound the Egyptian establishment with the European imperial order. Towards the end of his career, Qutb would Islamicize his condemnation of these collaborating elements by branding them "*jahili*", ignorant of the divine commands. In despair, Qutb evoked the heroic leadership of the previous generation: "Where are you, Oh, Mustafa Kamil? Where are you to teach the leaders of today how to parry the disgrace visited upon the country on 4 February [1942], just as you repulsed the oppression that embraced Egypt on the day of Dinshaway?"[64] In common with increasing numbers of Egyptians, Qutb believed the time was ripe for change.

At a time when many dissenting Egyptians were turning to Marxist-inspired analyses of imperialism and national liberation, Qutb's explanatory framework was closer to that of the Muslim Brothers, at least in its emphasis on the unification of morals and politics. All of Qutb's politically oriented writings of the period point, either directly or indirectly, to the presence of a deep moral flaw planted in the heart of the Western character. According to Qutb, Western nations acted the way they did because, in contrast to the ethically discerning cultures of the East, their populations lacked a moral conscience (*damir*), a trait essential for just and responsible behaviour in both the public and private spheres of human activity.[65] Having wilfully turned away from the spiritual dimension of life, Westerners adopted policies and attitudes based on abject materialism and selfish gain. Westerners, simply put, were not in harmony with the cosmos. This simple explanation of imperialism grafted comfortably onto Qutb's nationalism.

The renewal of nationalist agitation was triggered by the Sa'dist-led coalition government of Mahmud Fahmi al-Nuqrashi. Seeking to gain the political support of the masses, Nuqrashi approached the British Labour Government in December 1945 with a view to revising the 1936 Treaty to Egypt's advantage. The mild tone of the request, together with Britain's non-committal response, triggered a vociferous reaction by the nationalist opposition. On 21 February 1946, after several weeks of mounting tension, a large demonstration of students and workers demanding immediate British evacuation clashed with British army troops near the Qasr al-Nil Barracks. There were deaths and many injuries. Qutb marked the "Martyrs' Day" that followed by extolling the sacrifice of the "innocent victims". "Blood," Qutb wrote, "is the pledge of freedom in every time and place, and martyrdom is always the price of respect, both today and tomorrow."[66] In Qutb's opinion, 21 February 1946 stood with 4 February 1942 as testimony to Britain's intentions in the colonial world; Muslims must be on guard. Qutb's condemnation of the British and their domestic sympathizers was to the point: "Egypt is our Motherland, the East is our uncle, and the Nile our Fatherland. Death to imperialism and woe betide the colonialists!"[67]

Following the events of February 1946, Nuqrashi's coalition was replaced by a Palace-led coalition of independents and Liberal constitutionalists cobbled together by the old strong man of Egyptian politics, Isma'il Sidqi. Sidqi also attempted to negotiate with the British, but the talks bogged down over the issue of the Sudan. Like Nuqrashi, Sidqi was unable to contain popular passions that continued to simmer. On 16 November 1946, university students representing various political persuasions formed a "National Front of Students of the Nile Valley". Within a week, the demonstrations exploded "into orgies of fire—English books, stores, trams, and trees—and attacks on security and British forces in all the major centers."[68] Emerging from its wartime hibernation, the Muslim Brotherhood re-entered the political arena. According to Richard Mitchell, by 1948 the Muslim Brotherhood could claim to speak "in the name of a million Egyptians".[69] Whether or not the figure is accurate, it does reflect the Brotherhood's success in reaching beyond its core *effendi* constituency to other sectors of the population, particularly the urban lower classes.[70] An important role in popular mobilization was played by the system of "cooperative families" established in 1943 to facilitate indoctrination and the process of recruitment. In contrast, Young Egypt had only a "miniscule active following" in the immediate postwar years, a consequence of its inability to regroup following its suppression during the War.[71]

Violence became a defining feature of the political landscape. While Sidqi negotiated with the British, "pitched battles" erupted between the youth of the Muslim Brotherhood and the Wafd who "attempted to break up each other's meetings in Isma'ilyya and Port Sa'id."[72] In February 1945 a member of the Watani Party assassinated Qutb's hero Ahmad Mahir for his part in Egypt's declaration of war against the Axis. On 26 January 1946, a young nationalist shot dead Amin 'Uthman, wartime Minister of Finance. Attempts were made on the life of Nahhas.

Special significance attaches to the role of the Muslim Brotherhood's "Secret Apparatus (*al-jihaz*)", founded, probably, in 1940.[73] Al-Banna's role in the creation of this organization is debated. What is undisputed, however, is that its ranks included prominent Brothers such as Salih 'Ashmawi. Like the Watanist and Wafdist underground organizations that preceded it, the apparatus was meant to supplement the mass-based activities of the Brotherhood's mainstream by striking directly at the obstacles in its path. In the mid-1940s, this translated into grenade and gelignite attacks against British personnel and installations, and assassination attempts against selected members of the political establishment. Such activities were a consequence of the general mood of discontent current in Egypt at the time, in which caution and restraint increasingly surrendered to the temptation of violence. As we shall see, in 1965, shortly after his release from prison, Qutb would emulate the example of Egyptian underground organizations, including the Muslim Brotherhood's secret apparatus, in proposing tactics to be used against the 'Abd al-Nasser regime.

Meanwhile, the conflict in Palestine heated up. Qutb had long kept an eye on events in Palestine, home to close to a million Arabs and site of the Haram al-Sharif, the third holiest sanctuary in Islam. Yet it was only after World War II, when the conflict came to a head, that he gave the issue his full attention. In Qutb's opinion, the struggle of the Arabs in Palestine was at the heart of the Afro-Asian reaction to the colonial order; as such, it merited the support of Egyptians and other Muslims. As Qutb wrote, the conflict in Palestine was a pivot in the "struggle between the resurgent East and the barbaric West, between God's law for mankind and the law of the jungle."[74]

In 1947 Egyptian volunteers, including many Muslim Brothers, flocked to al-'Arish and the Negev desert to join Palestinian Arabs in battle against the Zionist militias. During the Arab armies' invasion of the newly declared state of Israel in May 1948, the Brothers distinguished themselves by rendering assistance to besieged Egyptian army troops in the Faluja pocket. This action earned them the respect of many Egyptian officers, including Gamal 'Abd al-Nasser. For Qutb and other Egyptians, the lacklustre performance of the Egyptian army against Israel was deeply humiliating. The people blamed the defeat on the Egyptian government, particularly King Faruq who personally had made the decision that the country should go to war despite the poor preparedness of the Egyptian army. Because of Egypt's defeat, the political establishment suffered a further loss of political legitimacy.

On the home front, the conflict sparked a fresh outburst of terrorist attacks, this time targeting Jewish establishments and foreigners in addition to the government. The government held the Muslim Brotherhood responsible for most of these attacks. Its suspicions were seemingly confirmed when it discovered several of the Brotherhood's arms caches. Nuqrashi, once again in office following Sidqi's 1946 resignation, took advantage of the martial law imposed during the Palestine war to dissolve the Brotherhood and seize its assets. This was done on 8 December 1948. In retaliation, on 28 December a member of the Brotherhood assassinated Nuqrashi. On 12 February 1949 political agents acting on behalf of the new Sa'dist Prime Minister, Ibrahim 'Abd al-Hadi, shot Hasan al-Banna in retaliation as he was getting into a taxi outside the headquarters of the Young Men's Muslim Association. Only in May 1951 did the government see fit to allow the Brotherhood once more to resume its activities.

Qutb derided the British and Americans for their complicity in the Zionist project. He was particularly chagrined at the 1946 report issued by the Anglo-American Committee of Inquiry, which recommended, at US President Truman's insistence, the immediate entry into the Palestine Mandate of 100,000 Jewish refugees from Europe and the creation of a unitary Palestinian State into which Jews would continue to be welcome. In Qutb's view, the committee blatantly ignored the right of Arab primacy in Palestine. On this point, there could be no debate, just as there could be no compromise on the issue of Egypt's sovereignty over the Canal Zone. It was only right that Arab people should be in control of their own territory.

Qutb says that he was not surprised at Britain's hand in the recommendations. However, the support given to Zionist "settler-colonialism" by the United States took him aback. He had shared with other Arabs the belief that as a country dedicated to international justice, the United States would support the self-determination of the Arab peoples, including the Palestinians, after the war. According to Qutb, America's refusal to support the creation of an independent Arab Palestine demonstrated that it was, in fact, no different from the British, French, and the Dutch in its attitude towards Eastern nations. Qutb wrote, "All [the Western nations] take their bearings from one source, and that is the materialistic civilization that has no heart and no moral conscience. It is a civilization that does not hear anything except the sound of machines, and does not speak of anything but commerce... How I hate and disdain those Westerners! All of them, without exception."[75] Qutb was in equal measure angered by the Soviet Union's decision to recognize the provisional Jewish government immediately upon its declaration of Israel's creation on 14 May 1948. In his mind, the Soviets also based their decision on a materialistic philosophy devoid of principle.

Despite his misgivings about Jewish territorial nationalism, Qutb was impressed at the Zionists' political success through the tactics of assassination and sabotage perpetrated by the extremist Zionist militias, the Irgun Zvi Leumi and LEHI. Writing in 1946, Qutb noted that Britain was prepared to reconsider the restrictions in the 1939 White Paper upon Jewish immigration into Palestine, but only because it had received a bloody nose from these violent groups. According to Qutb, the Arabs must learn from the Zionists and likewise adopt direct action, even if it earns them the censure of the Western nations. "The only language the modern world understands is the one used by the Jews [in Palestine], namely, force."[76] Qutb enjoined Arabs to take matters into their own hands. They must determine their destinies independently of their ineffectual political leaders. "Oh, Arab masses, be careful! Our own politicians, who are Arabs, may betray the Arab people because they are able to be deceived. The situation in Palestine requires that the Arab masses, rather than their leaders, take action."[77] Qutb drew his readers' attention to a 1946 play, *The New Shylock* by 'Ali Ahmad Ba-Kathir, an Egyptian-based writer of Yemeni–Indonesian background. In its reference to the problematic portrayal of the Jewish character in William Shakespeare's play *The Merchant of Venice*, the play's title conjured for its audience the anti–Semitic tropes of Jewish duplicity and cunning. Nevertheless, the play's contents impressed Qutb. He wrote that it provided a straightforward account of Palestinian dispossession and that he appreciated its concluding call for a comprehensive boycott of Zionists by Arabs everywhere. Displaying the same concern for the effect of words that figured in his book *Artistic Depiction in the Qur'an*, Qutb wrote, "[the play] excites human emotions and sympathies and awakens the spirit of Arabism." According to Qutb, the restoration of Arab dignity was contingent on hardnosed policies of self-reliance and national sacrifice.[78]

The growing awareness of socioeconomic issues spurred the radicalization of the non-parliamentary forces. The ongoing migration of rural people to Cairo, wartime inflation, the chronic problem of *effendi* unemployment, and the example of the Soviet Union combined in the 1940s to propel elements of the literate strata towards an economic understanding of Egypt's predicament. One manifestation of this trend was the re-emergence of Communism, which had been quiescent since the crushing of the Egyptian Communist Party by the Wafd in the mid-1920s. Now, in the wake of World War II, several Communist organizations vied with one another for local leadership of the Communist cause. These organizations included the Democratic Movement for National Liberation (DMNL), Iskra, and the New Dawn.[79]

Still more significant to the rise of a nationalist left wing was a variegated group of socialist intellectuals, including men such as the folklorist Rushdi Salih, the literary critic Luis Awad, the economist Rashid al-Barrawi, and Naguib Mahfouz, Taha Husayn and Muhammad Mandur (1908–1965). Mandur was especially important. A literary critic and protégé of Taha Husayn, in late 1945 he founded the Wafdist Vanguard, which sought to influence the party of Zaghlul in a leftist direction. Through their organs *Sawt al-Umma* (*Voice of the Nation*) and *al-Wafd al-Misri* (*The Egyptian Wafd*), Mandur and his colleagues drew attention to the economic dimensions of imperialism, especially the role of native elites in perpetuating the poverty of the masses. This was something new. With the exception of the Communists, no Egyptian nationalist or Islamist group had until then criticized the class of indigenous capitalists. Foreign-owned enterprises alone had borne the brunt of the nationalists' displeasure.

However, the efforts made by the leftist forces to reach the wider society were largely unsuccessful. The Communist organizations suffered because of the minority status of their leaderships (most were Jews), and because the alien terms of their Marxist discourse did not resonate in the large traditional sectors of the population. An additional liability was the Communists' decision, following the example of the Soviet Union, to accept the terms of the 1948 partition of Palestine, a move that directly contravened Egyptian majority opinion.[80] For its part, the Wafdist Vanguard never succeeded in transcending its status as a minority voice within the parent body of the party. The scattered support it received from workers, students and leftist intellectuals was not sufficient to propel it to the forefront of the national stage.

Yet the leftist forces were not without their influence. By challenging the body of mainstream nationalism in terms emphasizing that economic and political issues were inseparable, they precipitated an important change in the prevailing discourse.[81] The persuasive logic of the left's internal critique affected all of the opposition forces one way or another. Eager to offset mass defection from their ranks, the Wafdist and Sa'dist leaderships responded with a series of palliative economic reforms in precisely those areas that were the focus of leftist concern: land reform, health care, and education. According to Khalid Muhammad Khalid (d. 1996), a socialist critic of the government, talk about the concept of social justice "overwhelmed" Egyptians after World War II.[82]

The Muslim Brotherhood also answered the ideological challenge. Fearful of losing out to the Vanguard-Communist coalition in its struggle for influence in the Shubra al-Khayma textile workers' union, the Brotherhood devoted more attention to workers' issues, for instance, introducing "vast social welfare schemes into [its] activities: insurance for workers, medical care and others."[83] According to Joel Beinin, the Muslim Brotherhood's "activities during the period 1944–48 were motivated as much by the perceived ideological threat posed by communism as they were by the desire to expel the British from Egypt and establish an Islamic order."[84] In October 1949, Young Egypt responded to the economic concerns by changing its name to "The Socialist Party of Egypt". Accordingly, it changed the movement's old slogan, "God, Nation, King", to the more appropriate dyad, "God and the People".[85] The popular movements' greater awareness of socioeconomic issues was accomplished without sacrificing their moral-political focus. In contrast to the forces of the left, which regarded economic inequity as the product of structural forces, the Muslim Brotherhood and Young Egypt saw the problem as issuing from alien, non-Islamic norms and values that had infiltrated Egyptian society on the heels of imperialism.

The Islamic alternative

Qutb also responded to the heightened awareness of socioeconomic issues. He had always been aware of social injustice and economic disparity. As a boy growing up in Musha he was sympathetic to the plight of the itinerant field hands who worked his father's land. Now, encouraged by leftist critique, he called attention to issues of *effendi* unemployment, rural poverty, monopoly capitalism, the inequities of the taxation system, and the substandard quality of education.

Qutb advocated the creation of a "comprehensive social programme" that would drive "economic, cultural and legislative activity." "Social justice is non-existent in Egypt," he wrote. "We are in need of new parties with a creative mentality that will look to the complete unity of Egyptian society...and prescribe political renewal and social reconstruction capable of curing Egyptian society of its sickness."[86] He called upon the political establishment to legislate for better working conditions in the factories, reduce tariffs on necessities, and encourage a new spirit of social service among the population.

Qutb cautioned against implementing hastily conceived plans derived from Western models. Arguing from the viewpoint of culturally grounded nationalism, he suggested that only projects suited to the worldview of the people and to conditions on the ground could deliver Egyptians from the curse of poverty. Government officials had to go to the countryside and the urban slums to learn, first hand, about the challenges facing the people. Statistics had to be collected, surveys made and reports written before appropriate development projects could be undertaken.[87] As a man for whom identity concerns were central, Qutb understood that Egyptians had to separate modernization from Westernization for development to succeed.

Towards the end of the decade, Qutb began to frame his understanding of Egypt's predicament in terms that owed much to Islamism. He rendered his new orientation explicit in a journal called *al-Fikr al-Jadid* (*New Thought*), which he conceived in October 1947 with seven others, including his brother Muhammad, Naguib Mahfouz, and the Azhari–trained Muslim Brother Muhammad al-Ghazali. Qutb set himself up as the journal's chief editor. Like other progressive journals of the day, *New Thought* was concerned primarily with social questions. According to the British Egyptophile J. Heyworth-Dunn, the editorial staff aimed to "show up the real situation amongst the poor" and published reports and photographs detailing the desperate conditions of the peasant population. The journal put Qutb "in the forefront of those who [advocated] a system whereby large estates should be reasonably diminished in size, and the land distributed among the completely landless, in order to eliminate destitution."[88]

Each issue of the journal had a section that drew attention to the abuses, scandals, and contradictions perpetrated by the governing classes and their "wealthy friends". Did you know, Qutb asks his readers, that the Ministry of Social Welfare plans to build a shoe factory that will meet a paltry one-fifth of the nation's need in that area, or that unemployed Egyptian workers recently demanded that the police imprison them, so that might be fed three meals a day? Or that the European section of the Egyptian Broadcasting Company employs a Jew who routinely sketches the Star of David alongside his signature? Events such as these take place daily in our county and around the

Middle East. We must be aware, on guard and ready to challenge all forms of injustice and national humiliation.[89]

However, it is the way this journal looked to the primacy of Islamic ethics and morality that attracts notice. In the inaugural issue, Qutb wrote that the journal aimed to "bring justice, reveal the truth, and bring back God's religion", seeking to "translate the principles of this religion and its commandments into laws, ways, and structures, so that we can bring social justice to the highest level."[90] He went on to warn his readers against the "violent, destructive and oppressive" currents of materialist Communism, and encouraged them instead to look to the cultural resources of their own Islamic civilization in addressing current problems, namely, "that religion (*din*), which disapproves of the current situation and warns against those who would do injustice to the people."[91] "Our duty," Qutb continues, "is to believe in ourselves. We must instil within the generous and spirited youth of pure conscience, confidence in their country, religion, and glorious past." We must encourage them to "change the evil that we live amongst."[92]

According to Heyworth-Dunn, the Muslim Brothers viewed the independently produced *New Thought* as a challenge to their near monopoly of Islamic-oriented publications in the country. Accordingly, representatives of the Muslim Brotherhood approached Qutb and his colleagues "several times", asking if they could purchase the journal. When the editorial board spurned the Brothers' offer, the Brotherhood boycotted the journal, preventing its sale through the normal channels. Thus weakened, *New Thought* succumbed easily to the ban upon "subversive" literature issued by the government during the Palestine war, and closed down in April 1948 after a short run of only twelve issues.[93]

Unfazed by the Brotherhood's high-handed behaviour, Qutb proceeded to flesh out the Islamic roots of socioeconomic justice in three books. These were *al-'Adala al-Ijtima'iyya fi al-Islam* (*Social Justice in Islam*), *Ma'rakat al-Islam wa al-Ra'smaliyya* (*The Battle of Islam and Capitalism*), and *al-Salam al-'Alami wa al-Islam* (*Islam and World Peace*), published in April 1949, February 1951 and October 1951 respectively. These works, his most popular to date, put him on the map as an important spokesman of the Islamic movement.

The books represent a sea change in Qutb's ideological orientation. Up to this point, he had expressed his hope for Egypt's future in terms of secular nationalism, believing that the Egyptian people had a spiritual disposition that set them apart from the materialism and aggressiveness of the Western nations. Islam, in his previous understanding, stood with the Arabic language and Egyptian history as a marker of Egypt's collective identity, but was not sufficient itself. As Qutb had written in 1946, "The question for me is my honour, my language, and my culture."[94]

However, writing in 1948, he began explicitly to base his call for a just political, economic and social order on the teachings of the Qur'an and the example of the Prophet. Drawing on these sources, he began to fashion a theological argument that addressed the contemporary Egyptian contexts of political and social strain, especially the extreme social-class inequality that existed at the national level. At the heart of his discussion was an explicit moral and ethical concern for disenfranchised and downtrodden Muslims in Egypt and the wider *umma*. In the manner of the Muslim Brothers, Qutb came to define Islam as an "action-oriented force not only in the traditional areas of morals but also in the areas of collective ethics, domestic politics and international relations."[95] Nevertheless, Qutb's Islamism tended, at first, to buttress rather than supersede the discourse of cultural belonging that had dominated his earlier thinking. Despite his strong appeal to scriptural and prophetic authority, his concern at this stage remained to enhance the identity of the virtuous national Self against the different and competing Other of the West. It would not be until the mid-1950s that he began to employ, without undue reference to cultural and political arguments, the strictly theocentric[96] and imperative views upon which his fame as an Islamist ideologue chiefly rests.

In the absence of an explanation from Qutb himself, it is difficult to account for his turn to a political, as opposed to a purely cultural, understanding of the role of Islam in state and society. Almost certainly, however, he adopted the Islamist approach in response to an existential need for ideological certainty in a time of political crisis and social agitation. In common with opposition-minded Egyptians, Qutb sought an ideological solution to the problems that faced his country. While some turned to leftist organizations, such as the DMNL, as alternatives to the discredited liberal government, Qutb quietly gravitated to the programmatic discourse of Islamism. Already reasonably well formulated by the Muslim Brotherhood, Islamism provided Qutb what he needed: teachings that looked to the wellbeing of the community rather than the individual; which, in their evocation of the Prophet's career, called for an end to tyranny and wickedness; and which effectively distanced Muslims from the culture of the colonizing West. Employing Islamic vocabulary, codes and symbols that he perceived as untouched by the Western experience, Qutb gained in Islamism the ideological autonomy he had missed as a follower of Egyptian nationalism. Following the Muslim Brothers, he found texts in the Qur'an and the Prophet's Traditions to justify opposition to the regime in Cairo.

But it would be both condescending and misleading to suppose that Islamism fulfilled in Qutb a political need only. One must also take into consideration the deep spiritual need that Islamism fulfilled in Qutb. Based on the divine revelation, Islamism awakened in him energies and meanings tied to core aspects of his interior life. Since boyhood, Qutb had displayed a spiritual temper and a relentless desire for self-transcendence. Islamism captured and disciplined his native disposition, enabling him to indulge his nature in ways that were politically creative and authentic to the person he was.

Qutb's literary engagement with the Qur'an reinforced, and perhaps precipitated, his new orientation. It will be recalled that upon completing his literary study *Artistic Depiction in the Qur'an*, he had experienced within himself a "rebirth of the Qur'an". That "rediscovery", occurring in the context of the popular malaise, ignited in him emotions, moods and motivations linked to enduring aspects of society and the cosmos.[97] Because of his appreciation of the Qur'an, he was susceptible to the idea that Islam could, and should, govern the myriad affairs of men.

Referencing the Qur'an, Qutb now appreciated worldly experience and the Word of God in the same terms, one reflecting the other. If the scripture pointed to God's truth, so did the harmony inherent in the world mirror the Divine Reality.[98] Surveying the conditions of Egypt's malaise from a position of doctrinal anchorage, he was able to identify the struggle for political and cultural independence with a "sacred and transcendent cause", which insulated the propositions and preferences of self-determination "against criticism by mere mortals".[99] He understood that Islamism held a qualitative advantage over its nationalist and Marxist competitors, which could not claim divine sanction.

Qutb's was not the only case of a mid-career conversion to Islamism. There have been other instances of Muslim thinkers and activists abandoning secular nationalism for a religious frame of reference. Rashid al-Ghannushi (b. 1941), founder and leader of Tunisia's Islamic Tendency Movement, wrote an account of his conversion to Islamism that is suggestive of Qutb's experience. As a student in Damascus in the 1960s, Ghannushi had become disillusioned with Nasserism and Ba'thism, the two major strains of secular Arab nationalism. Searching for a camp that could accommodate both his Arab identity and his Islamic faith, he talked at length with a Muslim Brother named Jawdat Sa'id and attended lectures at Damascus University's Shari'a College. One night in June 1966 Ghannushi had an epiphany:

> That was the night I embraced true Islam. That very night I shed two things off me: secular nationalism and traditional Islam. That night I embraced what I believed was the original Islam, Islam as revealed and not as shaped or distorted by history and tradition. That was the night I was overwhelmed by an immense surge of faith, love and admiration for this religion to which I pledged my life. On that night I was reborn, my heart filled with the light of God, and my mind with the determination to review and reflect on all that which I had previously conceived.[100]

And here is the Moroccan Islamist Shaykh 'Abd al-Salam Yasin (Abdessalam Yassine) (b. 1928) describing, in conversational tone, his conversion experience, which took place about the same time, in 1965:

> I had what we can call a "spiritual crisis," a spontaneous awakening....In my conscience it was a pure quest for God. Very simply. I am someone who asked himself existential questions, who told himself: "Here it is. I am forty years old, what have I done with my life? Where am I going?" Anxiety over death, anxiety over having lost something. (...) So I began this spiritual quest....It is not so much my reading of Islamic or Islamist books which determined my action...but an internal logic which holds that Islam must lead to the *imane* [*iman*—"faith"], and the imane must go to the summit of *ihsan* [perfection], and the summit of *ihsan* is the *jihad*.[101]

Qutb did not adopt the Islamist position suddenly, as Ghanuushi and Yasin appear to have done. Rather, his new understanding of Islam gelled over the course of a year or so, and continued to evolve in relation to the circumstances of his life. Yet Qutb might well have written several of the phrases in the above passages. What Ghannushi, 'Abd al-Salam Yasin and Qutb have in common is the absolute sincerity of their beliefs. After years of incertitude and psychic confusion, Ghannushi was "overwhelmed by an immense surge of faith." 'Abd al-Salam

Yasin experienced an "awakening" in his conscience. Although Qutb's new, political understanding of his faith did not arrive in so dramatic a fashion, in referring all aspects of life, individual and collective, to the Qur'an and the Sunna, he found himself for the first time in his life on solid ground.

"Holism" is the core idea in Qutb's triad of books. In all of them, Qutb refers to Islam as a "*nizam*", an "integrated system" or "closed order" encompassing the realms of society, the economy, and politics. Qutb was certainly not the first Islamist to apply the term "*nizam*" in this way. Hasan al-Banna, for example, defined Islam as a comprehensive order, characterized by the application of Shari'a and operationalized in the form of a state.[102] So did the South Asian Islamist Abu l-A'la Mawdudi. Yet considered within the long history of Muslim peoples, the equation is of relatively recent provenance, dating from no earlier than the turn of the twentieth century. As Wilfred Cantwell Smith explained some four decades ago, the term "*nizam*"

...does not occur in the Qur'an, nor indeed does any word from this root; and there is some reason for wondering whether any Muslim every used this concept religiously before modern times. The explicit notion that life should be or can be ordered according to a system, even an ideal one, and that it is the business of Islam to provide such a system, seems to be a modern idea (and perhaps a rather questionable one).[103]

In Smith's assessment, prior to the early twentieth century Muslims, with few exceptions, tended to interpret the word "Islam" in accordance with its grammatical status as a verbal noun. Thus, "Islam" signified the action of personal faith and commitment. This was the sense of the term employed, for example, by the tenth century Persian exegete al-Tabari, for whom "Islam" denoted "the personal relationship of faith that unites a free moral agent with his creator."[104] Although, Smith explains, aspects of Islam's reification were present in the Middle Ages, it was only after the West challenged Muslim societies in the modern era that Islam became synonymous with the notion of a separate, abstract and competing entity. The change in meaning reflected a shift in the balance of Muslim piety from a spiritual to a this-worldly focus. In articulating his emergent Islamism, Qutb latched on to, and further developed, the modern tendency to reify the religion in order ideologically to confront the countervailing "system". It is interesting, in this regard, that when Qutb and Mawdudi compared Islam and other systems, they did not compare it with Christianity,

Judaism or Hinduism, but rather with the competing ideologies of Communism, Capitalism and Liberal Democracy.[105]

Equally significant is the books' stylistic manner. Combining Hasan al-Banna's down-to-earth coffee house preaching with the prosaic and didactic literary mode of the *effendi* intelligentsia, Qutb produced an accessible, highly readable and incisive discourse that avoided the complex methodologies, rhetorical devices and flourishes characteristic of the legal writings of the higher *'ulama*. Instead of engaging the reader in carefully crafted discussions of *fiqh* (jurisprudence), as was the norm among Azhari scholars, Qutb cut to the point, providing his readers with insights and practical advice, gleaned from scripture, which were relevant to their position as colonial subjects. However, in fashioning a discourse that paid scant regard to the conventions of classical and mediaeval Islamic learning, Qutb challenged the edifice of Islam that the *'ulama* had constructed, thus earning him the censure of many mainstream scholars whose social status derived from their command of the religious texts.

Of the three early books, *Social Justice in Islam* proved to be Qutb's most popular, as evidenced by the fact that it went through five Arabic editions, each which was revised to reflect the state of Qutb's thinking at the time of writing,[106] and has been translated into a number of languages. The work's dedication page renders explicit the book's motivational purpose. Focusing on the role of Egypt's youth in the moral, political, and cultural regeneration of Islam, Qutb writes:

> To the youth whom I behold in my imagination coming to restore this religion as it was when it began…striving in the way of God, killing and being killed, believing profoundly that glory belongs to God, to His Apostle and to the believers…
>
> To those youth in whom, I doubt not for an instant, the strong spirit of Islam will resurrect the spirit of past generations to serve coming generations in a day almost at hand…
>
> I dedicate this book.[107]

Recasting his old argument, Qutb begins by chiding Muslims who would ignore "their own spiritual capital or intellectual heritage" in favour of imported "principles and plans" which they have repeated "like parrots" and copied "like apes".[108] Rather, Qutb states, Muslims must live by the "native universal philosophy" of Islam, "which is to be found only in its own familiar authorities: the Qur'an and the *hadith*, the life of its Prophet and his everyday customs." Like al-Banna,

Qutb regarded these sources as covering "the whole of life, spiritual and material, religious and worldly."[109] In his view, all creation is a unity comprising different parts; it has a common origin, a common direction and purpose, because a single, absolute and comprehensive will deliberately produced it. In charting the paths of right and wrong, Islam restores man's linkage with what is true and enduring. It makes available God's justice, which is perfect, eternal, and applicable to all people, at all times, and in all places.

According to Qutb, justice arises from the Islamic *manhaj*, the "methodology" of belief and practice, which stems from uncompromising recognition of "the Testimony (*shahada*) that there is no God but God."[110] Belief in God's unity provides Muslims with complete "freedom of conscience" (*al-taharrur al-wijdani-al mutlaq*).[111] It liberates the human mind from subservience to anyone, or anything, other than God. Once released from the shackles of greed, priestcraft and political sycophancy, people will rise above their base desires to do what is best both for them and for society as a whole. Justice thus emerges naturally from an inner conviction of the spirit.

In practical terms, social justice is regulated by the Islamic principle of "mutual social responsibility" (*al-takaful al-ijtima'iyya*) which balances the ideal of individual responsibility against that of individual freedom. Such responsibility, according to Qutb, exists "between an individual and his self, and between the individual and his immediate family, and between the individual and the nation (*ummah*) and other nations, and also between one generation and all successive generations."[112] Thus, the individual has a responsibility to perform his work conscientiously and to put an end to any incidence of "evil" that may occur within his purview. For its part, the community has a corresponding duty to look after the poor and destitute by means of the Islamic mechanisms of *zakat* and *sadaqa*, the former obligatory and the latter voluntary, by which individuals put aside portions of their wealth for the needy. The Islamic *umma* is one body and feels as one body; whatever happens to one of its members, the others are also affected.[113]

Given an individual's responsibilities to others, Qutb thought it wrong that great disparities should exist among members of society. In confirmation of this point, he drew attention to Prophetic traditions and verses in the Qur'an expressive of the principle of "complete human equality" (*al-masawa al-insaniyya al-kamila*). Thus, according to the well-known *hadith*, "people are all equal as teeth of a comb." God declared in the Qur'an that He created all alike "out of an extract of clay" (35:12). For Qutb, the implications were clear: "If it is to be denied that one individual can be better than another individual by nature, then there can be no race of people that is superior by its origin or blood, as some races continue to boast even today."[114]

The principle of parity applies to dealings between nations, as for example, between Western and Muslim countries, as it does to social groups within a particular country. Fairness and equity also govern relations between the sexes, although the physical natures of men and women require that the principle of balance, rather than absolute sameness, governs these relations. "Wherever the physical endowments, the customs, and the responsibilities are identical, the sexes are equal; and wherever there is some difference in these respects, the discrimination follows that difference." So while men and women are strictly equal in religious matters and in affairs of "economic and financial competency", in social life important differences pertain: the Qur'an states clearly that men are the managers of women's affairs (4:34), and that in a court of law the testimony of a man is worth that of two women (2:282). Qutb explains these discrepancies, pointing to a man's practical experience in the world and to his "reflective and deliberative side", which contrast with a woman's relative naivety and emotional nature. These female characteristics, Qutb says, derive from the condition of motherhood, which requires a woman to spend most of her time at home, as opposed to the public realm, and nurture her family. Thus, writes Qutb, the status of women in Islam "is a question of the practical circumstances of life, not a question of preferring one sex as such over the other or an absence of equality."[115]

Yet, according to Qutb, there are societies in which the precepts of social equality appear to be absent. While Americans engaged "in an organized extermination of the Red Indian race", and white South Africans introduced racial laws that discriminate against coloured people,[116] employers in Western societies hired women to work in "shops, embassies, consulates and the news media", in order that they might use their sexual allure to attract clients or customers. These employers "The employer knows that hungry passions and treacherous eyes flicker about" the woman's body, "and take in her words, and he exploits this hunger for material gain and petty success, because honorable human values are far, far from him."[117] Only Islam, Qutb tells us, treats all humans fairly and honours their inherent dignity.

Because God is Lord of the universe, all property necessarily belongs to Him. Nevertheless, God has granted men and women the right to possess and enjoy property: "Men shall have a portion of what they have earned, and women shall have a portion of what they have earned" (Qur'an 4:36). Qutb therefore recognized that trading, buying, selling and the acquisition of land and goods are practices natural to the human species, and are therefore entirely legitimate. Further, he understood that a man "has a natural love for his posterity and a desire to pass on to them the results of his labor."[118] Yet, at the same time, he understood that Islam prohibits a person from profiting at the expense of others. "Justice demands that the social order serve the desires of the individual and satisfy his inclinations—within limits such that they do not harm the community."[119] In other words, while Islam rewards the individual's effort to make money, it severely restricts the "invisible hand" of the free market, which in Egypt and elsewhere resulted in a class of capitalist freebooters that had no regard for the human cost of its economic activity. Qutb explained how Islam qualified individual gain though charity, the prohibition of usury, and inheritance laws. With reference to these principles, Qutb wrote that Islam's textual sources demand that people govern their economic relationships in an ethical manner, looking to the interests of the common person and the community against predatory capitalism. Wealth should not be retained in the hands of a particular group of people, circulating only among them, the rest having no access to it, "So that it be not a thing taken in turns among the rich of you" (Qur'an 59:7).

Qutb understood that there was need for a political authority to oversee the framework of social justice. Thus, he addressed the issue of Islamic government. Following the traditional discourse, Qutb viewed Islamic political theory as resting "upon the basis of justice on the part of the rulers, obedience on the part of the ruled, and consultation [shura] between rulers and ruled. These are broad basic lines from which branch out other lines that lay out the shape and form of government after the preceding principle has laid out its nature and essence."[120] Qutb reminded his readers that consultation and obedience are divinely mandated. Thus Qur'an 3:159, "Take counsel with them in the affair." Fleshing out this command, Qutb explained that the Prophet would listen to the opinions of his companions in matters for which there was no revelation, and in which "they were more knowledgeable than he". And Qur'an 4:59: "O believers, obey God and obey the Apostle and those in authority among you" (Qur'an 4:59). Qutb makes clear that "the one who holds authority in Islam is not obeyed for his own sake, but is obeyed only because he submits to the authority of God."[121]

Qutb was not explicit as to the mechanisms of consultative governance. This is largely because, as he understood, the Arab-Islamic juridical tradition had very little to say about the matter. No particular system had been specified. The attention of the jurists had focused on the affairs of the community (*umma*), not the state (*dawla*), which they conceived strictly as a custodial agent for the implementation of the Shari'a. The chief duty of government was simply to allow the Muslim to lead a proper Muslim life. Because "Islam presents independent solutions to the problems of humanity, deriving them from its unified thought,"[122] the mechanisms of government and social ordering are therefore flexible, and thus able to address the exigencies of the time. Qutb asserts that a ruler should take the initiative in tackling problems pertaining to the general welfare for which "there is no guiding precedent in existence within the bounds established in Islam and on the condition of justice, which must characterize the leader (*imam*)."[123]

Against Western detractors, Qutb was keen to present Islam as a tolerant religion: "Islam does not compel others to embrace it, 'No compulsion is there in religion (Qur'an 2:256). Islam's tolerant attitude, he wrote, is especially apparent in relation to Christians and Jews, to whom Islam grants "the fullest freedom and protection in conducting their religious rites." Although, Qutb goes on to explain, Islam requires *dhimmis* (Jews and Christians under Islam's protection) to pay *jizya* (a poll tax) to the Muslim state, this is in lieu of *zakat*, and is the price for the protection that they gain as residents of the Islamic polity. Thus does Islam display "sensitive concern for justice in dealing with others":

In granting others their freedom to this extent, Islam is influenced by its broad spirit of humanity trusting that when they have the opportunity to examine Islam carefully without the interference of physical force or mental ignorance, their human nature will lead them to Islam, which achieves the perfect balance among all the goals that the previous religions aimed at as well among all the tendencies and desires of human nature, guarantees to all absolute equality and complete solidarity, and aims to achieve human unity at the level of the social system.[124]

Would Qutb have accepted an Islamized version of the existing monarchical-parliamentary system, one in which God-fearing Muslims replaced corrupt officials? He probably would. As a ministry employee, Sayyid Qutb retained investment in the state order. He was therefore uninterested in establishing anything as radical as, for instance, a new caliphate; in fact the term "caliph", in its political meaning, does not appear in the book. Although Qutb leaves the door open for options, it is clear that he would have accepted a reformed parliament as an arena for consultative activities. However, Qutb did not outline a method of checks and balances. There are no procedural guarantees ensuring that a chosen leader remained just. In the end, in his mind, all is contingent upon the ruler and his subjects bowing down together before the authority of God.

Qutb rounded out *Social Justice in Islam* by measuring the historical experience of the Muslim peoples against the ideal of Islamic social justice as practiced by the early community of Muslims at Medina. Here we find at work the universal motif of renewal, common to both nationalist and traditional Islamic discourses. Drawing upon the historical works of Haykal, al-'Aqqad and others, Qutb explained how the just rule of the first Caliphs lapsed into the tyranny of Mu'awiyya and the Umayyads. Qutb placed much of the blame for this state of affairs upon 'Uthman, the third Rashidun caliph, whose advanced age and inability to take control encouraged the rounds of civil war that ensued. According to Qutb, 'Uthman's political failure opened the way for a series of unstable and power-hungry dynasties whose inattention to Islamic principles eventually invited the intervention of the West. This Western colonization of Muslim countries, Qutb stated, is the most serious calamity ever to have befallen the Islamic world. Not only has the West been intent upon political subjugation, it has also succeeded through the more insidious process of cultural colonization in divorcing Muslims from their beliefs and sense of social responsibility, which had up to the modern era remained intact. Europe "devoted all its forces to Crusader hostility and from the material and cultural strength it bears."[125]

In composing *Social Justice in Islam*, Qutb attempted to undercut the claims of Western socialism, which was gaining adherents through its promise to impose distributive justice upon free enterprise. In large part, the book's effectiveness resided in the way it blended old and new concepts. In pre-modern Islamic discourses the term "justice" (*'adl*) referred to a condition of "balance" or "equilibrium" that resulted when a just prince was able to maintain the proper order of society:

hence the frequent use in mediaeval political discourse of holistic metaphors that spoke of the polity in terms of a living organism.[126] The obverse of justice was *zulm*, "a term which modern scholars usually translate as oppression" but has the etymological meaning of "transgressing the proper limit".[127] Thus the Egyptian historian 'Abd al-Rahman al-Jabarti (d. 1825) explained that the "common good" is contingent upon a state of affairs whereby all of the components of society—*'ulama*, rulers and ordinary people—accomplish the tasks expected of them and respect the established order, in so far as it conforms to the laws imposed on mankind by God.[128] In his narrative, al-Jabarti measures the turbulent and factious fighting among the Mamluk households against the ideal of divinely directed justice.

Although Qutb, like al-Jabarti, regarded strong individual belief as the key to social harmony and balance, he also emphasized the equitable distribution of wealth within a framework of mutual social responsibility and solidarity. This was because, rather than conceive the polity as a hierarchically arranged order, he thought in terms of "society", a congeries of culturally defined individuals who inhabited the space of the nation-state. By presenting Islam as the solution to real economic, social and political grievances, Qutb's book had an implicit reference to emergent Third World populism.

The work's central argument, that Islam provides answers to situations facing Muslims in all times, placed him squarely within the tradition of modern era Muslim reform. In contrast to the strict fundamentalism of earlier revivalists, such as Muhammad 'Abd al-Wahhab (d. 1793) and Muhammad Ahmad (The Sudanese Mahdi, d. 1885) who sought to replicate pristine Medina, Qutb followed the trend of the Turkish Namik Kemal (d. 1888) and Egypt's Muhammad 'Abduh (d. 1905), in accommodating Islam to the requirements of global modernity. Like these men, he fashioned historically specific, metaphorical, and even purely apologetic understandings of the Quran. These reformers expressed the regenerative dimension of their thought in terms of "progress", an Enlightenment concept that influenced the names they used to describe their particular movements.[129]

Like the reformers, Qutb interpreted Islam as a rational, practical and scientifically sound religion that was in accord with human nature. Thus, he adopted from the *usul al-fiqh* the juridical concept of the general interest of the community (*al-maslaha al-'amma*) and like 'Abduh, he applied it in a way that called to mind the utilitarian thinking fashionable in Europe.[130] Yet unlike the reformers and in common with the Muslim Brothers, he reacted to the reversal of Muslim fortunes in a way that bred a sense of distance from the West rather than accommodation with the foundations of its civilization. In Qutb's view, as in al-Banna's, far from being a benevolent mentor to Muslim peoples, the West and its domestic agents were adversaries intent on the political and cultural conquest of the Islamic world.

4

AMERICAN SOJOURN

The Shallow American

Qutb did not remain in Egypt long enough to witness the favourable response accorded *Social Justice in Islam* in Islamist circles. Soon after completing the manuscript in the late summer of 1948, he left for the United States on a government-sponsored mission to study American educational curricula and pedagogy.[1] He entrusted the manuscript to his brother Muhammad for publication. Qutb was at the time of his departure forty-two years old, beyond the usual age for educational missions, and some have wondered why the Ministry should have chosen him. 'Abd al-Fattah Khalidi, Qutb's Arabic biographer and a supporter of the Islamist cause, suggests that in sending Qutb to the US, the Ministry of Education was acting in concert with the Palace. Both were eager to muzzle Qutb's sharply stated displeasure with the political regime; the journal *al-Fikr al-Jadid* (*New Thought*) had been of particular concern to the authorities.[2] Another source contends that the mission was an attempt by the Ministry to temper Qutb's growing criticism of its foreign-based educational curricula "by putting him in closer touch with the West". According to this view, the Ministry hoped that familiarity, far from breeding contempt, would instil in Qutb a greater respect for the Western educational models that the Ministry was intent on adopting.[3] Whatever the actual reason, the Ministry allowed Qutb considerable freedom in determining the length of his visit and choosing the educational institutions in the United States that he would attend. His assigned mission was not to obtain a higher degree but simply to investigate American methods and curricula in the areas of primary and secondary education, a task for which his career as an educator had well prepared him.[4] During his trip and immediately afterwards, Qutb wrote letters and journal articles that detailed his impressions of the United States.

Qutb was certainly not the first Egyptian to visit a Western country and write about it. As early as the 1830s Rifaʻa al-Tahtawi (1801–73) provided his countrymen with an account of his five years in France as imam of the first large-scale Egyptian study mission sent to Europe by the reform-minded Muhammad ʻAli.[5] Some twenty years later, the state technocrat ʻAli Mubarak travelled to Paris on another of Muhammad ʻAli's missions, an experience that found an echo in his voluminous, semi–fictional travelogue *'Alam al-Din* (1882).[6] In the twentieth century, Taha Husayn fashioned an account of his studies between 1915 and 1919 at the French universities of Montpellier and the Sorbonne.[7] Mention might also be made of the Anglophile Luwis ʻAwad (1915–90) who wrote a memoir of his studies at King's College, Cambridge between 1937 and 1940. In his reminiscence, ʻAwad relates how on his way to England he stopped in Paris where he met another Egyptian studying abroad, Muhammad Mandur, who like ʻAwad was destined to become one of Egypt's leading literary figures in the 1950s.[8]

Although Qutb shared many things with these other Egyptian sojourners, including a penchant for reflective social analysis, he stood apart from them in the fundamental meaning that he ascribed to his mission in the West. Tahtawi, Mubarak, Taha Husayn and Luwis ʻAwad drew upon their experiences abroad as a way of expressing their admiration for Western culture and the form of the Western nation-state, which they generally regarded as appropriate models for Egypt's march to modernity. Tahtawi and Mubarak were attracted especially to the technical and organizational aspects of the Western nation-state, while twentieth century travellers like Husayn and ʻAwad were drawn to the ideological underpinnings of Western civilization. All recognized that Egypt's success was contingent on absorbing the lessons of Europe. As Rasheed El-Enany has stated with reference to ʻAwad, their purpose abroad was "Promethean" in that it hinged on the acquisition and application to Egypt of the sources of Western power.[9]

In contrast, Qutb infused his reporting of life in America with commentaries and images that were altogether critical of Western civilization. He believed that history in general and the Qur'an in particular had stamped Egyptians and other Muslim peoples of the East an outlook on life different from that of the Western countries, including the

United States. Although at the time of his departure he did not yet have a hard view of America, he was well aware that the country was starting to flex its muscles globally and was preparing to slip into the shoes of the severely weakened, but not yet dead, empires of Europe. Equally, he was aware of the growing influence in the world of American popular culture—a seemingly unstoppable trend propelled by the advertising might of Madison Avenue.

Qutb left Alexandria for New York City in early November 1948. From the moment that he settled into his first-class cabin, he was alert to the deeply personal significance of his journey to the "New World". Writing years later in *Fi Zilal al-Qur'an* (*In the Shade of the Qur'an*) Qutb recalled how the voyage elicited in him a heightened sense of destiny and moral purpose. Viewing the wintry seas from the deck of the ship, he contemplated Qur'an 2:164, which speaks of the

ships which sail through the sea with that which is of use to mankind, and the water (rain) which Allâh sends down from the sky and makes the earth alive therewith after its death, and the moving (living) creatures of all kinds that He has scattered therein, and in the veering of winds and clouds which are held between the sky and the earth, are indeed *Ayât* (proofs, evidences, signs, etc.) for people of understanding.

Surrounded by these manifest signs of God's power, Qutb explained how his thoughts gravitated to the majesty of the Divine Reality and to the "music" of God's creation: "I felt like a small speck in the immense ocean, among the crashing waves and the infinite blue surrounding us. And nothing but the will of God and his solicitation, and the laws He laid down for the universe, could have guaranteed the safe passage of that small speck among the terrible ocean waves."[10] As never before, he came to comprehend his life unfolding within the largess of God's providence. If we were to place Qutb's recollection of his sea journey to the West within a theoretical context, we could do no better than to evoke Victor Turner's symbolic analysis of the pilgrimage experience.[11] Like the generic pilgrim of Turner's study, Qutb sensed that his outward journey was leading him to the very centre of his existence, to a place animated by the divinely inspired truths.

As with every "heroic" quest, tribulations beset Qutb's journey. *In the Shade of the Qur'an* he tells how his attention was drawn to a Christian missionary who proselytized among the ship's passengers and dared even to direct his attention at Qutb and five other Muslim passengers aboard. Chagrined, Qutb approached the captain and received permission to lead the Muslim passengers and Nubian service staff in the Friday congregational prayer. Qutb recalled with satisfaction how this overt display of piety attracted the attention of the other passengers, including a Yugoslav woman:

After the prayer, many congratulated us on our "service"—this was the extent to which they understood our prayers. But a lady from the crowd—we learned afterwards that she was a Christian Yugoslav escaping the hell of Tito's Communism—was emotionally affected and moved. Her eyes swelled with tears and she could not contain her emotions. She clasped my hand warmly and said in weak English that she could not help but be touched by the humility, order, and spirituality contained in our prayers.

Qutb and his fellow Muslims were "in awe" of this woman who knew no Arabic yet sensed in the Qur'anic phrases of the prayers a spiritual power "like that of the Holy Spirit". Qutb concluded that the woman was responding to the *i'jaz*, the Qur'an's miraculous ability to move sensibilities by means of the sonorous power of its language, a topic that a few years earlier he had discussed in his literary study of the Qur'an.[12]

More disconcerting to Qutb than the activities of the missionary was the sudden appearance at his stateroom door of a "beautiful, tall, semi–naked" woman who asked if she could spend the night with him. Qutb writes that he had to ask the woman forcefully to leave his room. He heard her fall on the floor outside and realized that she was drunk. We may dismiss Qutb's assertion, reported by his Arabic biographer, al-Khalidi, that the woman was an American agent sent to engineer his moral collapse. However, we may take seriously Qutb's conviction that the encounter tested his resolve to resist temptations damaging to his identity as an Egyptian and a Muslim.[13] Alone and surrounded by non-Muslim strangers, Qutb spent the voyage sharpening the vertical line of distinction that separated his authentic moral self from its corruption from Western otherness.

Qutb made landfall at New York as the city prepared for the holiday season of Thanksgiving and Christmas. He checked into a hotel room with a friend, possibly one of the Muslim passengers from the ship, and wandered through the snow-dusted streets of Manhattan jostling with festive shopping crowds at Times Square and Fifth Avenue. Holiday decorations festooned the broad avenues and shop windows. Perhaps he passed by the jazz clubs on West 52nd Street and the string of theatres on Broadway, which in 1948 featured musicals like *Kiss Me,*

Kate, a revival of *Showboat* and performances by Billy Holiday and Maurice Chevalier. New York was then entering the peak of its post-war prosperity and the city's energy would have been palpable to a visitor like Qutb.

Yet Qutb was uneasy. He confided in a letter to his friend Muhammad Jabr, president of the Dar al-'Ulum Society, that the long sea journey and subsequent acclimatization had exhausted him. His thoughts were on home: "Is there anything I can do for you while I am here," Qutb asked Jabr. "Can I buy something for you, or inquire about some matter on your behalf?" In the letter, dated 19 December 1948, Qutb expressed concern that he had not heard from his brother Muhammad in three weeks. "Why hasn't he written? Why does he put me in this condition of worry?"[14]

Qutb had never been to a Western country before. However, his previous journalistic efforts to evoke the essential characteristics of Western society provided him with a template with which to understand and assess what he was experiencing. In much the same way as many modern-era Europeans who travelled to or wrote about the "Orient", Qutb would either purposefully ignore or simply not see anomalies that contradicted his view of Orient and Occident as essential and opposed entities. Over the course of his study mission, Qutb viewed the United States not with fresh eyes but rather through the tinted spectacles of a man long captive to a particular view of the world.[15]

The city's frantic pace confirmed his preconception of the West's hard-nosed, materialistic ways. Qutb explained that he pitied the city's pigeons, which, like the city's human inhabitants, lived joyless lives amid the hustle of the urban landscape:

I said: is this a place for peaceful pigeons? In New York, this crazy place, a place that's never still? Is New York the place for meek creatures like you? They turned their calm, translucent eyes right and then left, not understanding a word that I said. But I understood them very well.

It was a flock of pigeons that had landed on the curb of the main road, quite undisturbed by the clamouring noise around them, by the roaring cars and thunderous traffic, which surged forward as if it were the Judgment Day, or by the hurrying crowds rushing feverishly in search of their prey. Nor were they disturbed by looks so hard and cold they appeared to belong to the executioner, nor by those sharp and sparkling looks filled with greed, desire, and lust.

The pigeons were not interested in any of this. It was as though they were saying to this stormy, furious human herd: Easy! Have some leniency and peace. Ponder the meaning, beauty and the music of life. Pursue life's higher ends, rather than this life of gluttony, indulgence, craving, and consumption.[16]

Qutb did not stay in New York long. Early in 1949 he went to Washington, where he enrolled at the Wilson Teacher's College, a four-year institution that in 1976 would merge with three other schools to form the University of the District of Columbia. At the college, Qutb focused on improving his English language skills. Ever since his days at Dar al-'Ulum, Qutb felt intellectually handicapped by his inability to function adequately in English, knowledge of which was necessary for understanding the wider world. Now, when he lived in the United States, there were the added, practical needs to communicate with the American people and successfully complete his course work. Qutb stated in a letter that he was making "good progress" in English at Wilson College's International Center. However, he went on to say that the teaching methods of his American instructors did not impress him. In fact, Qutb told his friend, he had felt compelled to correct his teachers' "defective pedagogy" on a number of occasions. He boasted that he was able to convince the instructors to modify permanently the structure of the college's English language programme.[17]

Despite reservations about the college, Qutb was comfortable in his new surroundings. "Life in Washington is good," he wrote Jabr, "especially as I live close to the library and my friends." Thanks to the generous terms of his Egyptian government bursary, he maintained a decent standard of living: "A regular student can live well on $180 per month. I however, spend between $250 and $280 monthly."[18] Yet Qutb's stay in Washington was not without challenges. Qutb suffered an undisclosed illness that required treatment at the city's George Washington University Hospital. During his convalescence at the hospital, Qutb learned of the 12 February 1949 assassination in Cairo of Hasan al-Banna, Supreme Guide of the Muslim Brothers. According to Qutb, the hospital employees openly rejoiced upon hearing the news.[19]

It is difficult to believe that Americans of the time were aware of or interested in a political killing in far-away Egypt. More believable is Qutb's assertion that he was impressed by the seriousness with which informed Westerners regarded the Brotherhood and its late leader. He mentioned a conversation he had at the Washington residence of the

British Arabist John Heyworth-Dunn. Heyworth-Dunn, who was then on the verge of completing a privately-published study on Islamic trends in Egypt, told Qutb that the Brotherhood stood as a bulwark against the advance of Western civilization in the Muslim East. "Egypt," he said, "will not progress if the Muslim Brotherhood comes to power." Heyworth-Dunn's assessment of the Brotherhood's strength reinforced Qutb's growing belief that the movement was, indeed, a force to be reckoned with. His growing admiration of its faith-driven activism would prove instrumental in his joining the movement in 1953.

During their meeting, Heyworth-Dunn offered to pay Qutb for the privilege of translating al-'Adala al-Ijtima'iyya fi al-Islam (Social Justice in Islam) into English. Qutb refused the offer. He says that he was suspicious of Heyworth-Dunn's probing questions about the situation in Egypt and believed that the Englishman was trying to recruit him into the American intelligence network.[20] As it turned out, the American Council of Learned Societies took up the task of rendering the book into English. In 1948, the council had initiated a translation programme to afford Americans entry into the thought of the modern Near Eastern world, and included Qutb's work in the first group of twenty-two books to be so translated. It gave the assignment to the Rev. John B. Hardie, a scholar of Semitic languages at the ecumenical Atlantic School of Theology in Halifax, Nova Scotia. Hardie commenced work on the project some time in 1950 or 1951.

It was also in Washington that Qutb experienced his first real pang of homesickness. In a letter addressed to Tawfiq al-Hakim, the outstanding dramatist and novelist for whom he felt affinity, Qutb admitted to feelings of isolation and loneliness. Writing at a local restaurant, he thanked al-Hakim for sending him an autographed copy of his newly published adaptation of the Oedipus story, al-Malik Udib (1949). In the book, al-Hakim argued for a melding of Hellenic and Arab ideals against the materialism of the West. The book's central message impressed Qutb. However, the emotions that it evoked troubled him. As he explained to al-Hakim, the volume had revived the "spirit of the familiar East". He confided that he yearned for a friend with whom he could discuss literature and the world of ideas: "How much do I need someone to talk to about topics other than money, movie stars, and car models." Americans, Qutb opined, were crass people who were generally disinterested in life's spiritual dimension.

Indeed, they were more interested in the invention of new dishwashing technologies than they were in the Bible. As evidence of Americans' low aesthetic standards, he painted for al-Hakim a vivid verbal picture of an American youth standing nearby whose sweater was inscribed with gaudily coloured pictures of a leopard and an elephant. "Such," Qutb states bluntly to his friend, "is the taste of Americans."[21] He knew al-Hakim would understand; selfish and vulgar behaviour similarly bothered al-Hakim.[22]

Qutb's feelings of estrangement deepened as he travelled by train across America's heartland to Colorado. After a stopover in Denver, he made his way to Greeley, a prosperous agricultural and ranching community nestled in the Front Range of the Rockies where he enrolled at the Colorado State College of Education, an institution of some renown in the Central Plains states. Greeley was obviously a very different kind of place from New York and Washington. Established as a utopian community in 1870, the city proudly maintained in the late 1940s the moral rigour, temperance and civic-mindedness of its founding fathers. In the words of the 1949 Summer Session College Bulletin, Greeley was a place "where the handshake is [...] firm and the greeting is sincerely cordial." Greeley's first settlers had imposed a total ban on alcohol that was still in effect during Qutb's stay. In the view of many Americans of the era, the qualities of Greeley represented the best that the United States had to offer. In fact, such thinking would lead in 1989 to Greeley's inclusion on the Chicago's Civic League's list of "All-American cities".

But Greeley's highly touted civic virtue made little impression on Qutb. From his perspective the outlook of Greeley's inhabitants did not differ substantially from that of the larger US cities he had visited. Far from representing a kinder and gentler population of Americans, the people of Greeley carried within themselves the same moral flaws of materialism and degeneracy that characterized Occidental civilization in general. It was an assessment that would have been incomprehensible to Nathan Meeker, Greeley's idealistic founder, but one that fitted well with Qutb's overall picture of the world.

Qutb arrived in Greeley in time for the college's summer session and settled into what would turn out to be a six–month stay—the longest of his mission. The 1949 summer session was one of the best attended in the college's history. The session attracted a number of other international students. The college engaged James Michener, a former faculty member and author of the then recently published *Tales of the South Pacific*, to teach at the Department of English. The attractive green campus hummed with activity. Qutb's official college transcript reveals that he spent the eight-week session auditing a course in Elementary English composition.[23] The course led to a breakthrough in Qutb's knowledge of English. He wrote in a published letter that it was during his Colorado stay that he finally became comfortable in the language,[24] a real boon for a man who hitherto had been dependent on Arabic translations of foreign works. During the autumn Quarter, he audited courses in American Education, Secondary Education, and Oral Interpretation.

On 1 December 1949, just days before the period of final examinations, Qutb withdrew from all of his autumn Quarter courses. As an audit student, Qutb perhaps felt little compunction to trouble himself with the arduous examination process. The terms of Qutb's study mission did not require that he receive college credit for the courses that he attended. One searches Qutb's American writings in vain for references to strenuous academic challenge of the kind that feature prominently, for instance, in Taha Husayn's account of his studies in France.[25]

With a population at that time of just over 10,000, the city of Greeley was small and compact enough for Qutb to get to know it reasonably well. Qutb wrote how he would spend the summer evenings walking the quiet, tree-lined streets of the residential streets. "Each house," he writes, "appears as a flowering plant and the streets are like garden pathways." He expresses surprise at how few people ventured beyond their homes to enjoy the bucolic landscape. Indeed, according to Qutb, garden work appeared to be the most popular way of spending one's free time in this small Western city: "As one observes, the owners of these houses spend their leisure time working hard, watering their private yards and trimming their gardens. This is all they appear to do." It was, in his opinion, symptomatic of the American preoccupation with the external, material, and selfishly individual dimensions of life. Rather than engage in spirited local exchange and community interaction, Americans, in Qutb's view, chose to live within the confines of closed circles, symbolized by the residential year, which protected the private spaces of homeowners against the unwelcome intrusions of neighbours. Qutb writes, "I stayed there six months and never did I see a person or family actually enjoying themselves, even on summer nights when breezes waft over the city as in a dream."[26]

Such social behaviour was disconcerting for Qutb, who had grown up within a nurturing endogamous village and, as an adult, had been accustomed to the vibrant street life and closely packed neighbourhoods of Cairo.

Qutb probably had little in common with his teenaged and twentysomething classmates, but he did manage to have a social life in Greeley. He was a member of the International Club and presumably participated in its events, perhaps even the club's annual "pot luck" dinner, which featured dishes prepared by students from around the world, including what the club advertised as "Arabian cuisine". A former member of the club, a Palestinian, remembered Qutb as "a lovely person. He was quiet, but his intelligence was apparent. He had the personality of a politician. Once he met you, he never forgot your name." According to the classmate, Qutb was fond of Western classical music and played it "night and day". He did not regard Qutb as an overtly religious man: "In my time at Colorado," he says, "I never saw him pray."[27]

The college's administrators noted Qutb's presence on campus. They were pleased to have enrolled an international student of some repute in his native land. In the college's 17 October 1949 bulletin there is a photograph of Sayyid Qutb and Dr William Ross, the President of the college, examining together one of Qutb's works, possibly a copy of his then newly published *Social Justice in Islam*. Qutb had only recently seen a copy of his published work, which his brother Muhammad had sent to him. The caption beneath the photo identifies Qutb as a "famous Egyptian author...of both novels and textbooks" who is "an outstanding authority on Arabic literature and...a noted educator in his homeland." Qutb, the proud literary man, no doubt cherished the recognition.

In Greeley, Qutb had at least one encounter with "Jim Crow". Qutb and another Egyptian student named Muhammad 'Abbas, a PhD candidate in Mathematics, were denied admission into one of Greeley's four cinemas. The ticket seller misidentified them as African-Americans because of their dark complexions. After 'Abbas explained that they were, in fact, Egyptians the manager apologized and offered to let them in. However, Qutb did not accept the apology. A man of principle, he departed the scene angry and indignant.[28]

Qutb may have experienced racism, either overt or subtle, on other occasions during his American sojourn. After he returned to Egypt, he wrote an article in *al-Risala* that condemned the "White man" for his racist imperialism. It was the first time Qutb used such an epithet, and it almost certainly related to his experience in the pre-civil rights United States:

In America they talk about the white man as though he were a demi–god. On the other hand, they talk about coloured people, like the Egyptians and Arabs generally, as though they were half human....

The white man, whether European or American, is our first enemy. We must take this into account and make it the cornerstone of our foreign policy and national education.

We must nourish in our school age children sentiments that open their eyes to the tyranny of the white man, his civilization, and his animal hunger.[29]

At the same time, he wrote about the Americans' preference for the Turks "on account of their white skin".[30] It appears that the racism then current in America provided Qutb, perhaps for the first time in his life, with a degree of racial consciousness.

'The world is an undutiful boy!'

Qutb was not afraid to voice his critical attitude towards the United States and its role in world affairs before his hosts. In his Islamist tract *Milestones*, which he wrote in the early 1960s, he says that he was not afraid to argue with Americans on points of Islamic belief and practice. In these exchanges he drew attention to West's "shaky religious beliefs, its social and economic modalities, and its immorality." "These facts," Qutb goes on, "made the American people blush."[31] A simply written, one-page essay that Qutb contributed to *Fulcrum*, the magazine of the college's literary society, illustrates Qutb's tact. Entitled "The World is an Undutiful Boy!", it relates what Qutb purports to be an "ancient legend in Egypt" about a beautiful woman who represents a wise, all-knowing "Egypt" and her charge, a little boy who represents "The World". "Why did those ancient Egyptians hold this belief?" Qutb asks. "Because they were very advanced and possessed a great civilization before any other country. Egypt was a civilized country when other peoples were living in forests. Egypt taught Greece, and Greece taught Europe." As Qutb relates, when the little boy (i.e. "the World") grew up, he threw out his kind nurse (i.e. "Egypt") and even attempted to kill her. Qutb makes the point that the ingratitude shown by the boy toward his mentor is not, as some might believe, "a figure of speech", but is "what has actually happened" in history:

When we come here to appeal to England for our rights, the world helped England against the justice. When we came here to appeal against Jews, the world helped the Jews against the justice. During the war between Arab and Jews, the world helped the Jews, too.

Oh! What an undutiful world! What an undutiful boy![32]

The meaning of Qutb's allegory is straightforward; *Fulcrum's* mostly student readership would immediately have understood what Qutb had attempted to impart, that despite Egypt's gifts of the spirit and intellect, history has passed it over. The culturally inferior West has marginalized Egypt and dominated it politically, economically and in every other way.

Qutb wrote that he was surprised at the number of churches in Greeley; in his estimation, there were at least twenty, representing a variety of denominations. But in the plethora of churches there was a paradox. "Nobody," he writes, "can compete with the Americans in building churches...Yet, despite all this, no one is as distant as the Americans from appreciating the spirituality and sanctity of religion." According to Qutb, Greeley's pastors competed among themselves for congregations in the same fashion that shop or theatre managers competed for customers. As evidence, he cites an advertisement for a church function that was posted at the college: "Sunday October 1, 6:00 PM: Light Dinner; Magic Show; Puzzles; Contests; Entertainment..." In Qutb's mind, one should expect such efforts, for, as he says, "The American is naturally fascinated by greatness in size and number. For him, it is the first measure of feeling and appreciation."[33]

In order to experience something of Greeley's community life first hand, Qutb joined a church club (he is not specific as to the denomination) and participated in its social activities. "I belonged to church clubs wherever I was [in the United States], because these were important aspects of the country's social life that deserved close study from the inside." One such club activity was a dance that was held after the regular service in an adjacent hall. Qutb describes the seductive atmosphere of the occasion: "The dance hall was illuminated with red, blue and a few white lights. It convulsed to the tunes of the gramophone and was full of bounding feet and seductive legs. Arms circled waists, lips met lips, chests met chests, and the atmosphere was full of passion."

Much to Qutb's dismay, the church minister hosted the event. Indeed, he went so far as to dim the lights in order to create a "romantic, dreamy atmosphere". The minister then "advanced toward the gramophone to choose a song appropriate to the atmosphere, which would encourage those seated to get up on their feet." The song he chose was the popular Big Band dance tune, *Baby it's Cold Outside*,[34] from the 1949 Hollywood film *Neptune's Daughter*. Qutb, we may assume, remained on the sidelines, an uncomfortable spectator.

In America, Qutb stood face to face with the cultural source of the degeneracy that he held responsible for eroding the ethics and values of Egypt and the wider Muslim world. Qutb laced his American writings with anecdotes that reveal an almost obsessive concern with moral issues, especially matters of sexuality. He tells of a woman at the college who told him that sexual relations, far from being of ethical concern, "were a purely biological matter." He relates also how a nurse at the George Washington Hospital attempted to excite him by detailing the characteristics she desired her lovers to have. He draws a disapproving picture of the American woman's seductive appearance ("thirsty lips...bulging breasts...smooth legs...") and flirtatious demeanour ("the calling eye...the provocative laugh..."). He castigates Arab mission students who gave in to these wiles and dated American girls.[35] Although Qutb meant his sharply expressed critique of American sexual mores to distinguish American "primitivism" from values that he considered constitutive of the Egyptian nation, it also reflects the consternation of a man beset with encounters and temptations that challenged the ethic of public morality upon which his own sense of personal worth and integrity depended.

A little over a year of his arrival in New York City, Qutb crossed the Rockies and Sierra Nevada for California, where he spent the remainder of his time in the United States. His first stop on the West Coast was San Francisco, a city that he found physically beautiful but whose cool, misty climate proved detrimental to his health. Suffering from an undisclosed illness, possibly a relapse of the condition that had affected him in Washington, Qutb was admitted briefly to a local hospital.[36] After recovering, he moved to nearby Palo Alto whose drier and warmer climate reminded him of home. "I moved to Palo Alto," he wrote his friend 'Abbas Khidr, "where I smelled Egypt and became well."[37] By early summer, he moved again, this time to San Diego, the last stop on his American odyssey. Qutb's activities in California, educational and otherwise, are obscure; he did not document this stage of his journey to the same degree that he did his stays in Washington and Colorado. Although some sources claim that while in Palo Alto Qutb enrolled at Stanford University,[38] Stanford's Registrar has not been able to produce records suggesting that he ever attended that institution.

Qutb saw much of the United States during his twenty-one–month stay. Always he took time to take in the sights and experience what he could of American life. The vastness of the land and the beauty, inventiveness and organizational expertise of its people impressed him. However, Americans had gained all of these traits and accomplishments, he believed, at the expense of basic human values and moral depth. "I am afraid, "Qutb wrote, "that there is no correlation between the greatness of the American material civilization and the men who created it...in both feeling and conduct the American is primitive (*bida'a*)."[39] For Qutb, this deficit was nowhere more apparent than in the realm of American popular culture, which he considered shallow and fixated on muscular strength, material power, and sensuality. As examples, he pointed to American football, which had little to do with kicking the ball with the foot and much to do with physically harming one's opponent, and to the popular craze of professional wrestling that was then sweeping the country.[40] Americans, he says, must import their high culture from Europe, and this is possible only because of the country's great wealth. Qutb explains how during his "tenth visit" to the San Francisco Museum of Modern Art he was transfixed by a certain French painting, and bothered by the fact that so many Americans passed by it without interest, casting only cursory glances. For Qutb, it was only natural that the one art form in which Americans excelled should be films, which combined "craftsmanship and primitive emotions". Qutb derided the Westerns and police thrillers that were staples of the American film industry, and compared them unfavourably with what he considered the more sophisticated films of France. Still, he confessed to liking some Hollywood films, and singled out two stormy romances, *Gone with the Wind* and *Wuthering Heights*, and the more wholesome *The Song of Bernadette*, as personal favourites.[41]

Qutb took snipes at other manifestations of the American way. He disparaged American social etiquette. According to Qutb, party conversation consisted of "superficial" and "empty" talk. He also took a swipe at the weather. At best, he said, the physical climate of the United States was mediocre, especially compared to Egypt's. In his view, a person could not even get a decent haircut in America. Invariably, Qutb says, he would have to touch up his hair upon returning from the barber's shop to his lodgings.[42]

How did Qutb explain what he purported to be the shallowness and spiritual vacuity of American life? He looked to the imprint on the American character of history and the environment. The daunting challenge of taming the land and fighting the elements faced America's early settlers. They cleared forests and exploited mountains for their minerals, as Qutb observed in the mountain towns of Colorado. The practical requirements of pioneer life encouraged in Americans an aptitude for applied science, which submerged any spiritual tendency they might have had. Having never, it appears, read Thoreau and the nineteenth century New England Transcendentalists, Qutb wonders how the rugged landscape of the North American continent failed to awaken in Americans awe for nature and the divine spirit behind it. The American focus on the mundane was reinforced by the early settlers who fixated on the need to improve the material quality of their lives, not on "opening windows to the spirit and to the heart." The result of this imbalance between the material and the spiritual was a "deformity" in the American soul. "I fear," wrote Qutb, "that when the wheel of life has turned and the file of history has closed, America will have contributed nothing to the world heritage of values."[43] It was a strong indictment, but one consistent with Qutb's tendency to divide the world into culturally distinct and ethically unequal categories.

Qutb's discourse on the United States can be pegged as an example of "Orientalism in Reverse", a phrase coined by the Syrian cultural critic Sadiq al-'Azm in reference to the ways by which Easterners validate the Self in relation to the Other in the modern period.[44] As in the Orientalist tradition, Qutb documented encounters that confirmed cultural difference and inferiority. No doubt he "cherry picked", exaggerated and even invented some of his accounts of American life.[45] But he did so in order to make a grand point. As Egyptians continued to follow the example of Western secularism, Qutb was eager to communicate the damaging effects of materialism and individualism. Egyptians, he seemed to be saying, would do well not to follow America's lead. No doubt his concern on this point prevented him from reporting any positive encounter with American society that he may have had, and almost certainly his experiences were not all bad. As an international student at various colleges around the United States, he would have reached out to people, and they would have responded kindly, as people do in accordance with human nature.

Nevertheless, Qutb's negative impressions of America were rooted in deep, genuine sentiment. How else to understand this damning appraisal taken from his Qur'an commentary, *In the Shade of the Qur'an*, which he composed after his return to Egypt? Seizing upon the ancient prophetic motif, prominent in the Qur'an, of the corrupting effects on society of wealth and excess, he provides his readers with a hellish vision of a country alienated from God's truth. Racism, Qutb writes, is a particularly salient feature of this society. It is both a product and a justification of America's new power in the world, which has begun to target Muslims. William Shepard provides the translation:

During my stay in the United States of America, I saw with my own eyes the confirmation of God's (S) statement: "When they forgot the warning they had received, we opened to them the gates of everything (Qur'an 6:44)—the scene depicted by this verse is one in which all necessities and luxuries pour forth without limit! This hardly happens anywhere as it does in the United States. I also saw the conceit and luxury produced in the people, their feeling that this was the White Man's endowment. I saw the way they treat the colored people with despicable arrogance and disgusting barbarity. Their swaggering in the face of the rest of the world is worse than that of the Nazis, whom the Jews have denounced to the point where they have become the by-word of racial arrogance, while the white Americans practice racism against the colored in an even harsher form, especially if these colored people are Muslims. When I saw all of this I remembered this verse, as I trembled thinking of the law of God and could almost see it advancing step by step toward the unwary.[46]

Qutb's writings signal the moment in modern history when the United States' glossy image began to tarnish, not only in the eyes of Muslims, but in the view of many Americans and Europeans, too. Once viewed as a beacon—a champion of the self-determination of nations and advocate of cultural freedoms—in the post World War II era many perceived in America the political swagger and cultural insensitivities that William J. Lederer and Eugene Burdick captured so well in their 1958 novel *The Ugly American*.

Qutb discerned this change in America, first from the distance of Egypt and then first hand, prompting him to categorize the country as an oppressor of peoples and a polluter of universal standards of morality. Since the late 1940s, critical assessments of American policy and the pervasive US popular culture have become common to Muslims, and others, including many on the left, who chafe at the imbalance of

power in the world. In the dark
ture resulted in the appearance
the world. Although genuinely
nevertheless suggested gingerly,
with Cairo Metro passengers c
weeks following the 9/11 terror
While they generally condemned
ently focused on what they consid
can policy, especially regarding th
appreciated these viewpoints, even
secular frames of reference. He wo
since he had reported on America.

5

IN THE ORBIT OF THE MUSLIM BROTHERS

The battle of Islam and capitalism

Qutb returned to Egypt on 20 August 1950. The journalist 'Abbas Khidr announced his arrival at Cairo's Faruq airfield in advance in *al-Risala's* weekly arts column.[1] Among those who gathered at the airfield to greet him were several Muslim Brothers.

Qutb's first days back were exciting ones, filled by meetings with friends and literary colleagues who brought him up to date on events in Egypt. He resumed employment with the Education Ministry as assistant inspector of schools[2] and in the autumn arranged to perform the Hajj, the great pilgrimage to Mecca. For Egyptian pilgrims the sea route from Suez to Jeddah was still the most practical approach to the holy city. Qutb may have taken this route, or he might have bought an air ticket.

At the Hajj, he networked with Muslims from around the world. Later, in the city of Ta'if, he met separately the Indian Muslim scholar Sayyid Abu Hasan Nadwi (d. 1999) and the Hijazi writer 'Abd al-Ghafur 'Attar. Qutb was familiar with 'Attar's writings and the two men spent time discussing the state of Arabic literature. During his meeting with the Arabic-fluent Nadwi he passed on to him a copy of his *Social Justice in Islam.*[3] The clarity and decisiveness of the work impressed Nadwi, who was leader of the famous Nadwat ul-Ulema *madrasa* in Lucknow, a revivalist school that grew out of the Hanafi–oriented Deoband movement. He wrote later that he found in the book "a new style of writing, of research and exposition that I have not found in the writings of the Islamist writers in general, and in the writings of the Arabs in particular." Some time after their meeting Nadwi invited Qutb to write the introduction to the 1951 edition of his own

signature work, *Madha Khasira al-'Alam bi al-Inhitat al-Muslimin?*
(*What Has the World Lost with the Decline of the Muslims?*) .[4]

In the book, Nadwi expounded an idea derived from his mentor,
Abu l-A'la Mawdudi: that the Muslim world was steeped in *jahiliyya*,
"ignorance" of the divine mandate. Influenced by the West, Muslims
were captive to materialism and the false idol of nationalism, which
divided them and made them weak. "It is a tragic fact of modern life,"
he wrote, "that there exists no community worth the name in Europe,
Asia, Africa or America genuinely opposed to the Pagan [*jahili*] philosophy of materialism...What is to be regretted is that the traditional
enemy of Paganism, the Muslim, too, has become its ally and is serving
as its devoted camp follower in many parts of the world."[5] According
to Nadwi, without the assertion of their Islamic identity, Muslims will
not be liberated from foreign rule and regain their global leadership
role. Moreover, he wrote, the Arabs, the people from amongst whom
God chose the last prophet, must lead the revival.

Qutb noted with approval Nadwi's characterization of the world as
covered by a membrane of atheism, illusion, and darkness. It fitted
well with his own long-standing view that modern people, including
many Muslims, were alienated from the truth. Shortly after his meeting
with Nadwi, Qutb started reading Arabic translations of Mawdudi.
He found that the South Asian exposition of the modern *jahiliyya*
helped to clarify his critique of Western modernity. In the first rendition of his Qur'an commentary, he used the term in reference to the
application of non-Islamic legislation.[6] Qutb's collaboration with
Nadwi constituted a small yet significant encounter of the two creative
poles of Islamic thought in the modern period: Egypt and India.

Qutb returned from Saudi Arabia to Egypt in December 1951, just
as his second major Islamist work, *The Battle of Islam and Capitalism*,
was appearing in bookshops. In contrast to *Social Justice's* conceptual
approach, his new work focused on the concrete social and economic
problems that faced Egyptians. In so doing, it captured the mounting
anger and disillusionment of the Egyptian people.

Qutb begins his book with a bang, straight away accusing the ruling
classes of paralyzing the development of Egypt's human and material
resources and hence of perpetuating the country's "backwardness".
"The land," he wrote, "is still distributed as it was in feudal times. It
is held in the monopoly of the few who do not exploit it properly and
do not distribute it to those who can."[7] Deprived of economic oppor-

tunity, the people stagnate and waste their lives in cafes drained of dignity and initiative,[8] while the rich "squander their wealth at green gaming tables and on the laps of beautiful women."[9] Qutb inveighed that such conditions turn "the ideal of equality of opportunity into a myth, and the ideal of reward for effort into a legend." For "what equality is there between a lump of flesh born in a hut...and thrust into an environment of deprivation and neglect, and his sister who, delivered by a doctor and taken into the care of a nurse, is given every advantage?" In fact, Qutb wrote, rather than progressing, Egyptians were going backwards. In the quarter century since Egypt surrendered its traditions and handed power over to the political parties, the situation had worsened. "We look with nostalgia to the British Occupation. This is a disaster." Such conditions, he declaimed, go against the "nature of things" and cannot persist.[10]

Qutb rode the wave of the post-war leftist critique: "The State does nothing to protect the interests of the majority of the country's inhabitants. Rather, it is concerned only with the interests of a limited few."[11] Qutb evoked the example of the industrial magnate 'Abbud Pasha to prove his point. The state allowed 'Abbud to smash the union of his employees after they requested a small pay increase commensurate with the level of inflation.[12] Qutb followed the secular left in positing a relationship of dependency between Egypt's political class and the colonial power. "It is natural that colonialism, dictatorial rule, and money should be in alliance. Each depends on the others." The "internal exploiters" do not favour the termination of colonialism, because to do so would bring them face to face with the masses whose interests are in direct opposition to their own.[13] Consequently, Egypt's political parties will "stand together as one" in defence of the current capitalist order.[14]

Supporting Egypt's political elite was an ancillary echelon of opportunists and hirelings: "mercenary writers and journalists" and "professional men of religion who sold themselves, not to God or the homeland, but to Satan."[15] Chief among the latter were the men of al-Azhar who had failed to impart a "constructive and creative message—the resurrection of the Islamic idea and prepare it for practical application and propagate it." In Qutb's opinion, the *ulama* hindered the establishment of a new, just order by holding fast to the status quo. Previously tolerant of the scholars, he now regarded them as co-opted spokesmen of the political regime. Rather than push for change, the Azharis encouraged idleness; rather than construct innovative Islamic solutions to the problems facing Muslims, they were obscurantist. Indeed, writes Qutb, Islam has no need of a clerical class. *Fiqh* (religious understanding) is a skill potentially available to everyone. Just as a person can potentially master the knowledge required to become a medical doctor, so does religious authority derive from a person's hard work in mastering the sources of the Shari'a. Echoing the methods and purposes of the modernist reformers, men such as Jamal al-Din al-Afghani and Muhammad 'Abduh, Qutb declared that Muslims must cut though the dry and irrelevant "explanations and footnotes" of the Azharis and focus on the fundamental sources of the faith, the Qur'an and the traditions of the Prophet: "These have been enough for me to write my two books" (i.e. *Social Justice in Islam* and *The Battle of Islam and Capitalism*).[16] Although Qutb's criticism of al-Azhar was harshly phrased, it had some merit. The Mufti of Egypt at the time, Hasanayn Makhluf, was a man of the Old Regime, a staunch royalist whose most prominent *fatwa* (juridical opinion) was a 1951 judgment that permitted Muslims to imbibe Coca Cola and Pepsi.[17]

However, the edifice of political power was not the only factor standing in the way of justice. The secular and humanistic culture propagated by the government and other elite agencies was also to blame. According to Qutb, the Westernizing tendencies had raised up a generation of "brown English" (*al-Ingliz al-sumr*) intent on perpetuating the materialist and aggressive values of the foreign power. Those infected with the "Western disease" followed the British and other Westerners in disparaging Islam as a "relic of backwardness and decline".[18] Qutb echoed the emerging postcolonial critique in holding that ideological dependency prolonged material dependency.

But it was only a matter of time before the political regime collapsed under the weight of its inequity. Besieged by opposition factions and movements, the liberal order was on its last legs. "All of us," Qutb intoned, "recognize that the present situation cannot continue." "In the long term there is no avoiding an organized struggle... a struggle of the pen, of research and of organization."[19] The only question was which of the opposition groups would emerge victorious.

Qutb was adamant that the regime should not fall to any of Egypt's Communist organizations, whose atheistic philosophy would rob Egyptians of their native spirituality.[20] Although, according to Qutb,

Communism promised to clothe bodies and feed stomachs it was bankrupt when it came to the disbursement of moral values. True freedom, he wrote, was available only through Islam, which combined uniquely the egalitarian emphasis of Communism and the spiritual depth of Christianity. Moreover, unlike Communism, Islam is authentic to the Egyptian soul. It has been a "friend" to Egyptians for over 1,300 years, through thick and thin. The Egyptian people respond to the truth of Islam's comprehensive message of reform more readily than to systems of legislation and organization imported from abroad. "Our specific form emerges from roots deep within us."[21] He had treated this theme at length in *Social Justice in Islam*.

Previously, in the 1940s, Qutb had advocated Arab unity within a wider Eastern world. In this view, Egypt shared with other Arab, Muslim and Oriental countries an indigenous spiritual disposition. Not a religious exclusivist yet, he had been fond of evoking the Hindu poet-sage Rabindranath Tagore·who wrote compellingly of man's connections with the realm of the spirit.[22] The East produced such men.

Now, writing in the early 1950s, Qutb's transnational vision focused on Egypt's place within the distinctive and geographically expansive "bloc of Islam, which, strengthened by the new states of Pakistan and Indonesia, represented the dignity of the Muslim East."[23] Qutb still regarded himself an Egyptian "son of the country", and he continued to feel a deep connection to the wider Arab world. However, he now felt passionately that Islamic identity should trump all other articulations of belonging, including Egyptian territorial patriotism and the secular pan-Arab nationalism that had gained ground in Egypt since the 1940s. This was the period when influential Arab nationalist writers like Constantine Zurayk (1909–2000), Zaki al-Arsuzi (1899–1968), and Sati 'al-Husri (1879–1967) were theorizing, preparing the ground for the emergence of 'Abd al-Nasser and the Ba'thists. A person's primary loyalty, Qutb wrote, was to the "larger homeland of Islam (*al-watan al-Islamiyya al-akhbar*)", not to linguistic, ethnic or cultural collectivities.[24] Imperialism had torn up the unity of the Islamic World by creating petty states, each with the stamp of nationhood. Now, in the emergent struggle between capitalism and communism, America and the Soviet Union were attempting to gather these artificial statelets into their respective zones of influence. In Qutb's opinion, only through the creation of a distinctive zone of Islamic countries would Muslims be in a position to excise themselves from their "terminal positions in the caravans of Communism and Capitalism". Liberated from Great Power subservience and aware of their common Islamic identity, the Muslim countries would function as full, active and leading participants in global politics. They would have a say in war and peace and play leading roles in the destiny of the world. As Qutb put it, "We [Muslims] have something to offer."[25]

Qutb's definition of Islam as a corporate entity in competition with other ideologies reflected the sharply polarized categories of the Cold War. Here again we note the influence on his thought of the emergent Third Worldist tide. The original idea of an independent, actively anti–colonial bloc of African and Asian nations goes back to the early decades of the twentieth century. The Persian activist Jamal al-Din al-Afghani (1838–1897) may have been the first Muslim to stress "Oriental solidarity" against the West.[26] However, in the 1920s with the convening of the Congress of the Peoples of the East in Baku (1920), and the First Congress of the League Against Imperialism in Brussels (1927), an idea of anti–Western unity took definitive theoretical shape, sponsored by the Bolsheviks, who saw the utility of supporting anti–imperialist liberation movements. Among the contributors to the movement were the Soviet Tartar Sultangaliev (1892–1940) and Manabendra-Nath Roy (1897–1954) of India. Each, in his own way, blended ethno-linguistic nationalism, pan-Asian unity and Socialism in order to empower the "scorned, exploited and ignored" masses of the colonial world against the metropole.[27]

The "transmission belts" by which this mix of national liberation, socialism and cross-sectional unity was spread to the regions of the developing world, including many Muslim-majority countries, are difficult to ascertain with precision. What is clear is that by the early 1950s, it had become an important aspect in the post-colonial landscape. So, for example, we find the Algerian independence leader Ahmed Ben Bella (b. 1918) ruminating on Sultangaliev's doctrine of the "Colonial International" as he served his sentence as a political prisoner in a French jail cell in the mid-1950s. We find these ideas expressed, in concrete institutional form, in the Non-Aligned Movement whose first meeting in 1955 was at Bandung in Indonesia. Among the participants were Sukarno, Jawaharlal Nehru, Ho Chi Minh, Kwame Nkrumah and Egypt's President Gamal 'Abd al-Nasser. "More than any other single event, this conference in a hitherto obscure city...

symbolised the moment of arrival for the Third World."[28] We also discern aspects of those ideas, in an Islamist mode, in Sayyid Qutb's designation of Islam as a justice-oriented third force in geopolitics. Like much else in Qutb's body of work, his ideas on pan-Islamic unity constitute a creative adaptation of traditional Islamic concepts to contemporary trends.

As before, Qutb's emphasis on extra-territorial styles of identity did not mean negation of the nation-state as an appropriate and legitimate arena of struggle; he had yet to employ the very strict, Manichaean dichotomy between Islam and nationalism that would characterize his radical Islamist thought. Given the reality of the international state system, he believed that Muslims had no choice but to work through existing nation-states. He conceived the goal as capturing and colonizing the space of the state to build foundations for new forms of Muslim inter-state cooperation and unity. Echoing Hasan al-Banna, he stated, "There is no conflict between Arab nationalism (al-Qawmiyya al-'Arabiyya) and Islamic patriotism (al-wataniyya al-Islamiyya), only if we understand Arab nationalism as a step on the road. All the Arab land is part of the land of Islam. If we liberate the Arab land, we liberate part of the body of the Islamic homeland."[29]

Qutb's book was more condemnatory than prescriptive. Nevertheless, it did highlight a number of Qur'anic principles necessary for a just and compassionate social order. With an eye on the Pashas and foreign concessionaires, Qutb explained that Islam regards labour as the only legitimate means of making a profit: "Islam prevents the excessive accumulation of wealth not based on personal effort and work." The unregulated ownership of capital, he continued, results in class disparity of the kind "we see today in Egypt". To guard against economic injustice, Islam entitles workers to half the profits accruing from capitalist enterprise, and calls for the abolition of all monopolies, including the Suez Canal concession and those relating to transport and utilities. All of these enterprises, Qutb goes on, "must be the property of the people." Drawing once again on the Islamic principle of the general welfare (maslaha), Qutb recognized the right of the state to intervene in the economy on behalf of the people, as for instance, in the adjustment of land rents or of cotton prices.[30]

Qutb concluded The Battle of Islam and Capitalism by calling upon the downtrodden masses to take heed of his message and take matters into their own hands: "Oh, you masses, the path of human dignity and of social justice has been laid out for you. It is a path that the Islamic nation knew once before and is in a position to know again."[31]

In general, both *The Battle of Islam and Capitalism* and *Social Justice in Islam* continued the aspirations toward national integration and independence initiated during the Wafdist-oriented mobilizations of the immediate post-war era. In common with the variants of Egyptian nationalism, Qutb's discourse centred on the political and economic victimization of the Egyptian people at the hands of foreign predators and their domestic allies. In the manner of earlier figures such as Mustafa Kamil and Sa'd Zaghlul, he sought to enlighten the masses as to their condition and point the way to their salvation. Not yet a revolutionary, he recognized the primacy of politics in the reconstruction of state and society. It was for this reason that he continued to engage in advocacy journalism.

What distinguished Qutb's Islamist thought from secular nationalist discourses was, of course, his effort to frame these populist notions in terms of the Qur'an and prophetic *hadith*. Whereas Egyptian and Arab nationalists regarded the nation as sovereign and territorially bounded, Qutb drew upon a millennium-old Islamic theological tradition that attributed ultimate authority to God. By drawing on aspects of the Islamic heritage, Qutb was able to cast the people's struggle against the Western-oriented political and economic elite in terms that were in accordance with the precepts of a higher ethical and metaphysical order. In Qutb's interpretation, Islam was a transformative ideology designed to purge Muslim countries of imperialism and instil in them the divinely mandated system of virtuous conduct.

The religious overtones of Qutb's two books, as well as the third, *Al-Salam al-'Alami wa al-Islam* (*Islam and World Peace*), struck responsive chords among the Islamist-oriented sectors of the *effendi* opposition, and inspired several analyses that likewise emphasized the Islamic principle of social justice. Prominent among these were two works composed by Muslim Brothers, *al-Islam...la Shuyu'iyya wa la Ra'smaliyya* (*Islam...Not Communism and not Capitalism*) by al-Bahi al-Khuli, and *al-Islam wa Manahij al-Ishtirakiyya* (*Islam and the Methods of Socialism*) by an Azhari scholar with Muslim Brotherhood affiliations, Muhammad al-Ghazali, both published in 1951.[32] Each writer followed Qutb in stating that ownership and production must benefit the community as a whole. They viewed nationalization, land tenure restriction and cooperative societies as in accord with the Islamic spirit of social justice. Later, in 1960, Mustafa al-Siba'i (1915–64), leader of the Syrian branch of the Muslim Brotherhood (called "the Islamic Socialist Front"), composed a study entitled *Ishtirakiyyat al-Islam* (*The Socialism of Islam*) that drew heavily upon Qutb's notion of "mutual social responsibility" (*al-takaful al-ijtima'i*), balancing the ideal of individual responsibility against that of individual freedom.[33] Significantly, al-Siba'i sanctioned 'Abd al-Nasser's economic reforms—an irony, given that 'Abd al-Nasser became Qutb's implacable enemy. Hamid Algar mentions the influence of Qutb's works on the Indonesian Muslim thinker Hamka (Abdul Malik Karim Amrullah, 1908–81) and on the Iraqi Ayatollah Muhammad Baqir al-Sadr (1935–80) whose multi–volume work *Iqtisaduna* (*Our Economics*), published in 1961, also examined moral ways of producing and managing wealth.[34] Like Qutb, these writers drew upon economic analysis and populist rhetoric in order to monopolize the ideological space of the left.

Qutb's 'paranoid style'

Like Islamists of today, Qutb highlighted the victimization of Muslims at the hands of foreign nations and domestic "imperialist agents". Qutb believed that the Western powers, including now the United States, were attempting to undermine the project of Islamic empowerment by deliberately infecting key segments of the native population with a twisted, "reactionary" version of Islam—he called it "American Islam" (*Islam Amrikani*) . Their methods were devious and seditious. Employing liberal doses of money and political influence, the United States followed the example of Britain in encouraging Muslims to ignore the public dimension of their faith. Qutb railed at this instrumentalist use of Islam:

The Islam that America and its allies desire in the Middle East does not resist colonialism and tyranny, but rather resists Communism only. They do not want Islam to govern and cannot abide it to rule because when Islam governs it will raise a different breed of humans and will teach people that it is their duty to develop their power and expel the colonialists.

Like the expressions of Christianity he witnessed during his stay in the United States, "American Islam" emphasized piety and ritual at the expense of social and political activism. As such, it possessed little capacity to invest the spectrum of life with transcendent meaning. "American Islam," Qutb continued,

is consulted on the issues of birth control, the entry of women into parliament, and on matters that impair ritual ablutions. However, it is not consulted on the matter of our social and economic affairs and fiscal system, nor is it consulted on political and national affairs and our connections with colonialism.

Qutb went on to explain how "Americanized Muslims" dominated Egypt's press organs and intellectual life. They talk much about Islam, these would-be Americans, but they neglect Islam's holistic nature. Consequently, they have separated themselves from the true meaning of the creed and so opened doors to Egypt's further degradation.[35] Qutb included among these "Fifth-Columnists" dozens of the men he had worked with in the public sphere since the 1930s, whose intellectual culture he now found remote, unsatisfying and even repugnant. Like other post-colonial writers of the time—for instance Albert Memmi, a Tunisian of Jewish-Berber descent—Qutb understood that the colonial relationship bound the Colonized to the Colonizer in a relentless dependency, which shaped the features and dictated the conduct of the colonized.[36] Qutb wanted Egyptians to break free of this debilitating relationship.

Qutb laid much of the blame for this state of affairs at the feet of the Orientalists (Western scholars of Islam), several of whom had made careers in Egypt. For instance, the Italian Orientalist Carlo Alfonso Nallino (1872–1938) had taught Arab astronomy and Arabic literature at the Egyptian National University and introduced his students, most notably Taha Husayn,[37] to modern methods of historical and philological inquiry. Through other channels, Orientalism influenced writers such as Zaki Mubarak and Salama Musa. Qutb was somewhat familiar with the Orientalists' scholarly methods and general outlook; for example, he had read in Arabic translation *Whither Islam?* by the noted British scholar H.A.R. Gibb.[38] However, he was suspicious of their motives. He vigorously denounced the claim, which Taha Husayn and others had voiced, that the philological methods that Orientalists employed were scientifically objective and politically disinterested.[39] Qutb argued that Western studies of Islam facilitated the imperialist project. Orientalists constructed a false identity for Muslims through a series of libels and negations, and then attempted to impose that identity on Muslims, who then internalized it, believed it, and lived it to the point that the falsehoods became reality. If, says Qutb, some Orientalists say good things about the Prophet, it is to make Muslims sleep—lull them to let down their guard, so that the conquering Western culture can transform them in its image.[40]

Qutb resented that these outsiders were intent on defining his identity. As an educator, he was inclined to believe that Egypt's modernizing school system was the primary conduit of Islam's distorted image. This was by design, and he traced it to the British educational advisers and native disciples who propagated "a general mentality that scorns the Islamic elements in life."[41] Qutb writes that Muslims must win back their Islamic identity from the imperialists. Teachers must replace Eurocentric accounts of history with ones that privilege Islam as the driving force of history. Most important, teachers must cultivate in students "an inward (*wijdani*) idea of life" that pays special attention to Islamic values.[42] Muslims, says Qutb, should remember that the West's representation of Islam manifests an enduring "Crusader spirit that all Westerners carry in their blood... to which is added imperialism's fear of the Islamic spirit and the effort to destroy the strength of Islam, whereby the Westerners are all linked by a single feeling and a single interest in destroying it."[43]

Qutb viewed Jews, both within Egypt and abroad, as particularly hostile to Muslim success in the world. It was not intrinsic to Qutb's Islamism that he should single out any particular group, such as the Jews, for special condemnation. In Qutb's works, as in the writings of other Islamist ideologues, Jews stand with British, French and American imperialists as enemies of Islam. That is to say, the object of Qutb's ire was dependent on contingent factors, such as the existence of imperialist intervention, which he then incorporated as an integral part of his vision and as an instrument of mobilization against the Egyptian regime.

Nevertheless, Qutb's representations of Jews do stand out from those of other non-Muslim peoples for the textual support the Jews receive in the Qur'an and the Islamic tradition. Jews figure in the canonical sources of the Islamic heritage in a way that Christians and other religio-cultural groupings do not. The reason has to do with history—the Prophet Muhammad's troubled relations with the Jewish tribes of the oasis town of Medina, site of the first Islamic community in the 7th century CE.

The great ninth century compilations of redacted tradition upon which historians rely for a reconstruction of Islam's sacred history relate how Muhammad attempted to incorporate the three Jewish tribes of the oasis into the nascent Islamic community. Muhammad, we are told, went so far as even to allow the Jews to retain their distinctive religious beliefs and practices, provided they recognized him as religious-political leader of the Medina tribal ensemble. The Jews, however, dismissed Muhammad's claim to be a prophet in the tradition of Moses and the Torah and refused to cooperate with him against his pagan Meccan enemies. Moreover, the Jews stood behind the Arab "hypocrites" (al-munafiqun) of Medina who publically supported Islam while secretly conspiring against it. Resentful of the Jews' rejection of him and believing them to be a security risk, Muhammad had two of the Jewish tribes exiled and had the males of the third tribe massacred, although in circumstances that absolved him of direct culpability.

What is notable is that these negative images of the Jews did not, for the most part, translate into an entrenched persecutory posture on the part of Muslim authorities. Despite the inauspicious beginnings of Jewish Muslim relations, the Jews enjoyed a relatively secure position as a recognized and tolerated community in pre-modern Islamdom, especially compared to the situation faced by their co-religionists in the Latin West.[44] In the twentieth century secular Arab nationalists, particularly those inspired by the liberal ideal, drew attention to these relatively good relations as a way of highlighting the disharmonious effects of Jewish settlement in modern Palestine. According to this line of argument, best represented by George Antonius, "Arab hatred and anti–Semitism would end, and the ancient harmony would be restored, when Zionism abandoned both its 'colonialist' and 'neo-crusader' quest."[45]

Other considerations prompted Qutb's interpretation of Arab-Jewish history. Qutb saw himself as living in an age in which the divinely ordained order of Muslim supremacy had been overturned. Muslim land was occupied and its inhabitants humiliated by followers of the Jewish scriptural faith who, in league with others, were intent on engineering Islam's eclipse in the world. In these circumstances, Qutb focused his attention not on the alleged inter-faith utopia of the mediaeval period, as did the Arab liberals, but upon the history of interfaith contestation as exemplified in the relations between Muhammad and the Jewish tribes of Medina. In Qutb's view, the obstinacy of the Medina Jews in the first century of the Hijra had its direct analogy in the nefarious purposes of Zionism in his own day.

Qutb's compulsive urge to recapitulate the Arab-Jewish present in the guise of the past is fully exposed in a tract, written in the early 1950s, entitled *Ma'rakatna ma'a al-Yahud* (*Our Struggle with the Jews*).[46] It constitutes Qutb's only focused treatment of Jewry, although his Qur'an commentary, discussed above, also has much to say about Jews in reference to certain Qur'anic verses. Qutb begins this short work by observing how "the Muslim community continues to suffer from the same machinations and double dealing which discomfited the early Muslims."[47] Like the Jews of Medina, the Jews of today work tirelessly to distort God's truth and seduce Muslims from their faith in order to weaken and, ultimately, destroy the Islamic community.[48] One must take seriously the Qur'anic verse, which states: "One segment of the People of the Book shall lead you astray" (Q 3:69).[49] Qutb reproduces mediaeval exegetical materials that accuse the Jews of inventing bogus tales (*Isra'iliyyat*) about the Prophet's life and of falsifying Qur'anic commentary. Today, Qutb continues, this distortion of Islamic doctrine in performed by a vast array of Jewish philosophers and writers whose protégés are found everywhere in the Muslim world sowing lies and deception.[50] Indeed, the Jews stand behind an entire range of modern-day calumnies, including Freudian psychology and Marxist socialism.[51] Expanding on references in the Qur'an and Tradition, he writes how the Jews are naturally ungracious: selfishness lives strongly in them, they do not feel the connection that binds humanity together.

The gist of Qutb's message is clear: the Jews did not honour their compact with Muhammad, therefore one cannot expect of them compliance with treaties in the present age, least of all with regard to Palestine. Qutb reduces inter-group struggle to a zero-sum game in which dedication to faith and action is the prime criterion for success. All of this evil arises from their destructive egoism grudging that "Allah should send his bounty to whom He pleases" (Qur'an 2:90).[52] The Jews' aggression can be contained and their nature disciplined only if they place themselves under the protection (*dhimma*) of the Muslims.

How should we explain Qutb's "paranoid" style, his proclivity to see the world through the lens of conspiracies and collusions? Ervand Abrahamian identifies the factors behind the presence of conspiratorial thinking in Iran during the Pahlavi and Revolutionary eras, and these are helpful for understanding the situation in Egypt.[53] Abrahamian points to "Iran's experience of imperial domination", but also to the "wide gap" that existed in Iran between the state and civil society, one of whose manifestations was the close relationship of the indigenous elite with the imperial powers.[54] Faced with imperious foreign domination and government opacity, ordinary citizens were prone to reduce Iranian politics to a "puppet show in which foreign powers control the marionettes—the local politicians—by invisible strings."[55] In the popular Iranian view, "the intelligent observer should ignore appearances and focus instead on the hidden links; only then can one follow the plot, understand the hidden agendas, and identify the true villains."[56]

Egyptians, like their Iranian counterparts, were likewise aware that their nation's destiny was in the grip of others—the British, the Americans and the economic elite, many of the latter with roots outside the country, who, directly or indirectly, were connected with the monarchical-parliamentary regime. In common with Abrahamian's Iranians, ordinary Egyptians did not feel that they were in control of their destiny. Critics, such as Qutb, therefore found it easy to lay the blame for the ills of state and society at the feet of particular agents or institutions, which they then identified with the colonizing Other. Whereas previously Qutb saw the difference between Self and Other as cultural in nature, in the 1950s he viewed it as premised on the absolutes of religion: God's unassailable truth vs. its opposite whose agents were bent on Islam's destruction. Richard Hofstadter comments written in 1964 about the "paranoid style" in American politics are applicable to Qutb: "the paranoid spokesman sees the fate of conspiracy in apocalyptic terms—he traffics in the birth and death of whole worlds, whole political orders, whole systems of human values."[57]

The essentialism inherent in Qutb's presentation of Jews, Orientalists, Westernized elites, Communists and other "enemies" of Islam is basic to the structure of his thought over the course of his career as a writer. As both an Egyptian nationalist and an Islamist, he attempted to create in Egypt a new sense of community. He did this, on the one hand, by conceptually distancing certain groups, such as Westernized elites, Jews and Orientalists whose otherness he highlighted and mythologized, and on the other, by elaborating a set of common cultural attributes appropriated from the past that provided the illusion of continuity. Qutb's construction of enemies confirms Albert Memmi's point that the colonized cannot be expected to emerge from the colonial experience with a liberal or internationalist conscience. More than likely, they will be chauvinists of one kind or another.[58]

Yet, for all of its cartoonish imagery of Islam's "enemies", Qutb's discourse is not without a certain perverse logic. Beneath the exaggerations and historical reductionisms there lay a number of truths that discomfited Qutb and other Muslim Egyptians. These truths included the dominance at the political level of the British and the elite echelon of large landowners, and the creation of the State of Israel, which Qutb and others equated with the larger phenomenon of European imperialism. On a larger canvas, they also included America's new tendency to augment its "soft power" with other, more direct methods of control and manipulation in securing US geostrategic goals. In 1953, two years after Qutb wrote his essay about "American Islam", US Secretary of State John Foster Dulles cooperated with Britain to overthrow Iran's populist Prime Minister, Mohammed Mossadegh.[59]

As Terry Eagleton has said of the myths that undergird other manifestations of communalist struggle, "however retrograde and objectionable [these might be] they are not pure illusions: they encapsulate, in however reductive, hyperbolic a form, some substantial historical facts." Following Eagleton, we may regard Qutb's budding Islamism as providing Egyptians with a motivating ideology for their struggle against forces that many blamed for the sad condition of Muslims in modern times. For "men and women engaged in such conflicts do not live by theory alone...it is not in defense of the doctrine of base and superstructure that men and women are prepared to embrace hardship and persecution in the course of political struggle." They require collective symbols that encapsulate and define their social being. Qutb appears to have recognized this fact, if only intuitively, in his negative portrayal of "enemies", both domestic and external, which facilitated the setting of community boundaries and defining the nature of the political struggle in which he was enmeshed.[60]

Musings on the Qur'an

Although "reactionary forces" were afoot in Egypt and other parts of the Islamic world, Qutb was not without hope. He scanned the horizon and saw evidence of a great pan-Islamic awakening. He expressed his optimism in a 1951 letter to the anti–imperialist Iranian Ayatollah Abu al-Qasim Kashani: "One united cry echoes in all parts of the

Islamic world, calling to the banner of Islam, crying out for Islamic unity and Islamic government." The cry, he continued, emanated from Pakistan, from Iran, from the Malay States and Somalia. It came from Ahmad Husayn, leader of the Egyptian Socialist Party (formerly Young Egypt), from Allal al-Fasi and Muhammad Hasan al-Wazzani of Morocco, and from Abu al-Nadwi and Abu l-A'la Mawdudi. "The day that this vast world extending from the shores of the Atlantic to the shores of the Pacific Ocean [escapes from the clutches of imperialism], then 'the earth will become strait for them, for all its breadth'" [Qur'an 9:118].[61]

Qutb understood that his anti–establishment views were bound to attract the attention of the authorities. Already, on at least two occasions, the state had censored his writings. Afraid for his safety, a colleague cautioned him against continuing his tirade. saying that powerful forces confronted him and, because he lacked the backing of a political party, he was vulnerable. Not only that, his health was frail; indeed, he might as well commit suicide. Qutb understood the danger to his security and appreciated the concern of his friend. However, he insisted that fear should not deflect him from speaking truth to power. He responded to his friend that he had no desire to die; indeed, he wanted "to live a long life", especially as he "had not accomplished" all his goals. For a long period, he had been "far away from God". Now, in the heat of the political battle, he was trying to make up for lost time. "Death and life are in the power of God. These should not impede or distract one from duty."[62] Qutb had referred to his freedom from fear in *Social Justice in Islam*: "When the inward soul is liberated from the feeling of servitude and sanctification to any of God's servants and is filled with the feeling that it is in complete contact with God, then it does not suffer from any fear for its life, or any fear for its livelihood, or any fear for its reputation."[63]

In 1950–51 Qutb was still content to remain free of organizational ties. He was happy to remain in the mode of intellectual rebellion. However, given his Islamist bent, it was inevitable that he should gravitate to the Muslim Brotherhood. Since coming to Islamism, Qutb had felt a strong emotional connection to the Brotherhood. Others noted the affinity. During the late 1940s, Egyptian cultural analysts and political commentators tended to lump him with the Brothers. Now, as the political struggle heated up, Qutb involved himself more directly in the movement's activities, although it would take another two years before he declared his formal membership. He signalled his growing attraction by contributing regularly to two of its leading organs: the weekly *al-Da'wa* (*The Call*), founded in 1951 by the firebrand Salih al-'Ashmawi; and *al-Muslimun* (*The Muslims*) established by Sa'id Ramadan in November of that same year.[64] The Muslim Brotherhood signalled its own interest in Qutb by sponsoring reprints of *The Battle of Islam and Capitalism* and *Social Justice in Islam*.

In the January 1952 issue of *al-Muslimun*, Qutb began a monthly column entitled "Fi Zilal al-Qur'an" ("In the Shade of the Qur'an").[65] His first article contained commentaries on the Qur'an's opening chapter—*Surat al-Fatiha*—and parts of chapter two, *Surat al-Baqara*. He contributed six more articles for the journal, making his way up to verse 103 of *Surat al-Baqara*. On the surface, the series approximated the purpose of the traditional Qur'anic *tafsir* ("exegesis"). Like earlier commentaries, it aimed to elucidate and interpret the scripture for believers. But Qutb was aware that in both methodology and intention his effort differed significantly from the Qur'an commentaries of old.

Traditional commentaries were written by *'ulama* and were highly technical in nature. Exegeses like Abu Ja'far Muhammad al-Tabari's *Jami 'al-Bayan fi Tafisr al-Qur'an* (*Collection of Explanations for the Interpretation of the Qur'an*), or the *Anwar al-Tanzil wa Asrar al-Ta'wil* (*The Lights of Revelation and the Secrets of Interpretation*) of 'Umar al-Baydawi (d. 1286) had subjected the Qur'anic text to painstaking grammatical analyses based on the linguistics of Kufan and Basran scholars. Traditional exegeses also made liberal use of the traditions of the Prophet Muhammad and his Companions, and of Isra'iliyyat, Jewish stories of Mishnaic and Midrashic origin. In the words of Hugh Galford, "The discussions were erudite, scholastic, and beyond the understanding of most Muslims."[66]

Sayyid Qutb wanted to liberate discourse on the Qur'an from the dead weight of this tradition. As he wrote in his introduction to the series, "I did not want to drown myself in matters of language, diction, or *fiqh* ("jurisprudence") that would shield the Qur'an from my spirit, and my spirit from the Qur'an."[67] He designed his commentary as a vehicle for his personal ruminations on the meaning and implications of the Qur'an for Muslims living in the current period. It would speak to the existential and practical concerns of modernizing Muslims for whom al-Azhar's scholasticism was both irrelevant and obscure. Unlike al-Tabari, who packed his commentary with variant interpretations, traditional and arcane, Qutb aimed at a thematic approach that would be conversational in tone. He would provide summaries of the *sura*s and break them into topical units, drawing the reader's attention to pertinent points. He would discuss the Qur'an's ethical teachings but also draw attention to the political implications of the divine message. Moreover, he aimed to incorporate into his analyses the aesthetic concerns of his *Artistic Depiction in the Qur'an*, paying close attention to the harmonized structure of the scripture in the effort to understand its literary affect. Unlike the mediaeval exegetes, he would shy away from the *Isra'iliyyat* and other extra-Qur'anic materials. He would use only sound, reasonable traditions of the Prophet and trusted sources such as Ibn Ishaq's biography of the Prophet, Ibn Hisham's rendition of Ibn Ishaq's *Sira* (biography of the Prophet), and the *tafsir* and history of Ibn Kathir, and he would use these only sparingly. In short, he would attempt to understand the Qur'an principally though its own expression, using the Qur'anic text as the primary reference point for every single matter. His goal was to approach the "unadorned but complete Islamic idea" without the encumbrance and complications of the layers of received tradition.[68]

There was, of course, a precedent for this kind of "modern" *tafsir*, and that was the *Manar* (*The Beacon*) commentary of Muhammad 'Abduh and his Syrian disciple Rashid Rida (d. 1935).[69] 'Abduh's contributions to the exegesis drew from his lectures at al-Azhar and from the juridical opinions (*fatawa*) that he issued in his capacity as Mufti of Egypt. Rashid Rida later revised and continued the exegesis all the way up to *sura* 12:107. The *Manar* commentary almost certainly inspired Qutb's effort. Like *In the Shade of the Qur'an*, al-Manar similarly began as a periodical published at intervals, in its case, bi-monthly and then monthly. Like Qutb, 'Abduh and Rida were interested in crafting an exegesis that spoke to the challenges facing Muslims in the modern era; they wrote in terms of *hajat al-'asr* ("The need of the times").[70] To this end, they sought to demonstrate how the Qur'an is compatible with the rational foundations of modern civilization. Like Qutb, Rida, in particular, endeavoured through his commentary to promote Muslim unity. Nevertheless, despite the similarities, Qutb's commentary, even in its first edition, is more concerned than 'Abduh's and Rida's with questions of political legitimacy, that is, the need for Muslims to establish the Islamic *nizam*.

The popularity of the *al-Muslimun* series encouraged Qutb to write his *tafsir* separately as a thirty–volume set of books, which Dar Ihya al-Kutub al-'Arabiyya published in Cairo. Between October 1952 and March 1954, Qutb produced commentaries on fourteen out of the Qur'an's thirty designated parts, including, in the first volume, materials that had originally appeared in *al-Muslimun*. He continued working on the *tafsir* while in prison (1954–59). In its final form, *In the Shade of the Qur'an* is Qutb's finest and most expansive expression of his radical Islamist ideas. We will have occasion to return to this important work below.

The burning of Cairo

In the autumn and winter of 1951–52, popular elements in Egypt rose up to challenge directly the forces and symbols of foreign domination and economic exploitation. Qutb watched the events unfold with a sense of anticipation. He had a sense that something big was going to happen. As in 1947, the Wafd, in power since January 1950 after winning elections notable for the apathy of the electorate, inadvertently precipitated the demonstrations.[71] Hoping to build popular enthusiasm for its mandate, the party boldly decided to abrogate unilaterally the 1936 Anglo-Egyptian Treaty. This it did on 8 October 1951. However, rather than secure the Wafd's position among the people, the abrogation had the unintended effect of unleashing popular passions that threatened to go their own way, especially after it became clear that the British would not be budged from their remaining military bases.

Eager to enforce Britain's compliance, the Egyptian street mobilized with an intensity of purpose extraordinary even for the period of post-war radicalization. The British braced for conflict by increasing the number of their troops in the Canal Zone to 80,000. Egyptian workers withdrew their services to British personnel in a massive strike action and anti–British demonstrations flared up in Cairo, Isma'iliyya and Port Sa'id. After witnessing demonstrations that erupted in the Cairo business district on 23 October, Richard Mitchell, then a Fulbright student in Egypt, reported to the US embassy that "the feelings of the Egyptian populace have become exacerbated to a dangerous degree" and that there was a "do-or-die attitude", an "unreasoning determination to see an end to British occupation regardless of cost." He went on to report that at a mass meeting at Fu'ad al-Awwal University "educated Egyptians publicly proclaimed their willingness to sacrifice themselves, their wives and families in the national struggle."[72] Qutb joined with other nationalists in calling for "the full mobilization of the people for armed struggle against the British", and wrote fiery articles against the "feudalists" who ran the country.[73]

Over the course of the next three months "liberation battalions" consisting mainly of ill-equipped peasants, workers and students infiltrated the Canal Zone to harass and ambush British forces. Unwilling to escalate hostilities by committing Egyptian army troops to the struggle, the Wafdist government chose instead to provide the battalions with moral encouragement, both to maintain pressure on the British and to augment its legitimacy in the eyes of the people.

Since October 1950, a lawyer named Hasan al-Hudaybi had led the Muslim Brotherhood, although the Constituent Assembly of the movement did not officially elect him to the post of Supreme Guide until a year later. The sixty–year-old Hudaybi was a political moderate who believed that the Brotherhood should wait until it had clear majority support before taking overt actions of the sort demanded by the movement's rank and file.[74] The Brotherhood's activities at the Suez Canal appeared to him as precipitate and risky. Disobeying Hudaybi's orders, an estimated three hundred Brothers made their way to the combat zone where they distinguished themselves in several skirmishes.[75] Among the combatants was a twenty-four–year-old Yusuf al-Qaradawi, destined in the 1990s to become one of the most popular preachers in the Muslim world. The Brothers produced one of the first martyrs of the struggle, a student named 'Umar Shahin whose funeral provided the occasion for a massive demonstration.[76]

The Brothers' courage impressed Qutb, a sidelines observer. In his view, their dedication to the task stood in contrast to the inaction and "pacifism" of the government. He extolled the Brothers for their willingness to sacrifice themselves for the sake of social justice and the homeland (*al-watan*). According to Qutb, the Brothers were living testimony to the need for action driven by faith. He cited for his readers Qur'an 9:111:

Verily, Allâh has purchased of the believers their lives and their properties; for the price that theirs shall be the Paradise. They fight in Allâh's Cause, so they kill (others) and are killed. It is a promise in truth which is binding on Him in the Taurât (Torah) and the Injeel (Gospel) and the Qur'ân. And who is truer to his covenant than Allâh? Then rejoice in the bargain which you have con-cluded. That is the supreme success.[77]

Speaking as a "friend of the Islamic movement," he urged the Mus-lim Brotherhood's leadership officially to sponsor the activities of the *fida'iyyun*. Qutb said that it was important for Islam to lead the anti–imperialist struggle, for the country was in need of spiritual leadership. Others agreed. In a passionate letter penned to the newspaper *al-Masri* (*The Egyptian*) the Muslim Brother Shaykh Muhammad al-Ghazali, the author of the book on Islamic socialism, urged his colleagues to "fight with all their might" against the British.[78] Feeling the pressure, Hudaybi relented. On 13 January 1952, the Supreme Guide officially sanctioned the Brothers' Canal Zone activities.

Events came to a head on 25 January 1952. In an effort to clear the Isma'iliyya area of armed Egyptians, British troops instigated a firefight with the local gendarmerie, the *buluk al-nizam*. Heeding the orders of Fu'ad Siraj al-Din, the Wafdist Minister of the Interior, to defend the barracks "to the last man", the police held out for five hours armed only with rifles and a few sten guns before finally succumbing to the superior fire power of the British. When the smoke cleared, fifty Egyp-tians lay dead with many more wounded.[79]

The battle exacerbated the already tense situation. For the British it was a harsh wake up call to what they were up against in Egypt. One British commentator urged his countrymen to "face up to an undeni-able fact, whether we like it or not: the Egyptian police, both regular and auxiliary stood and fought to a degree that our authorities had not for one moment expected."[80] For Egyptians, particularly anti–estab-lishment Egyptians, it provoked feelings of outrage and anger that would presently translate into an escalation of violence.

The first overt signs of Egyptian public reaction to the battle occurred at about 2 a.m. the following morning when workers at Faruq Airfield surrounded four BOAC aeroplanes and prevented them from leaving.[81] By mid-morning demonstrations of policemen, work-ers, Azharis, and students from Fu'ad Awwal and Ibrahim Pasha uni-versities converged on the Prime Minister's office where they protested the aggression at Isma'iliyya and demanded arms for the fight in the Canal Zone. Leaving the Prime Minister's office, the demonstrators dispersed into the heart of the capital. Almost immediately, fires broke out throughout the downtown area.

Specific targets included foreign-owned establishments such as Shepheard's Hotel, the Egyptian headquarters of Barclay's Bank, Cairo Motors Studebaker Agency, and the offices of BOAC. They also included businesses catering to the wealthy or identified by the rioters with moral corruption and alien values, including the Diana, Metro and Rivoli cinemas, the Groppi restaurants, the Casino Opera, and over one hundred bars and dance halls. All told, the mob burned or looted over 700 establishments at a cost estimated at between forty and fifty million Egyptian pounds.[82] Twenty-six persons lost their lives, including the Canadian Trade Commissioner who was burnt to death with ten others in the Turf Club.[83] The message of the fire was clear.

In the course of an afternoon vast portions of the visionary city of Isma'il and his master planner 'Ali Mubarak, the city of *étoiles* and department stores, buses and tramways, upscale restaurants and cafes, had been reduced to cinders. The accusatory reports that followed placed blame squarely on the shoulders of Young Egypt and the Muslim Brotherhood, despite the lack of hard evidence.[84]

There could not have been a more telling expression of the popular mood. In a single dramatic gesture, the fire that had long resided "in the minds of men" had leaped into the richly adorned streets of Cairo's downtown core. Revolution was in the air and there was a palpable sense of expectation.[85]

However, with no force willing or able to take matters into its own hands, the months following Black Saturday brought no decisive denouement. As armoured personnel carriers scoured the streets for insurrectionists, the King attempted to defuse the situation by deposing the Nahhas government and appointing in its place a series of independent and Palace-sponsored ministries. He set up and dismissed three Prime Ministers in quick succession: 'Ali Mahir (27 January to 1 March), Ahmad Najib al-Hilali (2 March to 29 June and 22–23 July), and Husayn Sirri (2 to 20 July). But although the Hilali government was successful in clearing the Canal Zone of remaining rebels, and the 'Ali Mahir ministry managed to initiate a number of remedial social and economic reforms, the post-fire governments functioned as little more than holding operations.[86] Tensions continued to boil beneath the surface. It was at this point that an unexpected force emerged to break the cycle of ministries. In the early morning hours of 23 July 1952 motorized infantry columns under the command of Colonel Gamal 'Abd al-Nasser seized control of key installations in Cairo, thus initiating the events that would finally topple the old regime.

Free Officers and Muslim Brothers

The mythology of the 1952 revolution has it that 'Abd al-Nasser was destined from early on to assume the mantle of national saviour. In reality, 'Abd al-Nasser was slow in coming to his historical role. Born in 1918, he was part of what P.J. Vatikiotis called the "historical generation" of Egyptian national assertion.[87] Nourished by the historical romances and myths of national resurrection penned by Tawfiq al-Hakim and al-'Aqqad, he joined the great street demonstrations of 1935 that called for restoration of the 1923 Constitution, and in one of these was wounded by the police.[88] In a letter written during this period to his friend, Hasan al-Nashshar, Nasser wrote:

Who can cry halt to the imperialists? There are men in Egypt with dignity who do not want to be allowed to die like dogs. But where is the growing nationalism of 1919? Where are the men ready to give their lives for the country's independence? Where is the man to rebuild the country so that the weak and humiliated Egyptian people can rise up and live as free and independent men?[89]

Sayyid Qutb, 'Abd al-Nasser's older contemporary, asked these questions at the very same moment.

In his 1953 treatise *The Philosophy of the Revolution*, 'Abd al-Nasser evoked the conspiratorial mood current in the 1930s: "[O]ur activities in those days very much resembled those depicted in a detective thriller. We possessed important secrets. We had symbols and signs. We moved under cover of darkness and stored stacks of pistols and bombs, the anticipated use of which represented our sole aspiration." He confesses to his part in a failed assassination attempt, after which he escaped to his home and threw himself on his bed, the victim of wild and exhilarating emotions: "Rays of light filtered into my turbulent thoughts as I said to myself: 'the important thing is that he who should come be enabled to do so. We dream of the glory of the nation, and this glory must be established.'" The messianic tone of his nocturnal deliberations is clear. The country was in need of a saviour, and it was imperative that one should come.[90]

In March 1937, 'Abd al-Nasser joined the Military Academy for officer training, which had only then opened to social classes other than that of the landowning Pashas. Upon his graduation, his superiors sent him to a remote posting at Manqbad, near Asyut. There he established abiding friendships with other officers. As both nationalists and professional soldiers, these men experienced acute shame at the 1948–49 defeat of Egyptian arms in Palestine and blamed it on the corruption and ill preparedness of the government.[91] Convinced of the need to take decisive action, in late 1949, eight of them secretly organized as the constituent committee of a Free Officers' movement. In January 1950, the committee elected 'Abd al-Nasser as Chairman.

The ideological orientations of these young officers spanned the gamut of Egyptian oppositional discourse. 'Abd al-Nasser himself had flirted in the mid-1930s with Young Egypt, although to what extent is not clear. Between 1945 and 1947, he followed other dissident officers, including Kamal al-Din Husayn and 'Abd al-Hakim 'Amir, in joining an underground cell in the army organized by an operative of the Muslim Brotherhood, Mahmud Labib. Others in the group, notably Khalid Muhyi al-Din, had links with the Marxist-oriented DMNL.[92] However, two overriding factors compensated for the ideological variation: a shared nationalism that was both anti–imperialist and anti–feudal, and a strong desire, perhaps fostered by the exclusionary framework of the army's internal organization, to remain independent of other dissident organizations. Therefore, although the officers might establish links and enter into dialogue with other oppositional figures and groups, when the time came for open rebellion they would act alone on behalf of the nation.

In the spring of 1952, the Free Officers made their plans for a coup d'état. Eager to avoid the potentially dangerous effects of a mass-based revolt, they decided early on to adopt the Leninist-style strategy of the vanguard: a quick surgical strike aimed at the purge of corruption within the ranks of the political parties, the eviction of the British from the Canal Zone and an end to the domination of power by wealth. Beyond these general goals, the officers seem not to have had a specific plan, preferring to leave the mechanics of governance in the hands of a reformed parliament. In the words of Raymond Baker, "The Free Officers intended to wield decisive power, but to wield it indirectly. They would rule through the captured military establishment, acting as a kind of political stage manager—above politics yet preserving the monopoly of decisive power."[93]

Shortly before the coup, the officers approached the Muslim Brotherhood with the aim of harnessing its influence with the masses in support of the coming action. In the evening of 19 July, 'Abd al-Nasser and other Free Officers secretly met select Brothers at Sayyid Qutb's

Hulwan home.[94] Qutb was known to many of the officers. Several, including Ibrahim 'Atif, the secretary of the Free Officers' Club, had read *Social Justice in Islam* and admired it.[95] In the officers' opinion, Qutb was someone in tune with the oppositional spirit of the times, especially its Islamist dimension.

At the meeting, the officers briefed Qutb and the Brothers on the coming coup and requested assistance in the event of a harsh British response; it would be useful, the officers suggested, if the Brothers could take charge of the streets until the soldiers had established full control in Cairo. According to Mahmud al-'Azab, an officer with close connections to the Brotherhood, Qutb's special role was to facilitate communications between the officers and the Brotherhood.[96]

Qutb was still only a close associate, not yet a member of the Muslim Brotherhood. However, that did not matter to the officers. He was the leading light in an up and coming cadre of mostly young Islamists over whom they might gain influence. In 'Abd al-Nasser's opinion, men like Qutb were malleable and stood in contrast to Supreme Guide Hudaybi, who the officers feared would attempt to impose his will on events as the soldiers' new order unfolded. But if the officers believed that Qutb and other younger Islamists would be putty in their hands, they were mistaken. Although Qutb and his Islamist colleagues declared their support for the officers at the Hulwan meeting, they did so with a view to their own dream of the future. In their opinion, they represented the true conscience of the nation. Under their influence, the Free Officers' movement would function as the vehicle of the Islamic resurgence.

Despite the anticipatory mood among the people, the events of 23 July took most Egyptians aback. Few people knew what to make of the military perpetrators. In the days following the coup, Egyptians of all political persuasions stood by anxiously as the officers began to overturn the ranks of the political establishment. On the morning of the coup the soldiers deposed Prime Minister Naguib al-Hilali and replaced him with the "clean politician" 'Ali Mahir. On 26 July they forced the discredited King Faruq into exile and established a three-man Regency Council to rule until the Crown Prince, Ahmad Fuad, came of age. The officers consolidated their watchdog role by organizing as the Revolutionary Command Council (RCC). Only when the officers announced on 12 August their plans for land reform did Egyptians of the lower orders of society perceive 'Abd al-Nasser and his fellow officers as viable guardians of the people's will against the monarchy and pashas.

Relations between the Muslim Brotherhood and the officers were generally cordial during this period. Days after the coup, the Brotherhood's Consultative Assembly endorsed the officers' "Blessed Movement", exclaiming that it had restored dignity to the Egyptian people. In a show of solidarity with the RCC, the Brotherhood applauded the officers' suppression in early August of the striking textile workers at Kafr al-Dawwar, near Alexandria, denouncing the workers as dangerous "counter revolutionaries" intent on establishing in Egypt a Communist Soviet. On their side, the officers curried favour with the Brothers by reopening the unresolved case of Hasan al-Banna's assassination and by appointing a Brotherhood associate, Rashad Muhanna, to the Regency Council and a top ranking Brother, Ahmad Hasan al-Baquri, to head the Ministry of Religious Endowments (*awqaf*). In an additional gesture of goodwill, they granted amnesty to many of the Brothers jailed between 1936 and 1952. The officers and the Brothers were not prepared at this critical stage to alienate each other.[97]

Qutb was eager to cooperate with the Revolutionary Command Council. He saw that the junta's emerging reformist programme had much in common with his own demands for social justice and national independence. In an open letter addressed to General Naguib, the senior Free Officer and figurehead of the Revolution, Qutb encouraged the officers to cleanse the country of political corruption, even if this required the imposition of a "dictatorship" over the country.[98] Qutb had tinged his remark with a degree of sarcasm. Like many early supporters of the coup, indeed like the officers themselves, he supposed that the basic structure of government would remain intact. He had no way yet of knowing his statement's prophetic quality.

In an effort to cultivate Qutb as an ally, the RCC invited Qutb in August 1952 to address the Officers' Club in Cairo's island suburb of Zamalik. Qutb delivered his talk, entitled "Intellectual and Spiritual Liberation in Islam", to a packed house. 'Abd al-Nasser attended, as did several of the nation's leading intellectuals, including Taha Husayn and the venerable Ahmad Lutfi al-Sayyid, who introduced him.[99] Few in attendance were surprised at the content of Qutb's message. In intellectual and political circles his Islamist views were well known. Elaborating upon themes treated in *Social Justice in Islam*, he declaimed that the men of the revolution should bring the country to Islam. The regime should strive to instil moral rectitude in the nation, in addition to fighting for political freedom.

If the officers were displeased at Qutb's stance, they did not show it, at least publicly. Qutb was still too valuable as a potential ally to merit a reprimand. Following the lecture, the officers hosted a party in Qutb's honour during which 'Abd al-Nasser mounted the podium and offered him the officers' protection against his political enemies.[100] Qutb was glad that the soldiers embraced him. Over the years, his biting journalism had earned him the enmity of many individuals attached to the Old Regime. He knew that he had barely eluded imprisonment.

Over the months that followed, Qutb worked tirelessly for the officers—"up to twelve hours a day" according to his own estimate.[101] He attended RCC meetings as a cultural adviser. The officers provided Qutb with office space and asked him to lay down plans for the reform of Egypt's educational curricula. On at least one occasion, they publicly referred to him as the "tribune of the Revolution".[102] Qutb took advantage of the situation. He used radio air time, which the RCC granted him, in order to explain to listeners the Islamic foundations of Egypt's new order.[103] The officers still did not feel threatened by the Islamist propaganda and allowed Qutb to continue his broadcasts.

It is a measure of Qutb's dedication to the Free Officers' regime that on 18 October 1952, some twelve weeks after the July coup d'état, he announced his resignation from the Ministry of Education. In his view, the Ministry's Old Regime associations had tarnished it. Moreover, his new political responsibilities required extra time. Although his superiors at the Ministry regarded him as a troublemaker, they urged him to reconsider his decision. Qutb ignored their appeals and followed through with his decision—two years short of his eligibility for a pension. In the months that followed, Qutb felt the financial pinch.[104] Yet, as a man of ideals, Qutb put duty ahead of material considerations. He envisioned himself as a leading architect of a re-born Egypt.

By late 1952, the Free Officers' relations with the Islamists and remaining political parties and movements began to sour. Recognizing that these groups wanted a say in setting the national agenda, the RCC assumed greater control over the country's political life. This heightened control, in turn, made the political forces dubious of the officers' intentions. The result was a spiral of mistrust that led inevitably to a showdown with the Islamists, the most powerful of these forces.

Already in September 1952, the officers had forced 'Ali Mahir to step down from the premiership because of his refusal to sanction the planned land reforms. They replaced him with the senior member of their group, Muhammad Naguib, who assumed the presidency. The officers handed over key government portfolios to sympathetic technocrats and younger nationalists. In response to the Wafd's reluctance to purge itself of corrupt members, the officers decided on 10 December 1952 to eradicate the party system altogether.[105] On 18 June 1953, the officers went a step further by abolishing the monarchy, declaring Egypt a republic and thus ending the venerable Muhammad 'Ali dynasty.

The officers next brought the Communist organizations to heel. Fearing the Communists' proclivity for working class agitation, and aiming to appease the Americans whose political support the RCC sought, the officers suppressed in turn the Egyptian Communist Party, the Workers' Vanguard, and finally the DMNL between March and November 1953. Although Communist cells continued to eke out a precarious existence, the proscriptions effectively negated the possibility of a leftist opposition front directed against the officers.[106]

Hudaybi and others in the Muslim Brotherhood watched these developments with growing unease. They became more strident in asserting the movement's interests, fearing that the regime might target them next. Hudaybi criticized 'Abd al-Nasser's intention to negotiate with the British over the status of the Suez Canal, holding that such discussions should take place only after British forces had withdrawn from the Canal Zone. In addition, the Muslim Brothers began openly to advocate the promulgation of an Islamic constitution and insisted on their right to veto legislation introduced by the RCC.

The RCC regarded the Brothers' statements as provocations. For the Free Officers, Islam was important at the level of individual faith and as a component of the national personality. However, they were against having the laws of the country revamped to conform to Qur'anic principles, not least because such laws would discriminate against the Copts and other religious minorities: "Religion is for God and the nation for all," 'Abd al-Nasser said.[107]

Added to the officers' concern was the practical matter of the Muslim Brotherhood's political programme, which by its "very similarity to the Free Officers' rhetoric indicated that the country did have options other than military rule."[108] The two movements shared the common goals of social justice and independence. Moreover, the Brotherhood's desire to link Egypt to the wider Arab-Islamic world closely approximated 'Abd al- Nasser's desire, enunciated in his 1953 treatise *The Philosophy of the Revolution*, to situate Egypt within the three spheres of Africa, the Arab world and Islam.

The congruence of goals was not lost on outside observers. In a February 1953 dispatch to the State Department, US Ambassador Jefferson Caffery commented on the "striking similarity" between the Muslim Brotherhood's programme and the one currently being carried out by the regime: "Point by point the government has initiated measures to put into effect at least part of each of the policy aims of the Brotherhood."[109] In a context in which old power bases were crumbling, it was imperative for the officers that they should not lose their grip on power to a competitor, especially one with a large popular following, like the Muslim Brotherhood.

Troubled by the Muslim Brotherhood's independent spirit, the RCC took measures to curb its influence. On 23 January 1953, it established the Liberation Rally (*Hay'at al-Tahrir*) in order to mobilize support for the regime. As the sole legitimate party organization, the Rally organized mass demonstrations in favour of the regime and encouraged national solidarity. In an effort to draw in the Islamists, 'Abd al-Nasser suggested to the Muslim Brother Baha al-Khuli that he take up the position of liaison officer between the Muslim Brotherhood and the Rally. At the same time, 'Abd al-Nasser offered Qutb the post of general secretary of the Rally. Qutb was at first interested in the offer, viewing the Rally as a potential instrument for the spread of the Islamic message to the masses. In the end, however, neither al-Khuli nor Qutb took up the post offered him. Both men came to understand the offers as transparent attempts to co-opt them into the new system. After a month or so, Qutb cut off all contact with the Rally.[110]

In fact, Qutb's suspicions about the officers' intentions had been growing over the months leading up to the offer. Since late 1952, he had shared with others the concern that the RCC intended to dominate the politics of the country without significant reference to Islam. In Qutb's view, it was imperative that the collective will must follow the divine prerogative. If many Egyptians remained ignorant of this imperative, no matter, "for the need of the patient for a doctor does not depend on his being aware [of this need]." "We often see the patient refuse medicine, shrink away from the doctor and claim to be fit and healthy when medicine and the doctor's treatment are needed most."[111] According to Qutb, it was important that caring physicians be on hand to take care of the patient, even though the patient is not aware of his condition. The RCC showed dereliction in its refusal to apply the required "medicine" of Islam to the people. Like many in the Islamist movement, Qutb felt fooled by military men who sullied their vision for the country by the love of political power.

Not only that, Qutb was also worried that American intelligence services had infiltrated RCC policy.[112] Since his sojourn in the United States, Qutb had been aware of America's geostrategic interests within the context of the Cold War. He understood, correctly, that the Eisenhower Administration was concerned that the Middle East was vulnerable to Communist penetration, and that the US embassy in Cairo maintained close relations with the new regime in the hope of cultivating a new Cold War ally. After the 1952 coup, the CIA did assist the officers in reorganizing the *mukhabarat* (Egypt's intelligence service).[113] Qutb was wrong, however, in supposing the Free Officers to be malleable puppets of Washington; this was a product of his paranoia, discussed above. Indeed, within a year of Qutb's statements on the matter, 'Abd al-Nasser would distance his regime from the influence of Washington to the extent of becoming a founding member of the Non-Aligned Movement and exchanging ambassadors with Communist China.

Qutb expressed his unhappiness with the new regime by formally joining the Muslim Brotherhood. In his testimony, written prior to his execution in 1966, he wrote that his official membership in the movement dated from February 1953.[114] Having been an engaged but independent contributor to the Islamist cause, Qutb saw the widening chasm between the RCC and the Brotherhood as presaging a political showdown, and he wanted to mark out clearly his position on the side of "virtue". In his view, it was important that Islamists of all stripes close ranks and actively support the Brotherhood, the only organization capable of challenging the 'Abd al-Nasser regime and other enemies of Islam. "No other movement," he wrote, "can stand up to the Zionists and the colonialist Crusaders."[115]

Qutb may have had another reason for joining the Muslim Brotherhood. Following his resignation from the ministry, he was without institutional mooring. Formal membership in an organized community of shared ethics would give him a renewed sense of political belonging and purpose. In joining the Brotherhood, Qutb differed from his brother Muhammad, who habitually avoided membership in organizations of any kind.

As a new Muslim Brother, Qutb was a stalwart supporter of Hudaybi at a time when the Supreme Guide was under siege by a dissident faction within the Brotherhood. Led by Salih 'Ashmawi, these dissident Brothers pointed at what they alleged to be Hudaybi's dictatorial ways, in addition to his reluctance to adopt political activism as opposed to advocacy politics. In their view, Hudaybi did not measure up to Hasan al-Banna and was generally ill suited to the task of leadership. In the autumn of 1953 Salih 'Ashmawi and his confederates brought their dispute to the Guidance Council but were repudiated by a solid majority of Brothers, including Qutb, who appreciated the leader's stabilizing influence in a political context that required caution. In face of the danger posed to them by the RCC, a majority of Muslim Brothers believed that unity within the ranks was of paramount importance. Subsequently, the Guidance Council expelled four of the dissidents, including Salih 'Ashmawi, from the Brotherhood's ranks.[116]

The great respect in which Qutb was held by the Society, coupled with Qutb's loyalty to Hudaybi, gained him a coveted place in the Brotherhood's prestigious Guidance Council. His appointment inflamed the dissidents who saw Hudaybi's recruitment of outsiders as coming at their expense. However, the appointments of Qutb and others, including 'Ali 'Ashmawi (not to be confused with Salih), Salah Shadi and Munir al-Dilla, injected a new vitality into the Brotherhood. In what may be an oblique reference to Qutb and other new faces in the Brotherhood hierarchy, a 12 March 1954 intelligence report filed at the US embassy in Cairo claimed that the "true leadership" of the Brotherhood had passed to "the virtually unknown secondary 'intellectual'" cadre within its ranks.[117]

Shortly after his election to the Guidance Council, Qutb was put in charge of the Brotherhood's "Propagation of the Call Department" (*Qism Nashr al-Da'wa*). This was one of the Brotherhood's most important offices. According to Richard Mitchell, the Propagation of the Call Department was "the ultimate arbiter of the materials which were the stuff of the movement's ideology; its responsibility was to oversee the intellectual and spiritual tone of the members' reading."[118] In order to maintain doctrinal purity and organizational harmony, the Department had the final say on anything published in the name of the Brotherhood. As a Hudaybi supporter, Qutb made sure that the Brothers heard the Supreme Guide's voice alongside that of the venerated martyr Hasan al-Banna, whose works the Department edited and republished. In his capacity of department head, Qutb initiated and was the prime contributor to a series of publications called "This is Your Message" (*Hadhihi Da'watukum*), which was, however, soon discontinued owing to the 1954 confrontation with the RCC. He also edited the Brotherhood's long anticipated weekly journal, *al-Ikhwan al-Muslimun*, which first appeared in May 1954. After only twelve issues, the censorship imposed by the regime forced it also to close.

Qutb's duties as official propagandist of the Brotherhood took him beyond the borders of Egypt to Damascus and East Jerusalem. These were Qutb's first journeys to the lands of Greater Syria, and he revelled in the attention accorded him there as an important intellectual. At Damascus he attended a conference on social issues and on 2 March 1953 delivered a lecture entitled "al-Tarbiyya al-Khuluqiyya ka-Wasila li–Tahqiq al-Takaful al-Ijtima'i" ("Ethical Education as a Way of Realizing Mutual Responsibility"), which was a rehash of ideas more fully explored in *Social Justice in Islam*.[119] He also delivered a number of lectures at the Damascus headquarters of the Muslim Brothers. As a guest of Damascus University he lectured "for two hours without notes" on the topic of the Qur'anic *i'jaz*. At the university, he attended a lecture by a "former Governor of the German Central Bank" and noted with approval how his condemnation of usury "from the purely economic point of view" dovetailed with the Islamic position.[120]

Qutb next travelled to Jordanian-controlled East Jerusalem with a fellow Muslim Brother, Sa'id Ramadan, to deliver a lecture at the General Islamic Conference. The conference explored the possibility of establishing an Islamic university in the city, and formulated official responses to the state of Israel. In recognition of Qutb's growing stature in the Islamic world, the delegates paid him the honour of appointing him General Secretary of the conference. It is worth noting that conventional *'ulama* had dominated previous international Islamic conferences, such as those that met to discuss the revival of the Caliphate in the 1920s and 1930s, but this one was dominated by Muslim Brothers and other Islamists from around the Arab world. Amjad al-Zahawi (d. 1967), a leading figure in Iraq's Society of the Islamic Brotherhood (Jamiyyat al-Ukhwa al-Islamiyya), was there, as was 'Allal al-Fasi of Morocco's Islamist Independence (Istiqlal) Party. Amid these well-known Islamic leaders, Qutb showed a humble face.[121] According to Skovard-Petersen, Qutb's and the Brothers' "vision of the conference was clearly to establish a network of Islamic groups which could act as an intellectual avant-garde at home and then meet and coordinate their strategies abroad."[122] While in the Hashimite Kingdom, Qutb made contact with the local version of the Muslim Brotherhood. He was concerned that the Jordanian Brothers were overly involved in politics at the expense of missionary activity.[123]

Showdown

The simmering tensions between the Muslim Brotherhood and the RCC erupted into open conflict on 12 January 1954 when young people attached to the Liberation Rally confronted Muslim Brothers at the gates of Cairo University. The Brothers were demonstrating against the RCC's negotiations with Britain over the Canal Zone. They had been fired up by a speech delivered by Seyyed Mojtaba Navvab-Safavi, the founder of the Iranian underground Shi'i Islamist organization Feda'iyan-e Eslam (Devotees of Islam), who was visiting Cairo; at the time of his visit Navvab-Safavi was close to Ayatollah Kashani, who was well respected by many Egyptian Islamists. The clash between the two groups, which resulted in injuries on both sides, provided the RCC with the pretext it needed to move against the Brotherhood. Three days after the disturbance the officers dissolved the organization, claiming that it was a political, not simply a religious group and thus subject to the January 1953 ban on political parties.

The authorities arrested over 450 Brothers. Qutb and Hudaybi were among those apprehended.[124] Yet, despite the officers' precipitate action, there is little evidence to suggest that they intended at this time to eradicate the movement. As Joel Gordon explains, "The crackdown was more a propaganda campaign against Hudaybi and his allies than a concerted effort to destroy the Brotherhood."[125] By chastening the Brothers, the officers hoped that upon their release they would adopt a more cooperative attitude towards the regime.

Qutb, however, did not come around in the way the officers had intended. His taste of prison had the effect of hardening, rather than softening, his heart toward the soldiers. In the damp and cold of his cell, Qutb reflected on the events that had transpired and began to channel his brewing anger in the writing of volumes seventeen and eighteen of his Qur'an commentary, *In the Shade of the Qur'an*.

However, beyond the prison walls events were moving in a direction that afforded Qutb some hope. For several months, tensions had been mounting between Colonel Gamal 'Abd al-Nasser, the moving force behind the Junta, and General Muhammad Neguib, president of the new Egyptian republic and the figurehead of the Free Officers movement. At issue was the direction of the Egyptian revolution. Having implemented structural changes in Egypt's political and social systems, 'Abd al-Nasser and his close associates concluded that permanent military dictatorship over the apparatus of state was the logical next step. Neguib, concerned at his colleagues' tendency to autocracy, began to advocate a return to the constitution and political pluralism. To facilitate this, Neguib opened channels of communication with Mustafa al-Nahhas, the former leader of the Wafd whom he regarded as a potential ally against 'Abd al-Nasser.

'Abd al-Nasser decided to nip Neguib's challenge in the bud. In February 1954 army units loyal to the regime placed the general under house arrest. This, however, had the effect of turning Muhammad Neguib into a symbol of opposition to 'Abd al-Nasser. Muslim Brothers, Communists, Wafdists—all those whom the Free Officers had proscribed—demonstrated on behalf of Neguib, believing that his avowed allegiance to the constitution would allow them again to be political players. Leading the charge was the mutinous cavalry corps under the command of the Free Officer Khalid Muhyi al-Din, an old supporter of the Marxist DMNL, whose predilection for democratic socialism remained strong. Taken by surprise, the Liberation Rally, now denuded of its Muslim Brother contingent, was unable to contain the outrage.

'Abd al-Nasser faced the challenge head on. In a brilliant piece of political manoeuvring, he placated the dissenters by allowing Neguib to reassume his duties, but stripped him of all effective power and made sure that posts formerly held by him were given to officers loyal to the regime. Backed by loyal regiments, he forced the mutinous Khalid Muhyi al-Din into exile. And, in order to placate the Brothers, in late March he announced that Qutb, Hudaybi and other imprisoned Brothers would be released from prison and allowed to regroup on the condition that the Brotherhood did not engage in politics. "Calm, under virtual military occupation, returned to the streets of Cairo."[126]

The Muslim Brothers paid lip service to the "truce" but behind the scenes stepped up their anti–regime activity. Several Brothers, including 'Abd al-Qadir 'Awda, clandestinely met Muhammad Neguib, whom the Brothers continued to regard as the champion of an open political system. In late May Hudaybi left Egypt for Saudi Arabia, Syria, Lebanon and Jordan to drum up support for the Islamist cause among sympathizers in those countries.

Meanwhile, Sayyid Qutb resumed his responsibilities as head of the Propagation of the Call section. Each Tuesday, during the Brotherhood's weekly meeting, he delivered an inspirational talk at the movement's Cairo headquarters.[127] He began to write secret pamphlets criticizing the RCC's plan to reach an agreement with Britain that would recognize the self-determination of the Sudan and allow British technicians to remain in the Canal Zone "as a nucleus for the return of British troops in case of an attack by the USSR against any part of the Middle East."[128] In the view of Qutb and the Muslim Brotherhood, these stipulations diminished Muslim interests by privileging parochial nationalism and aiding imperialism.

In July, the remnants of Egypt's Communist Party secretly approached the Brotherhood with a plan that called for the two organizations to join forces. Although philosophically opposed, both Communists and Muslim Brothers shared a common interest in bringing down the hard-nosed government of Gamal 'Abd al-Nasser. Qutb stepped into the ensuing discussion. As the Brotherhood's representative, he discussed with the Communists tentative plans for a joint demonstration that would spark an uprising among the people. Each organization helped the other distribute its pamphlets, although nothing came of the proposed alliance of convenience.

The most consequential hub of Brotherhood activity during this unsettled period was the movement's semi–independent secret apparatus. Dating back to the early 1940s, the secret apparatus had always had a testy relationship with the Brotherhood's Supreme Guides. As advocates of cautious and gradualist bottom-up approaches to political change, al-Banna and Hudaybi were habitually wary of the apparatus's penchant for revolution. They knew from experience that precipitate action could very well bring down the wrath of the government on their heads. Consequently, they tried to monitor the activities of the apparatus. Usually, however, the secret apparatus was one step ahead.

In the evening of 26 October 1954, a week after the government's signing of the evacuation treaty with Britain, a member of the secret apparatus, a "round-faced shock-haired man" named Mahmud 'Abd al-Latif, rushed the podium and fired eight shots at 'Abd al-Nasser as he addressed a supportive throng of a quarter million at Alexandria's Manshiyya Square. 'Abd al-Nasser was not harmed in the attack—all of the shots missed. However, the failed assassination prompted the response Hudaybi had feared. "In Cairo, a mob surged through narrow, shabby back streets" to the Brotherhood's headquarters and set it on fire.[129] With the people apparently on his side, 'Abd al-Nasser took advantage of the incident to destroy the Muslim Brotherhood once and for all. Qutb, who like Hudaybi had no prior knowledge of the attack, would later claim that the Manshiyya Square episode was a "Zionist-Crusader" conspiracy designed to sink the only movement able and willing to stand up to the West and its colonial outliers.[130]

In the following month, state authorities rounded up Muslim Brothers all over Egypt. Officials arrested Hindawi Duwayr, the Imbaba section-leader who recruited 'Abd al-Latif, in addition to other members of the secret apparatus. On 30 October, they arrested Hudaybi along with members of the Muslim Brother's Guidance Council. Sa'id Ramadan, who was in Syria at the time, eluded arrest and in 1956 made his way to Geneva, where he eventually helped to establish a Muslim Brotherhood presence in Western Europe; today his son Tariq Ramadan, author of numerous works aimed primarily at European Muslims, carries on the work of *da'wa*. By the end of November 1954, over a thousand Muslim Brothers were in custody.

One of those arrested was the thirty-three–year-old Muhammad Yusuf Hawwash. Recently married and with a young daughter, Hawwash had been active in the Brotherhood since his student days in the 1940s. He lived on the same block as the Free Officer Anwar Sadat and was on friendly terms with the guards who watched his house. So, when Hawwash approached his street during the police sweeps, the guards warned him away, indicating that the security services were looking for him. Eventually the police caught up with Hawwash at his place of hiding.[131] Hawwash had no way of knowing it then, but soon he would enter into a close relationship with Sayyid Qutb.

In one fell swoop, the Free Officers closed the limited political space that had been available to the Muslim Brotherhood over the period of the Old Regime and the years that immediately followed. In severely curtailing dissent, 'Abd al-Nasser and his Free Officers foreshadowed the eventual appearance in Egypt of a police state. Although the military men would soon implement other methods to ensure political compliance, including the re-socialization of the population, political cooptation and the imposition of state controls over society, outright repression of the kind that was visited upon the Brothers remained integral to his regime over its duration, a black mark on an otherwise noble, if imperfectly conceived endeavour.[132]

In order to facilitate the trial of the Brothers, the RCC established a People's Tribunal, consisting of Gamal Salim, who functioned as the chief prosecutor, and Salim's assistants, Anwar al-Sadat and Husayn al-Shaf'i, men dedicated to preserving the direction in which 'Abd al-Nasser was taking the Egyptian Revolution. The prosecution charged the prisoners with planning a bloody insurrection against the regime. By all accounts, the court-appointed defence represented them poorly. The prosecutor often interrupted the prisoners and the courtroom audience jeered at them.

Qutb managed to elude the RCC dragnet for about three weeks. Finally, on 18 November, the authorities tracked him down at his family home in Hulwan. Four days later, frail and feverish, he was put on the witness stand in the trial of Hudaybi whose links with the secret apparatus the Prosecution was keen to establish. The authorities were rough, even violent, with Qutb and the other detainees. They placed some in a cell with attack dogs and beat them. According to a British Foreign Office report, "several of the accused appeared in court bearing signs of heavy handling."[133] However, none made an issue of the matter in the various opportunities made available to them. The same source says that in contrast to Hudaybi, who wilted under the pressure of the courtroom interrogation, Qutb answered the questions put to him calmly and without hesitation.[134]

The prosecutor read from captured Brotherhood documents and named Qutb as the Muslim Brotherhood's contact with the Communist organizations. He then asked Qutb about Hudaybi's contacts with General Neguib. Forthrightly, Qutb admitted that Hudaybi had informed him of Neguib's intention to lead sections of the army against the RCC in the hope of transferring rule back to civilian hands. Qutb also disclosed that he had bought a duplicating machine at Hudaybi's behest to print the Brotherhood's secret memoranda.[135] Following his testimony, the Tribunal returned Qutb to Tura prison to await the second round of trials for lower-level Brotherhood operatives, which was scheduled to commence following the trials of the Brotherhood's leadership.

On 4 December 1954, the People's Tribunal delivered its verdict. Seven members of the Brotherhood hierarchy, including Hudaybi, 'Abd

al-Qadir 'Awda, and members of the secret apparatus, were condemned to die on the gallows. Seven members of the Brotherhood's
Guidance Council received sentences of life imprisonment with hard
labour, and two others, including the future Supreme Guide 'Umar
Tilmisani, sentences of fifteen years each. Soon after the sentencing,
officials set aside Hudaybi's death sentence on the grounds of his
advanced age and supposed susceptibility to the bad influence of the
secret apparatus; they placed him under house arrest. The executions
of his six colleagues were carried out on 9 December. In Egypt, news
of the hangings was greeted with "Stunned and horrified silence".[136]

Qutb's turn to be tried came in January 1955. The case against him
and the remaining Brothers was based on the vague charge of "anti–
government activity". As he waited his turn in the dankness of his
prison cell, he was roughed up. When the time finally arrived for his
preliminary hearing, he lifted his shirt to show the Prosecutor the
traces of torture etched on his body. "Abd al-Nasser has applied to us
in jail the principles of the revolution," he said.[137]

The harsh conditions experienced by Qutb led to a rapid decline in
his overall health. Arthritis and angina pectoris, conditions he had long
suffered, were particular problems. In addition, he had lung problems
and it is possible that by this time he was also in the early stages of
tuberculosis, which was endemic in Egyptian prisons. Concerned lest
the health of their charge deteriorate further, on 3 May 1955 the
authorities transferred Qutb to the infirmary at Cairo's Military Prison
(*Sijn al-Harbi*) where about four hundred of the Brothers were incarcerated. Qutb's illness prevented him thereafter from attending court.
As a result, the authorities delayed his sentencing. Finally, on 13 July
1955, Qutb was well enough to appear before the court and hear its
verdict: it sentenced him to fifteen years' hard labour, served at the
Tura prison.[138]

Meanwhile, over the period of the trials and beyond, 'Abd al-Nasser
and his fellow army officers proceeded to implement the lofty goal of
"a purified, developed, and strong Egypt, purged of its colonial
past."[139] Toward this end, they implemented programmes that aimed
to transfer large degrees of social, economic and political power to the
state, thus winning back "for the people" a measure of the wealth that
had been concentrated in the hands of the feudalists and foreigners
since the time of Muhammad 'Ali. The officers also began plans to
expand education at all levels and in 1958 dramatically lowered uni-

versity tuition fees. The Minister of Education, Kamal al-Din Husayn, Taha Husayn's replacement, altered the school curricula by introducing a new ideology that built up 'Abd al-Nasser as a regional anti–Western populist leader. The regime initiated a programme of industrialization, of which the construction of a high dam at Aswan was to be the driving force. In 1955, the year Qutb was sentenced, 'Abd al-Nasser snubbed Western overtures to join the British-sponsored Baghdad Pact and attended the Bandung Conference in Indonesia as a founding member of the Non-Aligned Movement, as noted above—an organization that approximated the "third bloc" of Afro-Asian nations that Qutb and others had advocated.

A year later 'Abd al-Nasser earned praise throughout the colonial and post-colonial worlds for his nationalization of the Suez Canal Company, a move that elicited the aggression against Egypt of Britain, France and Israel. By surviving the onslaught of western and Israeli armies, 'Abd al-Nasser's star rose higher. In the early 1960s, Egypt's President began to implement socialism in the country. He founded the Arab Socialist Union (ASU) in 1962 as a successor to the mass-based Liberation Rally, with which Qutb was briefly affiliated, and the short lived National Union, the purpose of which was to gain the loyalty of the population. The 1964 National Charter called for universal health care, the provision of housing to the poor, and providing all Egyptians, including the long-suffering *fellahin*, with clean drinking water.[140]

Qutb, who was aware of these developments through conversations with family and friends and by limited access to the press, was bitter and pained that the state did not carry out its policies in ways that referenced the purity of the Islamic creed. He was even more distressed that the people of Egypt, whom he had earlier rallied to the regime, appeared to acquiesce in the "tyranny".

6

RADICALIZATION

The narrowed world of the prison

Qutb was just short of his fiftieth birthday when he walked though the gates of Tura prison.[1] There he was to spend the following nine years. Built in the later part of the nineteenth century, the prison was a grim place that afforded no cheer. Giant cockroaches appeared and disappeared in the small holes that peppered the moist brick walls.[2] The prison's toilets were filthy, and for long periods there was no running water. The daily fare of lentils, rice and beans, occasionally supplemented with an egg, barely sustained the prisoners' health. Most of the inmates had been caught up in the great police sweeps of 1954. But there were other political types, too, including communists and the Egyptian Jews whom the state had indicted for their role in the "Lavon Affair". Named after Israeli defense minister Pinhas Lavon, the "Lavon Affair" was an Israeli covert action in 1954 to blow up US and British targets in Egypt in the hope that Egyptian nationalist elements would be blamed. Israel's goal was to alienate the 'Abd al-Nasser regime from the Western powers. A number of Egyptian Jews cooperated with the Israeli intelligence in planning the attacks. Ordinary criminals occupied cells at the prison's far end. Because of his continuing health problems, the authorities consigned Qutb to the prison's hospital where conditions were only slightly better. Over the following years, whenever Qutb's condition worsened, the prison authorities would take him to the prisoners' ward at Qasr al-'Aini Hospital for treatment.[3]

Torture and mistreatment were common, and were meted out especially to new arrivals whose will, confidence and Islamist identity the guards sought to break. Guards suspended prisoners with their arms tied behind their heads, beat them with clubs, or subjected them to the viciousness of attack dogs. As the guards marched arrivals down the gloomy passageways in chains, they could hear the cries and desperate shouts of fellow Muslim Brothers. Evoking the mediaeval-type prison experience of the fundamentalist jurist Ahmad Ibn Hanbal, the incarcerated Islamists spoke of their *mihna* ("ordeal"), a test of faith and perseverance for the sake of God. Wounded physically, but also psychologically, they transferred the odium they had previously directed at the politicians of the Old Regime to Egypt's new government, and sharpened it.[4]

In the summer of 1956, the government released Muslim Brothers whom it had not yet brought to trial. Many of those released were jobless and unable to take care of their families. Khalida al-Hudaybi, wife of the Supreme Guide, and Zaynab al-Ghazali responded to the need by putting into action Islamic principles of charity. At one point, al-Ghazali donated her jewellery and 500 Egyptian pounds to aid the families in their need.[5] Al-Ghazali, who from here in looms large in Qutb's story, had been a teenage disciple of Huda Sha'rawi, founder of the European-inspired Egyptian Feminist Union in the 1920s. However, in 1935, one year after joining Sha'rawi's organization, she took a different path and dedicated her life to Islam. In 1936 she founded her own group, the Society of Muslim Women (Jamaa'at al-Sayyidat al-Muslimat), whose purpose was to help women study Islam and to engage in welfare activities. Although she admired Hasan al-Banna and believed in the mission of the Muslim Brotherhood, she resisted al-Banna's invitation to join her group with his.[6]

The incarcerated Muslim Brothers held their fellow inmate Sayyid Qutb in high esteem. Although their praise of him is effusive, and often indistinguishable from hagiography, it is clear that they recognized him for what he was—an established Islamist thinker who stood up to the political authority. This reputation provided him with eminence. When arguments broke out, the prisoners were quick to defer to his opinion on the matter at hand. They called him the "The Judge" (*al-Hakim*). During visits to the prison, Qutb's sisters and brother would sometimes pass on to him gifts of food—"grilled chicken or duck wrapped neatly in paper". Qutb would always invite his comrades to share in the small feast. When an inmate suffered a dislocated disc that kept him motionless on his back, Qutb kept a vigil at his bedside. His compassion extended to a mangy cat, which he fed and nurtured,[7] no doubt prompting among inmates comparisons with Abu

Hurayra, the Prophet's Companion and beloved narrator of *hadith*, who similarly loved cats.

Those on the outside did not forget Qutb, least of all his family. His sisters, Amina and Hamida, regularly delivered messages from well-wishers, including a note from a young American woman named Maryam Jameelah who was a recent convert to Islam (her name prior to converting was Margaret Marcus).[8] Qutb's critique of the materialist philosophies of the West had inspired Jameelah in the direction of Islam, and she attempted several times to communicate with him by post. Then finally, in June 1961, a month after her formal acceptance of Islam, she received a response, although not from Sayyid Qutb. She explained in a letter to Abu l-A'la Mawdudi, her mentor in far-away Pakistan, that it was Amina Qutb who contacted her:

Although he has not been able to write to me himself, just yesterday I received a beautiful letter from his sister, Amina Qutb, who told me that my letters had been delivered to her brother in his prison cell and that she wanted to write to me on his behalf. Sayyid, a scholar and the author of a number of books, is a great admirer of you [i.e., Mawdudi] and especially recommended your books to me. How tragic it is that in the so-called "Muslim" countries, Islam is much more severely persecuted than in the non-Muslim lands!

Jameelah noted Qutb's admiration for Mawdudi. Qutb, as we have seen, had become familiar with Mawdudi's ideas primarily through al-Nadwi's books. But the admiration was mutual. In his reply to the letter, Abu l-A'la Mawdudi agreed with Jameelah that Qutb was someone special:

I am happy to learn about your contact with Sayyid Qutb and his relations. Although we have had so far no opportunity to meet each other face to face, yet each one of us knows the other fully. He sent his books to me from prison and I met his brother, Muhammad Qutb when I visited Cairo in 1960. Ordeals of fire and sword through which the Ikhwan and in fact, all genuine Muslims everywhere must endure, should not surprise you. When a Muslim is nursed and raised under the influence of *Kufr* [disbelief] and he holds aloft the banner of *Kufr* in both hands, he goes to such extremes in persecuting his co-religionists as even non-Muslims would not dare to do, but sooner or later the time is sure to come when everybody must reap what he has been sowing.[9]

Qutb, as we shall see, was coming more and more to concur with Mawdudi's judgment on the disbelief of the age, modifying the concept slightly to reflect his increasingly dark vision of the world. Not long after the exchange of letters, Maryam Jameelah left the United States to take up residence at Mawdudi's family compound in Lahore. There, she eventually married one of Mawdudi's Islamist protégés, Mohammed Yusuf Khan, becoming his second wife. Although she never formally joined Mawdudi's organization, the Jamaat-e Islami, she nevertheless wrote books expressive of its views.

Qutb received messages from other supporters, which Zaynab al-Ghazali and the wife and daughters of Supreme Guide al-Hudaybi delivered to him. By means of these communications, Qutb remained reasonably informed about events outside the prison.

At the same time, his faith deepened. Cut off from the distractions of everyday life, with only the Qur'an and other Muslim Brothers to keep him company, his faith assumed a calm certainty unencumbered by sentiments of pride and personal ambition. Estranged from the nationalist society that was taking form outside the prison walls, he felt like a foreigner in the world, and in every act of reflection, his alienation grew. He realized that his punishment had a larger purpose and was leading to some kind of dramatic conclusion. Subjected to a limited range of experiences and influences, he focused his mind. He understood that non-Islamic sources had colonized his thinking; even as an avowed proponent of the Islamic cause in the late 1940s and early 1950s he had whored after false idols. The influence of these sources had distorted his personality and life. He admitted as much in his seminal prison work, *Milestones*. Adopting the third person he writes how he had spent "forty years of his life with books and research on almost all topics of human knowledge." He continues: "He specialized in some branches of knowledge and studies others due to his personal interest. Then he turned to the fountainhead of his faith. He came to feel that whatever he had read was as nothing in comparison to what he found here.[10]

Reading this, one gets the sense that these years in prison constituted Qutb's "true conversion" to Islamism—the moment when the scales fell from his eyes and he saw the stark truth staring him in the face. Unlike his turn to political Islam in the late 1940s, which did not constitute a radical rupture with his previous views, here Qutb repents and explicitly breaks with his past, a behaviour common to the conversion experience across cultures.

He developed an intense relationship with the Qur'an, greater than anything he had previously known. "I lived in the shadow of the Qur'an," he wrote, "filled with appreciation of that perfect harmony and balance inherent in God's creation, between man's actions and the movement of the Universe around him."[11] Refreshed by his daily encounters with the Qur'an, he experienced an inner happiness.[12] The scripture was a balm that healed the inner scars of torture and humiliation. Such was the depth of his faith that when overtaken by doubt and anxiety, he would sleep soundly and awaken in the morning with a "comforted heart". He compared this experience with that of the Prophet and the first Muslims, whom God had covered the night before the traumatic Battle of Badr "with a slumber as a security from Him" (Qur'an 8:11).[13]

The narrowed world of the prison enabled Qutb to appreciate God's simple blessings. When a beam of light, "no bigger than a penny", penetrated the darkness of the Tura prison cell, Qutb and the Islamist prisoners took turns standing in the way of the comforting ray. "I will never forget the day when we found the sun...or the excitement on our faces...How often on a daily basis, as we bathe in light and warmth and swim and dance in God's blessings, do we waste these rays that provide life? How often do we appreciate this overwhelming and accessible 'commodity' that is available without a price, without effort or suffering?"[14] Qutb's writings of the period are replete with observations and testimonials that show the poetic and mystical aspects of his nature. Adopting Sufi usage, he writes that by means of the Qur'an, he was able to "taste" (*dhuq*) God's favour.[15] Living in the "shade of the Qur'an," he felt assured and contented. "I could see God's hand in every event and everything. I lived in God's care and custody and His attributes, as given in the Qur'an, came alive before my eyes."[16]

Granted, there is much here that smacks of martyrology. Thus, Islamist accounts present Qutb as an exemplary figure, one who through struggle and suffering "creates a boundary between two belief systems".[17] However, even if one dismisses the exaggerations and rhetorical flourishes, there is enough to confirm Qutb's capacity to live an essentially moral life in an environment of immoral and inhumane conditions. In ordinary gestures of dignity and care for others, he evinced an ability inwardly to transcend the dismal conditions of his incarceration.[18] In choosing to live wholly committed to divine principles, he exposed the moral debris accumulating at the feet of Pharaoh.

In 1957, an event occurred that impressed upon Qutb the high stakes of the drama of which he was a player. The prison officials subjected Islamists who were reasonably fit to the hard labour of breaking stones at the quarries that flanked the prison. It was arduous work, and the prisoners were exhausted and angry. Their morale worsened with the arrival at the prison of a guard who deliberately ratcheted up the level of mistreatment. When rumours circulated among the prisoners that the guards planned, in fact, to massacre them at the quarries, they refused to go to work. The guards responded to the strike by opening fire on them in their cells. They shot dead twenty-one Muslim Brothers and wounded twice as many.[19] Qutb, whose frail condition had exempted him from the forced labour, was in the infirmary when the guards brought in the injured. The floor would have been covered with his comrades' blood.

The massacre elicited terrible emotions in Qutb. He was convinced that 'Abd al-Nasser's agents had encouraged the Brothers to strike in order to justify their murder. Qutb carried within him intense anger and bitterness at the Free Officers. Because of them, he and other Muslim Brothers had endured arrest and torture. He had come to believe that the regime was atheistic and in the grip of Zionists and Western "Crusaders", most especially the United States. All of this rankled. However, the 1957 massacre was the last straw. In his mind, it revealed the true, naked character of the Nasserist revolution. Qutb was full of indignation and outrage—"the righteous anger that puts fire in the belly and iron in the soul."[20]

How should Muslim Brothers react to the horrors foisted on them? During the last years of the monarchy, Qutb had argued that Islam was the panacea to bad socio-economic conditions. He designed his arguments to mobilize the people in the direction of change within the framework of the state. This was the tactic he had adopted in *Social Justice in Islam* and *The Battle of Islam and Capitalism*. Now, in the wake of the massacre, he understood that advocacy politics were ineffective against a regime that not only failed to put itself forward as the champion of justice, but was also prepared to eradicate, without compunction, its Islamist critics.

Qutb therefore shifted his emphasis from equating Islam with social justice to the fundamental issue of political legitimacy. Accordingly, his demand for the construction of an "Islamic order" lost its apologetic tinge and became emphatic, with strong appeals to core doctrines and principles. No longer did he pay heed to the rebirth of national or even transnational collectivities—markets that 'Abd al-Nasser had cornered with his three circles of Arab, African and Islamic identity. Instead, he took the whole of humanity as his subject. In Qutb's refurbished view, however much 'Abd al-Nasser claimed to represent the interests of Egyptians and other Arab peoples, his refusal to implement the Shari'a qualified him as a usurper of God's sovereignty, which it was incumbent on all the peoples of the world to recognize. Qutb appeared to be saying, ignore the reality of universal divine rule and Muslims are trapped, doomed to act only on a tactical level; but focus on the deep issue—the totalitarian imperative of the monotheistic creed—and they will be free. In this way, he undercut the parochial focus of the Nasserite project.

Qutb believed in his bones that victory was within reach. Although Islam had suffered a crippling blow, he understood that it was no more serious than the reversal of fortune endured by the Prophet and his Companions at the Battle of Uhud; in that battle the Meccan army, led by the pagan Abu Sufyan, severely bloodied, but did not destroy, the Muslim army, allowing it to fight another day. In Qutb's view the proscriptions, imprisonments and massacres amounted similarly to a setback, not a permanent defeat. The road remained open to complete victory. The Islamic movement would spring back to life, just as the early Muslims did following their defeat.[21] But now, as Qutb came slowly to see, success would stem not from the mobilization of the Muslim masses, which Nasser had co-opted, but rather from the raising up of an elect group of purified persons whose efforts would change not only Egypt, but the world also. So great was the global cultural, political and economic oppression that only a circle of adepts could awaken the masses from their slumber. In coming round to this tactic, Qutb had in mind the model of the Prophet Muhammad and the first Muslims who, from an initial position of weakness, had gradually built up their power so that they could confront the oppressors head on.

Soon after the massacre, Qutb penned a poem. In the gloom of the prison corridor, he saw a waving hand poke out of the barred window. Qutb could not identify the person, but the occasion moved him to write these lines. They capture his defiant mood: "Brother, I am not finished with the struggle."

> And I have not surrendered my weapon
> If the armies of darkness encircle me,
> I believe that the sun will still rise
> I will avenge my Lord and my Religion

I will stand firm on my way to victory
Or I shall return to the Paradise of God.[22]

To a large degree, Qutb's uncompromising dualism emerged from his long held belief in a superior supernatural realm separate from the dross and imperfections of everyday life, which only extraordinary insight could apprehend. However, it was also the product of objective circumstance. It confirms a contention of historians that the totalistic quality of revolutionary movements owes much to the authoritarian nature of the regimes against which they operate.[23]

Such had been the case, for example, in nineteenth century Russia where nihilist and anarchist groups converged on the complete triumph of their idea against the tyranny of the Tsarist system. It was also true of the savage insurgencies in Egypt and Algeria in the 1990s, which pitted radicalized Islamists against the state. In each case, bureaucratic-authoritarian regimes helped to spawn the maximalist intentions of various *jihadi* groups by the repressive nature of their response. Seen in this light, Qutb's gravitation to ideological totality anticipated, and in part inspired, the "friend-enemy" distinctions that drove the Islamist-state conflicts of the late twentieth century. Like the participants in these conflicts, Qutb understand that attitudes of compromise and negotiation were ineffectual against a strong opponent bent upon the annihilation of ideological competitors.[24] Towards the end of his life Qutb wrote, "All while the Islamic movement is busy with local and limited political activities such as opposing a treaty, bickering with this or that party, or supporting this or that party during elections," the "Zionist, Crusader and imperialist forces" are working in league with local Arab regimes to destroy the Islamic *da'wa*. Muslims must stop such forces in their tracks.[25]

The modern Jahiliyya

Qutb enunciated his revised discourse in works written between 1958 and 1964 under the watchful eyes of a government censorship committee headed by Shaykh Muhammad al-Ghazali.[26] Qutb knew al-Ghazali slightly, having worked with him briefly in the late 1940s in conjunction with the short-lived journal *al-Fikr al-Jadid* (*New Thought*); with Qutb, al-Ghazali had been a founder and contributor.[27] A graduate of al-Azhar, al-Ghazali had been a member of the Muslim Brotherhood, but he was expelled from its ranks in 1953 for having joined other

Muslim Brothers in opposing Hudaybi's leadership.[28] Subsequently he chose to work with the 'Abd al-Nasser regime, hoping thereby to encourage Islamic-oriented change from within the emerging system rather than from a position of dissidence. In the 1980s, al-Ghazali's moderate stance attracted the attention of Algeria's president Chadli Bendjedid who, eager to establish a counterweight to the growing influence of politically assertive Islamism, would have invited the scholar to be chairman of the Academic Council of al-Amir 'Abd al-Qadir University, Constantine.[29]

The most important of Qutb's prison works is, undoubtedly, *In the Shade of the Qur'an*. As noted, Qutb had begun the work years earlier. Upon entering prison, he picked up where he had left off at *sura* thirty-three. When he completed the commentary in 1959, he set about to revise *sura*s one to thirty-two, which had been published prior to his incarceration, to match his new, more radical mood. Yet he only succeeded in reaching *sura* fifteen. Therefore, in the published editions of the work, *sura*s sixteen to thirty-two remain in the form in which they had originally appeared in the journal *al-Muslimun*. Qutb found a publisher for his commentary in the person of Hagg Wahba, who was a long-time sympathizer of the Muslim Brotherhood. After Qutb completed a section of his commentary, he would hand it over to his friends and sisters who delivered it to Muhammad Qutb. Muhammad would then proofread the manuscript with Hagg Wahba "from 5–9 every day". Eventually, the published work appeared on the shelves of Wahba's modest shop in eight large volumes.[30]

Remarkably, the prison authorities allowed Qutb to work on the commentary so that he could fulfil his contractual obligation to the publishing house. According to al-Khalidi, the publisher had mounted a legal challenge against the government for the losses it had incurred during Qutb's imprisonment in 1954. The court ruled that the government should pay 10,000 Egyptian pounds, the amount demanded as compensation by the publisher, or permit Sayyid Qutb to complete his work in prison. The government chose the latter option. However, there may have been another reason for the concession. Islamists abroad, including many from Pakistan, had launched a barrage of protest at the Egyptian government because of its treatment of Qutb.[31] By allowing Qutb to write and publish, the regime could dismiss charges that it was maltreating Qutb and, by inference, other prisoners.

Over and beyond ideological issues, Muhammad al-Ghazali found Qutb's commentary wanting. Although he admired Qutb's literary style, he deemed the work "shallow from a scholarly point of view". Moreover, he judged sections of the commentary based on *fiqh* (jurisprudence) to be overly derivative from Ibn Kathir, the fourteenth century Hanbali *mufassir* (Qur'an commentator). According to al-Ghazali, Qutb "was not a scholar of Islam but only a rebel against injustices committed against him."[32] Muhammad al-Ghazali's harsh verdict on Qutb's Qur'an commentary remains typical of Muslim scholars who are mindful of traditional *fiqh* methodologies and interpretations, which they accuse Qutb of having ignored. Regardless, from the 1960s to the present day few Muslims, even those with quibbles, have doubted that *In the Shade of the Qur'an* is a remarkable intellectual achievement.

Other titles Qutb penned during this period included: *Hadha al-Din* (*This Religion*, 1962), *Khasa'is al-Tasawwur al-Islami wa Muqawwimatuhu* (*The Characteristics and Components of the Islamic Concept*, 1962), *al-Mustaqbal li–Hadha al-Din* (*The Future Belongs to this Religion*, published shortly after his release in 1965), *al-Islam wa Mushkilat al-Hadara* (*Islam and the Problems of Civilization*, 1962), and *Ma'alim fi al-Tariq* (*Signs on the Way*; translated as *Milestones*, 1964). In addition, Qutb substantially revised his earlier work, *Social Justice in Islam* to match his new thinking.[33] Of these works, *Milestones* is probably his most direct, concise and uncompromising statement.

In composing these works, Qutb had few written sources at his disposal. He received some materials from his sisters and was able to access the prison's modest library. Of course, he also possessed a copy of the Qur'an. As he wrote, he depended on the feedback of a fellow prisoner, Yusuf Hawwash. The authorities had sentenced Hawwash to a term of fifty-five years following the 1954 proscription. During much of the time Hawwash was ill, the consequence of damage done to his kidneys when during a period of imprisonment in the 1940s he endured the damp cold of a cell over the span of a winter.[34] His visits to the infirmary gave him the chance to form a close bond with Qutb. Each man possessed a mystical temperament. Moreover, each had endured torture and humiliation at the hands of jailors. They understood, as outsiders could not, what it meant to feel broken and alone. Hawwash looked up to the older Qutb; he claimed to have read all of his Islamic writings to that date. During the calm that followed the massacre of the Muslim Brother prisoners, the two passed the time ruminating on the implications of what had occurred.[35]

From Hawwash, Qutb gained detailed information about the history and personalities of the Muslim Brotherhood—an organization he joined relatively late in the game. He also received from Hawwash confirmation that the path of ideological strictness upon which he now embarked was sound. According to an oft-repeated story, Hawwash had a dream one night in which the Prophet Joseph addressed him: "Tell Sayyid Qutb that in my *sura* he will find what he seeks."[36] A tyrant—Pharaoh—had imprisoned Joseph, just as 'Abd al-Nasser had incarcerated Qutb. In the *sura*, Joseph preaches God's unity to his fellow prisoners:

And I have followed the religion of my fathers,—Ibrahîm (Abraham), Ishâque (Isaac) and Ya'qûb (Jacob) and never could we attribute any partners whatsoever to Allâh. This is from the Grace of Allâh to us and to mankind, but most men thank not (i.e. they neither believe in Allâh, nor worship Him). O two companions of the prison! Are many different lords (gods) better or Allâh, the One, the Irresistible? You do not worship besides Him but only names which you have named (forged), you and your fathers, for which Allâh has sent down no authority. The command (or the judgment) is for none but Allâh. He has commanded that you worship none but Him (i.e. His Monotheism), that is the (true) straight religion, but most men know not (12:38–40).

Could there be a more direct affirmation of God's authority over the wiles of men? Although these prison writings do not mention 'Abd al-Nasser by name, it is clear that the president of the Egyptian Republic is their intended target.

It may be useful at this point to provide a composite view of the main ideas contained in these works. These ideas do not depart radically from what Qutb previously had enunciated; rather, the differences are of emphasis. The prison works bring to conclusion concepts that had long been integral to Qutb's discourse.

As before, Qutb's starting point is the Qur'an, the "first source" (*al-nab' al-awwal*) for ordering the practical and spiritual affairs of individual and community life.[37] In Qutb's strict view, the fundamental principles of Islam do not change nor do they evolve. Rather, they are "constant" (*thabit*), unaltered by historical transformation and environmental variation. This is true, for example, of the *'ibadat* (devotional duties owed to God), "which cannot be affected by the requirements of any time or generation."[38] In their constancy, the divine principles reflect the law (*namus*) of the universe that governs human nature (*fitra*) and the nature of existence in general.[39] Consequently, the man of true faith is "the complete man (*insan kamil*)", a man who unites his thought and action in daily life with the light of divine guidance.[40] Islamic principles are also "comprehensive" (*shamil*) in that they make no distinction between religion proper and worldly affairs.[41] Indeed, Qutb upbraids those who would distinguish between the *'ibadat* and the *mu'amalat* (aspects of the Shari'a relating to interpersonal relations). "No one who ably understands religion," Qutb writes, "could conceive of a divine religion which limits its influence to people's emotions (*wijdan*) and exercise no [influence] over their daily activities," for "it is not natural for religion to be separated from [the affairs] of the world."[42]

Yet, Qutb tells us, there are those who would negate the Islamic fundamentals of divine lordship (*rabbaniyya*) in order to gain wider latitude in determining the shape of modern society. He accuses both Muhammad 'Abduh and the South Asian poet philosopher Sir Muhammad Iqbal (1875–1938) of having "poured Islam into the foreign mould" of philosophy. While Iqbal erred in conceiving Islam in terms of categories borrowed from Hegel and Kant, 'Abduh's mistake was to elevate reason to a status equal to that of revelation. Consequently, they ended up limiting truth to the judgment of rational discourse. In addition, and for the same reason, Qutb refuted the efforts of mediaeval Muslim philosophers such as Ibn Rushd, Ibn Sina and al-Farabi whom he regarded as mere imitators of their Greek predecessors. In Qutb's judgment, philosophical equations are dangerous. Not only does philosophy diminish the status of the Qur'an as first source, in the modern period it also legitimizes the entry into Islam of dangerous extraneous elements, namely, Western secular culture. In Qutb's view, any system (*nizam*) of belief and practice grounded in human as opposed to divine judgment is faulty and unsound owing to the volatile and imperfect nature of human reason. There is no intellect, Qutb tells us, that is not affected by shortcomings. Reason (*'aql*) and revelation (*wahy*) each has its designated sphere of influence and activity, but they are not equal, as no human faculty can ever hope to contain within itself any of the divine attributes.[43] Qutb asks the rhetorical question, "Who knows better, you or God?"[44] Qutb may have agreed with 'Abduh regarding the importance of *ijtihad*—independent judgement based on the Qur'an and the Traditions from the Prophet—but on the question of reason's ability to understand the divine Will, he was close to the fundamentalist Hanbalis.

More than his earlier works, Qutb's prison works totally reject rational exchange or argument as the chief means of disseminating truth. Faced with the charm and veracity of the Qur'an and the vision of the ideal life espoused in it, he saw no need for reasoned, philosophical argument. Instead, one finds him declaring that faith is sufficient for all that is required in life. Man, he says, discerns truth through the beauty and inevitability of the Islamic worldview, not by intellectual endeavours or philosophical speculations. Thus knowledge dealing with the mind is not his concern. His main interest is the marriage between religious knowledge and praxis. As he stated in *Milestones*, "Islam is not a "theory" based on "assumptions", but is rather a way of life working with "actuality".[45]

Qutb's doctrinal fundamentalism is reminiscent of the positions held by the eleventh century Asharite theologians. Visceral opponents of the rationally inclined Mu'tazilites, the Asharites subordinated reason to revelation. Like them, Qutb denied that the laws of causality governed the universe. Rather, the universe is the product of ever-renewed acts of divine creation. What appear to be laws of nature are actually conventions that God has created in nature. Events do not follow by necessity but occur because God wills them. Qutb explains: "[N]othing happens in this world without God's authority. Cause and effect are only valid by the will of God. When you put your hand in the fire it is burnt, but the burning itself only occurs with God's leave; for it is He who gave fire the property to incinerate and gave human skin susceptibility to burn."[46] By projecting the image of an omnipotent and transcendent creator God, Qutb aimed, once again, to distinguish the unique Islamic system from all other systems of belief and social organization.

But a problem arises from the fact of God's absolute power. Does not God's omnipotence call into question His justice? How could God allow his people to be defeated? Qutb was aware that strict determinism could easily lead Muslims to a condition of defeatism and paralysis. This possibility had been a concern of mediaeval Muslim theologians, too. In fact, Qutb wrote his book *al-Mustaqbal li–Hadha al-Din* (*This Religion Belongs to Islam*) in part to soothe the concerns of those incarcerated Brothers who were troubled by the fact that an enemy of Islam had proscribed their movement.[47] Qutb provided an answer in the book, and again it is similar to the solution that the Asharite theologians developed centuries earlier: God has created a power within humans that allows them to strive, or not to strive, to bring about God's Kingdom on earth. "He chose to grant him a will and the ability to respond; He chose to make guidance dependant on effort and perception."[48] In order to encourage Muslims in the right direction, God imposes tests on them: the defeat at Uhud, for example, but also, as Qutb implies, the current ordeal faced by the Brothers. God will reward those who meet the challenge, certainly in Heaven, perhaps in this world. "God," Qutb writes,

has chosen thereby to raise men to a point of excellence corresponding to the exertions he has made, the abilities he has applied, and the patience within which he has met misfortune for the sake of realizing the divinely ordained path, of removing evil from himself and from life around him: "Did the people imagine that they would say: we have tested those before them, and they would not be tested"? (Qur'an 29:2).[49]

In the end, no man has the right to ask God why he has chosen a certain thing; faith accepts that justice lies in what God commands. Qutb's message to the disheartened Brothers is clear: Forge ahead and do not look back. Show unblinking commitment to the project of Islam's revival. God "has chosen to make the divinely ordained path for human life to be realized through human existence, rather than enforcing it miraculously, through obscure, hidden means."[50] The believer may not know the outcome of his efforts, but by the very fact of conforming to the divine path, he comes closer to God.

In Qutb's view, man's dignity and life unfolded in accordance with a universal *tasawwur*, a "conception" or "ideological ideal" from which all of Islam's primary characteristics (*khasa'is*) are derived. These included, in addition to constancy of divine purpose, divine origination (*uluhiyya*), comprehensiveness, balance, dynamism, realism and divine unity (*tawhid*). Qutb fleshes out the meaning and implications of each of these in his 1962 book *Khasa'is al-Tasawwur al-Islami wa Muqawwimatuhu* (*The Characteristics and Components of the Islamic Concept*). Together these characteristics cover the range of human experience: "The Qur'an presents this comprehensive explanation to people in such a complete form that it takes into consideration all aspects of human nature, and satisfies its need in every dimension."[51] Thus, among true Muslims, Islam's characteristics are manifested naturally in a social order (*nizam*). There is no distinction between the practice of the social subject and his intellectual awareness of that practice. As long as theory is not the judge and determinant of social action, there is no rift between God's plan and its actual implementation. To eradicate the division between the idea and the action is to involve oneself existentially in the reality of Islam.

In confirmation of this point, Qutb draws attention to the example of the early Muslims of Medina. For them, the organization of community affairs was the natural concomitant of the faith that was planted in their hearts at Mecca: "Those of the first generation did not approach the Qur'an for the purpose of acquiring culture or information. Rather, they "turned to the Qur'an to find out what the Almighty Creator has prescribed [for them]."[52] Building upon this firm foundation of belief, the *umma* was able to mature dynamically in ways relevant to its changing circumstances.

This point led Qutb to counter critics who disparaged the Islamic movement for not fashioning a precise blueprint detailing what a fully-fledged Islamic order in the modern world would look like. While Qutb reiterates time and again that Islam is a comprehensive, practical *manhaj* ("method") covering all aspects of life, he insists that legislatively it is concerned only with concrete situations faced by a particular society accepting the sovereignty of God. "When [such] a society in fact exists, it will have an actual life that will require organization and laws...Only at that time will this religion begin to establish institutions and laws for people who surrender to such institutions and laws."[53] In the meantime, true Muslims should work to establish among the people belief in the creed. Qutb reminded his readers that the Prophet spent thirteen years preaching in Mecca before he attempted to establish the workings of a viable Islamic society.

Qutb's mature Islamism thus makes the revolutionary process central to its concerns. In other words, the horizons of Qutb's revised Islamism do not extend beyond the stage of struggle to envision precisely what a "proper" Islamic state should look like. In this sense, it is much like European fascism, which focuses on change at the expense of a fully thought-out "orthodox stage when the dynamics of society settle down to becoming 'steady-state,' namely when its internal and external enemies have been eliminated and new institutions created."[54] What is clear is that for Qutb, many different forms of social organization are possible. While the foundations of human existence are constant, "the forms (*ashkal*) of Islamic civilization" are necessarily difference in accordance "with the degree of industrial, economic and scientific progress", for like science and technology, the apparatuses of state are ethically neutral. What matters is the use to which one puts them.

On one point, however, Qutb is clear: when the time for legislation comes, Muslims must enact Islam in totality. One cannot implement its precepts piecemeal: "we cannot simply take one legal provision of one principle of Islam and try to implement it in a non-Muslim social set-up."[55] That is because Islam's myriad beliefs and practices are interrelated and mutually reinforcing. They all issue from the same divine source and thus have the same purpose—the liberation of man from tyranny, poverty, fear, and vice. It would make no sense—indeed, it would be a travesty of God's justice—to enforce one aspect of God's law but not others. Thus, for example, although the enforcement of the *hudud* punishments—specific penalties for certain crimes, such as the amputation of a hand for theft—is Qur'anically binding, the penalties cannot be applied outside the framework of an Islamic *nizam*. Qutb explains that because the structure of the Islamic system takes care of all of the economic and sustaining needs of the people, the only motive for theft is greed, which issues from a bad moral character. In such an Islamic framework, it is only right to impose a decisive penalty. Where an Islamic *nizam* is not fully manifested, the severing of a hand at the wrist would be simply barbaric.

Any similarity between the synchronization of theory and practice and Qutb's earlier expressive inclinations is probably not coincidental. It will be recalled that under the influence of al-'Aqqad, Qutb was attracted to an understanding of poetry that stressed its emotive effect upon individual consciousness. True art, according to this school of thought, has the ability to touch the soul and transform human sensibility. We noted that this understanding influenced Qutb's reading of the Qur'an, in which he identified its stylistic and rhetorical characteristics. Now, writing in a political environment that rendered useless the spirited argumentation of his previous Islamist works, Qutb returned to romanticism in order to spur individuals to action through the evocative power of Qur'anic imagery. As in *Artistic Depiction in the Qur'an*, he takes the Holy Book to be a source of aesthetic power, only now he sees the purpose behind its words as to propel individuals to action. What mattered to Qutb was the political effect of a word, image, or notion upon the community of believers.

In emphasizing the catalytic power of the religious imagination, Qutb was close to several Western thinkers who examined the nonrational and inspirational forces that underlay ideologies. The Italian economist Vilfredo Pareto (d. 1923), for example, argued that ideological structures are little more than rationalizations of deeply held, non-logical "sentiments". Carl Schmitt (d. 1985), the one-time Nazi collaborator, endeavoured to uncover the existential dimensions of the political realm, which he believed had been superseded by rationalistic and abstract categories originating in the Enlightenment. Georges Sorel (d. 1922), one of the chief proponents of the Anarcho-Syndicalist movement in late nineteenth century France, similarly discussed non-discursive modes of apprehending the world and acting upon it.[56] Like other anti–establishment theorists of the late nineteenth and early twentieth centuries, Sorel despised the edifice of Enlightenment thought, which rationalized bourgeois liberalism and diminished the heroic qualities of virtue and honour that had been hallmarks of European civilization in the past. In his writings, by evoking the ideal of a "the general strike", he aimed to tap the emotional realm and articulate the "epic state of mind" without which acts of struggle and sacrifice were impossible. As mentioned in relation to Alexis Carrel, there is a degree of common ground between Qutb's Islamism and those European-generated discourses that aimed to diminish or eradicate the cold, exploitative, mechanical machine of modern civilization.

However, there is an important, and obvious, difference between Qutb's and Sorel's formulations. Whereas in Sorel's view the mythic élan lay within subjective consciousness, for Qutb it was the expression of the individual's faith in God and of unquestioning obedience to His will. In this sense, Qutb lived the purported truth of ideology rather than conceiving it, as did Sorel and others, as an instrument of expediency whose grounding in truth was unimportant. For Qutb, belief preceded understanding and was the primary mode of self-alteration.

Qutb argued that God's judgment over the universe was constitutive of His *hakimiyya* ("sovereignty" or "dominion"). Qutb, who was an avid reader of Abu l-A'la Mawdudi, adopted the term from Mawdudi's small book *The Four Key Concepts in the Qur'an*, which was available to him in the form of Nadwi's 1955 Arabic translation. In the 1940s, Mawdudi had used the concept to nullify the claims of India's Muslim League sponsors who were intent on establishing a secular Muslim state in the subcontinent.[57] Nevertheless, for reasons of expediency, Mawdudi migrated to Pakistan as soon as the state came into being in

1947, where he continued his struggle against secularism, agitating for God's rule over laws created by men. In the debate that erupted over Pakistan's identity, Mawdudi vigorously claimed that the new state ought to be Islamic in character, rather than a secular state for Muslims.

Despite Qutb's obvious attraction to Mawdudi's ideas, we must be careful in ascribing a precise genealogy. As with other influences originating from Mawdudi, Qutb's reception of the term reinforced an already existing tendency in his thought. As noted, already we find Qutb emphasizing God's divine judgment in *Social Justice in Islam*. So too did Hasan al-Banna refer to God as standing above individual, party and class interests. Indeed, the basic idea of divine authority or judgment is the natural starting point of all Islamist discourse. We agree with Ibrahim Abu Rabi that Mawdudi's influence on Qutb in this and other matters was "secondary, and that both the historical situation of Egypt while he was writing and his understanding of the Qur'an were the primary influences upon his intellectual life and its development."[58] Nevertheless, the term helped Qutb to crystallize the concept of God's ultimate majesty over the universe.

The term *hakimiyya* derives from the trilateral Arabic root *h.k.m*, which carries the basic meaning "to judge", "decide" or "pass a verdict". Various derivatives of the root "are used in more than a hundred places" in the holy text.[59] Thus, "God is the final judge (*hakam*), seated on a throne and ruling his creation from its inception (cf. Q 7:54). He strikes those who transgress his order (cf. Q 6:124) [and] sets a path to be followed (Q 6:153)."[60] In classical Islamic jurisprudence, *al-hukm al-Shar'i* is a ruling derived from God's word in the Qur'an or the *sunna* pertaining to a specific facet of human behaviour.[61] According to the classical jurists, such rulings constitute the foundation of all legitimate judgment in the universe.

However, the word "*hakimiyya*" itself does not appear in the Qur'an. As Shahrough Akhavi points out, it is an Arabic neologism coined by Hasan al-Nadwi to render Mawdudi's Urdu phrase "*hukumat-i ilahiyya*" ("divine government").[62] Nevertheless, as both Mawdudi and Qutb were aware, the concept of divine judgment and decree has a solid Qur'anic pedigree. Especially important, in Qutb's perspective, are several verses of the Qur'an's *surat al-Ma'ida*, which communicate the absolute imperative to implement God's law over all of human life. Thus, God instructs the Prophet Muhammad to "judge between them by that which Allah hath revealed, and follow not their desires away from the truth which hath come unto thee" (Q 5:48); again, "Whoso judgeth not by that which Allah hath revealed: such are disbelievers" (Q 5:44); and again, "Is it a judgment of the time of (pagan) ignorance that they are seeking? Who is better than Allah for judgment to a people who have certainty (in their belief)? (Q 5:50)." Commenting on these verses, Qutb writes, "The criterion for rulers is to judge in accordance with what God has revealed, and for people to accept such a judgment and not to prefer anything else to it."[63]

Qutb drew upon this Qur'anically justified concept of God's judgment and dominion in order to undermine the theory and practice of state sovereignty, an important principle undergirding the Western-dominated global order. Modern state authorities exercise sovereignty because, unlike their mediaeval counterparts, they are able "to make laws and effectively sanction [the state's] upkeep; exert a monopoly over the disposal of the means to violence; control basic policies relating to the internal political or administrative form of government; and dispose of a national economy that is the basis of its revenue."[64] Recognized in the normative statements of international law, "sovereignty" legitimized the discrete political units that emerged first in Europe and later in Egypt and other parts of Africa, Asia and the Americas from the early modern period onwards. The independence movement that took root in Egypt under the leadership of Sa'd Zaghlul, which Qutb had supported during the period of the Old Regime, no less than the emergent nationalisms in China, Korea and India, took its inspiration from the idea, traced back to the seventeenth century Treaty of Westphalia, that nations were inherently autonomous and thus deserving of self-determination.[65]

Although Qutb's Islamist writings had long challenged the secular authority of the state in the name of divine authority, it was not until his confrontation with the coercive arm of the 'Abd al-Nasser regime that he began explicitly to follow Mawdudi in standing the modern concept of state sovereignty on its head. In Qutb's view, as in Mawdudi's, *hakimiyya* is the exclusive prerogative of God who alone is qualified to fashion principles appropriate to the proper functioning of a social, political and economic order. God is the legal sovereign as well as the Lord of nature. This message is especially clear in the verses revealed at Mecca when God called the people to the true faith. Commenting on Qur'an 2:159–62, Qutb writes: "The One God is the only deity to be adored and worshipped, and He is also the sole source of man's moral codes and norms, and the origin of all the laws and regulations that govern and control man's social, political and economic life and the life of the whole cosmos.[66]

To submit to the control and supervision of secular authorities and humanly devised institutions is to surrender to the worldly whims and selfish interests of individuals and governing elites. The rule of man over man, according to Qutb, leads inexorably to oppression and the stifling of man's God-given nature. Qutb states in his commentary on Qur'an 5:44, 5:45, and 5:47:

> God (limitless is He in His glory) says that this whole issue is one of faith or unfaith, Islam or non-Islam, Divine law or human prejudice. No compromise or reconciliation can be worked out between these two sets of values. Those who judge on the basis of the law of God has revealed, enforcing all parts of it and substituting nothing else for it, are the believers. By contrast, those who do not make the law God has revealed the basis of their judgment are unbelievers, wrongdoers and transgressors.[67]

For Qutb, "Belief and faith are the only worthy and legitimate ties that can bring men together. They override all other incidental ties of nationality, race or ancestry."[68]

The *qibla*, the direction of *salat* (obligatory prayer) towards the Ka'ba at Mecca, symbolizes Islam's liberation from the parochial identifications of territorial nationalism, tribal lineage, and ethnicity. As such, the *qibla* speaks to the manifest destiny of Muslims in the world, "which is suffering under the tyranny of false religions, oppressive and arrogant ideologies, flawed political and economic systems and heedless leadership." The *qibla* stands as a reminder to the faithful "that their standards in life must...be derived from the Divine revelations...." The *qibla*, directs "man's senses, heart, soul and body towards God," allowing him to fulfill God's mandate on earth.[69]

Qutb directed the concept of divine sovereignty against the nationalist regime that had imprisoned him and outlawed the organization to which he belonged. By constructing the individual Muslim as a juridical subject beholden to the exigencies of the Shari'a alone, Qutb sought to delegitimize the legislative and executive authority held by the Free Officers and all other systems of government based on worldly interests and ties. In this absolute negation of the legitimacy of the system of politics and nation-states, Qutb heralded the appearance within Islamism of an ideology based uniquely on universal moral purpose.

The *hakimiyya* doctrine looks ahead to Al Qaeda's abstract and deterritorialized utopia of the global caliphate.

Qutb underscored the purported illegitimacy of the Egyptian Republic, and by extension all other non-Islamic regimes and societies, by equating its moral universe with the condition of *jahiliyya* ("ignorance"). As we noted in the previous chapter, Nadwi's book *What the World has Lost with the Decline of the Muslims* introduced Qutb to this novel application of the term. However, it was only towards the end of his prison experience that he began to expound on the concept. *Jahiliyya*, as Qutb was fully aware, is a Qur'anic term well placed within the body of classical Islamic discourse. In pre-Islamic times and in the Qur'an the Arabic trilateral root j.h.l. carried the basic meaning of "barbarism"; its antonym was h.l.m., "conveying the meaning of gentility and civilization".[70] Famously, the first Umayyad Caliph, Mu'awiyya, was a man of *hilm*. However, from early in the Islamic era, most Muslim commentators took the word to refer to the condition of disbelief, that is, ignorance of the divine mandate, current among the Arabs of west-central Arabia prior to the advent of Islam's "civilizing mission". *Jahiliyya*, in this sense, had a temporal designation that served to distinguish Islam from the pre-Islamic age of heathendom.

Following Mawdudi and Nadwi, Qutb applied the term more widely. Excising *jahiliyya* from its original temporal context, he applied it to those forces that worked against the implementation of the divine directives throughout history, which were especially prevalent in his own time.[71] In Qutb's words, "Today too we are surrounded by *jahiliyyah*. Its nature is the same as during the first period of Islam, and it is perhaps more deeply entrenched. Our whole environment, people's beliefs and ideas, habits and art, rules and laws—is *jahiliyyah*...."[72] According to Qutb, all the societies of the world that exist today— without exception—are to be classified as *jahili* ("ignorant") on account of their wilful ignorance of the divine guidance. These include societies in which paganism or idol worship prevails, for example India, South East Asia, and regions of Africa. In addition to the Christians, they include the Jews whose allegedly corrupted scriptures put forward the false notion of the separation of Church and State. Communist societies are also, obviously, *jahili* in nature because of their atheism and all that follows from it, including their worship of the political party.

Qutb upbraids all of these *jahili* societies, especially those of the modern West, the chief purveyors of *jahiliyya* in his time. He identifies a number of common traits. In *jahili* societies, the strong oppress the weak, materialism and selfish individualism prevail over concern for the common good, and populations resort to decadent and immoral behaviour, especially of the sexual variety. In fact, states Qutb, sexual permissiveness has been a factor in the decline of entire civilizations, including those of Athens, Rome, and Persia. As he had observed first hand in the United States, it enfeebles the countries of the West, including most especially France, the progenitor of all vice and licentiousness:

The same factor is now working for the destruction of Western civilization. Those effects appeared first in France. One can now see them in America, Sweden and other Western civilized countries. France is foremost because she took the lead in shedding moral inhibitions. She succumbed in every war she fought since 1870.[73]

Qutb cites the telling example of the 1963 Profumo Affair, an event that was then in the news, in which Britain's Secretary for War had an affair with a call-girl named Christine Keeler. According to Qutb, British officials did not consider the affair serious "because of its sexual aspect"—they evidently considered such behavior "normal" and inconsequential. Rather, they took notice of the scandal only because it put state security at risk; before her fling with Profumo, Keeler had been the mistress of the Russian naval attaché, and there was concern that she might divulge state secrets to the Russians.[74] These and similar manifestations of immoral behaviour, says Qutb, are reflections of the *jahili* societies' alienation from God.

However, Qutb breaks new ground by regarding Muslim societies as *jahili*. He says of these "so-called" Muslims:

Although they believe in the oneness of God, still they have relegated the legislative attributes to others and submit to this authority, and from this authority they derive their systems, their traditions and customs, their laws, their values and standards, and almost every practice of life. God Most High says concerning such rulers: "And whosoever does not judge by what Allâh has revealed, such are the *Kâfirûn* (i.e. disbelievers—of a lesser degree as they do not act on Allâh's Laws(Q.5:44)."[75]

Qutb explains that some *faux* Muslims openly declare their secularism, while others pay lip service to Islam, "but in their social life have completely abandoned it". These latter "say they do not believe in the

'Unseen' and want to construct their social system on the basis of 'science', since science and the Unseen are contradictory!"[76]

When, exactly, did Muslims begin to lose their religion? Qutb followed the standard Muslim view that the best generation of Muslims was that of the Prophet and his companions. "This generation drank solely from [the spring of the Qur'an] and thus attained a unique distinction in history."[77] Subsequently, some Muslims reasserted old pre-Islamic customs or, like the philosophers, mixed their Islam with foreign Greek and Persian sources, thus corrupting the faith. Nevertheless, despite the corruption, mediaeval rulers and populations continued to recognize God's lordship, sometimes in practice, at the very least in theory. Therefore, although Islam fell from the height of its prestige at pristine Medina, it continued to exist over the next few centuries. It was only with the onset of Western imperialism in the nineteenth century and the universal spread of secularism that Muslims came gradually to ignore God's sovereignty completely and a deep, unfettered *jahiliyya* began.[78]

Qutb came late to this understanding. In the early editions of *Social Justice in Islam*, dating to the late 1940s and 1950s, he adopted the conventional reformist stance of reviving religion in state and society. "We call for the restoration of an Islamic life governed by the Islamic spirit and Islamic law (*al-qanun al-islami*) in which the Islam we preach is combined with a genuine Islamic environment."[79] Although he explicitly condemned the shallow commitment to Islam current among some of the ruling elite, he saw Islam as still operative in the larger society. "If the spread of the Islamic spirit had stopped in governing circles—indeed in some of these circles but not others—it continued operative in other aspects of the life of society and individuals, realizing many of its ideals and reaching many high levels. Right up to the present hour it still functions in those areas that are not influenced by the official course of the state."[80] In other words, in his earlier works, including the first edition of his Qur'an commentary, Qutb did not deny the existence of Islam in either state or society. Only in the early and mid-1960s, most notably in the last rendering of *In the Shade of the Qur'an* and its spin-off, *Milestones*, did he take the step of declaring not only the governments of the Muslim world, but also ostensibly Muslim populations, to be beyond the pale of Islam.

It was a harsh judgment, but one that followed logically upon the premise of God's *hakimiyya*. Either a Muslim recognizes and accepts

God's legislative prerogative, or he does not. There can be no middle ground: "Do they then seek the judgment of (the Days of) Ignorance? And who is better in judgment than Allâh for a people who have firm Faith." (Qur'an 5:50).[81] Muslims may believe in God and His prophet, pray, fast, perform the Hajj, and dispense *zakat*, but as long as their lives "are not based on submission to God alone" they are steeped in *jahiliyya* and cannot be reckoned as Muslims. Qutb states plainly that the "position of Islam in relation to all *jahili* societies, including those that claim to be Muslim, can be described in one sentence: it considers all these societies un-Islamic and illegal."[82] That is because "Islam knows only two kinds of society, the Islamic and the *jahili*."[83]

Still, as William Shepard observes, Qutb refrains from "labeling 'so-called Muslims' individually as *kafirs* ["unbelievers"]."[84] Perhaps this was because Qutb was aware of the seriousness of labelling someone a *kafir*. As we shall note at greater length in the following chapter, the scholars of Islam had long ago castigated the practice of *takfir* (the pronouncement of disbelief on a person). It is more likely, however, that Qutb discerned a significant conceptual difference between the two terms. Whereas the *kafir* is a person who intentionally disbelieves in God, the *jahili* individual sees himself as a believer yet dismisses Islam's prerogative to govern all aspects of life.[85]

Regardless of this difference, describing the Islamic world as "ignorant" was a serious indictment. In claiming that Islam did not exist in the modern period, Qutb went further than any of his contemporaries. Hasan al-Banna never made such an allegation. For al-Banna, the society and the state were categorically Islamic, even though in the current period the Western cultural onslaught had diminished the quality of Islam. As noted, he had set himself the task of reviving the Islam among the backsliders, hypocrites, and transgressors. In his view, Islam had not disappeared. And although both Mawdudi and Nadwi asserted that the *jahili* culture of the West had influenced contemporary Muslim societies, they did not brandish Muslim societies as completely given over to modern forms of paganism. Soon, Qutb's harsh verdict on the Muslims of his era would raise eyebrows in conventional Islamic circles. Qutb's concept of the modern *jahiliyya* would be a factor in his eventual condemnation to death at the hands of the state authorities.

Jihad

Given the dire condition of the world, Qutb said that Muslims had a duty to reactivate the principle of *jihad* (literally, "striving") against the *jahili* forces responsible for humankind's "misery and confusion". Like all Islamic thinkers, Qutb knew that the injunction to *jihad* comes from divergent and even contradictory texts in the Qur'an. While some verses caution Muslims against confronting enemies, and others allow fighting disbelievers only in defence, a select few verses appear to sanction *jihad* in all circumstances. This is true, for example, of *sura* 9:29, one of four so-called "sword verses". It enjoins Muslims to "Fight against those who (1) believe not in Allâh, (2) nor in the Last Day, (3) nor forbid that which has been forbidden by Allâh and His Messenger (4) and those who acknowledge not the religion of truth (i.e. Islâm) among the people of the Scripture (Jews and Christians), until they pay the *Jizyah* with willing submission, and feel themselves subdued." The mediaeval exegetes regarded these divergent texts as corresponding to the "occasions of revelation" (*asbab al-nuzul*), in other words, to the changing circumstances of the Prophet Muhammad's career. According to this method, the divine revelations encouraged Muslims to avoid physical conflict during the Meccan stage when they were weak, but expanded the conditions under which they could wage war once the Muslims attained a position of strength at Medina. Furthermore, most jurists held that the latter "sword verses" abrogated, or replaced, the verses regarding *jihad* revealed earlier. In their view, the earlier verses related to specific situations, while the later verses were enduring and universal in scope. Therefore, according to the jurists, aggressive combat was the norm. Drawing on the jurists, Qutb explains the progression: "[T]he Muslims were first restrained from fighting; then they were permitted to fight; later on they were commanded to fight against the aggressors; and finally they were commanded to fight against all the polytheists."[86]

The classical doctrine grew out of this aggressive interpretation of *jihad* and served to justify conflict with idolaters and followers of non-Muslim scriptural faiths. During the early and later mediaeval periods, scholars such as 'Abd al-Rahman al-Awza'i (d. 774), 'Abdullah Ibn al-Mubarak (d. 797), Muhammad al-Shaybani (d. 804), Ibn Taymiyya (d. 1328) and his Hanbali disciple Ibn Qayyim al-Jawziyya (d. 1350) constructed a raft of rules and advice regulating combat against unbelievers. These included stipulations regarding the equitable division of spoils, the fate of prisoners and the harming of women, children and old people (normally prohibited). Objectively, the rulings legitimized in Islamic terms the great the Muslim conquest movements of the eighth, ninth and tenth centuries CE, a period in world history when "conquering and vanquishing the weak was an accepted part of the customs and practices of nations and empires."[87]

Sayyid Qutb honoured the classical jurisprudence on *jihad*, viewing it as a template for sustaining and directing the struggle against Islam's enemies in the modern period. He was particularly impressed by what Ibn al-Qayyim had to say on the topic in his compendium of traditions, *Zad al-Ma'ad (The Provisions of the Hereafter)*.[88] In deferring to the hallowed literature of militancy, he followed al-Banna and Mawdudi in rescuing the practice from what he deemed modernist and apologetic definitions that regarded *jihad* primarily as a spiritual struggle aimed at the taming of base desires and inclinations—the so-called Greater *Jihad*—or as a purely defensive operation against aggressors. The Indian Sir Sayyid Ahmad Khan (1817–98), as well as Rashid Rida and Muhammad 'Abduh, had each emphasized the spiritual, defensive, and non-aggressive characteristics of *jihad* over its triumphal aspects. In the effort to normalize relations between the British and Indian Muslims following the 1857 Mutiny, Sir Sayyid wrote that Muslims should fight only in situations in which the unbelievers positively oppressed them or prevented them from practicing their religion.[89] Qutb argued that such definitions neutralized Islam's universal mission. "If we insist on calling Islamic *jihad* a defensive movement, then we must change the meaning of the word "defense" and mean by it 'the defense of man' against all those forces that limit his freedom."[90]

In his prison works, especially his revised Qur'an commentary and in *Milestones*, Qutb says explicitly that Islam is essentially expansionist. *Jihad*, he writes, is the instrument of the universal Islamic revolution—the means by which people will attain their freedom. Not freedom in the Western sense of the individual's right to choose, but the freedom that comes with the realization of one's God-given nature (*fitra*). Nothing will stand in the way of Islam's manifest destiny, inscribed in the natural curve of historical evolution. "Some enemies of Islam may consider it expedient not to take any action against Islam, if Islam leaves them alone in their geographical boundaries.... But Islam cannot agree to this unless they submit to its authority...."[91]

Muslims do not fight to gain military honour or on behalf of nations, territories or kings. Rather, they fight to realise "God's universal Truth" in the world.

Again following the classical doctrine, Qutb wrote that faced with the imperative of Islamic conquest, non-Muslims have but three options. They may yield to the Muslims and enter into Islam (i.e. convert); if they are Jews and Christians, they may forego conversion and instead pay the *jizya* (poll tax), which gains them *dhimmi* (protected) status; or, if recalcitrant, they may fight the believers and pay the consequences in terms of lives lost and property confiscated. For Qutb, as for the classical jurists, it is important that Islam be elevated to a position of power over the peoples of the earth. Dispensing God's justice, Islam's rule will be wise and benevolent, unlike the pagan, Christian or imperialist empires. "Islam does not force people to accept its belief, but it wants to provide a free environment in which they will have the choice to believe. What it wants to abolish are those oppressive political systems under which people are prevented from expressing their freedom to choose whatever beliefs they want, and after that it gives them complete freedom to decide whether to accept Islam or not."[92] Qutb was confident that given the choice, non-believers under Islam's sway would accept the true creed sooner or later.

Qutb looked back at previous efforts to stem the *jahili* tide. In the Middle Ages the heroes of Islamic reassertion were the Mamluks who, under the spiritual guidance of the Damascene scholar Ibn Taymiyya, successfully confronted the ravages of the Tartars, even though the latter (like 'Abd al-Nasser) professed to be Muslim. In recent times the Mahdi of the Sudan, 'Umar al-Mukhtar of Libya, and 'Abd al-Hamid Ibn Badis of Algeria preserved the "spirit of resistance" (*ruh al-muqawama*). Each in his specific way struggled against the usurping authority of tyrants and colonial overlords. Their example beckons Muslims in the present era.[93]

However, Qutb was living in an era of darkness in which so-called Muslims were ignorant of Islam's intentions. How else to explain the people's easy co-optation by the oppressive *taghut*? Qutb does not, as Ayman Zawahiri would in his 1991 book *al-Hasad al-Mur* (*The Bitter Harvest*), offer a retrospective analysis of the "shortcomings" of the Muslim Brotherhood (in al-Zawahiri's view, the Muslim Brotherhood made far too many accommodations with the "iniquitous" political order).[94] Throughout the period of his imprisonment, Sayyid Qutb continued to admire Hasan al-Banna and the movement that he founded. However, reading between the lines it is clear that Qutb now doubted the ability of the Muslim Brotherhood to recoup and succeed by means of conventional missionary efforts and advocacy politics in the face of a regime that was intent upon maximizing its control. Ruminating on the general failure of the Islamist mass movement to achieve its goals, Qutb saw the need for a new approach to the problem of the contemporary *jahiliyya*. Writing in his Qur'an commentary and in *Milestones*, he explains that the restitution of God's *hakimiyya* is dependent on the formation of a vanguard (*tali'a*) of believers who will excise themselves from the corrupting influences of the surrounding *jahili* culture. The vanguard will imbue the people with Islamic consciousness and lead them to eventual victory against the corrupt political order. Qutb's vision of a small, highly organized and ideologically dedicated cadre of "professional revolutionaries" takes us far from his earlier formulations about disaffected Egyptian Muslims rising in spontaneous anger against the political establishment.

Qutb explains that the beliefs and conceptual grounding of this select group must be pure and its members devoted to serving God alone. This, in turn, requires that they separate themselves completely from the corrupting influence of the *jahiliyya*. "Thus there would be a complete break between the Muslim's present Islam and his past *jahiliyyah*." Although the vanguard will have to deal occasionally with "polytheists" for practical reasons related to business and commercial dealings, by and large it will remain aloof from society. Working in jobs and living in neighbourhoods, the members of the vanguard will focus their minds and spirits solely on God's universal truth. All guidance will come from God's Word and the example of the Prophet. Surrounded by vice, their bare and moral ways of life will strengthen them against temptation and weakness. Qutb does not say so, but one imagines that the renunciation he envisages might include even the severing of relations with family members who choose to remain ensnared by the illusions and deceits of the world.

Qutb is explicit that such a group, once formed, will constitute the only true and legitimate Muslim community on earth, an island of righteousness in a sea of disbelief. By "preaching and persuasion", it will work hard to spread the fundamental message of God's sovereignty to others, all the while tackling the "material obstacles" in its path. The ranks of true Muslims will swell. But the vanguard will need to be patient. It will take a long time before a true Islamic society comes into being. "If only the masses could be converted to Islam all at once by preaching and explaining the laws of Islam, but this is a vain hope. The masses will convert from *jahiliyya* and the service of oppressive tyrants to Islam and the service of God alone only by that long slow road that the mission of Islam has always followed."[95] Qutb is not explicit as to how the vanguard should relate to the powers-that-be during the rebuilding phase. But his radically dichotomous world view, which explicitly called for Islam's victory, in conjunction with his reminder that *jahili* powers have historically chosen to fight rather than submit to God's way (most notably in 1954), leaves the reader no doubt as to the inevitability of the confrontation ahead. Qutb wrote:

Preaching alone is not enough to establish the dominion of Allah [*mamlakat Allah*] on earth, to abolish the dominion of man, to take away sovereignty from the usurper and return it to Allah, and to bring about the enforcement of the Divine shari'ah and the abolition of man-made laws. Those who have usurped the authority of Allah [*sultan Allah*] and are oppressing Allah's creatures are not going to give up their power merely through preaching.[96]

Yet Qutb understood that the militant phase of the rebuilding process was still a long way off. Probably he did not expect to see the *jihad* unfold in his lifetime. It was in order to provide the future vanguard with guidelines that he composed *Milestones*. "The Muslims in this vanguard must know the landmarks and the milestones on the road to this goal so that they would know the starting point as well as the nature, the responsibilities, and the ultimate purpose of this long journey."[97]

Qutb provided the practice of the *tali'a* Islamic legitimacy in referring to the example of the Meccan Muslims who separated themselves from the surrounding pagan society as a prelude to their eventual victory. For thirteen years, Muhammad and the "unique Qur'anic generation" preached the fundamental lesson of God's lordship before striking out in pursuit of victory. As Qutb was aware, the paradigm of the Prophet's career had inspired previous generations of Muslims in their confrontation with oppressive states. In the prophetic model, he discerned a tactical option born of necessity. In the manner of the first Muslims, the vanguard would evade the risks and uncertainties of open, mass-based confrontation by resorting to preparatory activities appropriate to the situation at hand. No doubt Qutb's preference for this tactic found reinforcement in the examples of other, temporally more immediate revolutionary movements and groups. The Watanist and Muslim Brother secret societies, no less than the Egyptian Free Officers, had each adopted to its specifications the pattern of professional revolutionaries orchestrating from above the toppling of the old order, a model that the Bolsheviks made famous.[98]

Nonetheless, for Qutb and his followers, it was the Islamic prototype that carried weight. Given his cultural framework, Qutb's deference to the Islamic tradition is understandable. Islam emerged on the world scene in the seventh century CE as a revolutionary force concerned with justice, equity and compassion—potentially world-transforming ideals that were, in the first instance, at variance with the worldliness and tribalism of the *jahiliyya*, what Toshihiko Izutsu referred to as the "pessimistic conception of earthly life."[99] So, although other, more recent models of revolutionary activism were available to Qutb, in the context of persecution he responded to Islam's original message to spread justice and peace, which resonated in him at a deep emotional level.

There is one other aspect of Qutb's activist ideology that deserves notice, and that is his belief in the transforming effect of struggle itself. Qutb writes that Muslims will benefit from the act of fighting in God's way regardless of the outcome. That is because the true Muslim, "while struggling against other people", also "struggles against himself". Thereby "horizons are opened to him in the faith which would never be opened to him if her were to sit immobile and at rest....His soul, feelings, his imagination, his habits, his nature, his reactions and responses—all are brought to a point of development which he could not have attained without hard and bitter experience."[100] This spiritual dimension of military combat has a distinct Islamic pedigree. It was appreciated by mediaeval "holy warriors", for example by the "Men of the Ribat" (*Al-Murabitun*) who under the eleventh century Sanhaja warrior-scholar 'Abd Allah Ibn Yasin conquered the western Sahara and Morocco.

At the same time, it once again calls to mind other, non-Islamic sources, for example, the angry deliberations of Franz Fanon (1925–61), the post-colonial theorist from Martinique, who famously argued that violent struggle was "a cleansing force. It frees the native from his inferiority complex and from his despair and inaction; it makes him fearless and restores his self-respect."[101] Although Qutb consciously placed himself within the religious tradition that gave birth to the Sufi–oriented *jihad* of Ibn Yasin, his theorizing is close to Fanon's and that of the international left. Theorizing under similar conditions of colonialism, each presented struggle as the key not only to resistance but also to the awakening of the true self. Qutb's case confirms the French scholar François Burgat's adage that "the forms of political appropriation of a religion are explained less by the essence of dogma than by the sociology of those who practice it."[102]

In introducing the dyad of *hakimiyya* and *jahiliyya* into the heart of his Islamist discourse, Qutb sharpened the division between the Self and Other that had long been a fundamental feature of his worldview. Whereas previously he had distinguished between virtuous Muslim Easterners and self-centred Western and Westernizing materialists, during the final few years of his incarceration he articulated the division in terms of the stark, theological categories of Islam vs *jahiliyya*. Significantly, the latter category included confessing Muslims who had succumbed to the selfish individualism that sprang from the secular policies championed by the 'Abd al-Nasser regime. Contemptuous of Muslims and Peoples of the Book who chose to live benumbed, asleep, or intoxicated by the poison of the modern *jahiliyya*, he called for the release of the "inner man" from the grip of false consciousness. People must be brought to understand that an enduring bond, regulated by the Shari'a, linked humankind and the cosmos. Surveying the wreckage of the Muslim Brotherhood from his jail cell, he advocated the creation of a select group of individuals whose transformed consciousness would make possible the resurrection of the Islamic movement.

Qutb's prison works thus continue the process of discursive mutation apparent in his earlier writings. Through the Islamization of new concepts like *tali'a*, and the reformulation of traditional Islamic concepts such as *jahiliyya* and *jihad*, Qutb was able to give point to his political concerns without compromising the cultural foundations of his dissent. By demonizing the political and cultural moorings of the Other, and by giving absolute value to its conceptual opposite, Qutb managed radically to circumscribe the range of legitimate political discourse. In so doing, he implemented a "closure", which excluded latitudinarian interpretations of the Qur'an in the interest of maintaining fixed meanings. Ultimately, Qutb's mature Islamist discourse had the purpose of turning Islam's struggle with its "oppressors" into a cosmic battle between good and evil. Implicit within the scheme was the modern dream of revolutionary transformation.

MARTYRDOM

A new secret organization

While Qutb was writing in prison, Muslim Brothers on the outside took steps to rebuild the Islamic movement. In 1957 Zaynab al-Ghazali met a Brother named 'Ali 'Abd al-Fattah Isma'il at the port city of Suez. Both were on their way to Mecca to perform the Hajj. A former member of the Brotherhood's Guidance Council, Isma'il was a fiery Muslim who believed absolutely in the righteousness of the Islamic cause. Caught up in the 1954 proscription, he had endured two years of prison before the authorities released him and other Brothers held without charge.[1]

Once he arrived in Mecca, Isma'il took al-Ghazali aside and told her about his ambition to put the Muslim Brotherhood back on a solid footing. Al-Ghazali agreed that this was a desirable goal and swore with Isma'il to "fight and die for the sake of His *Da'wa*."[2] Upon returning to Egypt, they presented the idea to the Supreme Guide Hasan al-Hudaybi, who remained under house arrest in Alexandria.[3] Against the cautions of the Muslim Brother Munir al-Dilla, also a prisoner, Hudaybi endorsed the plan.[4] However, Hudaybi set the condition that that they must accomplish their goal by means of education and conventional missionary activity. Violence, he said, would compromise the integrity of the Brotherhood's mission and jeopardize its future.[5]

In an effort to spark the revival, Isma'il travelled around Egypt searching out former Brothers and new recruits. His efforts bore fruit. By 1961, he had identified committed Islamists in towns and cities around the country. These, in turn, recruited other supporters, including a young man from al-Mahalla Kubra named Muhammad Badi'a who would become Supreme Guide of the Muslim Brothers in 2010. Soon, small branches of committed activists were established in the Delta and the provinces of the Sa'id, in addition to Cairo. Thus were sown the seeds of a secret organization (*tanzim*) dedicated to the task of reestablishing the Muslim Brotherhood. In addition to 'Abd al-Fattah Isma'il, the organization's core members included 'Ali 'Ashmawi, Ahmad 'Abd al-Majid 'Abd al-Sami, Majdi 'Abd al-'Aziz Mitwalli, and Sabri 'Arfa al-Kawmi.[6] They loosely modelled their activities on the Muslim Brotherhood's old underground paramilitary arm, the Secret Apparatus, which had engaged in subversive activities between its founding in the early 1940s and its demise in 1954.

Meeting at Zaynab al-Ghazali's Heliopolis apartment, they prepared themselves intellectually. They studied the exegetical and juridical works of Ibn Kathir, Ibn Hazm, Ibn al-Qayyim and Muhammad Idris al-Shafi'i and read the published portions of Sayyid Qutb's work in progress, *In the Shade of the Qur'an*.[7] Taking their ethical responsibilities seriously, they dispensed material support to the families of imprisoned Muslim Brothers.[8]

They also discussed possible courses of action. Contrary to the directive of Hudaybi, 'Abd al-Fattah Isma'il and several other members of the organization talked about forming a commando to overthrow the regime. Specifically, they considered hurling an explosive device at 'Abd al-Nasser's motorcade as it passed in the street. Al-'Ashmawi and 'Abd al-Majid demurred, however. They reminded their colleagues that 'Abd al-Nasser's motorcade was usually armoured. Moreover, it would be almost impossible to get close enough to the vehicles to throw a bomb accurately. After considering these points, the militants in the group decided to put their plans on hold until they could work out the details.[9]

On occasion, Muhammad Qutb would attend the organization's Cairo meetings.[10] With his published books, *Doubts about Islam* (*Shubuhat Hawl al-Islam*, 1954), *The Jahiliyya of the Twentieth Century* (*Jahiliyyat al-Qarn al-'Ishrin*, 1964), Muhammad was already a recognized Islamist thinker in his own right. In the early 1970s, his reputation would gain him a distinguished position as a teacher of Islamic Studies in Saudi Arabia. Yet, despite their hard deliberations and Muhammad Qutb's help, the organization's leading members floundered in their attempts to conceive concretely the path before them. It was obvious that they needed expert advice.

Supreme Guide Hasan al-Hudaybi, released from house arrest in 1961, was an obvious contender for this role. Yet, although he had approved of the organization, he did not step forward to lead it. Another possibility was 'Abd al-'Aziz 'Ali. He was a strong supporter of the Islamist cause, and his participation in the 1919 Uprising had also gained him expert knowledge of the workings of secret cells. Moreover, he had the endorsement of Hudaybi. Yet, despite these credentials, most in the organization did not feel comfortable with 'Abd al-'Aziz 'Ali. They did not like his autocratic style and suspected that he would abandon the organization should the state authorities press him. The members of the fledgling organization were therefore compelled to consider the only other viable candidate, Sayyid Qutb. Qutb was still in jail. However, through his sisters and Zaynab al-Ghazali who visited him regularly, he would be able to provide them with the practical advice and spiritual direction that they sought. Qutb received the organization's invitation through his sister Hamida. Much to the delight of the members, he consented. However, he told them that he wanted to keep his relationship with them low key. Given his precarious position as a prisoner, he did not want his name bandied about. He urged them to read the works of Abu 'Ala Mawdudi and Abu l-A'la Mawdudi, the Indian scholars who had so impressed him, until he was able to meet them face to face.[11]

In 1962 Hamida and Amina Qutb presented Zaynab al-Ghazali with pages of a new manuscript that their brother Sayyid was writing; the sisters told al-Ghazali that he "did not mind" if they circulated this work-in-progress among the organization's members.[12] Quite obviously, Qutb meant the draft to guide the incipient organization in its deliberations, believing it had the potential to jell into the vanguard that he had conceived.[13] Al-Ghazali dutifully distributed the pages. When the members finished reading what they received, Qutb's sisters brought additional pages, until the organization had read all of what Qutb called *Ma'alim fi al-Tariq* (*Milestones*). We have already made note of this important work. It is Qutb's seminal treatise and it provides a concise summary of his mature Islamist thought. In fact, its diagnostic élan and call to action bear comparison with Lenin's tract *What is to be Done?* Qutb derived much of *Milestones* from his Qur'an commentary, including sections that the censorship committee at the Tura prison had formally excluded. He took four of its thirteen chapters directly from the commentary, and then modified them slightly "to suit the topic".[14] Its ringing lines continue to inspire Muslim activists the world over. The opening lines of the work speak of the despair of the current age. The world has lost its moral bearings, to the extent that nuclear war threatens to obliterate the peoples of the earth. Islam stands as the salvation not only of Muslims, but also of humanity as a whole.

Mankind today is on the brink of a precipice, not because of the danger of complete annihilation which is hanging over its head—this being just a symptom and not the real disease—but because humanity is devoid of those vital values for its healthy development and real progress. Even Western scholars realize that their civilization is unable to present healthy values for the guidance of mankind and does not possess anything to satisfy its own conscience.[15]

Qutb spelled out his scheme for the world's salvation: to reconnect the human being to his or her place in the natural order through the efforts of a vanguard of true Muslims that will set out "with determination" to confront "the vast ocean of al-jahiliyya which encompasses the entire world" and then "keep going".[16] Qutb writes:

Our foremost objective is to change the practices of this society. Our aim is to change the jahili system at its very roots—this system which is fundamentally at variance with Islam and which, with the help of force and oppression, is keeping us from living the sort of life demanded by our creator.[17]

According to Qutb, the vanguard should spend long years of spiritual preparation before setting out to "smash the walls that stood between man and the truth".[18] Motivated by the belief that there is "no god but God", its members must preach the true understanding of Islam to others and build up the strength of the umma. In so doing, they must keep aloof from the corrupting influences of the jahili society and become independent of and distinct from it.[19] They must also adopt an attitude of diligence and patience. The Prophet Muhammad and the early Muslims prepared the ground at Mecca before challenging the established political and cultural order there. The vanguard of the current period should do the same. Qutb is explicit about Islam's right to rule:

Indeed, Islam has the right to take the initiative. Islam is not a heritage of any particular race or country. This is Allah's din [religion] and it is for the whole world. It has the right to destroy all the obstacles in the form of institutions and traditions that restrict man's freedom of choice. It does not attack individuals nor does it force them to accept its beliefs. It attacks institutions and traditions in order to release human beings from their pernicious influence, which distorts human nature and curtails human freedom.[20]

There is no doubt that *Milestones* advocates complete and uncompromising system change. Years later, Zaynab al-Ghazali had this to say about *Milestones'* sharply worded condemnation of the "usurpers" of God's sovereignty: "Read the *Ma'alim* to find out why Sayyid [Qutb] was executed!"[21]

Hudaybi saw the chapters as Hamida and Amina made them available. Although well aware of its radical and potentially incriminating revolutionary overtones, he was impressed with the work's vigorous defence of Islam and so gave it his blessing.[22] Satisfied that the chapters had the imprimatur of the Supreme Guide, the sisters passed them on to the publisher Hagg Wahba who published *Milestones* in January 1964. As it hit the bookstalls, *Milestones* attracted the notice of the state authorities. By this time, Egypt's media were in the process of coming under state control; already, in 1957, the government had entrusted the venerable daily *al-Ahram* to Muhammad Hasanayn Haykal, 'Abd al-Nasser's close friend and confidant. Then, in May 1960, as a prelude to the nationalization of extensive sectors of the economy, the government gave over publishing houses and the remaining newspapers to the National Union.[23] Thereafter, inspectors were on the lookout for books that were critical of 'Abd al-Nasser's government. Yet it took six months for the regime to ban the book. In the meantime, *Milestones* went through five reprints.[24]

Meanwhile, the organization continued its preparations. In 1961 or 1962, prior to Qutb's agreement to advise its members, 'Ali 'Ashmawi travelled to Saudi Arabia. Officially, his purpose was to perform the Hajj. However, he also wanted to open channels of communication between the organization and those Muslim Brothers who had settled in the Saudi Kingdom following the 1954 crackdown. Among the latter were Mana' al-Qatta', perhaps the first Egyptian Brother to recruit Saudi nationals to the Muslim Brotherhood, and Muyhi al-Hilal who had avoided capture by Egyptian authorities in 1954 by escaping to Libya before relocating to Saudi Arabia. Early in the trip, Muyhi al-Hilal arranged for 'Ashmawi to meet a number of Saudi–based Muslim Brothers at Jedda. Normally the Saudi authorities did not allow pilgrims to leave the pilgrimage route. Therefore, in order to avoid notice, 'Ashmawi dressed in a Saudi style robe (*thawb*) and headdress (*shmagh*).

At the Jedda meeting, Muyhi al-Hilal offered to provide the organization with funds to purchase arms; 'Ashmawi specified that the organization needed assault weapons, sniper rifles, grenades and explosives, "enough for a thousand-man force". The Brothers then arranged for Mustafa al-'Alam to purchase the weapons in southern Sudan before smuggling them into Egypt. Al-'Alam was experienced in such matters. He had procured large amounts of weapons during the Palestine War of 1948–49 and the Suez insurgency of 1951 for the Muslim Brother volunteers. During his visit to Saudi Arabia, 'Ashmawi took care to avoid unnecessary contacts. 'Abd al-Nasser's spies circulated freely among the pilgrims, especially the Egyptians, watching carefully for signs of anti–regime activity.[25]

'Properly equipped forces of goodness'

Over this period, Qutb continued to educate inmates at Tura prison in the "correct" understanding of Islam. The detainees now included Muslim Brothers from other prisons. The authorities had temporarily transferred these to Tura for medical treatment. Many came from al-Qanatir prison, located northwest of Cairo near the barrage across the Nile, others from the Wahat prison camp in the Western Desert where prominent members of the Brotherhood's Guidance Council were interned. The guards at these prisons had brutalized many of them, as they had the Brothers at Tura. Consequently, the arrivals carried with them into the infirmary wounds that were both physical and mental.[26]

Qutb would meet the newcomers in the exercise yard, or else in the infirmary, and engage them in discussion. He understood that the pervasiveness of the *jahili* culture made it difficult for even dedicated Muslim Brothers, such as these, to possess accurate knowledge of the faith. Therefore, he was gentle in correcting what he took as their misunderstanding of doctrine. He lent books to those who were enthusiastic and encouraged them to pass on what they had learned to others after they returned to the Qanatir and Wahat prisons. Helping him in this missionary endeavour was his close friend Yusuf al-Hawwash. Qutb estimated that "perhaps twenty-five" of these visiting brothers gained "an unambiguous understanding of the Islamic creed and its correct application". Already, he had begun to build up the new cadre of activist Muslims that he was writing about in *Milestones*. One man at a time, he was strengthening the "*umma* of believers".[27]

The Brothers back at Qanatir caught wind of Qutb's activities. Some of them, especially the older guard, were suspicious about his teachings. Chief among the critics was a contingent headed by Amin Sidqi and 'Abd al-Rahman al-Banna, Hasan al-Banna's younger brother. In their cells, they chastised Qutb for not deferring to the movement's established leadership. In their view, Qutb's habit of cultivating "young talent" at Tura undercut the authority of Hudaybi who alone was qualified to proffer spiritual guidance and practical advice. Equally if not more noxious, in their view, was Qutb's explicit condemnation of Muslim society as *jahili*. To them, it smacked of the long-discredited practice of excommunicating professed Muslims from the faith (*takfir*, literally, declaring a person a *kafir* or "disbeliever").

In their accusations, Qutb's critics upheld the established Sunni theological stance, which taught that only God knew the content of men's hearts. According to this majority position, failures in practice, whether they were crimes or omissions of worship, did not exclude a person from the community of believers. What mattered was that the person must confess the creed. Qutb, they said, had no right to pass judgment on the faith of fellow Muslims and declare them to be in a state of disbelief. In expressing this view, the critics drew upon arguments put forward by Sunni theologians during the first centuries of Islam, which carefully set the criteria for distinguishing *iman* ("faith") from *kufr* ("disbelief"). The theologian Abu Hamid al-Ghazali (d. 1111), for example, wrote a book that condemned the indiscriminate application of *takfir*.[28]

When word of these accusations reached Qutb, he forcefully denied them. He clarified his position to the prominent Muslim Brothers 'Umar al-Tilmisani and 'Abd al-Aziz 'Atiyya, close advisers of Hudaybi who were at Tura for medical treatment. He told them he did not excommunicate people but rather condemned the general ignorance of Islam that was a feature of the age. Al-Tilmisani (who in 1973 would become the third Supreme Guide of the Muslim Brotherhood) and 'Atiyya accepted Qutb's explanation, and passed it on to their colleagues in the Guidance Council at Wahat prison. After hearing Qutb's explanation, many of the critics withdrew their charges, but others did not. Already Qutb was becoming a source of division within Islamist ranks.[29] Differences of opinion regarding Qutb's ideas on faith and disbelief would continue among Muslim Brothers over the following years.

In 1964, shortly after he completed *Milestones*, Qutb suffered a heart attack. Severely weakened, his health rapidly deteriorated. He had already spent nine years in prison and had six more to go. It was clear to everyone that unless his circumstances changed, he would soon die.

It was at this point that Iraq's president, 'Abd al-Salam 'Arif, intervened on Qutb's behalf.[30] At first glance, 'Arif was an unlikely benefactor. One of the architects of the July 1958 coup d'état that toppled Iraq's Hashimite monarchy, he admired 'Abd al-Nasser and shared with him the dream of a unified Arab world able to stand up to the West. However, unlike the Egyptian president, 'Arif did not disparage the Islamist movement. In fact, he was sympathetic to its goal of moral rearmament, and was on good terms with the Society of Islamic Brotherhood (Jamiyat al-Ukhuwa al-Islamiyya), the Iraqi spin-off of the Muslim Brotherhood. But as a politician, he also understood the utility of cultivating an ally among the important Islamist sector of the Sunni middle class. These factors prompted 'Arif in 1963 to implement ordinances that enforced the stricter public observance of Islam.[31]

'Arif had learned of Qutb's dire condition from Shaykh Amjad al-Zahawi (1883–1967), the leader of the Society of Islamic Brotherhood,[32] and was immediately worried. Shortly after the 1958 Iraqi Free Officers' coup, 'Arif had been placed under house arrest by his co-conspirator 'Abd al-Karim Qasim who was loath to share power. During his incarceration, an edition of *In the Shade of the Qur'an* had consoled him. In taking up Qutb's case, the Iraqi president now wanted to repay his debt to the Egyptian writer.[33] At the same time, he sought to score points with Iraq's Islamist movement.

During a state visit he made to Egypt in May 1964, 'Arif petitioned 'Abd al-Nasser to release Qutb. The Egyptian regime complied with the request, citing as its official reason Qutb's ill-health. Yet, in all likelihood, humanitarian considerations were secondary to the regime's greater purpose of avoiding responsibility for what appeared as Qutb's impending death. 'Abd al-Nasser did not want to draw the ire of the many Muslims worldwide who sympathized with Qutb. On the other hand, the Egyptian president may also have believed that the ideologue's freedom would mollify the dissidence of "moderate" Muslim Brothers whose support he was eager to gain. It is a fact that Qutb's release took place at a time when 'Abd al-Nasser was attempting to co-opt the opposition to the regime.[34] However that may have been, Qutb's Islamist biographers suggest a darker motive. They say that the government set him free in order to "create the conditions for his re-arrest, trail, and final elimination."[35] There may be some merit in that charge.

Qutb walked out of Tura prison into the nurturing embrace of his sisters and brother. It must have been a heady, exhilarating moment. Iraq's Ambassador to Egypt immediately conveyed to him a congratulatory message from President 'Arif. Qutb responded with a telegram in which he thanked the Iraqi president for his intervention. In gratitude, he sent him, via Iraq's Cairo embassy, several of his books, "covered with the best bindings available."[36] Iraq's government-controlled newspapers noted Qutb's release.

Qutb was a free man, but changes in the urban landscape would have caught him off guard. There were now more cars on the road, and Cairo neighbourhoods such as Shubra al-Khayma, which were mostly farmland when he went to prison, were now thickly populated.[37] Scattered around the city were architectural and cultural markers of revolutionary intent—in Qutb's mind, shrines to the *jahiliyya*. Impossible to miss was the new latticework Cairo Tower, looming above the residential island of Zamalek, at 187 metres taller than the Great Pyramid, which heralded the regime's overall goal of socialist development. Qutb, who had a weakness for the cinema, would have noted gaudily painted movie posters and billboards advertising the creative work of directors like Yusuf Shahin, films that highlighted social injustices but without reference to the curative balm of Islam.[38] The electrified Bab al-Luq train on which he used to travel to his office now passed heavy iron and steel works as it lumbered into Hulwan station. Qutb could appreciate the necessity of industrial ventures such as this. He would also have understood the need for the regime's showcase project, the giant Aswan Dam, which promised hydroelectricity and increased cropland, and whose first stage was already complete. However, it must have galled him that the directing hand behind these developments was a new Pharaoh, a "transgressor of limits"[39] whose arrogance and cruelty knew no bounds. Not far from Qutb's Hulwan home stood a training camp of the Arab Socialist Union's Youth Organization. As if to mock Qutb, the camp disseminated a steady stream of "*jahili*" regime propaganda right under the noses of his family.[40]

Qutb also had to deal with the psychological consequences of incarceration. After years in prison, he felt like a "blind man".[41] He had to integrate into old and new social networks and rediscover the simple freedoms of everyday life.[42] Yet rather than settle down into a routine of normalcy, as many released Muslim Brothers did, he saw his freedom as an opportunity to continue the *da'wa*. When Iraq's Minister of Education offered him a job in Baghdad as a consultant for the Ministry, he politely declined the offer, stating that his natural place was in Egypt where he had many things yet to accomplish. Beneath his tired and broken visage, he remained a man on fire.

Qutb's reputation in international Islamist circles was now higher than it had ever been. In part, this was because of the speedy and wide-ranging dissemination of his writings. Already the House of Sa'ud and its Wahhabi clerical backers were interested in sponsoring the Brotherhood's ideology to counter the secular pan-Arabism of Egypt's president. To this end Saudi radio broadcast "on a regular basis" segments of *In the Shade of the Qur'an*. Islamists of various kinds were reading his works in Syria, Iraq, Algeria, India and Pakistan. Qutb began to receive modest royalties from his publications.[43] This money was a boon to a man who was essentially in the financial care of his family.

He entertained a steady stream of well-wishers at his family's Hulwan house. His brother Muhammad was often on hand at these meetings. The salon resembled a small court. As the visitor entered and made his way across the room toward Qutb, Muhammad or one of Qutb's nephews would whisper the name in his ear.[44] Qutb's growing reputation inspired in these guests a degree of obeisance. Many were Muslim Brothers from branches of the movement around the Arab world. Egyptians, or individuals influenced by the Egyptian Brothers, had founded these offshoots in the 1940s and 1950s. Already in 1945, Hasan al-Banna's close associate Sa'id Ramadan had opened the first Brotherhood office in Palestine. In Syria the Muslim Brotherhood had been active since 1944 under the leadership of Mustafa Siba'i.[45] Members of these and other branches looked to the Egyptian parent organization with reverence and sought the guidance of its thinkers, especially, now, Sayyid Qutb.

The questions related mostly to their organizations' troubled dealings with the nationalist dictators and ruling coalitions that had taken power all over the Middle East in the late 1950s and early 1960s. Many of these rulers were inspired by 'Abd al-Nasser or held to the similar nationalist ideology of Ba'thism, as in the case of Syria. Qutb, however, was cautious in proffering advice to the foreign Brothers. He was painfully aware that because of his long incarceration, he did not fully understand the political contexts in which these Brothers from abroad operated. Moreover, given his dismal view of Islam's position in the world ("the modern *jahiliyya*"), he was sceptical of any conventional, political attempt to assert Islam's profile within the context of the nation-state. Qutb's account of these encounters provides a snapshot of Islamism as it stood in the early 1960s, capturing the moment when Qutb's radicalized thought began to take hold of Muslims' imagination around the world.

One unnamed visitor was a Muslim Brother from Syria who relayed greetings from Issam al-'Attar, the leader of the Syrian branch. The visitor told Qutb that the Brotherhood in Syria was severely pressured by the Ba'thist regime, which had assumed power in Damascus in March 1963.[46] A month earlier Islamists and their sympathizers had risen up against the regime in the city of Hama, a Muslim Brother stronghold, following the fatal shooting of a student protester. Qutb records only the barest bones of the conversation. No doubt he was aware of the terrible retribution that the Ba'thist government had visited upon the city, retaliatory actions that included the shelling of the city's venerable Sultan mosque.[47] Clearly, in the view of the Brother, Islam in Syria confronted its conceptual opposite. How should Syria's Islamic movement respond to the challenge?

An Islamist from Jordan sought Qutb's counsel on the troubled relations between Jordan's Muslim Brotherhood and the Palestine Liberation Organization (PLO), which the Cairo-based Arab League had just created that year (1964) under the leadership of Ahmad Shuqairi. According to the visitor, the Jordanian Brotherhood was willing to cooperate with the secular-minded PLO, but Shuqairi did not allow Brotherhood members to participate in the PLO's Executive Council. As a result, the Muslim Brotherhood did not have the opportunity to contribute politically to the liberation struggle against Zionism. What course of action should the Brotherhood adopt in the face of this rebuff?[48]

Qutb advised both of these activists to refrain from playing the "political game". He explained that although the *taghut* ("idolatrous" tyranny) threatened their organizations, politics were futile in contexts in which governments did not know morality and were intent on the destruction of political opponents. He therefore encouraged them to focus on the religious and cultural mission (*da'wa*) and eschew electoral and other types of politics altogether. The Islamic movement must capture hearts and minds before it is able to establish itself in power. Regardless of local contexts, slow preparation at the grassroots must be the common strategy of true Muslims around the world.

Zaynab al-Ghazali put Qutb in touch with the Algerian representative on the Council of Muslim 'Ulama whose meeting took place in Cairo in 1965. During Qutb's imprisonment, Arab and Berber Algerians had waged an unrelenting war of independence against the French colonial establishment. For many Algerian revolutionaries, Islam and Arabism were cut from the same cloth, one indistinguishable from the other. It was a situation different from the Arab East where circumstances had ensured the secular orientation of Arab nationalism. Now, said the Algerian, "communist elements" within the National Liberation Front (FLN) leadership were threatening to undermine the revolution's Islamic foundations. Would Sayyid Qutb write a précis on the topic of Islamic social justice in order to subvert the secular leftist tendencies afoot in the country? It was important, he said, for Algerians to understand that principles of a just, modern society lay within their native Islam. However, the delegate continued, he would have to translate the précis into French; because of decades of French-colonial acculturation, most educated Algerians never had the opportunity to become proficient in literary Arabic.[49] The Algerian delegate left Cairo before he and Qutb could finalize plans for the précis and translation. Yet his interest in Qutb marks the Egyptian's emergence as the ideologue of choice among many Algerian Islamists, to the degree that Qutb supplanted in popularity even the native son Malek Bennabi (1905–73) by the 1980s.

Letters from the Indian Subcontinent arrived in Qutb's mailbox. One was from the secretary of the reform-inclined Indian *madrasa* Nadwat al-Ulama—the organization to which Abu al-Hasan 'Ali Nadwi belonged. The secretary suggested that Qutb and the scholars of the Nadwa exchange ideas about the methods by which to defend Islam from adversaries. He said that Islam's worldly success depended on Muslims uniting around a common vision.[50]

In January 1965, Qutb finally got in touch the core group of Islamists who had been meeting on and off at Zaynab al-Ghazali's flat and elsewhere. Earlier, while Qutb was in prison, these men had asked him to be their mentor and he had consented. The first meeting was with 'Abd al-Fattah Isma'il and 'Ali 'Ashmawi and took place at Qutb's Hulwan house. Soon, Qutb had met all five leading members of the organization.[51]

At these meetings, the men told Qutb that they were thinking about launching an attack against the regime to avenge the disastrous events of 1954. In fact, about two hundred would-be *fida'iyyun* were already training in Cairo, in al-Daqhaliyya and al-Sharqiyya provinces, and elsewhere precisely for this purpose.[52] They related how sympathizers in Saudi Arabia were funding their efforts. In fact, 'Abd al-Fattah Isma'il had already received from these sources about a thousand Egyptian pounds.[53] With this money, they had purchased weapons and were now learning how to make primitive bombs.[54]

The dedication of these young men impressed Qutb. In particular, 'Abd al-Fattah Isma'il struck him as capable. However, he understood that left to their own devices they would lead the remnants of the Islamic movement to disaster. Although they were ardent, the Egyptian state was simply too powerful. In his gloss of Qur'an 4:95, dealing with *jihad*, Qutb had written about the dangers of precipitate action: "The forces of falsehood, in their great numbers and heavy armament, must be countered with the properly equipped forces of goodness. Otherwise, it would be a suicidal situation or one that is lacking in seriousness. Either attitude is unbecoming of believers."[55]

Qutb warned them that hasty action would bring down the wrath of the government on their heads. Weakened and fragmented, the Islamic movement could not survive another hammer blow. Rather than prepare for a coup d'état, the organization should focus its energy in building up a spiritually enlightened cadre that could disseminate the Islamic message at the grassroots. "Our first objective should not be to establish an Islamic order (*al-nizam al-Islami*) or to implement the Shari'a. Rather, our primary task is to bring the society in its entirety, both rulers and the ruled, to a closer understanding of true Islamic principles." Effective regeneration could only issue from purified hearts, not the emotion of revenge. Only when the organization had strengthened and prepared society in the Islamic mode should it take concrete steps to replace the secular government with an Islamic one, forcefully if need be.[56]

Qutb worked to temper his followers' enthusiasm by expanding their understanding of the "Islamic method" (*minhaj*). He set about educating them about the meaning of the divine *hakimiyya* and the correct way of dealing with non-Muslim societies and powers. He met the chief members of the organization regularly, "sometimes once a week, other times once every two weeks," and led them in discussions about the political and cultural contexts in which they operated. He encouraged them to read newspapers and keep up with current events. He reviewed the history of the Muslim Brotherhood, including the reasons for the ordeals that befell the Brothers in 1948, 1954 and 1957.[57] In asking the men to think hard about the consequences of staging an attack, Qutb introduced an element of pragmatic political calculation into his assessment of violence.

Qutb overawed his young charges with his moral and intellectual prowess, especially his command of the sacred texts. "None of us could argue with him because of his great knowledge. He would quote the Qur'an and the *hadith* to prove his points", one of them said.[58] Qutb, who as a child had memorized the Qur'an and as a young man had explored its literary genius, who over the decade of his imprisonment lived incessantly in the comforting "shade of the holy book", did indeed know scripture. From his disciples' perspective, his calm and deliberate manner reflected his deep understanding of the divine message he preached.

Yet Qutb did not take military training off the table completely. In what would prove to be the most controversial aspect of his rebuilding programme, he told his followers that they could use force legitimately "to repel aggression if it occurs".[59] In other words, Qutb allowed them to deal immediate defensive, preventative and retaliatory blows against the government if it moved to crush the organization. Although Qutb cautioned against taking revenge for past wrongs, he was also determined that the Islamic movement should never again succumb to the kind of savage suppression it had earlier experienced. As he said, "Attacks had taken place during which we were arrested, tortured, severely humiliated, and stripped of our dignity. Our homes were destroyed and our families thrown into the streets."[60]

In order to defend the organization from possible attack, Qutb allowed the paramilitary training to continue. This mostly involved weapons handling and sports, which, we may suppose, included vigorous games of football. However, he insisted that only individuals "who had a mature level of awareness" should have access to the weapons. By the estimate of his close associates, there were about seventy who qualified in this regard.[61]

At the same time, Qutb joined the organization's five leaders in drafting a provisional plan that they would implement in the event of an attack by the state. Taking inspiration from the Qur'anic principle,

"Then whoever transgresses the prohibition against you, you transgress likewise against him" (Qur'an 2:194), they discussed the possibility of going for the state's jugular vein: assassinating 'Abd al-Nasser, Prime Minister 'Ali Sabri, and the directors of the General Intelligence (*Mabahith 'Amma*) and military security services (*Mukhabarat 'Askariyya*). The organization floated various scenarios: rake the president's motorcade with machinegun fire, blow up the train carrying his party from Cairo to Alexandria, or dynamite the grandstand from which he addressed a political rally in Alexandria. They also talked about destroying the Nile Barrage, the bridges that spanned the Nile at Cairo and the electricity generating station at Alexandria.[62] These attacks, they reckoned, would sow confusion and hinder the efforts of the security forces to search out and destroy the organization, thus allowing its members to escape and regroup. The attacks would also send a message to the regime that any effort to destroy it would come at a high price.[63]

However, on second thoughts, Qutb and his colleagues decided to shelve plans for the destruction of infrastructure. They might go ahead with assassinations, but the destruction of bridges and the barrage, they came to understand, would impose hardships on the innocent people of the city and its environs. Moreover, such attacks would weaken Egypt's economy and play to the advantage of Israel, the implacable enemy of the Muslims. However, it was clear to all in the organization that they had little chance of putting even their modified plan into effect. The concern that 'Ali 'Ashmawi had earlier expressed regarding militant action remained true: 'Abd al-Nasser and his ministers were too well protected and the organization too ill-prepared to undertake any kind of serious counterstrike against the regime. In the face of this lack of readiness, Qutb asked the organization to step up the pace of the paramilitary training.

Qutb admitted that the plan, though ill defined, was violent and harsh. Yet, he added, if anyone should criticize the plan's severity, he might compare it with the indiscriminate methods 'Abd al-Nasser employed against his Muslim opponents, including their families. Unlike the *taghut*, the organization only targeted select leaders, and in ways that upheld Qur'anic dictates. "Islam forbids Muslims from torturing and humiliating its enemies. It also forbids rendering women and children homeless, unable to provide for themselves."[64] He had explained in his commentary of *sura* 9, al-Tawba ("The Repentance"), which deals with issues of war and peace:

Reports are numerous which make clear the general method Islam adopts in fighting its enemies, as well as its commitment to a high standard of ethics in war, giving high respect to human dignity. Fighting is targeted only against real forces which prevent people's liberation from subjugation by other creatures, so that they submit to God alone.[65]

Qutb and his colleagues may have conceived their plans as a purely defensive action, yet it appears that they were ready to take advantage of a possible assault on their organization to seize power, taking advantage of circumstances to establish the beginnings of an Islamic order. Qutb was sincere in his derision of the Bolshevik tactic of the surgical strike. Yet, in the event of all-out defensive war, he was willing to consider the possibility of overthrowing the government sooner rather than later.

A complicating factor arose when the weapons that 'Ali 'Ashmawi had ordered three years earlier were set to be delivered. Qutb had only learned about the shipment after he joined the organization. Shipped via Sudan, the weapons were due to arrive shortly at a small town called Draw near Aswan in the south of Egypt. In order to ward off suspicion, the Muslim Brothers had packed them amid boxes stuffed with dates. From there, Muslim Brothers would transport the weapons to Cairo.

On the one hand, the weapons would give the organization a more realistic chance to implement its plan, should it become necessary. On the other hand; their existence raised the stakes in the game. No longer was the plan theoretical; numerous weapons were on their way, and they threatened to turn the organization into a runaway train. Qutb pondered. Would the ordinary members of the organization use them irresponsibly? What would happen if the authorities caught wind of the shipment? Qutb consulted 'Ali 'Ashmawi and others about the possibility of cancelling the weapons shipment. When the leaders replied that they could not halt the shipment, he suggested that they reroute the arms across the remote desert tracks of Libya in order to decrease the chance of interception. He said that he knew two Libyan Muslim Brothers who had good connections with truck drivers who plied the route; the drivers would be willing to help.[66]

Qutb had good reason to be concerned. In advance of the Soviet Communist Party chief Nikita Khrushchev's 1964 visit to Egypt, 'Abd al-Nasser had released most of Egypt's Communists from captivity. Seeking to win their support for his social policies, he encouraged the

Communists, men like Lutfi al-Khuli, to join his newly created Vanguard Organization, the core structure in the Arab Socialist Union.[67] Qutb believed, probably correctly, that the leftists had their ears to the ground and were intent on blowing the whistle on the Muslim Brothers' organization, both to curry favour with the regime and to satisfy an old grudge. Despite the brief honeymoon between the Communists and the Muslim Brothers at the time of the Muhammad Neguib imbroglio, the leftists bore ill feeling towards the Islamists. They regarded the Muslim Brotherhood as ideologically reactionary, accusing it of being the willing accomplice of the Palace during the Old Regime.[68]

Over the period of his freedom, Qutb was careful to recognize Hudaybi as the true guide of the Muslim Brotherhood.[69] He was sincere in doing so. He had always been a loyal supporter of Hudaybi and had defended him against challengers among the Muslim Brothers in the early 1950s. As far as Qutb was concerned, the pre-proscription leadership structure remained frozen in place, even while the regime made it difficult for Hudaybi to exercise his executive prerogatives in practice.

Yet, in face of Hudaybi's relative political impotence, Qutb had no choice but to make important decisions regarding the secret organization on his own. In order to ensure the continuing operation of the organization, he chose Yusuf Hawwash, his former prison companion, to succeed him in the role of spiritual adviser to the organization should he die or be killed.

'The red snake'

In early June 1965, Qutb traveled with his family to the Mediterranean seaside resort of Ra's al-Barr near Dumyat in the eastern Delta. Founded in the 1860s, Ra's al-Barr had originally attracted Cairo's well-heeled classes, but by the post-World War II era the town had became affordable, thus attracting increasing numbers of the petite bourgeoisie.[70] Qutb stayed in a chalet near the beach and settled in for a few weeks of restful vacation. The resort's famous sea breezes provided him with relief from the burgeoning summer heat of Cairo. He was anxious to put the business of the organization out of his mind, if only for a little while. His last meeting with the organization's members had been in May, some weeks before his departure for the Mediterranean.

Nevertheless, he had a nagging concern that something big was about to happen. In July, he summoned 'Abd al-Fattah Isma'il and 'Ali 'Ashmawi to meet him at the resort. 'Ashmawi had taken time off from his job at a construction company in order to celebrate his marriage; days earlier he had married the younger sister of a fellow organization member, Ahmad 'Abd al-Majid. To spur him on to come, Qutb suggested to 'Ashmawi that he bring his bride so that they might enjoy the summer beach life. Over lunch at a seaside restaurant, the three men discussed the business of the organization. Qutb said that he was uneasy; he was receiving reports that the authorities had obtained some information about the organization, although he did not yet know particulars.[71] 'Ashmawi took heed of the warning. A couple of days later, he and his bride returned to Cairo.

Qutb and 'Abd al-Fattah Isma'il remained at Ra's al-Barr. Qutb then had a troubling dream. He recounted to a visiting journalist named Mahmud al-Rakabi that in the dream, a red snake had wrapped itself around his body. It was an unnerving vision that left him puzzled and prevented him from sleeping soundly over the next few nights. In order to soothe Qutb, al-Rakabi suggested that snake represented the red ribbon on a gift that "one of the believers" would soon bestow upon Qutb. However, Qutb had his own interpretation. "Why can't it be that I am the gift presented to the believers?" Al-Rakabi protested, "Isn't the existence of the righteous more beneficial to the Islamic da'wa?" Qutb replied, "Not always. In fact, sometimes the departure of the righteous is more beneficial." He continued, "I do not intend to hasten my own end, but we must be firm in our stance, knowing that this firmness can hasten destruction."[72]

Qutb was already thinking about martyrdom. He knew that his association with the organization was risky business. One day soon the authorities would accumulate more intelligence and uncover its members. They would take him and the others away for trial and execution. Already he had deliberated on the meaning of martyrdom in his prison writings. The final chapter of *Milestones* examines Qur'an 85:1–9, which relates the paradigmatic story of the Companions of the Pit. These were believers who, in Qutb's words "encountered tyrannical and oppressive enemies who were bent upon denying the right of a human being to believe in the All-Mighty, the All-Praiseworthy Allah." According to Qutb, the tyrants "intended to deprive man of the dignity that has been bestowed upon him by Allah and without which he is reduced to a mere plaything in the hands of tyrants...." The verse in the Qur'an reads:

By the heaven, holding the big stars

And by the Promised Day (i.e. the Day of Resurrection);

And by the witnessing day (i.e. Friday),

And by the witnessed day [i.e. the day of 'Arafât (*Hajj*) the ninth of Dhul-Hîjjah]; Cursed were the people of the ditch (the story of the Boy and the King)

Fire supplied (abundantly) with fuel,

When they sat by it (fire),

And they witnessed what they were doing against the believers (i.e. burning them).

They had nothing against them, except that they believed in Allâh, the All-Mighty, Worthy of all Praise!

Who, to Whom belongs the dominion of the heavens and the earth! And Allâh is Witness over everything.

Qutb highlighted the verse's central message: that believers must prepare for fortitude and persecution, "whatever comes their way, as yet unknown to them."[73] Although tyrants may attain earthly gain, their victory is hollow and fleeting. Rather, the steadfastness of believers signals the real and enduring triumph of human nobility. Whereas God will chastise the "criminals and tyrants", perhaps in this world, certainly in the Hereafter, to the martyrs he has promised everlasting life. The martyrs go directly to the Garden and are not questioned or punished. In confirmation of the reward given the martyrs, Qutb quoted Qur'an 3:169–70, a verse that has molded Muslim understanding of martyrdom's rewards:

Think not of those who are killed in the Way of Allâh as dead. Nay, they are alive, with their Lord, and they have provision. They rejoice in what Allâh has bestowed upon them of His Bounty, rejoicing for the sake of those who have not yet joined them, but are left behind (not yet martyred) that on them no fear shall come, nor shall they grieve.

Qutb explained, "These martyrs are indeed alive, having all the essential qualities of life. They 'receive' their needs from their Lord, are happy with the grace God bestows on them, rejoice at the happy news of what is to befall their brethren whom they left behind, and they witness the events of the Muslim community."[74]

Qutb understood that, for him, the game was almost up. However, strengthened by the Qur'an's assurance of the martyr's reward, he soldiered on. He had long understood that the regime's worldly power was a façade without substance. What was real was the truth for which he was willing, even eager to sacrifice himself. His death would be a gift to humankind. He would become a living embodiment of the faith that was the salvation of humanity, and which was under attack by its enemies.[75]

The reckoning unfolded sooner than Qutb had anticipated. On 29 July, word came to Qutb that his brother Muhammad had been arrested without charge. He was expecting some kind of government action against the "true Muslims", but he did not expect that Muhammad would be a target. After all, his brother was not a member of the organization; in fact, he had never been a member of the Muslim Brotherhood.[76] There was only one explanation: the 'Abd al-Nasser regime was probing. Qutb put it this way: "The forces [of the state] feel the presence of the organization, but they lack meaningful information about it. So they strike, hoping to find a thread that will lead them to the organization."[77] Soon afterwards, the police arrested Muslim Brothers who had nothing to do with the organization at a village called Sanfa, confirming that the arrests were random.

Afraid of what might happen next, 'Ali 'Ashmawi dipped into organization funds, giving one member, Jabr Rizq, 500 Egyptian pounds to rent flats to use as safe houses in case the intelligence services uncovered the organization. He ordered organization members to contact their local leaders on a daily basis. Those who failed to report he would consider arrested. Members stepped up their training. They made petrol bombs and prepared their weapons.[78]

Two days after Muhammad's arrest, Qutb learned that police had searched his house in Hulwan while he was away. Then they showed up at his Ra's al-Barr chalet. The police had a brief look around and then left. Feeling the heat, Qutb cautioned 'Abd al-Fattah Isma'il to leave the beach resort as quickly as possible. On 2 August, Qutb rushed back to Cairo to find out precisely what had happened to his brother. He did not know it, but Muhammad was, in fact, in gaol at Marsa Matruh, a town on the Mediterranean coast to the west of Alexandria.[79] Taking care to avoid contact with the police, he asked one of his nephews to deliver a handwritten note to Ahmad Rasikh, the officer in charge of the investigation. In the letter, he complained about the arrest and the searches. The Egyptian regime should be ashamed,he said: even the British had the decency to reveal the location of Bertrand Russell following the philosopher's arrest in 1961 for his ban-the-bomb agitation. Qutb then arranged for his sister, Hamida, to contact 'Ali 'Ashmawi and tell him to cancel "at all costs" both the weapons shipment and the plans for any kind of retaliatory assault.[80] Qutb knew that the authorities would soon investigate everyone associated with the organization, and he did not want potentially incriminating evidence to surface. 'Ashmawi carried out Qutb's orders. Scurrying about the city, sometimes "in disguise", Qutb stopped by the bookshop of Hagg Wahba, his publisher, to bid him farewell before returning to Ra's al-Barr.[81] Qutb knew that the noose around him was tightening.

On 6 August, he returned to Ra's al-Barr and braced himself for the coming storm. He did not have long to wait. Just before dawn on 9 August, the authorities appeared at his chalet door. They took him to Cairo and interned him in the military prison. Once again, Qutb was compelled to breathe the dank, fetid air of a gaol cell. His newly found freedom had lasted less than a year.

With the Qutb brothers out of the way, the regime set about to uncover the organization's rank and file. Under interrogation, suspected Muslim Brothers and sympathizers began to divulge names. Learning that 'Abd al-Fattah Isma'il, 'Ali 'Ashmawi and another Brother named Mubarak 'Abd al-'Azim were preparing to visit an organization member at his flat in the Cairo suburb of Imbaba, the security services planned a sting operation in the early morning hours of 20 August. As the Islamists entered the flat, plain-clothed police appeared suddenly from behind the furniture with guns drawn. The captors took the three Muslim Brothers to the military prison. There a terrible scene awaited them: faces pressed against walls, shouts from distant rooms, young men splayed on the floors. One Brother, Muhammad 'Awwad, died after interrogators repeatedly smashed his head against a wall.

Soon enough, interrogators subjected the twenty-one–year-old 'Ali 'Ashmawi to harsh treatment. As 'Ashmawi recounted, they tied his hands and feet and suspended him from an iron bar, beating the soles of his feet. The torture continued for hours. "Rambling and hallucinating," he revealed the existence and whereabouts of those weapons already in the possession of the organization.[82] However, other accounts, including that of 'Abd al-Fattah al-Khalidi, claim that he revealed everything he knew about the secret organization, going so far as to claim that Qutb had ordered the organization to overthrow the government—a claim that is dubious.[83] It is a fact that his detailed confession, which ran to eight pages, earned him the leniency of the regime. Yet, if he "spilled the beans", it is unlikely, given his record, that he wilfully betrayed his colleagues. Rather, he would have succumbed to the coercive techniques of his interrogators, revealing to them the "information" that they wanted out of fear, pain or both.

With more names in their possession, the authorities stepped up the pace of arrests, which now extended to ordinary Muslim Brothers and sympathizers. Thousands were detained and questioned all over the country.[84] In a manner reminiscent of the police attack on Musha that Qutb described in his autobiography, police invested the village of Kardasa on the western outskirts of Giza on 22 August. Gilles Kepel paints the picture: "The Muslim Brethren had had a base there since the forties, when training camps for militants had been established in the nearby desert." They were looking for a member of the organization named Sayyid Nazili, but could not find him. "[H]ouses were sacked, and the village notables and their families were stripped and flogged in the public square. Hundreds of the villagers were taken away and interrogated."[85] In Cairo 'Abd al-Fattah Isma'il, Hamida Qutb and Hasan al-Hudaybi were taken into custody. Yusuf Hawwash had been spending time at his father's farm in Gharbiyya province when the security services arrived. He asked the police to wait until he finished his prayers. Then, taking with him a Qur'an that his wife intended to present to their son, and had inscribed with the son's name, he accompanied the officers to their vehicle. As he got in, he promised to return the Qur'an to her, no matter what.[86]

The blind Shaykh 'Abd al-Hamid Kishk, the popular Azhari–trained preacher, was another who was taken into custody. His ringing sermons on the divine *hakimiyya*, delivered at Cairo's government-sponsored 'Ayn al-Hayat mosque, had earned him the regime's displeasure and now this was a chance to silence him. Following his release in the 1970s, Kishk became "a strong critic of modernist orthodoxy and the materialist public morality of many in the political and intellectual elite."[87] The authorities arrested twenty-three–year-old Shukri Mustafa, a student of agriculture at Asyut University, for distributing leaflets on campus supporting the Muslim Brotherhood. Shukri Mustafa also re-emerged in the mid-1970s, in his case as ringleader of the extreme Islamist Jama'at al-Muslimin. The arrests extended even to Egypt's former Crown Prince, Muhammad Rashad Mahna; the authorities feared that the Muslim Brothers might attempt to install him as Head of State should they seize the reins of power.[88] The authorities dispersed the many suspects to Egypt's archipelago of prisons. Zaynab al-Ghazali later wrote, "Al-Qal'ah, the military prison, as well as Za'bal Prison, al-Fayyum and Tanta prisons and others were filled with our Muslim Brothers."[89]

The detainees experienced a replay of the ordeal of the mid and late 1950s. Zaynab al-Ghazali, who was arrested towards the end of August, provides a harrowing account of the tortures endured by the prisoners at the Military Prison in her autobiography *al-Ayyam al-Hayati* (*Days from Life*; translated as *Return of the Pharaoh*):

Almost unable to believe my eyes and not wanting to accept such inhumanity, I silently watched as members of the Ikhwan were suspended in the air and their naked bodies ferociously flogged. Some were left to the mercy of savage dogs which tore at their bodies. Worse still, I knew many of these pious, believing youth personally. They were as dear to me as my own sons, and had attended study circles of *Tafsir* and *Hadith* in my home, in their own homes and at Ibn al-Arqam house.[90]

Soon, al-Ghazali experienced similar ill-treatment: whippings, weighted suspensions and immersions in water by gaolers who invoked the name of 'Abd al-Nasser "before speaking just as Muslims invoke God's name before performing any action." Yet, she tells us, throughout the torment she was able to protect her virtue. Her will remained unbroken and in the manner of the Muslim saints, she was able by means of prayer to transcend the horror. "Inwardly, I prayed; 'I seek refuge in Allah from the accursed Satan. O Allah! Bestow on me Your tranquility.'" In her book, she asks simply, "What immorality or what *Jahiliyya* could allow this kind of behavior?"[91] As Timothy Mitchell noted, "Zaynab al-Ghazali's description of prison life becomes a detailed diagnosis of the state's methods of control. Thus, such memoirs can themselves show how these methods actually participate in producing the political discourse of Islam....these forms of opposition were not something external to the system of power, but the product of techniques and tensions within it."[92]

It is not surprising that, given the trauma that they inflicted on so many, the gaolers of 'Abd al-Nasser's Egypt became notorious in the

view of Egypt's public, especially as the stories of their atrocities surfaced over the course of President Anwar Sadat's "Corrective Movement" in the mid-1970s when prisoners were released and allowed to
tell their tales. "Even a Nasser loyalist had to write in August 1981: 'In
the years to come, all the suffering endured by numerous members of
the Association of Muslim Brothers under torture, in military prisons,
will remain a black stain on the white robe of the Revolution.'"[93]

Writers immortalized some of the gaolers in literature. The Egyptian
author Gamal al-Ghitani (b. 1945) remembered how in the late 1960s
he, Naguib Mahfouz and a group of friends gathered at the café 'Urabi
in Cairo's 'Abbasiyya district when they saw an imposing man enter.
"His eyes were strange, seeming to be turned toward the outside."

When he entered a strange silence fell, and the waiter hastened to bring a
waterpipe, which he placed next to him, setting in front of him a chess set on
which those present started playing with him.

....Mahfouz leaned toward me and asked me, "Who is that?" I didn't know
him, but I signaled to the waiter and whispered to him, "Who's that?" "It's
Hamza al-Basyuni, the former director of the military prison," he replied.

Mahfouz's eyes widened and he took to observing the man discreetly. I still
remember the way al-Basyuni looked, the way he held the waterpipe and bent
over the chessboard, and the atmosphere of gloom that his presence created in
the café.

As recounted by al-Ghitani, the encounter with Hamza al-Basyuni
inspired Mahfouz to write the novel *al-Karnak*, which provides an
unflinching account of the oppression and torture that targeted the
political opponents of 'Abd al-Nasser in the 1950s and 60s.[94]

'Abd al-Nasser was in the USSR as the arrests were winding down.
He was there to discuss with the new ruling triumvirate of Brezhnev,
Kosygin and Podgorny the Soviet Union's role in the new Afro-Asian
solidarity movement, of which Egypt was a leading member. It was the
sort of movement that Qutb had pushed for during the previous decade. 'Abd al-Nasser spent much of his time sequestered at the Zagi-
dova hunting lodge. In between meetings, his hosts took him out to
shoot ducks.[95] Then, returning to Moscow, he took advantage of a
meeting with Egyptian mission students to announce publicly the
thwarting of what he said was a coup attempt against the regime, thus
ending the news blackout that had prevailed in Egypt since the onset
of the arrests. The plot, announced 'Abd al-Nasser, had been carefully
orchestrated by Muslim Brothers whose objective was to assassinate

the head of state and high ranking officials and destroy key communication and transport facilities. In the ensuing chaos, they planned to take over the government. Thankfully, Egypt's security services had prevailed against the enemy.

The news of the conspiracy quickly travelled back to Egypt. The 7 September 1965 headline in the government organ *al-Ahram* proclaimed, "First Details of the Muslim Brotherhood's Recent Conspiracy." Other periodicals followed suit with government-slanted analyses of the events. The 15 and 22 September issues of the weekly news magazine *Akhir Sa'a* couched the organization's "subversion" and "terrorism" as typical of Muslim Brotherhood activities past and present. The Shaykh al-Azhar, Hasan Ma'mun, contributed a piece to the 15 September issue in which he laid bare the errors of the Brothers, especially ideas pertaining to the modern *jahiliyya* contained in Qutb's *Milestones*. According to Jeffery Kenney, the magazine gives "credit for the defeat of the Brothers to the Egyptian people (*al-sha'b*) and the revolution (*al-thawra*), a collective force that effectively leveled 'a shout in the face of the conspirators: Don't kill our children!'"[96] Shaykh 'Abd al-Latif al-Subki, president of the *fatwa* commission, likened Qutb's ideas to those of the Kharijites. He accused Qutb of counter-revolution. "If we draw the connection between Sayyid Qutb's preaching (*da'wa*) and recent events, and if we view it in the light of the Egyptian revolution [meaning Nasserism] and the stirring triumphs it has registered in all domains, then it becomes clear that the message of the Brethren is no more than a plot against our revolution under the guise of religious zeal, and that those who act to propagate it or who pay heed to it are seeking to prejudice the nation, to cause it to regress and to inflict calamities upon it."[97]

In coming down hard on Qutb, the *'ulama* of al-Azhar were dutifully fulfilling their assigned role of supporting the regime against detractors; in 1961 'Abd al-Nasser had put the administration of al-Azhar under the control of the state. However, one gets the sense that they were also acting in self-interest. Historically the *'ulama* were the custodians of the faith. Their command of Islam's textual tradition provided them with "cultural capital" that gained them status and prestige within society.[98] The Egyptian historian al-Jabarti (d. 1825), himself a religious scholar, had famously upheld this high status in his discussion of the five levels of chosen persons whom God appointed to dispense justice, placing the *'ulama* second, after the prophets and ahead of kings and rulers.[99] Jealous of their traditional prerogative, the *'ulama* regarded Qutb as an interloper, a religious charlatan whose lack of *'ilm* (religious knowledge) threatened the edifice of Islam that they had constructed.

'A life which will never disappear'

Why, in 1965, did the 'Abd al-Nasser regime come down hard on Qutb and the Muslim Brothers? It can be argued that the presence of any underground political grouping, especially one grounded in the subversive discourse of *Milestones*, was enough to provoke a strong response from a regime intent on consolidating its control over the people and resources of the country. Seen this way, the 'Abd al-Nasser regime was unwilling to countenance a revival of the Islamic movement and acted accordingly. However, did the existence of a small, ill-formed organization justify a repression that was so sweeping and severe?

Any attempt to address the question must take into account the regime's growing sense of vulnerability. In the early years of the socialist experiment, Egypt's economic growth had been steady, prompting the regime to boast that under its governance the lives of ordinary Egyptians were improving. There was substance to the claim; between 1960 and 1964, Egypt's economy grew steadily by 5.5 per cent per annum. But by the time of the arrests the growth rate had slowed considerably. One reason for the downturn related to the regime's inability to provide sufficient financial and material resources to sustain the policy of import substitution. Added to this was Egypt's involvement in Yemen's civil war, which by 1965 was costing the country some one million dollars per day.[100] 'Abd al-Nasser feared that the dismal economic indicators would derail the "social contract" by which the "regime provided goods and services to the public in return for their political support." Confirmation of "a silent current of frustration"[101] appeared on 23 August, just a couple weeks after the first arrests, when tens of thousands of Egyptians took to the streets of Cairo to join the funeral procession of the former head of the Wafd, Mustafa al-Nahhas.[102] It galled the president of the United Arab Republic that a politician of the Old Regime should receive honours from the masses in whose name he had come to power. In light of these reverses, the regime reckoned that the highly publicized suppression of a coup attempt would rally the increasingly disaffected population around it.

However, it was also true that the case against the organization was a product of exaggerations about its strength and intentions put forward by the intelligence services, especially the Military Intelligence (al-Mukhabarat al-'Askariyya) under the direction of Field Marshall 'Abd al-Hakim Amir and his cabinet chief Shams Badran. Aiming to enhance its influence within the state, the Military Intelligence pointed to "grave" threats, which, it claimed, the competing Interior Ministry's General Investigation Service (Mabahith 'Amma) ignored. As John Waterbury writes, "Nasser's underlings in the intelligence networks vied for the privilege of unearthing his enemies."[103] As it happened, the Military Intelligence's warning caught 'Abd al-Nasser's ear, with the result that it was Shams Badran who was mostly in charge of the operations against the Brothers. On the other hand, 'Abd al-Azim Fahmi, the Minister of the Interior under whose jurisdiction the General Investigation Service fell, was sacked.[104]

The authorities took Qutb to the Military Prison and held him in solitary confinement. His commentary on surah 2:49–50, which speaks of the persecution and trials of the Israelites in Egypt, must have seemed to speak to the occasion. Qutb writes that the believer's experience of "hardship, misfortune and tribulation" will not be in vain if he knows that they contain an "element of trial by God" to test one's "faith and resolve": "Once aware of this fact, one will develop more resilience and moral strength that will enable one to endure pain and overcome it much more easily."[105] Because of his frail health he had to spend time at the prison hospital ward where he was secluded from the other prisoners. There Zaynab al-Ghazali caught a glimpse of him as "the wind lifted the blanket which acted as the door" to his cell. "The hospital was immediately in an uproar, for Qutb was not allowed to be seen by other prisoners, and a fluke chance was no excuse."[106]

Over the course of that autumn, the Military Intelligence gathered information about the organization from the prisoners and delivered it to the Public Prosecutor so that it could prepare for the interrogation and trial of the suspects.

As he waited for the authorities to question him, Qutb wrote his confession. The censored version was later published as the pamphlet called Why Limadha A'damuni (Why Did They Execute Me?). According to 'Abd al-Fattah al-Khalidi, the authorities removed the passages in the pamphlet in which Qutb wrote about his torture and mistreatment. Yet, despite these omissions, the confession remains a valuable source for events relating to the last year of Qutb's life, and more particularly, for understanding the state of his thinking at this crucial juncture. Qutb writes that by the time he wrote the pamphlet in October 1965, the police had arrested all of the members of the organization and most of the detainees had already "talked". He therefore saw no danger in divulging details. In fact, he states that he regarded his confession as an opportunity to set the record straight.[107]

In this small work, Qutb spelt out his perception of the Muslim Brotherhood's dealings with the Nasserist state. First, he writes it was the violence by the state directed against the Brothers in 1954 that compelled the organization in 1964 to consider the option of defensive force. Indeed, if the state could have assured them that their arrest would result in a fair trial, then he and his followers would not have considered the option of defensive force. Further, he wrote, the regime's destruction of the Muslim Brotherhood in 1954 played directly into the hands of "Zionists and imperialist Crusaders" whose longstanding ambition has been been to destroy the Islamic creed. The regime should understand that the most effective way to combat Western hegemony over Muslim societies is to honour Islam. Alone among movements and groups in Egypt, the Muslim Brotherhood had worked to strengthen the faith against internal and external enemies. Finally, Qutb explained that because Islam is a complete way of life, the simple trappings of faith would never satisfy true Muslims. It is not enough that the government encourages Muslims to participate in the Hajj, provides mosques, Islamic conferences and religious television programming to the people. "Islam is bigger than all of these things." There needs to be a new generation of Muslims prepared to implement Islam comprehensively at the levels of both the society and the state. Indeed, according to Qutb, the raising of this new generation was the Muslim Brotherhood's historic task.[108]

In order to expedite proceedings, the regime promulgated extraordinary powers that gave it wide latitude in the arraignment and handling of suspects in times of "national emergency". It did this on 11 November. Islamists referred to the new measures collectively as "Pharaoh's Law". Armed with them, Salah Nasr, Director of the General Intelligence Agency, proceeded to interrogate the organization's principal members, including Qutb. In order to be closer to the action he moved his office to the Military Prison.[109] Over the course of three long afternoon and evening sessions conducted on 19–21 December 1965,

Nasr grilled Qutb about the organization's ideology, composition and intentions.

He asked Qutb if he really believed that Islam was in a state of eclipse. And was it true that he believed that his organization constituted the only legitimate community of Muslims in the world? Did he not want to change the government in Egypt? And where was his loyalty? Was it to Egypt and Islam, or to the Muslim Brotherhood? Finally, Salah Nasr accused Qutb of following Nafi' Ibn al-Azraq and the creed of the early mediaeval Kharijites (*Khawaraj*).

By identifying Qutb with the Kharijites, Salah Nasr tapped a powerful trope within Islamic discourse. Following the dictum "There is no judgment but God's" (*al hukm illa li–Allah*), the Kharijites had pronounced anathema both on the fourth Caliph 'Ali and his opponent Mu'awiyya for their alleged sins. According to Kharijite theology, Muslim rulers who did not abide by the Qur'an were disbelievers (*kuffar*). Because of their apostasy, they should be deposed. The radical wing of the Kharijites, the Azariqa, followers of Nafi' Ibn Azraq, stressed that apostates should, in fact, be killed. However, in the view of the emergent majority Sunni opinion, the Kharijite ideal of the "just imam" led invariably to war and bloodshed. Sunni theologians responded to Kharijite idealism by holding that a "grave sinner cannot be excluded from the community" even if his actions were sinful. By separating faith and works, the theologians provided justification for the existence of strong rulers capable of maintaining political order and communal unity.[110] "A bad Sunni ruler was still better than *fitna*."[111] In associating Qutb's thought with the extremism of the Kharijites, Salah Nasr depicted Qutb as a threat to the stability of state and the wellbeing of the country's social fabric, as someone who was completely at variance with the wise consensus of generations of Muslims.

Qutb explained his position to Salah Nasr. He admitted that his organization wanted to change the secular regimes in Egypt and elsewhere, but insisted that it wanted to accomplish this gradually through the "creation of a generation of young Muslims". Only if the regime discovered the organization or otherwise threatened its existence would it take up arms. He insisted that the revolutionary toppling of the government was not in the organization's sights, although it did seek the creation of an Islamic state in the long term.

Qutb also made clear to Salah Nasr his stance on patriotism: "Nationalism is a flag whose historical time has passed." The world, he said, is moving towards ideological complexes based on thought and doctrine. The Islamic movement is part of this global trend. *'Asabiyya* (group solidarity) which is based on tribal identity, race or land is a backward, *jahili* form of identity.[112]

As to the charge of "Kharijism", Qutb responded with the same answer that he had presented to 'Umar al-Tilmisani in prison, that the condition of *jahiliyya* applied to the prevailing global culture; in no way would he regard an individual Muslim as a *kafir*, even though he might be ignorant of the true meaning of the creed. As long as he confesses the creed, he is one of the faithful. Such a person might be "ignorant", but he would not be a an unbeliever.[113] He went on to explain that if there was a difference between the members of his organization and "ordinary Muslims", it lay in the fact that the former possessed a *minhaj*, a programme of action to bring a true Islamic order into being, whereas the latter did not. He was clear with Salah Nasr that, although he held the Muslim Brotherhood in high esteem, his only loyalty was to Islam.[114]

On 9–12 April 1966, Qutb and forty-two other Islamist defendants were brought to trial. It was a young group; twenty-eight of them were under thirty years of age.[115] Eight months had passed since the crackdown. The authorities took the prisoners in trucks to the court and there placed them in a large holding cell. One by one, the prosecutor asked the prisoners if they objected to the proceedings. All answered that they did not object to the individuals who presided, but did not recognize the legitimacy of the *jahili* law by which the prosecutor judged them.[116] The judge then separated Zaynab al-Ghazali and Hamida Qutb from the other prisoners and sent them back to the Military Prison; he had decided that they should be subject to a "special trial". As in the 1954 trial, Qutb appeared drawn and haggard. Those who saw him on the witness stand said that he had aged ten years.[117] Yet, despite his weakened condition, he maintained his composure. A short film clip of the trial shows Qutb attired in jacket and tie, sitting patiently with hands folded. There is a look of calm certainty on his face. He knows that the end is near and that there is nothing left for him to do but witness for the faith.

Qutb's lawyer, assigned by the state, argued that although his client did belong to a secret organization both in prison and after his release, his activities were "educational" in nature; there was no convincing evidence that he had been actively planning a terrorist strike against the state.[118] The prosecution disagreed, and energetically accused Qutb of subversion, the intention to commit terrorism, and the encouragement of sedition. Qutb had not only attempted to reconstitute the officially banned secret organization of the Muslim Brotherhood, but, with others, he had also hatched a bloody plan to overthrow the legitimate government of the country. Why else would Qutb have sanctioned the purchase of weapons? Had Qutb and the others succeeded in their plot, Egypt would have descended into chaos. To make its point, the prosecution drew heavily upon *Milestones*, pointing to its call for "true Muslims" to use physical power to abolish the organizations and authorities of the "*jahili*" system. Qutb calmly responded to the charges, again by emphasizing the long-range, gradualist nature of his programme and the entirely "prophylactic" purpose of the weapons acquisitions, but to no avail. The court had already made up its mind on the question of his guilt.

It is difficult to judge the validity of the regime's case against Qutb. In the dock, Qutb claimed that the weapons purchases and paramilitary training were in anticipation of persecution. That may have been the case. In his prison writings, Qutb had explained that educational preparation was required before the Islamic movement could be in a position to remove "the obstacles in its path". *Jihad* of the tongue and *jihad* of the pen had to precede "*jihad* of the sword" (*jihad bi-al-sayf*). Islam will come to power only after a sufficient number of Muslims understand the true meaning of the creed. In the meantime, the Islamic movement must protect itself from its enemies: thus the need for a strong defensive posture. Although Qutb spoke about the inevitability of conflict, nowhere in his writings did he advocate the tactic of the Leninist-style coup that would become the hallmark of some radical Islamist groups after his death, including the Islamic Jihad Organization to which Ayman al-Zawahiri belonged.

Nevertheless, Qutb belonged to an underground organization that emerged from the rubble of the outlawed Muslim Brotherhood. Combined with his long-range intention to establish a new order and his part in the drafting of a contingency plan to attack government personnel, this was enough to seal his fate. In the end, the state's case against him was relatively easy. Qutb may have regarded the secret organization as having a defensive purpose, but in the view of the court, the group was "a loose cannon" that had to be reined in.

Following the trial Qutb returned to prison to await sentencing. At least one high-ranking government official expressed concern at what appeared to be his impending execution. Kamal al-Din Husayn, one of the original members of the Free Officers Movement, thought that the court should display mercy. Kamal al-Din had been close to the Muslim Brothers in pre-revolutionary days, and no doubt he felt genuine sympathy for Qutb whose moral stance he admired. In a letter that he penned to 'Abd al-Nasser on Qutb's behalf, he evoked the Qur'an's solemn warnings to those who would do wrong. "Fear God," Kamal al-Din warned 'Abd al-Nasser: "Fear God and do not be amongst those whom God has described: "And if he was told fear God, pride carries him off to sin, therefore hell is sufficient for him" (Qur'an 2:206)."[119]

However, Qutb was at peace. In June 1966, he wrote to his friend the Saudi Arabian author 'Abd al-Ghaffar 'Attar. An intelligence officer who knew one of the prison guards made sure that the letter was delivered:

I have been able to discover God in a wonderful new way. I understand His path and way more clearly and perfectly than before. My confidence in His protection and promise to the believers is stronger than ever before. Moreover, I maintain my resolution to raise my head and not to bend it except to God. "And God has full power and control over His affairs, but most among mankind know it not" (Q. 12:21).[120]

On 21 August 1966, the court passed its verdict. Guards escorted each of the accused out of the prisoner's enclosure to an adjoining room to hear his sentence. Qutb and six of his companions—'Abd al-Fattah Isma'il, aged forty-two; Yusuf Hawwash, forty-four; Sabri 'Arfa, thirty-six; Ahmad 'Abd al-Majid, thirty-three; Majdi 'Abd al-Aziz' twenty-nine; and 'Ali 'Ashmawi, twenty-two—were all told that they were to die on the gallows. By all accounts, the men took the news stoically. Undoubtedly, different thoughts and concerns ran through their minds. On the way back to the Military Prison, Qutb casually mentioned to his colleagues that if 'Abd al-Nasser went ahead with the executions, within three years Egyptians would rise in revolution. Such talk did not impress Yusuf Hawwsh, who perhaps spoke for the others when he responded, "Brother Sayyid, let's not discuss about political matters now that we're closer than ever to meeting God. Instead, we should promise that whichever of the six of us is saved from punishment in the Hereafter should intercede with God on behalf of the others."[121]

Ten days later, 'Abd al-Nasser commuted the sentences on Sabri 'Arfa, Ahmad 'Abd al-Majid, Majdi 'Abd al-'Aziz and 'Ali 'Ashmawi to life imprisonment because of their relatively young ages. Islamists, however, charge that 'Ali 'Ashmawi's release was, in addition, a reward for his cooperative attitude to the authorities. Eventually he relocated to the United States. Twenty-five other defendants received life sentences and eleven more were given prison sentences ranging from ten to fifteen years. In the end, only Qutb, 'Abd al-Fattah Isma'il and Yusuf al-Hawwash were to be executed.

Upon receiving his sentence Qutb is said to have proclaimed, "Praise be to God, I performed *jihad* for fifteen years until I earned this martyrdom." In his Qur'an commentary, Qutb had followed generations of Muslim theologians and jurists in writing that God preordained the coming of death for each person. The end of one's life was predetermined; one could do nothing but accept God's decree. Qutb knew that he had lived by God's commandments. All that he could do was to accept his allotted fate knowing that God would carry out His will. The martyr's death was inscribed in his destiny.

Immediately messages protesting against the sentence streamed into Cairo from around the Muslim world. The future Grand Mufti of Saudi Arabia 'Abd al-'Aziz ibn 'Abd Allah Ibn Baz, then Vice President of the Islamic University of Medina, interceded on his behalf, as did the Saudi monarch, Faysal Ibn 'Abd al-'Aziz Al Saud.[122] Although we cannot doubt the sincerity of the Saudi concern for Qutb, it appears also true that the House of Saud and its Wahhabi backers were eager to make the point that, in contrast to the "Godless" Egyptian regime, they were prepared to protect true men of God. In fact, not long after the executions the Saudi monarchy allowed Egyptian Muslim Brothers to settle in the Kingdom. From Algeria, the Islamist group Jam'iyyat al-Qiyam al-Islamiyya (The Society of Islamic Values) publicly denounced the death sentences, prompting Algeria's President Houari Boumediene to ban the group's activities in the *wilaya* of Algiers before completely dissolving it by decree in 1970.[123] However, these and other entreaties did not have their desired effect. Upon receiving King Faysal's telegram, 'Abd al-Nasser is said to have replied, "I do not know why those sons of... care so much about Sayyid *zift*" (the literal meaning of *zift* is tar or asphalt, but in this context it might best be translated as "trash").[124]

The night before the executions, the prison official Hamza al-Basyuni convinced Hamida Qutb to relay to her brother the government's conditional offer to reduce the sentence. "No one," al-Basyuni said to Hamida, "has more influence over him than you." All her brother need do, said al-Basuyni, was to admit that the Muslim Brotherhood was allied with other subversive political forces in Egypt, and that he was sorry for what he had done.[125]

Upon hearing the offer from his sister, Qutb responded that he could not accept it. The alleged complicity with anti–government forces "did not happen, and I would never tell a lie." Moreover, God had already decided his fate: "Life decrees are in the hands of Allah. These despots can neither prolong nor shorten my life. All is in the hands of Allah, and Allah is behind us encompassing everything."[126] Although grieved by the coming execution, Hamida was pleased with her brother's decision. Like him, she understood that worldly advantage paled in significance to the bare truth of the All Powerful. There were only two ways: the way of the Lord and the way of Shaytan. Each was diametrically opposed to the other. Qutb had stated in *Milestones*: "Islam's ultimate aim is to awaken the 'humanity' of man."[127] He saw his coming execution as a means of accelerating that goal.

The prison authorities likewise granted Yusuf al-Hawwash the opportunity to recant. He too steadfastly refused the offer. After the sentencing, the authorities allowed him to meet his wife and two young children briefly. As the guards roughed him up he soberly explained to them, "The scales [of justice] are reversed, and they will not be corrected today." He then went on to quote the Qur'an's promise of eventual retribution: God says, "We shall set up the Scales of Justice for the Day of Judgment" (Qur'an 21:47).[128] Hawwash knew that at least on the Last Day, the mask of the illusory would fall and God would expose the injustice of the tyrants. To prepare for his coming demise he was fasting. If the authorities made an offer of respite to 'Abd al-Fattah Isma'il, there is no available record of it.

The sentences were carried out without warning, and sooner than anyone, including Qutb, expected. Late in the night of 28 August 1966, Sayyid Qutb, 'Abd al-Fattah Isma'il and Yusuf al-Hawwash were summoned and taken to the car that was to take them to the police headquarters in Cairo's old Bab al-Khalq neighbourhood where the executions were to take place. As Qutb left the prison, he smiled and shook hands with each of the guards. The car then made its way through Cairo's nearly deserted streets. Behind beamed the headlights of a small convoy of military vehicles. Awaiting the condemned men were three hanging posts. A story, which may well be apocryphal, relates that as Qutb stood on top of the scaffold, a "high ranking officer" approached Qutb with a final offer of clemency from the president: in return for his admission of guilt and an apology, 'Abd al-Nasser would be willing to commute his death sentence. "Sayyid looked up with his clear eyes. A smile, which one cannot describe, appeared on his face. He told the officer in a surprisingly calm tone: 'Never! I would not exchange this temporary life [for] a life which will never disappear!'"[129]

It is unwise to attempt to discern the private thoughts of an individual at any time, but especially in a circumstance such as this. What is certain, however, is Qutb's firm belief that he was about to go to "a better place." He had written in his commentary,

Death, whether natural or in battle, does not represent the end. Life on earth is not the best thing God bestows on people. There are other values and nobler considerations: 'If you should be slain of die in God's cause surely forgiveness by God and His grace are better than all the riches they amass. If you shall die or be slain, it is to God that you should be gathered' (Qur'an 3: 157).[130]

Speaking through the hoods that the executioners now placed over their heads, the men uttered the most profound of the Islamic obligations, the Profession of Faith: "There is no god but God, and Muhammad is His Messenger!" Then the platforms upon which they stood gave way. The execution took place 29 August at around 3 a.m. Immediately the presiding officials hoisted a black flag that signalled to the outside world that they had carried out the sentences. They then placed the bodies of Qutb and his companions in a black car. Flanked by motorcycles and police cars, the vehicle made its way directly for the nearby "Great Cemetery" (al-Qarafa al-Kubra), the resting place of the puppet-Caliphs of the Mamluk era and site of the mausoleum of Imam al-Shafi'i, the ninth century jurisprudent. Quickly, officials buried the three bodies in unmarked graves. Breaking with custom, the burial team did not recite the funeral prayer (janaza) over the bodies. Meanwhile, a heavily armed Special Forces unit patrolled the sleeping streets of Cairo's old city.[131] The authorities did not cremate Qutb's body and scatter his ashes in the river, as happened to the body of the executed tenth century Mesopotamian mystic-martyr Mansur al-Hallaj who had similarly defied religio-political consensus, in his case by espousing a doctrine of pantheism. Yet in acting surreptitiously, the government hoped to avoid the type of funeral demonstration that often accompanied a martyr's "triumph".

Egypt's state radio announced the executions hours after they had taken place. Yusuf Hawwash's wife was preparing breakfast when she heard the news. With tears in her eyes, she repeated the prayer, "To God we belong and to Him we shall return." Hamida Qutb and Zaynab al-Ghazali learned of the hangings in their shared cell at the Military Prison: "News of the executions fell on us like a dead weight, for those executed were all dear to us, good *mujahids* [fighters for the faith]."[132]

Muslim Brother Ahmad Ra'if recalled the moment when he and the prisoners at Abu Za'bal heard the news of the executions. Forbidden by the prison guards to speak to one another, they muffled their grief. "Terror was present in each cell." Then, allowed to gather in the court-yard for the evening prayer (*salat al-maghrib*), the men listened to the imam intoning Qur'an 5:27: "And (O Muhammad SAW) recite to them (the Jews) the story of the two sons of Adam [Hâbil (Abel) and Qâbil (Cain)] in truth; when each offered a sacrifice (to Allâh), it was accepted from the one but not from the other. The latter said to the former: "I will surely kill you." The former said: "Verily, Allâh accepts only from those who are *Al-Muttaqûn* (pious).""" Unable to contain their emotion any longer, the men responded with groans and cries.[133]

Salah 'Abd al-Fattah al-Khalidi remembered being in a coffee shop at al-Azhar University watching the morning news on the television when a clip of Sayyid Qutb suddenly appeared on the screen. The students watched transfixed as the doomed Qutb beamed at onlookers from a seat of the car in which he rode to the place of execution. They were emotional, but given the tense political atmosphere in the city dared not express their sorrow.[134]

To the south of Cairo in the leafy suburb of Ma'di, the news of the executions reached fifteen-year-old Ayman al-Zawahiri. The distraught teenager's grief turned to anger. Soon afterwards, he joined with several other young people in forming an underground Islamist cell. Years later, this small cell combined with similar small groups to form Jihad Group, the organization that was responsible for the assassination of President Anwar al-Sadat in October 1981. In his *Knights under the Prophet's Banner*, written in Afghanistan in 2002, al-Zawahiri explained the significance of Qutb's martyrdom:

Sayyid Qutb became an example of sincerity and adherence to justice. He spoke justice in the face of the tyrant (Jamal Abd al-Nasir) and paid his life as a price for this. The value of his words increased when he refused to ask for pardon from Jamal Abd al-Nasir. He said his famous words, "The index finger [which holds the prayer beads] that testifies to the oneness of God in every prayer refuses to request a pardon from a tyrant."[135]

Far away in Kabul in Afghanistan, an 18–year-old Pushtun named Gulbuddin Hekmatyar heard word of the executions over the radio. Like Zawahiri, Hekmatyar remembers Qutb's death as marking the moment when his mind turned to Islamic activism. Hekmatyar would go on to form the Hizb-i Islami, an organization much inspired by the ideas of Qutb and other Muslim Brother figures.[136]

In the Islamist perspective, the *mihna* of 1965–66 was a drama of good versus evil in which Qutb played the central role of martyr for the cause. By sacrificing his life, Qutb demonstrated publicly the vast gulf that separated truth from its opposite. For not only did his death communicate that Islam was an ideal worth dying for, it also highlighted the essential illegitimacy of the powers that ruled over Muslims in Egypt and elsewhere.

Islamist accounts of the events surrounding Qutb's sentencing and execution are replete with stories of visions, dreams and communications with the spiritual realm. The Islamists lived in a cosmos marked by open paths of communication between the material world and the realm of the spirit. For them, as for the culture generally, dreams and visions were "not thought of as mere products of the human mind, but [were] believed to be windows into the spiritual realm, and to provide insights that would otherwise be unavailable."[137] With roots in the rural practices of magic and saint veneration, most Egyptians were acutely aware of the numinous and, more particularly, of the immanence of the divine in their everyday lives.

For literate Muslims such as the Islamists, the classical doctrine provided a template for making sense of dreamscapes and visions. It held that visions are the products of meetings between the spirits of the living and the dead, which meet in *al-barzakh*, the intermediary zone "where the spirits dwell until the resurrection of the bodies on the Last Day."[138] The mediaeval Hanbali jurist Ibn Qayyim, whom Qutb and other Islamists were fond of citing, wrote, "The spirits of the living and dead meet in sleep and then question one another."[139] Similarly, the great thirteenth century mystical philosopher Ibn al-'Arabi wrote, "God has an angel who is in charge of visions, who is called the spirit, and who lives beneath the lowest heaven."[140]

This general understanding influenced the Islamists. They saw themselves as party to a social network that extended beyond the grave. In his Qur'an commentary Qutb clearly stated his own belief in the reality of the "unseen world" (ghaybiyyat), including "Paradise, Hell, angels, demons, jinn (jinn), and the earthly paradise of the first humans." These were "invisible realities that one should not try to prove scientifically or to deny as being fables, cosmogonic myths, or symbols of a literary type."[141] It bears repeating that Qutb constructed his concept of the modern jahiliyya around his observation that modern lives were unnaturally and tragically insulated from the metaphysical realm. It is a truism that religious ideology was the framework by which these men and women comprehended the universe. What we need to emphasize is the absolute belief of these Islamists in the reality of a supernatural realm.

In the manner of Sufis, Zaynab al-Ghazali relates that in a dream she saw Qutb, her recently executed spiritual guide, during the quiet following the Fajr (dawn) prayer. Qutb told al-Ghazali that although he had been present physically at the gallows, his spirit was far removed from the scene. "Know that I was not with them, I was in Madinah in the company of the Prophet (peace be upon him)." Soon afterwards, again following the dawn prayer, she heard the faint sounds of a mysterious voice: "Sayyid is in the highest Firdaus and his companions are in 'Illiyin."[142] Al-Ghazali immediately awakened Hamida, her cellmate, and related what she had heard. Hamida rejoiced and, in formal religious language, replied, "These visions are consolation, a strengthening from Allah, the Exalted, the High."

The twenty-nine–year-old Hamida had her own supernatural encounter shortly after the gaolers separated her from Zaynab al-Ghazali, her "Sister-Mother," and cast her into solitary confinement. It was a terrifying experience. Constant nightmares disrupted her sleep. According to her siblings, Hamida had always possessed a nervous disposition.[143] Now she was on the verge of a breakdown. One morning, before dawn, as the rest of the prison slept, she saw a "large man" enter the locked door of her cell. He was dressed in white and his face inscribed with "kind features". He took Hamida's hand and placed her finger over Qur'anic verses that read:

We recite to you some of the news of Mûsa (Moses) and Fir'aun (Pharaoh) in truth, for a people who believe (those who believe in this Qur'ân, and in the Oneness of Allâh). Verily, Fir'aun (Pharaoh) exalted himself in the land and made its people sects, weakening (oppressing) a group (i.e. Children of Israel) among them, killing their sons, and letting their females live. Verily, he was of the *Mufsidûn* (i.e. those who commit great sins and crimes, oppressors, tyrants, etc.). And We wished to do a favour to those who were weak (and oppressed) in the land, and to make them rulers and to make them the inheritors, and to establish them in the land, and We let Fir'aun (Pharaoh) and Hâmân and their hosts receive from them that which they feared (28:3–6).

The words put her at ease. She knew that God's justice would be done. Just as God had humbled Pharaoh, so too would He punish the tyrants of the modern *jahiliyya*. It was a vision uncannily similar to the one Yusuf al-Hawwash had had in prison years before.[144]

Yet like her brother Sayyid, Hamida understood that God's Judgment would not come about through the efforts of the Muslim masses. Pagan false-consciousness had infected their minds and they were incapable of making a difference in the world. In her memoir, she recalled the time when the authorities took her from the prison to the Qasr al-'Aini Hospital for medical treatment. Through the barred window of the lorry, she viewed the throngs of people in the streets and felt contempt for them. They were sheep, unthinking and unknowing, oblivious of the web of lies in which they lived. They knew nothing of the horrors foisted upon her and other true Muslims, and if they did know, they did not care. Her brother's strategic view was entirely correct: God would accomplish His work only though dedicated effort of a cadre of true believers, men and women whose acuteness of vision saw though the dross of the phenomenal world to the Reality beyond and were prepared to act.[145]

Yusuf al-Hawwash's wife also experienced a miracle, although she had to wait many years for it. In the mid-1980s, she visited her daughter and son-in-law at Medina after she had performed the Hajj; the young married couple was part of the wave of Egyptian Muslim Brothers and their sympathizers who relocated to the safety of Saudi Arabia during the 1960s and 1970s. At her daughter's Saudi home, she happened to notice the copy of the Qur'an that Yususf had carried with him on his way to prison. She was able to identify the Qur'an because it was inscribed with the dedication that she had made to her son in 1965. Her son-in-law told her that a woman he met by chance at the Mecca sanctuary had given it to him; the woman had known of his relationship through marriage to the Hawwash family. According to Yusuf's wife, "This *mushaf* (copy of the Qur'an) had been to France, London and Saudi Arabia, until it eventually reached us twenty-years later." In this way, she says, the martyr Yusuf al-Hawwash fulfilled through God his promise to return the Qur'an to the possession of his son.

'The Mother of the Light'

The vindication promised to Hamida Qutb in her vision came sooner than she could have imagined, although in a form that was painful to bear. Shortly after their transfer from Tura to the Qanatir women's prison on 5 June 1967, Hamida Qutb and Zaynab al-Ghazali heard "screaming and wailing" wafting down the corridors of the gaol. They inquired and learned that Israel's military forces had soundly defeated the armies of Egypt, Syria and Jordan in the space of a few short days. The defeat came after spurious reports that the Arab armies were driving the Jewish forces before them, all the way to the outskirts of Tel Aviv. The two women were not yet privy to the details of the short war. They did not know that all seventeen of Egypt's airfields were hit, and most of Egypt's air force destroyed on the ground; that in the Sinai, Egypt's armoured divisions were defeated and put to flight; and that the Suez Canal, since 1956 a top earner of income for the state, was shut down.[146] It was enough for them to know that "wickedness" had triumphed over "good".

Like every other Egyptian, the two women reeled under the shock of the Jewish state's spectacular victory. However, they soberly calculated that the defeat was inevitable. It was the consequence of the Muslims' disobedience towards God. Muslims had ignored His *hakimiyya*. Had the Arab states waged the war along Islamic lines, God would have assured their victory. Al-Ghazali cast rebuke upon 'Abd al-Nasser and the other Arab leaders: "Indeed, it is because of your departure from the Qur'an and the *Sunnah* that you are defeated, miserable and sinking in your set-backs. For there is nothing in disobeying Allah except humiliation, misery, defeat, weakness, fire and an everlasting punishment."[147] In her view, the Arabs under 'Abd al-Nasser were buried in shame.

Had he lived to see the defeat, Qutb surely would have endorsed al-Ghazali's judgment. Throughout his career as an Islamist, he believed that the Muslims' adoption of secularism and materialism had sapped the source of their historical strength. He wrote in his Qur'an commentary, "When the believers fall short...they have to meet the consequences. The fact that they are Muslims and believers does not mean that the laws of nature should be suspended or abrogated for their sake."[148] In other words, Qutb believed that Muslims were responsibility for the outcome of their actions.

In the months and years that followed *al-Naksa* ("The Setback"), Egyptians and other Arabs looked deep into their collective soul to discern the reasons for a defeat so grand and sweeping. While leftists such as Kamal Rif'at blamed the disaster on what they perceived as the regime's insufficient dedication to Socialist and even Marxist principles, others viewed the conflict through the lens of civilizational conflict. The latter read with "deepened understanding" Qutb's stern appraisal of "the Jews" (*al-Yahud*) as set forth in his Qur'an commentary and other writings. Comparing the "perfidy" of the Jews of Medina with the modern Israelis, he writes with reference to *sura* 2:31–39: "The war the Jews began to wage against Islam and Muslims in those early days has raged on to the present. The form and appearance may have changed, but the nature and means remain the same."[149]

Especially in the 1970s, a plethora of books and articles, many of them written by supporters of the Islamic cause, argued that by his secular polices, 'Abd al-Nasser had broken the fighting spirit of the army and the nation. As a result, the Arabs were unable effectively to challenge Israel whose citizens, many believed, adhered strongly to the religious principles of their forefathers. The 1967 *Naksa* was instrumental in driving home the Islamist message to ever-wider populations of Arabic-speaking Middle Easterners. "At the end of 1967, Shaykh 'Abd al-Latif Subki wrote: 'God gives our enemies their victory not because He does not love us, but in order to engulf them in their impiety. Their victory is our cure and His rebuke for demeaning ourselves... Now we are able to realize what we had left behind and remember what we had forgotten.'"[150]

'Abd al-Nasser was devastated by the defeat that he had presided over. In a televised speech delivered to the nation in the evening of 9 June, he tendered his resignation from the office of presidency and turned the reigns of government over to fellow Free Officer Zakariyya Muhyi al-Din. As soon as he completed his short announcement, hundreds of thousands of Cairenes flooded onto the streets demanding that he stay on to lead the nation. 'Abd al-Nasser agreed to do so, and then began to identify scapegoats. In short order he forced the Commander of the Armed Forces, General Hakim 'Amir, and members of his coterie, including Shams Badran and Nasr Salah, to step down from their positions; Badran was subsequently imprisoned. Fearful that 'Amir was plotting a coup, the Egyptian president had his erstwhile colleague placed under house arrest. Whether to preserve his honour or to escape trial, or both, on 14 September 1967 'Amir committed suicide. 'Abd al-Nasser eventually purged one thousand officers from the army and air force.

The fall of these men of the revolution was as dramatic as the sudden eclipse of the Barmakid viziers in the 'Abbasid age. Men who enjoyed status and power were in an instant denuded of both. Their demise stirred the imagination of Egyptians. While many were happy to lay blame for the Setback squarely at the feet of these dishonoured men, thus absolving 'Abd al-Nasser of responsibility, others, including most Islamists, regarded the sackings as indicative of a general unravelling of the secular order. Gradually, God was dismantling the tyranny.

During the dark days of his captivity, Yusuf al-Hawwash had caught a glimpse of these future happenings. According to his widow, once during the night prayer, as he wavered between sleep and consciousness, he saw the doors of the prison cells open. Through the doors entered the men of 'Abd al-Nasser's security services, men like Shams Badran. He then saw himself with a group of the Companions (*Sahaba*) giving *bay'a* (allegiance) to the Prophet. He asked the Prophet, "Messenger of God, have we changed things after you?" To which the Prophet replied, "No, but you are trustworthy, trustworthy, trustworthy."[151] The message in the vision was clear: Be patient and trust in the Lord, justice will be served and truth will prevail.

A similar reassurance was granted the nation as a whole. Beginning on 2 April 1968, ten months after the defeat, tens of thousands of Egyptians, both Muslims and Copts, witnessed a vision of the Virgin Mary over the Church of the Blessed Virgin in Zaytun, the same Cairo suburb where, four decades earlier, Qutb had lived briefly with his journalist uncle. Spotted initially by two garage mechanics, the luminous figure of Mary appeared almost every night over the next two and a half years. Large crowds gathered to catch a glimpse of "The Mother of the Light", as Egyptians call the Virgin. According to one witness, the apparitions "always took place at night and were generally preceded by mysterious lights, flashing and scintillating silently over the church like a canopy of shooting stars."[152] Many have explained the Marian vision at Zaytun as a collective psychological response to the trauma of the 1967 defeat. That may be the case. On the other hand, for those who witnessed the apparition and believed in it, the explanation was simpler: there is a divine truth, a rock of certainty constant over the ages that beckons man to liberation from human failing and the imperfections of the world.

Sayyid Qutb had understood that this divine truth was waiting for people to discover it and act upon it. He knew this in his bones. All that was required was the energy and determination of human will to realize the vision—nothing less than man's reconciliation with his Creator. He died before he was able to qualify his idea or refine it. However, the ideas that he did manage to articulate were taken up and pushed to extreme lengths by the next generation of radicals in Egypt: Shukri Mustafa, 'Abd al-Salam Faraj, 'Abbud al-Zumur, and especially Ayman al-Zawahiri who would carry his vision forward into the maelstrom of Afghanistan and beyond.

8

EPILOGUE

THE TRAJECTORY OF 'QUTBISM'

The elephant in the room

Following the execution of Sayyid Qutb the Islamists who remained in prison were despondent. They felt as thought they were living in a nightmare. To someone standing outside the Islamist ideological frame-work, the concept of the modern *jahiliyya* can seem abstract and vague. But for the Islamists, it denoted something very terrifying—a world where nothing was true and everything was permitted, in which deceit, double dealing and self gratification were the norms and people were allowed to do terrible things to one another. In the Islamist reck-oning, the modern *jahiliyya* represented a mode of life cut off from the wellspring of truth.

It is well beyond the scope of this book to treat Qutb's legacy at any length. The ways by which subsequent Islamists received and modified Qutb's ideas require a separate study. Nevertheless, because observers of the post-9/11 *jihadi* landscape often read Sayyid Qutb's works through the prism of these legatees, rather than on their own terms, some brief remarks are in order, to situate Qutb properly.

Over the few years following his death, Qutb's siblings faired badly. According to Islamist sources, Muhammad Qutb was tortured so severely that rumours spread about his death. When it turned out that he was very much alive, Islamists both inside and outside the prisons took to calling him the "living martyr".[1] With her close friend Zaynab al-Ghazali at her side, Hamida Qutb also continued to endure hard-ships and privations. As her martyred brother once did, she sought solace amid the gloom of her prison cell in the care of a cat.[2] The two sons of Nafisa Qutb, Sayyid's nephews, had also been arrested in 1965 and one died in prison.[3] Amina Qutb was spared captivity, but with one sibling dead and the remaining two incarcerated, she was bereft of the nurturing company of family. To make matters worse, her fiancé, a Muslim Brother named Kamal al-Sananiri, languished in a prison far away in Qina in Upper Egypt. He had been captured in the great proscription of 1954, and since then had repeatedly urged Amina to agree that they break off their engagement.[4]Although he loved Amina, he did not think it fair to her that she should waste what remained of her youth in expectation of his release. But she insisted on waiting and regularly made the overnight rail journey from Cairo to visit him.

The elderly Hudaybi also waited out his prison sentence. Earlier, almost alone among the old guard of Hasan al-Banna's supporters, he had stood by Qutb and had publicly endorsed his views as set forth in *Milestones*. He had taken Qutb at his word: that the reconstituted Islamic movement should establish an Islamic state only after concerted missionary endeavour had prepared the ground. However, now, behind bars, he was aware that the same extreme attitudes that he had earlier observed among some of Qutb's followers were gaining ground. In fact, one group of prisoners at Abu Za'bal had taken Qutb's *jahiliyya* theory to mean that the entire society was *kufr* (disbelieving).[5] Perhaps Qutb's ideas were dangerous after all, if only because they were ambiguous. It was against the developing, *takfiri* interpretation of Qutb's writings that Hudaybi composed a tract called *Du'at wa la Qudat (Preachers, Not Judges)*, which he aimed at these young radicals. Hudaybi hoped that by writing his book, which was published in 1969, he might dampen the ardour of the extremists and, at the same time, salvage the reputation of the Brotherhood in the eyes of the state, thus hastening its members' release.

In the book, Hudaybi explicitly targeted Mawdudi's contention that contemporary society was *jahili*, but, as Gilles Kepel noted, "reading between the lines it is not difficult to detect a refutation of certain passages of *Signposts* [i.e. *Milestones*]."[6] According to Hudaybi, ever since the Prophet's time, the Qur'an and Sunna have been available to guide Muslims. Although it is true that people have misinterpreted Qur'anic concepts, as long as these sources exist they provide light for mankind. It is therefore specious to suppose that this light has ceased to cast its beam in the contemporary period. Hudaybi emphasized the traditional consensus of the *'ulama*, that once the individual professes the faith (the unity of God and the Prophethood of Muhammad), he is categorically a Muslim, even though he sins. As for Mawdudi's (and Qutb's) doctrine of the divine *hakimiyya*, Hudaybi argued that the concept imposed "an essentialist view of law" that downplayed the creative role of human reason in discerning God's will. In writing the book, Hudaybi wanted to tell both the Brothers and the political authorities that the job of the Brotherhood was to preach, not to judge the faith of others.[7]

Hudaybi's book impressed at least one of the *takfiri* Brothers. Following the circulation of the book, Shaykh 'Ali 'Abdu Isma'il, leader of the nascent *takfiri* group, publicly renounced *takfir* and accepted the consensual view. However, Hudaybi's arguments did not win over most other *takfiri*s.[8] For its part, the state was not entirely convinced by Hudaybi's sincerity and remained sceptical of the Brotherhood's intentions.

But then 'Abd al-Nasser died on 28 September 1970. His death after humiliation and defeat was a bitter end for a man who regarded himself, and was accepted by the world, as the champion of Arab nationalism, a cause which he had pledged to maintain. His successor to the presidency, the Free Officer Anwar al-Sadat, was at first sight an unlikely candidate for the post. Although he had served as the secretary general of the Organization of the Islamic Conference and speaker of the National Assembly, he had held few positions of real authority. Nonetheless, he had grandiose plans of his own. Within a year of coming to power, he implemented what he called his "Corrective Movement" by which he began the slow process of changing the course of the Egyptian revolution. Immediately Sadat made plans to dismantle the large public sector that Nasser had built up—a daunting task that would take years. His intentions earned him the wrath of those attached to the Arab Socialist Union. In May 1971 Sadat thwarted a coup-in-the-making led by 'Ali Sabri, and then, in a surprise move, began to release the Muslim Brothers from their captivity. He hoped that the Brothers' strong anti–Marxist attitudes would counter what remained of the leftist "centres of power".

One by one, and then in clusters, the Brothers began to emerge from the prisons. The releases continued until 22 March 1975 when a general amnesty set free the last of the prisoners. Although the experience of incarceration made the Brothers angry and bitter, many were eager to get on with their lives. A handful had been radicalized; this was the case with the *takfiris*. Muhammad Qutb gained his freedom in 1972 and within a year relocated to Saudi Arabia where he obtained a teaching position at the Mecca branch of King 'Abd al-'Aziz University. At the age of fifty, he married and proceeded to raise a family.

In Saudi Arabia, Muhammad Qutb joined other Egyptian and Arab Muslim Brothers who had fled their countries, for example, the Syrian Muhammad Surur Zayn al-'Abdin who had arrived in 1965. As noted earlier, the House of Saud was pleased to sponsor the Muslim Brothers, regarding them as assets in its quest to gain legitimacy in the Muslim world at the expense of the secularizing Egyptian Republic. Muhammad Qutb quickly set about to accommodate his brother's thought with the generally apolitical discourse of the Wahhabi shaykhs. So, for example, he equated the concept of divine sovereignty (*al-hakimiyya*) with the Wahhabi teaching on Divine Unity (*tawhid*), and the dichotomy of Hizb Allah ("Party of God") and Hizb al-Shaytan ("Party of Satan") with Wahhabi exclusivity, as in the Wahhabi doctrine of *al-Wala' wa al-Bara'a* (loosely, "Friendship to Muslims and Enmity to Disbelievers"). As a concession to his Saudi patrons, Muhammad Qutb amended his brother's theory of the universal quality of *jahiliyya*. Only Saudi Arabia, he said, had gleanings of Islam within its system, but even so it was in need of correction in some areas. The exiles, many of whom were teachers, exerted a great deal of influence in their new home. Employed like Muhammad Qutb as teachers, they introduced their Saudi students to the activist impulse that Sayyid Qutb had popularized. Out of the confluence of radical Muslim Brotherhood and Wahhabi understandings emerged the *Sahwa* ("Awakening") movement, which became strong in Saudi Arabia in the 1980s in the wake of Juhayman al-'Utaybi's attempted takeover of the Mecca Grand Mosque in November 1979.[9] Muhammad Qutb was the teacher of one of the best known of the *Sahwa* shaykhs, Safar al-Hawali (b. 1950).[10] At first, the House of Saud sponsored the *Sahwa* scholars as a way of countering the "rejectionist", anti–Saudi attitudes of Juhayman and his followers Subsequently, however, that support trailed off as the *Sahwa* shaykhs adopted a dissenting attitude towards the royal family, largely in response to its cooperative attitude towards the US-led coalition's "occupation" of Saudi Arabia during the 1990–91 Gulf War.

Zaynab al-Ghazali was released in August 1971. During her imprisonment her second husband died. Childless, she thereafter devoted her time to writing and charitable activities. She remained especially interested in women's issues, detailing the special role of the mother in creating the conditions for a strong and pious household. Shortly after Zaynab's release, Hamida Qutb gained her freedom. She, too, continued to write. She married a medical doctor and eventually moved with him to France,[11] an unbelieving country, but in her mind no worse than Egypt whose leadership had mistreated her so. Amina's patience was rewarded when Kamal al-Sananiri was released in 1974; they married the same year.

Amina supported al-Sananiri's ongoing career as a "soldier of God". During the 1970s he travelled forging connections between the revived Muslim Brotherhood (discussed below) and Islamist organizations abroad. One of these trips took him to Afghanistan where, in 1979, he was one of the first Arabs to assist the Afghan Mujahidin against the invading Soviet Red Army. According to sources, he inspired 'Abdullah 'Azzam to devote his energies to the *jihad* in Afghanistan.[12] Back in Egypt, the police arrested al-Sananiri in the security sweeps that preceded the Jihad Group's assassination of President Sadat in October 1981. The police subjected al-Sananiri, who was an important, "second-tier" leader of the Brotherhood, to torture. During one torture session he died, although afterwards the Egyptian authorities insisted that he had hanged himself from a water pipe in his cell so as not to divulge out of pain the information they sought from him.[13] Amina Qutb then became a widow. Displaying literary gifts that were common to her family, she remembered her relationship with Kamal al-Sananiri in a poem. It reads, in part:

> Do you remember us meeting, or has it already,
> Taken place in the land of the mirage;
> Then it withdrew and its shadow vanished;
> And it turned into tortuous memories;
> Thus asks my heart whenever,
> The days grow long, after your absence;
> When your shadow stares, smiling,
> It is as if I am listening to the response;
> Did we not walk upon truth together,
> So that good can return to barren land;
> So we walked along a thorny path,
> Abandoning all our ambitions;
> We buried our desires deep within ourselves,
> And we strove on in contentment, expecting reward from Allah.[14]

Amina Qutb passed away in January 2007. Leading members of the Muslim Brotherhood's Guidance Council attended her funeral in recognition of her status as one of the "great missionaries" of contemporary Islam. Hasan al-Hudaybi took advantage of his newly found freedom to rebuild the Brotherhood. Putting into practice what he had preached, he focused on *da'wa* activities and went out of his way to establish good relations with the state, wanting to make the point that the Muslim Brotherhood was not a revolutionary organization. He was successful in making his pitch. In return for cooperation, Sadat allowed the Brotherhood breathing room, although he refused to lift the official ban on it. Thus the Muslim Brotherhood was illegal but tolerated. Upon Hudaybi's death in 1973, the Brothers recognized 'Umar al-Tilmisani (d. 1986) as Supreme Guide. Like Hudaybi, Tilmisani steered a cautious course, not wanting to upset the regime. He was an enemy of the *takfiri* tendency. The increasing religiosity of Egyptian society following the 1967 debacle, manifested for example in the landslide victories of Muslim groups in university student elections, buoyed up his efforts to spread the message of Islamic revival.[15]

But there was still the issue of Qutb's legacy to contend with. What attitude should the Muslim Brotherhood adopt in relation to its most famous thinker? In *Preachers, Not Judges* Hudaybi had excoriated the radical ideas with which some associated Qutb, without mentioning the ideologue by name. Tilmisani's tack was to "whitewash" Qutb, in effect to deny that he was in any way guilty of the charges that the state had laid against him, because of which some Brothers still held him in suspicion. According to this line of defence, Qutb's intentions had been deliberately misconstrued by his enemies.

This effort to secure Qutb's reputation is clear in the lead article of an early issue of *al-Da'wa*, the Muslim Brotherhood's new press organ, founded in 1976, which was devoted to "the martyr, Sayyid Qutb".[16] The article opened with a ringing endorsement of Qutb's thought by the respected Moroccan Islamic scholar and freedom fighter, Muhammad 'Allal al-Fassi (d. 1974), and went on to claim that Qutb was innocent of all wrongdoing. Qutb was a *da'i*, a missionary whose methods and purposes were entirely peaceful. He preached that Islam was a system of belief and practice that touched on all areas of life, but that Muslims of the current period were far away from this understanding. "Islam," the article quotes Qutb as saying, "came to organize the whole of life, and cannot be limited to devotional acts and rituals." So, the article asks, why the persecution of Qutb and other good Muslims? The author answers that it is because the powers-that-be recognize that Islam has a mandate to change the world at their expense. Thus the United States Ambassador Jefferson Caffery had approached 'Abd al-Nasser asking him to suppress the Muslim Brotherhood, which threatened US interests in the region, not least in relation to Israel, in return for US support for his regime. Given this collusion of interests, it is not surprising that the 'ulama and other state officials cooperated with 'Abd al-Nasser in "dressing the innocent [i.e. Qutb] in the clothes of evil."

Amid the historical distortions, there is no mention of Qutb's bolder declarations concerning the unbelief of Muslims or acknowledgment of his call to organize for the forceful toppling of the *jahili* order in cases when the Islamic movement "is infested by brute force and open violence".[17] There is, in other words, no admission that Qutb believed in the utter illegitimacy of the dominant order and the imperative need to "remove the obstacles in the path" of Islam's victory. Other comments on Qutb continued to downplay the uncomfortable aspects of his thought. For example, from his perch in Saudi Arabia, Muhammad Qutb addressed head on the charge of *takfiri* doctrine that hovered over his brother's legacy. There is nothing in Sayyid's writings, wrote Muhammad,

that contradicts the Koran and the Sunna, on which the mission of the Muslim Brethren is based,...There is nothing in his writings that contradicts the ideas of the martyr *Imam* Hasan al-Banna, founder of the Muslim Brotherhood, in particular al-Banna's comment on his letter "Teachings" (*Risalat al-Ta'lim*), chapter 20: "It is not permitted to excommunicate a Muslim who pronounces the two professions of faith, acts according to their requirements, and accomplishes the ritual obligations.[18]

Still, for the reborn Muslim Brotherhood, the subject of Qutb remained touchy. The ambiguity in his thought was partly to blame. Did his doctrine of *jahiliyya* imply the excommunication of Muslims? And did Qutb advocate the violent overthrow of the government? The unwillingness of Muslim Brothers to tackle Qutb head on was a consequence of their fear of opening a Pandora's Box that might compromise their still precarious position vis-à-vis the state. Consequently, most Muslim Brothers either ignored Qutb or explained him away. He was the "elephant in the room", a presence every Muslim Brother was aware of but of whom few dared to speak forthrightly. Even in the early and mid-1980s, when militants who made reference to the influence on them of Sayyid Qutb attacked the Egyptian state, most Muslim

Brothers remained silent on the issue of Qutb's alleged culpability, leaving such discussion as took place to the *'ulama*. Today the Muslim Brotherhood's leadership continues its skittish attitude, preferring to focus on his solid contributions to Islamic thought rather than his contributions to radicalism.

In the years that followed, those who succeeded 'Umar al-Tilmisani in the position of Supreme Guide continued his policy of political accommodation, electing to operate through formal structures such as party organizations, professional syndicates and the Parliament. To overcome the state ban on its functioning as a political party, the Brotherhood entered into an electoral alliance with the reborn Wafd Party in 1984 and with the Labour Party in 1987. In subsequent elections, the Brotherhood continued to field candidates on the Labour Party ticket.

The Jama'at

A more direct engagement with Qutb's ideas was undertaken by the *jama'at*, the small radical groups that emerged in Egypt during Sadat's presidency. As John Voll notes, these "did not represent a single unified movement but were instead a shifting and interacting collection of individuals and groups about whom little was known until some dramatic event would bring them to the attention of the police and the media."[19] Whereas the leaders of the *jama'at* were charismatic and adept at Islamist rhetoric, the ordinary members tended to be university students from campuses around the country, chiefly Cairo and Asyut, or else tradespeople and small merchants.[20] The members were mostly young, in their twenties, and had family roots in the villages. Although leaders and followers were middle class and reasonably educated, especially in science and technology, they were decidedly unintellectual inasmuch as they preferred straight-ahead thinking to analytical thought. In this they were quite unlike Qutb, the inveterate aesthete and social critic. Yet they shared Qutb's passionate anger at the way things stood: upward mobility blocked by poor economic performance, government indifference to the plight of the people, and the erosion of traditional Islamic virtues. Additionally, they were despondent at the inability of Egypt and the Arab World to defeat Israel. Although Egypt's army had managed to cross into Israeli–occupied Sinai during the 1973 October War, Egypt did not score a victory, and the shame of 1967 still hung in the air. Worse still was the insult of Sadat's 1977 peace initiative towards "the Jews". In the view of the *jama'at*, although Sadat had released the Muslim Brothers and had elevated Islam to a place of prominence in state affairs, at the deep level the condition of the country had not changed.

Of course, these festering problems affected the morale of all sectors of Egyptian society, including those who supported Sadat's new incarnation of the revolutionary spirit. Yet the socialization and experiences of the young men of the *jama'at* induced them to frame their understanding of events in terms of signs and symbols associated with the Islamic tradition.

Thus, they were quick to seize on the radical implications of Sayyid Qutb's thought. Like Qutb, they saw themselves as a force of renewal. They revered Hasan al-Banna and believed that the older generation of Muslim Brothers had neglected "true *jihad*", especially in their accommodating attitude to the Sadat regime. Like Qutb, too, they condemned the edifice of the contemporary order root and branch, although they differed among themselves about the degree of society's religiosity. In the words of Saad Eddine Ibrahim, these new radicals were convinced that "adherence to the purest sources will deliver them, their society, and the world from all the ills of our time—from the world's decadence, corruption, weakness, poverty and humiliation..."[21] Qutb's teachings provided their invective against the status quo with doctrinal substance and direction.

The earliest of these *jama'at* bodies was led not by a native Egyptian but by a Palestinian, Salih 'Abdallah Siriyya, who was alleged to be a disciple of Taqi al-Din Nabahani (d. 1977), founder and ideologue of the Islamic Liberation Organization (*Munazzamat al-Tahrir al-Islami*), established in 1953. According to Kepel, Siriyya arrived in 1971 in Cairo where he befriended Zaynab al-Ghazali and Hudaybi. Qutb's (and Mawdudi's) concept of the divine *hakimiyya* influenced him in the direction of radicalism.[22] Ayman al-Zawahiri remembered hearing him address an "Islamic jamboree" at 'Ayn Shams University in Cairo: "As soon as I heard the speech by this visitor I realized that his words carried weight and meaning on the need to support Islam."[23] However, unlike Qutb, he condemned only the regime, not the society, as being distant from Islam. In 1974, he and his followers took over the Technical Military Academy in the Cairo suburb of Heliopolis in preparation for a takeover of the Egyptian government. The putsch failed and the authorities executed Siriyya and one of his surviving followers, but the stage was set for the next armed underground leader to confront the tyranny.

This was Shukri Mustafa, the agriculture student imprisoned during the crackdown of 1965. He called his group Jama'at al-Muslimin, although outsiders referred to it as Takfir wa al-Hijra ("Excommunication and Withdrawal"). In prison, Shukri had read Qutb and absorbed his ideas on the vanguard and the *jahiliyya*. He had been a member of the fledging group of *takfiri*s in Abu Za'bal. Following his release in 1971, he set out to recreate the society of true believers that had taken form in the prison. Differing from Siriyya, he believed that both the state and the society were *jahili*, but he was more explicit than Qutb in branding the societies of the age to be in a state of apostasy. Heeding Qutb's advice, he encouraged his small band of followers to live in pious isolation from the surrounding *jahiliyya* in preparation for the *jihad*, first in the caves of Asyut province not far from Qutb's native village, Musha, and then in designated flats in Cairo. In their view, they were the only true Muslims. In part, they did this to evade the risk of detection, but physical separation was also their way to attain purity and resolution of purpose. The more isolated the group was, the more it would be aware of its special identity and calling, and the richer would its values become.

Although Shukri believed in the necessity of confrontation, he did not sanction an immediate coup d'état. Like Qutb he believed that the pervasiveness of the *jahiliyya* required preparing the ground first, just as Muhammad the Prophet had patiently worked for Muslim success at Mecca and later at Medina. Shukri planned to build up a model community of Muslims prior to taking action. As Saad Eddine Ibrahim explained, "After its completion, this Islamic community of believers would grow in numbers and in spiritual and material strength. When it had reached a certain point the true believers would march onward to bring down the crumbling sinful social order of Egypt at large."[24]

Qutb's influence over this strategy of action-oriented gradualism is clear. However, Shukri was far more "fundamentalist" than Qutb, as for instance in his "radical rejection of all previous interpretations of Islam",[25] including those of the imams of the four legal schools, especially Bin Hanbal and Malik Ibn Anas to whom Qutb often deferred.[26] Events forced the group to act sooner than Shukri had planned. In July 1977 the police captured several members. In an effort to convince the authorities to release their brothers, the group's members kidnapped the former Minister of Religious Endowments (*awqaf*) Shaykh Dhahabi, and when the government refused to give into the blackmail, murdered him. Within months of the assassination, the state authorities apprehended Shukri and four of his associates, tried them and sentenced them to death.

The Jihad Group (al-Jama'at al-Jihad) had origins going back to the 1970s in a number of scattered cells, one of which, we have noted, a young Ayman al-Zawahiri had organized. Its members hailed from both Lower and Upper Egypt and many had records of Islamist activism. The group's loose organization precluded tight operational control. However, two individuals arose to dominate its thinking, 'Abd al-Salam Faraj (d. 1982), a graduate of Cairo University with a degree in engineering, and the Azhari shaykh 'Umar 'Abd al-Rahman (b. 1938), who had a large following in Sayyid Qutb's home province of Asyut. Sayyid Qutb's call to action inspired both men.[27] Following Qutb, Faraj and 'Abd al-Rahman upheld the imperative of *jihad* against the forces of disbelief (*kufr*), including, most especially, infidels who held authority over Muslim lands; against such forces, *jihad* was incumbent on all Muslims. Yet Muslims in the modern period had neglected the duty of *jihad*; hence the title of Faraj's 1979 tract *al-Farida al-Gha'iba* (*The Neglected Duty*). Faraj wrote, "It is obligatory for the Muslims to raise their swords under the very eyes of the Leaders who hide the Truth and spread falsehoods. If (the Muslims) do not do this, the Truth will not reach the hearts of men..."[28]

Faraj's argument, which he backed with scattered quotations drawn from the Qur'an and mediaeval Hanbali jurists, led to one fundamental claim: that the current rulers of the Muslim lands were infidels and thus legitimate targets of Muslim wrath. "The rulers of this age," he wrote, "are in apostasy from Islam. They were raised at the tables of imperialism, be it Crusaderism, or Communism, or Zionism."[29] He backed up his charge of infidelity in drawing upon a juridical opinion (*fatwa*) by the fourteenth century Damascene scholar Ibn Taymiyya. Ibn Taymiyya had argued that, although the Mongol rulers of the mediaeval Middle East said they were Muslims, the fact that they continued to apply pagan Mongol law (*yasa*) qualified them as disbelievers, usurpers of God's sovereignty, whom Muslims ought to resist.[30] In Faraj's and 'Abd al-Rahman's view, Sadat was a ruler who similarly usurped God's prerogative, even while claiming to be a Muslim. In his treatise, Faraj argued that "apostate" leaders (such as Sadat) were the "Near Enemy" who must be fought prior to engagement with the "Far Enemies" such as Israel and America. "To fight an enemy who is near is more important than to fight an enemy who is far."[31]

Thus 'Abd al-Salam Faraj and 'Umar 'Abd al-Rahman explicitly described Egypt's governing class as irreligious.[32] However, unlike Qutb, they did not cast serious aspersions on the faith of common Muslims. Whereas Qutb had insisted on a prior period of preparation during which the vanguard would build up its resources and gain new converts, Faraj advocated an immediate and violent coup d'état without reference to the larger population of Muslims, "In this way," Gilles Kepel writes, "Faraj broke with the strategy of *Signposts* [i.e. *Milestones*] and its successive versions through the seventies."[33]

It did not take long for the Jihad Group to act on its vision. Egged on by two of its members, Khalid al-Islambuli and Karam Zuhdi, the group assassinated President Sadat on 6 October 1981 during a military parade marking the Egyptian armed forces' successful crossing of the Suez Canal into Israeli–occupied Sinai eight years earlier. The group had actually planned to murder the entire upper echelon of the leadership, hoping thereby to spark a popular uprising against the regime. But it had not been able to put the full plan into effect, and many within the Jihad Group's membership subsequently suffered imprisonment and execution; Ayman al-Zawahiri was one of those imprisoned, in his case for complicity but not direct involvement in the murder. However, the Group survived the crackdown and was able to reconstitute itself in the years that followed. In 1984 there was a schism in its ranks when one of its original components, al-Jama'at al-Islamiyya (the Islamic Group), composed mainly of Upper Egyptians, decided to go its own way. At issue was the question of leadership. The Islamic Group wanted one of its own to lead the unified group, namely, 'Umar 'Abd al-Rahman, while the core Jihad Group membership favoured a former military intelligence officer, 'Abbud al-Zumur. The debate raged over matters of Shari'a law: the Jihad Group argued that 'Abd-al-Rahman's blindness disqualified him from a leadership role, while the Upper Egyptians reminded everyone that al-Zumur was still in prison as a result of his role in the Sadat assassination: should not that fact disqualify al-Zumur?[34]

Additionally, there was the matter of tactics. The core members of the Jihad Group preferred to operate clandestinely and continued to prefer the tactics of the putsch. Biding its time, it prepared secretly to overthrow the regime in Cairo. The Islamic Group, on the other hand, worked to ingratiate itself among the local population, especially in Upper Egypt, and opened its doors widely to recruits. It favoured guerilla operations rather than the surgical strike. One of the motivations for the group's populist approach was its members' regional identification, which pitted Egypt's economically disadvantaged, and politically marginal, southern districts against the power centre in Cairo.[35] In the end the parting of the two groups was relatively amicable, but they competed vigorously for prestige and resources. During the late 1980s and well into the 1990s, Jihad, the Islamic Group and other smaller organizations such as the short-lived Salvation from Hell attacked high-ranking officials and police forces incessantly, ratcheting up the level of violence against them.

Similar groups emerged in Algeria. Following the army's coup on 11 January 1992 and its banning of the Islamic Salvation Front (French acronym, FIS), some disaffected elements of society found an outlet for their anger and humiliation in radical Islamist groups that had been formed or consolidated in the wake of the army takeover.

The 'ulama *weigh in*

In all of this violence, religious and political authorities in Egypt and elsewhere discerned the ghost of Sayyid Qutb, and not without reason: Qutb did in fact inspire numbers of dissenting Muslims to adopt an attitude of confrontation against the established state order. The murderous rampages of the 1980s and 1990s earned the groups the censure of religious scholars who supported the regimes in Cairo and Algiers against violent Islamism. One such scholarly critic was the conservative, Azhar-trained shaykh Yusuf al-Qaradawi (b. 1926), whose strong association with the Muslim Brotherhood went back to the late 1940s.[36] Adopting the standard argument, al-Qaradawi accused Qutb and his followers of challenging the integrity not only of the state but, more seriously, of the very fabric of Islamic civilization. In al-Qaradawi's view, the extremists broke with the received understanding of Islam—that Muslims are those who acknowledge God's unity and the prophecy of Muhammad. Muslims must heed the example of the pious ancestors (*al-Salafiyyun*) and postpone judgment on other Muslims. To do otherwise was to follow the community-destroying path of the Kharijites. He wrote, "If a Muslim in this age observes the *wajibat* [those things that are obligatory for Muslims] and eschews the most heinous of the *muharramat* [those things that are forbidden] he should be accommodated in the fold of God."[37]

Al-Qaradawi also challenged the militants concerning their overly aggressive attitude towards Christians and Jews. Such emphasis, he wrote, was bad *fiqh* (juridical understanding) and flew in the face of the Qur'an's conciliatory ethos. To make his point, he cited Qur'an 8:61: "And if they incline to peace, incline thou also to it, and trust in Allah, Lo! He is the Hearer, the Knower." This and other verses, taken in conjunction with the Prophet's example, communicate Islam's preference for establishing treaties with non-Muslims when possible.[38] Al-Qaradawi admitted that he shared many of the concerns of the militant groups, especially on issues relating to authoritarian rule in Arab countries, the growing materialism and hedonism of social and cultural life, and the inability of Arab governments to cope with Israel. Yet, he argued, Muslims must face these and other challenges with strategies of gradualism, patience and tolerance.

Other scholarly voices weighed in against the extremists. Jad al-Haq 'Ali Jad al-Haq, whom Egypt's new president Husni Mubarak appointed Shaykh al-Azhar in 1982, issued a *fatwa* against the Jihad Group in which he condemned Faraj's analogy between the Mongol rulers and Anwar Sadat. He asked, how can one compare the abject irreligion of the Mongols to a man who openly professed the faith? Such a comparison is absurd. One can apply apostasy only to someone who expressly abjures the creed. Moreover, according to Jad al-Haq, Faraj misinterpreted the Qur'anic "sword verse", 9:5: "Then when the Sacred Months (the Ist, 7th, 11th, and 12th months of the Islâmic calendar) have passed, then kill the *Mushrikûn* (see V.2:105) wherever you find them, and capture them and besiege them, and prepare for them each and every ambush. But if they repent and perform *As-Salât* (*Iqâmat-as-Salât*), and give *Zakât*, then leave their way free. Verily, Allâh is Oft-Forgiving, Most Merciful." Faraj had used this verse to justify aggression and warfare against all of Islam's enemies. Yet, as Jad al-Haq explained, the scholarly consensus held that God revealed this verse to refer specifically to the Meccan polytheists who had broken a treaty with the Muslims, not to unbelievers in general.[39]

Similarly, many Salafi shaykhs, including revered custodians of the Wahhabi tradition in Saudi Arabia, raised eyebrows at what they perceived as the *bida'* ("innovations") of Qutb and his followers. The venerable Grand Mufti 'Abd al-'Aziz Ibn 'Abd Allah Ibn Baz (d. 1999) and the renowned teachers Muhammad Ibn al-Uthaymin (d. 2001) and Salah Al-Fawzan (b. 1933) explained Qutb's interpretive distortions as resulting from his poor knowledge of *Usul al-Fiqh* (the principles of jurisprudence). Thus, for example, Ibn Baz accused Qutb of demeaning the character of ancient prophets and prophetic Companions; of being too harsh in his judgment of wayward Muslims; and of propagating the pantheistic Sufi teaching, distasteful especially to Salafis, of *Wahdat al-Wajud* ("the Unity of Being").[40] Clearly, Qutb's freewheeling discursive style, full of literary flourishes and allusions, was distasteful to these men of *fiqh*. But reading between the lines, one also discerns in their response a strong reaction against the individual they deemed most responsible for the open dissent of the *sahwa* shaykhs. The great Salafi shaykhs who once welcomed Qutb's ideas into the Kingdom, or at least turned a blind eye to them, by the 1990s came to regard Qutb's influence as disruptive to Saudi Arabia's social and political order.

The crux of the scholars' argument is that only qualified individuals can legitimately interpret the Qur'an and guide the impulse underlying the Islamic awakening. For instance, according to Qaradawi, the definition of Islam should emerge from public, critical discussion conducted by the leading *fuqaha* (jurists) only. Unqualified agents such as Qutb are apt to have their judgment clouded by emotion and selfish desires. Amateurs will be attracted to allegorical or excessively literal understandings of Islam's textual sources, or become preoccupied with controversial side issues. In the scholars' view, the attainment of the common good was contingent on society's acquiescence to their expert guidance. Indeed, it is against this ideal of directed social harmony that Qaradawi, Jad al-Haq and the Salafi shaykhs of Saudi Arabia measured the turbulence set in motion by Sayyid Qutb, the *jama'at*, and the *Sahwa*. Although many *'ulama* were quick to criticize the state as not sufficiently dedicated to Shari'a legislation, they nevertheless understood the need for a custodial authority. The *'ulama* therefore worked within the framework of the established order, even while they attempted gently to steer that order in the direction of Islamic change. It is no accident that, in recent decades, some *'ulama* (al-Qaradawi is a prime example) have made common cause with the new Muslim Brotherhood, which similarly aims to effect change within constitutional limits.

Yet, in arguing their case, Qaradawi and other critics perhaps missed the point. Although it is true that those who belonged to the extremist organizations did not, with few exceptions, possess profound knowledge of the Islamic sciences, the attainment of scholarly credentials was not their concern. What mattered to them was the plight of politically under-represented and economically marginalized Muslims. Alienated from the Western values of the establishment culture, and angered by the Egyptian government's Western-leaning policies, these groups' members fastened onto symbols of the Islamic culture that distinguished them from the dominating order. In the case of Egypt's militants, such symbols included styles of Islamic dress and the wearing of beards, in addition to veiling and relative seclusion of women, all of which, in the phrase of Aziz al-Azmeh, comprised a "discourse of authenticity whose primary epistemological instrument is the recognition and registration of difference."[41] But these markers were more than tokens of social identity; they pointed to the great religious truth that lay behind the obscuring curtain of the phenomenal world. Sayyid Qutb's ideas of *hakimiyya*, *jahiliyya*, and—in the case of the Jihad Group—the vanguard were goads for much of this conceptualization. Qutb's worldview of religiously justified cultural division and conflict is apparent in the discourse of the Jihad Group's 'Abbud al-Zumur. In prison in the mid-1980s, he experienced the same ill-treatment that guards had earlier meted out to Qutb and other Islamists. He wrote, "Anyone who observes the Islamic nation today as it groans from its wounds and stumbles through illusions, drunk on the false nectar of Western civilization, will ask the God of earth and heaven to cure the disease that captured Muslim leaders, the disease that resulted in their separation from religion and dismissal of God's Book."[42]

Conclusion

The core concepts on radical Islamist dissent constitute a political myth of Islam's rebirth in world affairs, attained by confrontation with allegedly corrupt and dysfunctional regimes and, sometimes, societies. I use the term myth not in the common meaning of an unfounded or false notion, but in the sense of a body of beliefs that express the fundamental, largely unconscious or assumed political values of a group—in short, a dramatic expression of ideology. Composed of simplistic images that speak to the despair and alienation felt by many Muslims, as well as to their hope for the future, the myth addresses the fundamental malaise of modern Islam, the "sense that something has gone wrong with Islamic history".[43] Not only does this myth function to mobilize activists in support of Islamic resurgence, it can also provide the necessary justification for acts of terror. As the British journalist Fergal Keane observes:

To be capable of sustaining a savage war against the enemy, to be able to subject him and his loved ones to a relentless campaign of terror—a war in which the normal rules, the concept of a 'warrior's honour' are abandoned—it is necessary to narrow the mind, make it subject to a very limited range of ideas and influences.[44]

We have already made the point that Qutb's radical Islamism shares points of similarity with political opposition movements of other times and places, including most notably the secular nationalist movements, which likewise call for collective reassertion or revolutionary activity. Keane cites the IRA gunmen of the 1920s whose political consciousness and willingness to adopt violence were shaped by the vision of a reborn Ireland, but other examples could be cited, including the Revisionist Zionist movement in British Mandate Palestine and the various expressions of Arab nationalism, such as Ba'thism and Nasserism. The Watani–inspired secret cell to which 'Abd al-Fattah 'Inayat belonged, described in chapter 1, would also qualify. These movements differ on a multitude of points, not least the level of their commitment to "direct action" and deference to divine authority. But all share the underlying premise of community regeneration through struggle.

Radical Islamism, as Qutb expressed it, is a fundamental, though disturbing aspect of the modern experience of Muslims, anchored in the historical record of suppression by imperialist outsiders. Through recourse to the power of images drawn from the cultural memory of Muslims, Qutb and other radical Islamists crafted an uncompromising understanding of Islam, one whose core myth aims to inspire a movement of purifying, cathartic community rebirth. By demonizing the political and cultural moorings of the Western, or Westernized, "Other" and envisioning principles for an as-yet-unrealized "community of virtue", they have narrowly circumscribed the range of legitimate political discourse. As Sayyid Qutb well understood, Qur'anic images possess sufficient power to transform theory into practice.

There is no need to discuss in any detail the paths by which global *jihadi*s of the present period have absorbed and modified Qutb's articulation of this deep-seated impulse. Such discussions are beyond the scope of this book and, in fact, redundant in face of the many excellent studies on these topics which, as noted in the Introduction, have appeared in recent years.[45] Here it suffices to note that the *jihad* against the Soviet Red Army in Afghanistan provided opportunities for the Saudi orientation within Salafism and Egyptian-style jihadism to co-mingle. Throughout the 1980s, Salafi fighters from Saudi Arabia linked up with *mujahidin* from Egypt, Algeria, Pakistan, Indonesia and elsewhere. Stymied in their home countries by police action, they considered Afghanistan an appropriate and inviting location to engage the principle of *jihad*. The merging of conservative and radical elements was evident in the Islamist organization Hizb-i Islami, which took much of its inspiration from Qutb and was also one of the chief beneficiaries of Saudi money and Salafi doctrine. It was also evident in the discourse of the Salafi–oriented Palestinian *mujahid* 'Abdullah 'Azzam, who accepted Qutb's premise that aggression against Muslims should be met and challenged.

In their efforts, the fighters received support in the form of money and arms from the CIA and the Saudi Intelligence Department, which those organizations channelled to the resistance through Pakistan's Inter-Services Intelligence Directorate (ISI). All three countries—the US, Saudi Arabia, and Pakistan—shared the common goals of containing communism in South Asia and strengthening Sunni Islam against the revolutionary Shi'ism spilling out of Iran.

The mix of Puritanism and *jihad* was potent. For the fighters in Afghanistan, the war was a source of heroism, solidarity and total devotion to the Shari'a. Many were already aware that the struggle against the Red Army was a school in which they might hone the violent techniques needed to topple their governments at home.

Certainly, the Afghan war was the defining experience of Usama bin Laden's life. A Saudi who grew up in the devotional environment of Saudi Arabian Salafism, bin Laden was one of the first Arabs to join the *jihad*. He saw his role there as facilitator and spent his personal fortune to build roads and tunnels for the *mujahidin* and provide pensions to the families of the fallen. His personal piety and willingness to sacrifice comfort for the cause of Islam endeared him to his fellows.

After the Soviet withdrawal from Afghanistan in 1989, Usama bin Laden returned home in triumph with other Saudi veterans. When the Ba'thist regime in Iraq invaded Kuwait a year later, he approached the

Saudi royal family and offered to raise a new army of believers to resist Saddam Husayn. When the ruling house rejected the offer, bin Laden became increasingly alienated from the elite social stratum of his birth. His loathing for the Saudi ruling family deepened when, with the sanction of bin Baz, it allowed the stationing of US troops in the kingdom during and after the war. In bin Laden's mind, in aiding and abetting the US occupation of the kingdom the House of Saud, whose legitimacy derived from its protection of Islam, had entered the circle of iniquity.

In his criticisms of the Saudi royal family, bin Laden had at his disposal both the radical articulations developed by Sayyid Qutb's followers and the traditions of rebuke of the Salafi–Saudi tradition in which he had been raised. Yet while bin Laden was willing in the tradition of Salafi–oriented dissent to brand the ruling family as unbelievers, he chose instead to attack the alleged American puppet master operating from behind the throne. In so doing he and Ayman al-Zawahiri reversed the order theorized by the Qutbist groups, which advocated as a first step the eradication of the perceived corruption at home. According to the standard view, the Western "other" should be engaged only once the Muslim World had been strengthened by the creation of a transnational Islamic state. Bin Laden and Zawahiri, on the other hand, appear to have desired global confrontation sooner rather than later. In so doing, they helped to reify Islam as an abstract faith and moral code distinct from national or cultural identities, traditions, and histories. In planning the 9/11 attacks, Al Qaeda had in its sight nothing less than the salvation of the *umma* broadly conceived.

We know that the 9/11 hijackers saw much of the United States during the months they were residents. Like Qutb years earlier, they viewed the country not with fresh eyes but through the filter of a preconceived vision. In contrast to Qutb, however, murderous purpose, more than simple contempt, animated their outlook. In Muhammad 'Atta's case, his dark vision jelled in Hamburg where he was a regular visitor to the Al-Tawhid mosque and met ideologically committed veterans of the Afghan *jihad*. Living outside his native culture in a foreign country, 'Atta found solace at the mosque but also a cache of ideas that enabled him to transcend his alienation.

Qutb, whom he assuredly read, would not have sanctioned the methods of extreme violence that 'Atta and his terrorist colleagues employed; as Qutb had pointed out in his writings, the killing of innocents finds no justification in the Qur'an. Nor would Qutb have understood Al Qaeda's desire to attack a Western power in such a fashion. In his mind, the *jihad* against the *taghut* at home was always paramount. However, he would have had little trouble understanding the underlying logic of their purpose. For in the September 11 attacks the hijackers underscored the same point that he made in his prison writings: that the World, as it stands, constitutes a conceptual realm of irreligion and vice that ought to be resisted in the name of God.

The hijackers defined their actions as the ultimate act of *jihad*, which called into stark relief the chasm in their minds between the forces of virtue and unbelief. They conceived their attacks as what Mark Juergensmeyer called "performance violence",[46] spectacular acts of carnage and death designed to have a searing effect on the consciousness of their television audiences, which in the case of the September 11 attacks numbered many millions. Indeed, this reading of the events is confirmed by bin Laden, who related in a videotape seized in the course of the anti–Taliban-Al Qaeda campaign how the hijackers "said in deeds in New York and Washington, speeches that overshadowed all other speeches made anywhere in the world. The speeches are understood by both Arabs and non-Arabs—even by Chinese."[47] Here is dramatic testimony of how events were understood by the perpetrators themselves, as metaphors for the confrontation between an absolute good threatened with destruction by its absolute opposite.

NOTES

INTRODUCTION

1. Following Graham Fuller, I define an Islamist as "one who believes that Islam as a body of faith has something important to say about how politics and society should be ordered in the contemporary Muslim world and who seeks to implement this ideas in some fashion": *The Future of Political Islam* (New York: Palgrave Macmillan, 2003), xi. The International Crisis Group has put forward another worthy definition: "Islamism is defined... as synonymous with 'Islamic activism', the active assertion and promotion of beliefs, prescriptions, laws, or policies that are held to be Islamic in character." "Understanding Islamism," *Middle East/North Africa Report* no. 37—2 March 2005, 1. Of course, Islamists do not apply the term to themselves. In their view, they are revivalists interested in the restoration of authentic, original Islam. Posters plastering the walls of the villages of Upper Egypt proclaim, "Islam is the solution" (*al-Islam huwwa al-hal*), not "Islamism is the solution."

2. Sayyid Qutb, *This Religion of Islam* (Delhi: Markazi Maktaba Islami, 1974), 9; Arabic original *Hadha al-Din* (Cairo: Dar al-Qalam, 1962).

3. Sayyid Qutb, *In the Shade of the Qur'an: Fi Zilal al-Qur'an*, vol. III, surah 4, Al-Nisa', translated and edited by Adil Salahi and Ashur Shamis (Leicester: The Islamic Foundation, 2001/1421), 349; Arabic original, Sayyid Qutb, *Fi Zilal al-Qur'an* (Beirut: Dar al-Shuruq, 1994), parts 5–7, vol. 2, 778.

4. François Burgat and William Dowell, *The Islamic Movement in North Africa*, new edition (Austin: Center For Middle East Studies, University of Texas at Austin, 1997), 94.

5. For example, in his *Fasl al-Kalam fi Muwajahat Zulm al-Hukkam* (n.p. Al-Jabha al-Islamiyya li–Inqadh [FIS] n.d.), 203 *et passim*.

6. Quoted in S.A. Arjomand, *The Turban of the Crown: The Islamic Revolution in Iran* (Oxford University Press, 1988), 97.

7. François Burgat and William Dowell, *The Islamic Movement in North Africa* (see note 4), 64.

8. Col. Francisco Cruz Jr., "Morojihad and the Islamic Vision of Ustadz Salamt Hashim: Understanding MILF's Politico-Religious Ideology," Philip-

pine Institute for Political Violence and Terrorism, Paper Series (August 2008), 3–4.

9. Quoted in Peter L. Bergen, *The Osama bin Laden I Know* (New York: Free Press, 2006), 19.

10. Olivier Carré, *Mysticism and Politics: A Critical Reading of the Qur'an by Sayyid Qutb, Radical Muslim Brother*, translated by Carol Artigues and revised by W. Shepard (Leiden: E.J. Brill, 2003), 9.

11. See, for example, the long list of blogs focused on Sayyid Qutb at: http:// en.wordpress.com/tag/sayyid-qutb/.

12. On Qutb's influence on the Syrian Brothers see Emmanuel Sivan, *Radical Islam: Medieval Theology and Modern Politics* (New Haven: Yale University Press, 1985), 40–7, and Brynjar Lia, *Architect of Global Jihad: The Life of Al-Qaida Strategist Abu Mus'ab al-Suri* (New York: Columbia University Press, 2008), 38–41.

13. On the Egyptian *Jama'at* see Gilles Kepel, *Muslim Extremism in Egypt: The Prophet and the Pharaoh* (Berkeley: University of California Press, 1984), 72–102.

14. Committee on Near Eastern Studies, *Report for 1950*. The assignment for the translation of *al-'Adala* was given to the Rev. John Hardie. Qutb's book was the first to appear in the Arabic series. I am grateful to Professor Leon Carl Brown for sharing the reports of the Committee on Near Eastern Studies dealing with the translation programme with me.

15. For Kepel see note 8 above; Carré's book has been translated into English as *Mysticism and Politics: A Critical Reading of the Qur'an by Sayyid Qutb, Radical Muslim Brother*, translated by Carol Artigues and revised by W. Shepard (Leiden: E.J. Brill, 2003). See also William Shepard, *Sayyid Qutb and Islamic Activism: A Translation and Critical Analysis of Social Justice in Islam* (Leiden: E.J. Brill, 1996); Youssef Choueiri, *Islamic Fundamentalism* (London: Pinter, 1989, rev. ed. 1997); Ibrahim M. Abu-Rabi, *Intellectual Origins of Islamic Resurgence in the Modern Arab World* (Albany: State University of New York Press, 1996); Ahmad Mousalli, *Radical Islamic Fundamentalism: The Ideological and Political Discourse of Sayyid Qutb* (Beirut: American University of Beirut Press, 1992); Leonard Binder, *Islamic Liberalism: A Critique of Development Ideologies* (University of Chicago Press, 1988), 170–205; Emmanuel Sivan (see note 6 above); Yvonne Haddad, "Sayyid Qutb: Ideologue of Islamic Revival," in John Esposito (ed.), *Voices of Resurgent Islam* (Oxford University Press, 1983), 67–98; Shahrough Akhavi, "Sayyid Qutb: The 'Poverty of Philosophy' and the Vindication of Islamic Tradition," in Serif Mardin (ed.), *Cultural Transitions in the Middle East* (Leiden: E.J. Brill, 1994), 130–52; Muhammad Hafiz Diyab, *Sayyid Qutb: Al-Khitab was al-Idulu-jiyya* (Cairo: Dar al-Thaqafa al-Jadida, 1989); Muhammad Tawfiq Barakat, *Sayyid Qutb* (Beirut: Dar al-Da'wa, n.d.); Hilmi al-Namnam, *Sayyid Qutb wa Thawrat Yulyu* (Cairo: Mirit li al-Nashr wa-al-Ma'lumat, 1999); Adnan Musallam, *From Secularism to Jihad: Sayyid Qutb and the Foun-*

dations of Radical Islamism (New York: Praeger, 2005); Roxanne
L. Euben, *Enemy in the Mirror: Islamic Fundamentalism and the Limits
of Modern Rationalism* (Princeton University Press, 1999); Sayed Khateb,
The Political Thought of Sayyid Qutb: The Theory of Jahiliyyah, London
and New York: Routledge, 2006); and *The Power of Sovereignty: The
Political and Ideological Philosophy of Sayyid Qutb* (London and New
York: Routledge, 2006).

16. Salah 'Abd al-Fattah al-Khalidi, *Sayyid Qutb: Min al-Milad ila al-Istishhad* (Damascus: Dar al-Qalam, 1991). This is an expanded version of his
earlier published book on Qutb, also based on his graduate work, entitled
Sayyid Qutb: Al-Shahid al-Hayy (Amma: Maktaba al-Aqsa, 1985).

17. Personal email communication from Lawrence Wright, author of the
Looming Tower and one of the very few individuals outside Islamist circles to have interviewed Muhammad Qutb. Since the late 1960s, Muhammad Qutb has been the primary custodian and official interpreter of his
brother's legacy.

18. See *al-Furqan* magazine's interview with al-Khalidi at: http://www.ikhwan.
net/vb/showthread.php?t=13479. Accessed 3/25/2009.

19. Thomas Hegghammer, "The Obstacles to Understanding Radical Islam
and the Opportunites to Know it Better," *Times Literary Supplement* (2
April 2008). Available on the www at: http://entertainment.timesonline.
co.uk/tol/arts_and_entertainment/the_tls/article3667505.ece. Accessed
4/4/2008.

20. Some of the most insightful of the recent studies which emphasize Qutb's
role include Lawrence Wright, *The Looming Tower: Al-Qaeda and the
Road to 9/11* (New York: Knoph, 2006); Malise Ruthven, *A Fury for
God: The Islamist Attack on America* (London and New York: Granta
Books, 2002); Daniel Benjamin and Steven Simon, *The Age of Sacred Ter-
ror* (New York: Random House, 2002); Paul Berman, *Terror and Liberal-
ism* (New York: W.W. Norton & Com, 2003); Anthony Shadid, *Legacy of
the Prophet: Despots, Democrats, and the New Politics of Islam* (Boulder:
Westview Press, 2002); Fawaz Gerges, *Journey of the Jihadist* (New York:
Harcourt, 2006); and François Burgat, *Islamism in the Shadow of Al
Qaeda* (Austin: University of Texas Press, 2008). Thomas H. Kean and
Lee H. Hamilton, *9/11 Report: The National Commission on Terrorist
Attacks Upon the United States* (New York: St. Martin's Press, 2004) goes
farther than other studies in establishing a relationship between Qutb and
bin Laden: "Bin Ladin also relies heavily on the Egyptian writer Sayyid
Qutb....Bin Ladin shares Qutb's stark view, permitting him and his fol-
lowers to rationalize even unprovoked mass murder as righteous defense
of an embattled faith." p. 51.

21. Quoted in Montasser al-Zayyat, *The Road to Al-Qaeda: The Story of Bin
Laden's Right-Hand Man*, translated by Ahmed Fekry, edited by Sara
Nimis (London: Pluto Press, 2004), 24–5; original title *Ayman al-Zawahiri
Kama 'Araftahu* (Cairo: Dar al-Mahrusa, 2002). An edited version of al-

Zawahiri's *Knights under the Prophet's Banner* was serialized in the Saudi–owned newspaper *Al-Sharq al-Awsat* (2 Dec. 2001). The translation of this document by FIBIS was formerly available on-line.

22. The book is *Al-Harb al-Amriki bi–Manathir Sayyid Qutb* (The American War from the Perspective of Sayyid Qutb). See the summary of LCDR Youssef Abdoul-Enein, MSC, USN, "Sheikh Abdel-Fatah Al-Khalidi Revitalizes Sayid Qutb: Inside the Adversary's Anti–American Ideology from the Cold War to Operation Iraqi Freedom," The Combating Terrorism Center, United States Military Academy, West Point, NY. At: http://www.ctc.usma.edu. Accessed 10/15/08. The first edition of the book is Salah 'Abd al-Fattah al-Khalidi, *Amrika min al-Dakhil bi–Nazar Sayyid Qutb* (Cairo: Dar al-Wafa', 1987).

23. For example, "Roots of Terrorism," *Greeley Tribune*, 24 February 2002; "Greeley Trip Was One of Islamist's 'Milestones'", *Rocky Mountain News* (Denver), 21 September 2002. "Greeley's Al Qaeda Connection: How 1940s Greeley Influenced Al Qaeda's Mastermind," *Fort Collins Weekly*, vol. 1, issue 5, 2–8 April 2003; and Mark Steyn, "The Church Dance that Snowballed," http://www.macleans.ca/culture/books/article.jsp?content=20060925_133309_133309. One can justify the standard narrative by arguing that it captures the essence of the subject. Indeed, some of the most insightful commentaries on the contemporary *jihadi* phenomenon have come from writers who weave artistic insight into hard-nosed analysis. Two works of exceptional quality are here relevant: Adam Curtis' three-part documentary, *The Power of Nightmares: The Rise of the Politics of Fear* (British Broadcasting Corporation, 2004), and Jonathan Raban's *My Holy War: Dispatches from the Home Front* (New York: New York Review of Books, 2005).

24. Tariq al-Bishri, *al-Haraka al-Siyasiyya fi Misr, 1945–1952* (Cairo: Dar al-Shuruq, 2nd edition, 1983), 41–2.

25. Roxanne Euben, *Enemy in the Mirror: Islamic Fundamentalism and the Limits of Modern Rationalism* (Princeton University Press, 1999), 20–48.

26. The nihilist Sergi Nechaev (d. 1882) was the prototype of one of the main characters in Dostoevsky's novel *The Possessed*.

27. Sayyid Qutb, *In the Shade of the Qur'an*, vol. 1, surahs 1–2, xxii; Sayyid Qutb, *Fi Zilal al-Qur'an*, parts 1–4, vol. 1, 15.

28. Carré, *Mysticism and Politics*, 56.

29. Sayyid Qutb, *In the Shade of the Qur'an*, vol. 1, surahs 1–2, xvii–iii; Sayyid Qutb, *Fi Zilal al-Qur'an* (Beirut: Dar al-Shuruq, 1994), parts 1–4, vol. 1, 11.

30. One of the primary themes in his *Mysticism and Politics: A Critical Reading of the Qur'an by Sayyid Qutb, Radical Muslim Brother*.

31. On the study of emotion in the social sciences, see Jeff Goodwin, James M. Jasper, and Francesca Polletta (eds), *Passionate Politics: Emotions and Social Movements* (University of Chicago Press, 2001), Catherine S. Lutz and Lia Abu-Lughod (eds), *Language and the Politics of Emotion* (Cam-

bridge University Press, 1990), and Barbara H. Rosenwein, "Worrying about Emotions in History," *American Historical Review*, 107/3 (June 2002), 821–45.

32. As in the introduction to his Qur'an commentary: Sayyid Qutb, *In the Shade of the Qur'an*, vol. 1, surahs 1–2, xxiv; *Fi Zilal al-Qur'an*, parts 1–4, vol. 1, 17.

33. James Billington, *Fire in the Minds of Men: The Origins of the Revolutionary Faith* (New York: Basic Books, 1980), 505.

34. I have found Talal Asad's essay, "Religion, Nation State, Secularism" in Peter van der Veer and Hartmut Lehmann (eds), *Nation and Religion: Perspectives on Europe and Asia* (Princeton University Press, 1999), pp. 178–96, useful in spelling out the disjuncture between nationalism and Islamism.

1. SON OF THE COUNTRY

1. Translated in a document of the British Foreign Office (henceforth FO) 371/62991, 16 April 1947. See also Malak Badrawi, *Political Violence in Egypt 1910–1925: Secret Societies, Plots and Assassinations* (Richmond: Curzon Press, 2000), 173 ff; and Donald M. Reid, "Political Assassination in Egypt, 1910–1954," *International Journal of African Historical Studies*, vol. 15, no. 4 (1982), 625–51.

2. 'Inayat's five-man cells appear to owe their distinctive form to the tradition of underground insurgency developed in the early 19th century by the French Philadelphians, Blanqui, the Russian Decembrists and others. See James Billington, *Fire in the Minds of Men: The Origins of the Revolutionary Faith* (New York: Basic Books, 1980), 110–11. The Wafdist secret apparatus was likewise organized into five-man cells. See Marius Deeb, *Party Politics in Egypt: The Wafd and its Rivals* (Reading: Ithaca Press, 1979), 65.

3. On the Darfur caravan see 'Ali Mubarak, *al-Khitat al-Tawfiqiyya al-Jadida li–Misr al-Qahira wa-Munduniha wa-Biladiha al-Qadima wa al-Shahira*, 20 vols. (Bulaq: al-Matba'a al-Kubra al-Amiriyya, 1303–1306/1886–1888), 17:32, and Charles Issawi, *The Economic History of the Middle East 1800–1914: A Book of Readings* (Chicago and London: The University of Chicago Press, 1991), 257.

4. Nicholas Hopkins, "Clan and Class in Two Arab Villages," in Farhad Kazemi and John Waterbury (eds), *Peasants and Politics in the Modern Middle East* (Miami: Florida International University Press, 1991), 257.

5. Sayyid Qutb, *Tifl min al-Qarya* (Beirut: Dar al-Hikma, n.d. [1967]), 180. Translated and edited by John Calvert and William Shepard as *A Child from the Village* (Syracuse University Press, 2004), 115. German translation as *Kindheit auf dem Lande: ein agyptischer Muslimbruder erinnert* (Berlin: Ed. Orient, 1997). References are to the 1967 Dar al-Hikma Arabic text followed by the 2004 translation.

6. Ahmad Ibn 'Ali al-Maqrizi, *Kitab al-Khitat al-Maqriziyya*, 3 vols. (al-Shiyya, Lebanon: Maktabat Ihya al-'Ulum,1959), III: 418.
7. *Tifl min al-Qarya*, 80; *Child from the Village*, 51.
8. Qutb provides a vivid description of the Sa'id's agricultural cycle, see Ibid., 168–9; 113–14.
9. Barry Kemp, *Ancient Egypt: Anatomy of a Civilization* (London and New York: Routledge, 1991), 10.
10. Sayyid Qutb made the claim of his father's Indian descent to the Indian scholar Abu Hasan al-Nadvi when the latter visited Egypt in 1951. See al-Khalidi, *Sayyid Qutb: Min al-Milad ila al-Istishhad* (Damascus: Dar al-Qalam, 1991), 28. My characterization of al-Hajj Ibrahim as a medium landowner is an inference based upon Qutb's report in *Tifl* that the land-holdings at Musha were relatively substantial in size, ranging up to 200 *faddan*s (170); *A Child from the Village*, 114. According to Nathan Brown, a "property of fifty faddans was considered medium to large..." *Peasant Politics in Modern Egypt* (New Haven and London: Yale University Press, 1990), 27.
11. The history of Musha's social configuration is briefly examined in Hopkins, "Clan and Class in Two Arab Villages," 252–76.
12. *Tifl min al-Qarya*, 15; *A Child from the Village*, 7.
13. Qutb dedicated his 1947 book *Mashahid al-Qiyama fi al-Qur'an* to his father: "Father, I dedicated this book to your spirit, you who impressed upon me fear of the Judgment Day in my early years..." p. 5.
14. Al-Khalidi, *Sayyid Qutb*, 40–49 provides sketches of Sayyid's siblings. It is worth noting that, with the exception of Nafisa, Sayyid's brothers and sisters were active in the Islamist movement in Egypt in the 1950s, 60s and 70s.
15. Ibid., 38. See also the dedication to *al-Atyaf al-Arba'a* (n.p., n.d. [1945], a book of poetry and personal musing jointly authored by Qutb and his siblings, which honours the memory of their mother; and Qutb's comments in the same work, 165–84.
16. On this point, see Nathan Brown, *Peasant Politics*, 79–81; Winifred Blackman, *The Fellahin of Upper Egypt* (New York: Frank Cass and Co. Ltd., 1968; first published 1927), 129; and Henry Habib Ayrout, *The Egyptian Peasant* (Boston: Beacon Press, 1963; first published in France under the title *Moeurs et coutumes des fellahs*, 1938), 109–10.
17. *Tifl min al-Qarya*, 153; *A Child from the Village*, 103.
18. *The Egyptian Peasant*, 111.
19. *Tifl min al-Qarya*, 144 ff.; *A Child from the Village*, 97 ff.
20. Bruce J. Malina, *The New Testament World: Insights from Cultural Anthropology* (Louisville, Kentucky: Westminster/John Knox Press, 1993), 50.
21. Andrea B. Rugh, "Reshaping Personal Relations in Egypt," in Martin E. Marty and R. Scott Appleby (eds), *Fundamentalisms and Society: Reclaiming the Sciences, the Family, and Education* (University of Chicago Press, 1993), 157.

22. On Weber, Tonnies and the sociological roots of modernization theory, see Jorge Larrain, *Theories of Development* (Cambridge: Polity Press, 1989), 87–94.

23. The following examine developments in Egypt's state and economy in the nineteenth century: Kenneth Cuno, *The Pasha's Peasants: Land, Society, and Economy in Lower Egypt, 1740–1858* (Cambridge University Press, 1992); Khaled Fahmy, *All the Pasha's Men: Mehmed Ali, His Army, and the Making of Modern Egypt* (Cambridge University Press, 1997); F. Robert Hunter, *Egypt under the Khedives, 1805–1879: From Household Government to Modern Bureaucracy* (Pittsburgh, PA: University of Pittsburgh Press, 1984); Afaf Lutfi al-Sayyid Marsot, *Egypt in the Reign of Muhammad Ali* (Cambridge University Press, 1984); Ehud Toledano, *State and Society in mid-Nineteenth Century Egypt* (Cambridge University Press, 1990).

24. Roger Owen, "Egyptian Cotton and the American Civil War," in Charles Issawi (ed.), *The Economic History of the Middle East* (University of Chicago Press, 1966), 417.

25. Lady Duff Gordon, *Letters from Egypt* (New York: [s.n.], 1903), 208–9.

26. Charles Issawi, "The Economic Development of Egypt," in Issawi (ed.), *The Economic History of the Middle East*, 364.

27. F. Robert Hunter, *Egypt Under the Khedives*, 106.

28. Following 'Ali Mubarak's *Khitat* (see below, note 30), Gabriel Baer provides the example of the 'Abaza family who as governors of al-Sharqiyya Province controlled more than 6,000 *faddans* in 15 villages. *A History of Landownership in Modern Egypt, 1800–1952* (London: Oxford University Press, 1962), 59.

29. Hunter, *Egypt under the Khedives*, 120–21. See also Charles Smith's discussion of the social paternalism practiced by one well-to-do family in the village of Kafr Ghannam in al-Daqahliyya Province. *Islam and the Search for Social Order in Modern Egypt: A Biography of Muhammad Husayn Haykal* (Albany: SUNY Press, 1983), 33–4.

30. The adoption of Western-inspired law codes in Egypt is treated in Hunter, *Egypt under the Khedives*, and Donald Reid, *Lawyers and Politics in the Arab World* (Minneapolis: Bibliotheca Islamica, 1981).

31. J.N.D. Anderson, "Law Reform in Egypt: 1850–1950," in P.M. Holt (ed.), *Political and Social Change in Modern Egypt* (London: Oxford University Press, 1968), 219.

32. The indispensable source for educational development remains J. Heyworth-Dunne, *An Introduction to the History of Education in Modern Egypt* (London: Luzac and Co., 1938). See also Timothy Mitchell, *Colonizing Egypt* (Berkeley: University of California Press, 1988), 68–80, and Gregory Starrett, *Putting Islam to Work: Education, Politics, and Religious Transformation in Egypt* (Berkeley: University of California Press, 1998), esp. 23–61.

33. Information on Mubarak's life is contained in the biographical notice inserted into his *Khitat* 10:37–61. See also Mitchell, *Colonizing Egypt*, 63–5 *et passim*, Lorne Kenny, "Ali Mubarak, Nineteenth-Century Egyptian Educator and Administrator, *Middle East Journal*, Winter 1967, 35–51, and Gilbert Delanoue, *Moralistes et politiques musulmans dans l'Egypte du XIX siècle (1798–1882)*, 2 vols. (Institut français d'archéologie orientale du Caire, 1982), 2:488–564.

34. 'Ali Mubarak, *Alam al-Din*, 4 vols. (Alexandria: Matba'at Jarida al-Mahrusa, 1299/1882), 1:319. French translation in Delanoue, *Moralistes et politiques*, 2:633.

35. See above note 2.

36. David Beetham, *Max Weber and the Theory of Modern Politics* (Cambridge: Polity Press, 1985), 84.

37. For colourful accounts, see David Landes, *Bankers and Pashas* (Cambridge, Mass.: Harvard University Press, 1958), 69–101.

38. J. Heyworth-Dunne, *An Introduction to the History of Education in Modern Egypt*, 343.

39. Robert Tignor, *Modernization and British Colonial Rule in Egypt, 1882–1914* (Princeton University Press, 1966), 126.

40. Abdel-Maksud Hamza, *The Public Debt of Egypt, 1854–1876* (Cairo: Government Press, 1944), 6–7.

41. For full accounts of the Urabi rebellion see Alexander Schölch, *Egypt for the Egyptians! The Socio-Political Crisis in Egypt, 1878–82* (St Antony's College: Ithaca University Press, 1981), and Juan Cole, *Colonialism and Revolution in the Middle East: Social and Cultural Origins of Egypt's 'Urabi Movement* (Princeton University Press, 1993).

42. Quoted in Issawi (ed.), *The Economic History of the Middle East*, 431–2.

43. Earl of Cromer, *Modern Egypt*, 2 vols. (New York: Macmillan, 1908), 2:279.

44. Roger Owen, "The Influence of Lord Cromer's Indian Experience on British Policy in Egypt 1883–1907, " *St Anthony's Papers*, 7 (1965), 109–39, and Tignor, *Modernization and British Colonial Rule*, 180–206.

45. Tignor, *Modernization and British Colonial Rule*, 181.

46. Jacques Berque, *Egypt: Imperialism and Revolution*, trans. Jean Stewart (London: Faber and Faber, 1972), 99.

47. Tignor, *Modernization and British Colonial Rule in Egypt*, 376–7.

48. See note 5.

49. On this point see Fedwa Malti–Douglas, *Blindness and Autobiography: Al-Ayyam of Taha Husayn* (Princeton University Press, 1988), 75–90. The journey from tradition to modernity is also treated in Ahmad Amin's *Hayati* (Damascus: Matba'at al-Mufid, 1928), trans. Issa Boullata, *My Life* (Leiden: E.J. Brill, 1978); and Salama Musa's *Tarbiyyat Salama Musa* (Cairo: Salama Musa li–Nashr wa-al-Tawzi, n.d.), trans. L.O. Schuman, *The Education of Salama Musa* (Leiden: E.J. Brill, 1961).

50. *Al-Ayyam* (Cairo: Matba'at Amin Abd al-Rahman, 1929), first published in serial form in *al-Hilal*, 1926–7; translated by E.H. Paxton as *An Egyptian Childhood* (London: Routledge, 1932). Indeed, Qutb dedicates *Tifl* to Taha Husayn: "To the author of *The Days*, Dr. Taha Hussein Bey. These, dear sir, are 'days' like your 'days,' lived by a village child, some are similar to your days and some are different. The difference reflects the difference between one generation and another, one village and another, one life and another, indeed the difference between one nature and another, between one attitude and another. But they are, when all is said and done, also 'days.'" *A Child from the Village*. Neguib Mahfouz also admired *al-Ayyam*, which he imitated with a work called *al-A'wam* (*Years*); see J. Brugman, *An Introduction to the History of Modern Arabic Literature* (Leiden: E.J. Brill, 1984), 296.

51. *Tifl min al-Qarya*, 168; *A Child from the Village*, 113.

52. Ibid., 42; 25–6.

53. Ibid., 198; 132.

54. *The Census of Egypt* (Cairo: Government Press, 1921) reports that in 1917 literacy among the total male population of Asyut Province was 104/1000; 141/1000 for males between the ages of 10–19; and 3/000 for females.

55. *Tifl*, 15; *A Child from the Village*, 7.

56. Ibid, 47–8; 29–30. Many of these scholars would, presumably, have been returning to their native regions, for we know that as late as 1966 fully half of the students at al-Azhar had origins in agricultural provinces such as Asyut. See Uri Kupferschmidt, "Reformist and Militant Islam in Urban and Rural Egypt," *Middle Eastern Studies*, vol. 23, no. 4 (Oct. 1987), 415 n.8. The Azhari effort to influence rural populations intellectually took on new meaning in the 1980s, when *qawafil* ("convoys") of Azhari scholars descended on villages in order to dissuade youth from joining militant Islamist organizations, such as the Islamic Group (al-Jama'a al-Islamiyya). See Malika Zeghal, "Religion and Politics in Egypt: The Ulema of Al-Azhar, Radical Islam, and the State," *International Journal of Middle East Studies*, 31 (1999), 385–6.

57. On the transmissive character of traditional Islamic scholarship, see Dale Eickelman, "The Art of Memory: Islamic Education and its Social Reproduction," in Juan Cole (ed.), *Comparing Muslim Societies: Knowledge and the State in a World Civilization* (Ann Arbor: University of Michigan Press, 1992), 97–132.

58. Richard C. Martin, *Islamic Studies: A History of Religions Approach* (New Jersey: Prentice Hall, 1996), 181–2.

59. *Tifl*, 95; *A Child from the Village*, 62.

60. Ibid., 96–100; 63–66. Compare with Winifred Blackman's discussion of the *qarina* in *The Fellahin of Upper Egypt*, 218 ff.

61. *Tifl*, 92; *A Child from the Village*, 61.

62. Ibid., 100; 66.

63. Ibid., 5–14; 1–6. Compare with Valerie Hoffman's discussion of *gazb* [sic] in her *Sufism, Mystics, and Saints in Modern Egypt* (Columbia: University of South Carolina Press, 1995), 208–13.

64. Ibid., 10; 4.

65. Ibid., 120, 132; 79, 88.

66. Ibid., 133–4; 89.

67. Ibid., 106 ff; 70 ff.

68. Ibid., 117; 77.

69. Ibid., 199; 133.

70. Nathan Brown, *Peasant Politics in Modern Egypt*, 43.

71. Qutb writes that the episode occurred "more than a quarter century" prior to the writing of his autobiography in 1946. *Tifl*, 167; 112.

72. Ibid., 158–67; 106–12.

73. Benedict Anderson, *Imagined Communities: Reflections on the Origin and Spread of Nationalism* (London: Verso, 1983), 33–46.

74. Reinhard Schulze, "Mass Culture and Islamic Cultural Production in 19th Century Middle East," in G. Stauth and Sami Zubaida (eds), *Mass Culture, Popular Culture, and Social Life in the Middle East* (Frankfurt: Campus Verlag, 1987), 195–204.

75. *Tifl*, 118; *A Child from the Village*, 78–9.

76. Ibid., 119–120; 79.

77. Ibid., 123; 81.

78. As Israel Gershoni and James Jankowski state: "'Effendi" (lit. *afandi*) was the term used in Egypt in the early 20th century to refer to the urban, educated class of native Egyptians. "In the Egyptian hierarchy of wealth and status the effendi on the one hand stood below both the indigenous political elite...and the often haute bourgeoisie who dominated the Egyptian economy; on the other side the effendis of Egypt definitely stood above the country's urban working classes (the *'ummal*) and the masses of its rural peasantry (the fallahin)." *Defining the Egyptian Nation, 1930–1945* (Cambridge University Press, 1995), 11. See also Lucie Ryzova, "Egyptianizing Modernity through the 'New Effendiyya,'" in Arthur Goldschmidt, Amy Johnson and Barak Salmoni (eds), *Re-Envisioning Egypt 1919–1952* (Cairo: The American University in Cairo Press, 2005), 124–63.

79. *Tifl*, 187–93; *A Child from the Village*, 125–30.

80. Qutb refers to the government officials who periodically visited his school to ensure that proper standards were met. Ibid., 43–4; 27–8.

81. Mitchell, *Colonizing Egypt*, 76–80.

82. On this point see the discussion in Barbara Daly Metcalf, *Moral Conduct and Authority: The Place of 'Adab' in South Asian Islam* (Berkeley: University of California Press, 1984), 1–20 *et passim*.

83. Michel Foucault, *Discipline and Punish: The Birth of the Prison*, trans. Alan Sheridan (New York: Vintage Books, 1979), 136–7.

84. Compare with Starrett's remarks, *Putting Islam to Work*, 57–61.

85. *Tifl*, 28–9; *A Child from the Village*, 16–17.
86. Ibid., 19; 10.
87. Ibid., 30–3; 17–21.
88. Ibid.
89. Ibid., 35; 21.
90. Ibid.
91. Ibid., 36–9; 23–4.
92. On Mustafa Kamil and the Hizb al-Watani see Arthur Goldshmidt, Jr., "The Egyptian Nationalist Party, 1882–1919," in P.M. Holt (ed.), *Political and Social Change in Modern Egypt* (London: Oxford University Press, 1968), 303–33; and Israel Gershoni and James Jankowski, *Egypt, Islam, and the Arabs* (New York: Oxford University Press, 1986), 3–13.
93. Samir Seikaly, "Prime Minister and Assassin: Butrus Ghali and Wardani," *Middle Eastern Studies*, 13 (1977), 112–23.
94. On the war's impact on Egyptian society, see Muhammad al-Rafi'i, *Thawrat 1919*, 2 vols. (Cairo: Maktabat al-Nahda al-Misriyya, 1946), 1:40–4; Marius Deeb, "The 1919 Popular Uprising: A Genesis of Egyptian Nationalism," *Canadian Review of Studies in Nationalism*, 1 (1973), 110–12, and Ellis Goldberg, "Peasants in Revolt—Egypt 1919," *International Journal of Middle East Studies*, 24 (1992), 261–80.
95. *Tifl*, 140; *A Child from the Village*, 92.
96. For Sa'd Zaghlul and the emergence of the Wafd see Afaf Lutfi al-Sayyid Marsot, *Egypt's Liberal Experiment, 1922–1936* (Berkeley: University of California Press, 1977); Marius Deeb, *Party Politics in Egypt*; and 'Abd al-'Azim Muhammad Ramadan, *Tatawwur al-Haraka al-Wataniyya fi Misr 1918–1936* (Cairo: Madbuli, 1983).
97. Joel Beinin and Zackary Lockman, *Workers on the Nile* (Princeton University Press, 1987), 100.
98. al-Rafi'i, *Thawrat 1919*, 150–2.
99. Reinhard Schultz, "Colonization and Resistance: The Egyptian Peasant Rebellion, 1919," in *Peasants and Politics in the Modern Middle East*, 203–10.
100. See Brown, *Peasant Politics in Modern Egypt*, 206–7.
101. *Tifl*, 144; *A Child from the Village*, 96.
102. Gershoni and Jankowski, *Egypt, Islam, and the Arabs*, 44–50.
103. Theda Skcopol, *States and Social Revolutions* (London and New York: Cambridge University Press), 4.
104. Qutb states his reformist intentions explicitly in the introduction page to *Tifl*: "These are pictures of the life of the village as it was in the time of my childhood, a quarter of a century ago….[m]ost of these images are still quite alive, but well-off city people have hardly any conception of them, whether as things in real life or even as imaginary things. This recording of them will give the new generation a picture of what is good

and what is bad in our nation's countryside. Perhaps they will have an opinion as to what should remain and what should be discarded."
105. Tetz Rooke, *In My Childhood: A Study of Arabic Autobiography* (Stockholm: Almquist and Wiksell, 1997), 173.
106. *Tifl*, 185–6; *A Child from the Village*, 124.

2. THE MAKING OF AN EGYPTIAN NATIONALIST

1. Sayyid Qutb, *Tifl min al-Qarya* (Beirut: Dar al-Hikma, n.d. [1967]), 201; *A Child from the Village*, translated, edited and introduced by John Calvert and William Shepard as *A Child from the Village* (Syracuse University Press, 2004), 135.
2. Ibid., 195; 130.
3. John Darwin, *Britain, Egypt and the Middle East: Imperial Policy in the Aftermath of the War, 1918–1922* (New York: St. Martin's Press, 1981), 74.
4. Quoted in Afaf Lutfi al-Sayyid Marsot, *Egypt's Liberal Experiment, 1922–1936* (Berkeley: University of California Press, 1977), 63.
5. Jacques Berque, *Egypt: Imperialism and Revolution*, translated by Jean Stewart (New York: Praeger Publishers, 1972), 466.
6. See Janet Abu-Lughod, *Rabat: Urban Apartheid in Morocco* (Princeton University Press, 1980), 131–73.
7. The development and layout of modern Cairo are treated in Janet Abu-Lughod, *Cairo: 1001 Years of the City Victorious* (Princeton University Press, 1971); Jacque Berque, *Egypt: Imperialism and Revolution*, 91 ff., 466 ff. *et passim*; Andre Raymond, "Cairo", in Mary Wilson, Philip Khoury and Albert Hourani (eds), *The Modern Middle East* (Berkeley, University of California Press, 1993), 311–37; Timothy Mitchell, *Colonizing Egypt*, 64–69; Magda Baraka, *The Egyptian Upper Class Between Revolutions, 1919–1952* (Reading: Ithaca Press, 1998), 95–207 *et passim*.
8. Baraka, *The Egyptian Upper Class*, 98–9.
9. Karl Baedeker, *Egypt and the Sudan: Handbook for Travellers*, 8th edition (Leipzig: Karl Baedeker Publisher, 1929), 44.
10. A point made by Amira Sonbol, *The New Mamluks* (Syracuse University Press, 2000), 85.
11. Andre Raymond, "Cairo", 323.
12. Baraka, *The Egyptian Upper Class*, 111.
13. Salah 'Abd al-Fattah al-Khalidi, *Sayyid Qutb: Min al-Milad ila al-Istishhad* (Damascus: Dar al-Qalam, 1991), 71–5.
14. Candidates for Dar al-'Ulum were initially recruited from the only place where high standards of literacy prevailed—al-Azhar. See Muhammad 'Abd al-Jawwad, *Taqwim Dar al-'Ulum (1872–1947)* (Cairo: Dar al-Ma'arif, 1952), and Lois A. Aroian, *The Nationalization of Arabic and Islamic Education in Egypt: Dar al-'Ulum and al-Azhar*, Cairo Papers in Social Science, 6 (Cairo: The American University in Cairo Press, 1983).

15. Donald Malcolm Reid, *Cairo University and the Making of Modern Egypt* (Cambridge University Press, 1990), 34.

16. Aroian, *The Nationalization of Arabic and Islamic Education in Egypt*, 30. See also Hasan al-Banna, *Mudhakkirat al-Da'wa wa al-Da'iya* (Cairo: Dar al-Tawzi' wa al-Nashr al-Islamiyya, 1986), 42.

17. Hasan al-Banna, *Mudhakkirat al-Da'wa wa al-Da'iya*, 52–3.

18. Aroian, *The Nationalization of Arabic and Islamic Education in Egypt*, 60–7.

19. Hasan al-Banna, *Mudhakkirat al-Da'wa wa al-Da'iya*, 43–53.

20. Aroian, *The Nationalization of Arabic and Islamic Education in Egypt*, 61.

21. Al-Khalidi, *Sayyid Qutb*, 100–1.

22. Sayyid Qutb, "Naqd Mustaqbal al-Thaqafa fi Misr," *Sahifat Dar al-'Ulum* (April 1939), 64–5.

23. Sayyid Qutb, "Ta'awun al-Thaqafi bayna al-Aqtar al-'Arabiyya," *al-Risala* 617 (1945), 442.

24. Salah 'Abd al-Fattah al-Khalidi, *Amrika min al-Dakhil bi–Nazar Sayyid Qutb* (Cairo: Dar al-Wafa', 1987), 31, 158.

25. Al-Khalidi, *Sayyid Qutb*, 44.

26. Rivka Yadlin, "The Seeming Duality: Patterns of Interpersonal Relations in a Changing Environment," in Shimon Shamir (ed.), *Egypt from Monarchy to Republic: A Reassessment of Revolution and Change* (Boulder, CO: Westview Press, 1995), 154.

27. For a chronology of Qutb's employment, see al-Khalidi, *Sayyid Qutb*, 85–8.

28. 'Ali Mubarak, *Al-Khitat al-Tawfiqiyya al-Jadida*, 10, 80–1.

29. Ralph M. Coury, *The Making of an Egyptian Arab Nationalist: The Early Years of Azzam Pasha, 1893–1936* (Reading: Ithaca Press, 1998), 30.

30. Karl Baedeker, *Egypt: A Handbook for Travellers*, 170.

31. The principle sources for al-'Aqqad's life include his autobiographical works *Ana* (Cairo: Dar al-Hilal, 1964) and *Hayat Qalam* (Cairo: Dar al-Hilal, 1964). See also Hamdi Sakkut, *'Abbas Mahmud al-'Aqqad* (Beirut: Dar al-Kitab al-Lubnani, 1983); Ibrahim Ibrahim, "Ahmad Amin and 'Abbud Mahmud al-'Aqqad: Between al-Qadim and al-Jadid: European Challenge and Islamic Response," in George Atiyeh and Ibrahim Oweiss (eds), *Arab Civilization: Challenges and Responses* (Albany: SUNY Press, 1988), 208–30. Qutb's early contacts with al-'Aqqad are treated in *al-Khalidi*, Sayyid Qutb, 135 ff.

32. See Qutb's glowing appraisal of al-'Aqqad, written about a decade after their first meeting, in his *Kutub wa Shakhsiyyat* (n.p., n.d. [1946]), 84.

33. Israel Gershoni and James Jankowski, *Egypt, Islam and the Arabs: The Search for Egyptian Nationhood, 1900–1930* (New York: Oxford University Press, 1986), 87.

34. For biographical sketches of these and other Egyptian men of letters of the period, see J. Brugman, *An Introduction to the History of Modern Arabic*

Literature in Egypt (Leiden: E.J. Brill, 1984), *passim*; also Gershoni and Jankowski, *Egypt, Islam and the Arabs*, 89–95.

35. M.M. Badawi, "The Background," in M.M. Badawi (ed.), *Modern Arabic Literature* (Cambridge University Press), 19.

36. Prior to the publication of their Diwan the group had called itself, appropriately, "Madrasat al-Tajdid" ("The School of Innovation"). See Badawi, *A Critical Introduction to Modern Arabic Poetry* (Cambridge University Press, 1975), 84ff.

37. S. Somekh, "The Neo-Classical Arabic Poets," in M.M. Badawi (ed.), *Modern Arabic Literature*.

38. On this point see Salama Khadra Jayyusi, *Trends and Movements in Modern Arabic Poetry*, vol. 1 (Leiden: E.J. Brill, 1977), chap. 4; and Mounah Khouri, *Poetry and the Making of Modern Egypt (1882–1922)* (Leiden: E.J. Brill, 1971), 139–75.

39. Al-'Aqqad's view on poetry are succinctly presented in David Semah, *Four Egyptian Literary Critics* (Leiden: E.J. Brill, 1974), esp. 3–18.

40. Quoted in Semah, *Four Egyptian Literary Critics*, 11.

41. Including patriotic poems by Thabit al-Jurjawi and Muhammad Bey Khudari. Qutb's teacher told him about the existence of Hafiz and Shawqi. See *Tifl min al-Qarya*, 140–4; *A Child from the Village*, 95.

42. Amina, Hamida, Muhammad and Sayyid Qutb, *Al-Atyaf al-'Arba'a* (n.p., n. d. [1945]), 3.

43. M.M. Badawi, *A Critical Introduction*, 128.

44. The most important history of the Apollo Group is 'Abd al-'Aziz al-Dasuqi, *Jama'at Abullu wa Atharuha fi al-Shi'r al-Hadith* (Cairo: Hay'a al-Misriyya al-'Amma li al-Ta'lif wa al-Nashr, 1971). See also Badawi, *A Critical Introduction*, 115–44.

45. Al-Khalidi, *Sayyid Qutb*, 93.

46. Sayyid Qutb, *Muhimmat al-Sha'ir al-Haya wa Shi'r al-Jil al-Hadir* (Beirut: Dar al-Shuruq, n.d. [1932]).

47. Ibid., 87.

48. Ibid., 61.

49. Ibid., 87–8.

50. Ibid., 13.

51. Ibid., 62.

52. Ibid., 9–11.

53. Sayyid Qutb, *Al-Shati' al-Majhul* (Cairo: Matba'at Sadiq, n.d. [1935]).

54. Ibid., 6–7.

55. Ibid., 18–20.

56. Ibid., 83–6.

57. Ibid., 51–2.

58. Mahmud al-Khafif, "Shati' al-Majhul: Nazm al-Sha'ir Sayyid Qutb," *al-Risala* (10 June 1935), 959–60.

59. *Al-Usbu'* 31 (June 1934), cited in Muhammad Husayn 'Abd al-Baqi, *Sayyid Qutb: Hayatuhu wa Adabuhu* (Mansura: Dar al-Wafa', 1986), 78.

For an overview of Qutb's involvements in these "battles" see ibid., 78–90.

60. S. Somekh, "The Neo-Classical Arabic Poets," 55. A famous case in point was Shawqi's scathing poem written upon the departure of Lord Cromer from Egypt in 1907; likewise the many political satires scattered in the *diwans* of al-Rusafi and al-Ghayati and others.

61. Referring to al-Rafi'i's attack on al-'Aqqad. See 'Adil Hamuda, *Sayyid Qutb: min al-Qarya ila Mishaqa* (Cairo: Ruz al-Yusuf, 1987), 51.

62. Brugman, *Introduction*, 153–4.

63. Dauqi, *Jama'at Abullu*, 485–6.

64. *Al-Usbu'* 43 (19 September 1934); ibid., 44 (26 September 1934). Qutb's views are presented in 'Abd al-'Aziz al-Dasuqi, "Qadaya wa Mulahazat"; *al-Thaqafa*, 91 (April 1981), 49–53. See also Adnan Musallam, "Prelude to Islamic Commitment: Sayyid Qutb's Literary and Spiritual Orientation, 1932–1938," *Muslim World*, 80 (July-Oct. 1990), 183–4.

65. Al-Dasuqi, *Jama'at Abullu*, 277 and Brugman, *Introduction*, 155.

66. Musallam, "Prelude to Islamic Commitment", 184.

67. On al-Rafi'i see Mustafa M. Shak'a, *Mustafa Sadiq al-Rafi'i* (Beirut Arab University, 1970).

68. Ibid., 8.

69. Ibid., 73–109, 205–6.

70. Al-'Aqqad, *al-Fusul* (Beirut, n.p., 1967), 346 ff.

71. In a series of articles entitled *'Ala al-Saffud* [On the Skewer] published under one cover (Dar al-'Usur, 1930). These "partisans of the heritage" included al-Rafi'i's biographer, the historical novelist Muhammad Sa'id Aryan, Isma'il Mazar, editor of *al-'Usur*, and the conservative religious writer Ahmad al-Ghamrawi.

72. Sayyid Qutb, "Bayna al'Aqqad wa al-Rafi'i", *al-Risala*, 257 (6 June 1938), 936.

73. Sayyid Qutb, "Bayna al-'Aqqad wa al-Rafi'i", *al-Risala*, 251 (25 April 1938), 694.

74. Sayyid Qutb, *Al-Risala*, 259, "al-'Aqqad 29 August 1938", 1019.

75. Al-Khalidi, *Sayyid Qutb*, 168–9, citing Sayyid Qutb, *al-Usbu'* (June 1934), 31–6.

76. Sayyid Qutb, "Bayna al-'Aqqad wa al-Rafi'i," *al-Risala*, 251 (25 April 1938), 693.

77. Sayyid Qutb, "Bayna al-'Aqqad wa al-Rafi'i," *al-Risala*, 263 (1 July 1938), 1179–80.

78. As Qutb stated to the Indian Islamic scholar Abu Hasan Nadwi in 1951. See Nadwi, *Mukhakkirat Sa'ih fi al-Sharq al-Arabi*, 2nd revised ed. (Beirut: Mu'assasat al-Risala, 1975), 96.

79. See for example Sayyid Qutb, "Dariba al-Tatawwur", *Majallat al-Shu'un al-Ijtima'iyya*, 6 (June 1940), esp. 44–6.

80. Anthony Giddens, *A Contemporary Ctitique of Historical Materialism*, vol. 1 *Power, Property and the State* (London: Macmillan, 1981), 193–5.

81. The politics of the post-World War I era are treated in Jacques Berque, *Egypt: Imperialism and Revolution* (New York: Praeger, 1972); Afaf Lutfi al-Sayyid-Marsot, *Egypt's Liberal Experiment, 1922–1936*; and 'Abd al-'Azim Ramadan, *Tatawwur al-Haraka al-Wataniyya fi Misr, min Sanat 1937 ila 1948*, 2 vols. (Cairo: Madbuli, 1983).

82. See the appendix in al-Sayyid-Marsot, *Egypt's Liberal Experiment*, 253–67, for the text of the Treaty of Alliance.

83. Joel Beinin, "Society and Economy, 1923–1952," in M. M. Daly (ed.), *Cambridge History of Egypt*, vol. 2 (Cambridge University Press, 1998), 323–8.

84. Marius Deeb, *Party Politics in Egypt*, 320.

85. Gershoni and Jankowski, *Redefining the Egyptian Nation*, 12.

86. Beinin, "Society and Economy," 328.

87. Eric Davis, *Challenging Colonialism: Bank Misr and Egyptian Industrialization, 1920–1941* (Princeton University Press, 1983), 3.

88. Al-Bishri, *al-Haraka al-Siyasiyya fi Misr*, 202; Joel Beinin and Zachary Lockman, *Workers on the Nile* (Princeton University Press, 1987), 14.

89. See Robert Vitalis, "On the Theory and Practice of Compradors: The Role of 'Abbud Pasha in the Egyptian Political Economy," *International Journal of Middle East Studies*, 22 (1990), 291–315.

90. Sayyid Qutb, *Muhimmat al-Sha'ir*, 92–3. Translated by the author.

91. Sayyid Qutb, *al-Shat' al-Majhul*, 188–94.

92. Matthew Ellis, "King Me: The Political Culture of Monarch in Interwar Iraq and Egypt," MPhil Thesis, Exeter College, Oxford University, May 2005. At: http://users.ox.ac.uk/~metheses/EllisThesis.htm#_ftn334

93. "Al-Mihrajan," *Sahifat Dar al-'Ulum*, 4–4 (March 1938), 52–4. Interestingly, Qutb crafted his poem as a panegyric (Arabic, *madih*), the ancient eulogizing genre associated in his own day with the neoclassicists, his artistic foes.

94. The 1935 student demonstrations are treated in Ahmad Abdalla, *The Student Movement and Nationalist Politics in Egypt* (London: Al Saqi Books, 1985), 39–42.

95. Partha Chatterjee, *The Nation and its Fragments: Colonial and Post Colonial Histories* (Princeton University Press, 1993), 5.

96. A point developed by Sami Zubaida, *Islam, the People and the State: Political Ideas and Movements in the Modern Middle East* (London: I.B. Tauris, 1993), 157–62.

97. Al-Banna's early life and career are recorded in his *Mudhakkirat al-Da'wa wa al-Da'iya* (see above n. 16). Studies of al-Banna and the Muslim Brotherhood include J. Heyworth-Dunne, *Religious and Political Trends in Modern Egypt* (Washington: published by the author, 1950); Christina Phelps Harris, *Nationalism and Revolution in Egypt: The Role of the Muslim Brotherhood* (Stanford, CA: Hoover Institution Press, 1964); I.M. Husayni, *The Muslim Brethren, the Greatest of Modern Islamic Movements*, trans. J.F. Brown and J. Racy (Beirut: Khayat's College Book Coop-

erative, 1956); Richard Mitchell, *The Society of the Muslim Brothers* (London: Oxford University Press, 1969); and most recently, Brynjar Lia, *The Society of the Muslim Brothers in Egypt: The Rise of an Islamic Mass Movement, 1928–1942* (Reading: Ithaca Press, 1998).

98. J. Spencer Trimingham, *The Sufi Orders in Islam* (Oxford University Press, 1971), 251.
99. Hasan al-Banna, *Mudhakkirat al-Daʿwa wa al-Daʿiya*, 53.
100. Ibid., 53–5. Among the prominent Egyptians who frequented the Theosophical society in Cairo were the politicians ʿAbd al-Khalaq Thawrat Pasha and Lutfi Bey Sayyid.
101. Ibid., 54.
102. Charles Wendell, *Five Tracts of Hasan al-Banna (1906–1949)* (Berkeley: University of California Press, 1978), 44.
103. Imam Hasan al-Banna, *Letter to a Muslim Student* (Leicester: The Islamic Foundation, 1999), 11.
104. Hasan al-Banna, *Mudhakkirat al-Daʿwa wa al-Daʿiya*, 55.
105. Richard Mitchell, *The Society of the Muslim Brothers*, 8.
106. Brynjar Lia, *The Society of the Muslim Brothers in Egypt*, 114–17. See also Abu Rabi, *Intellectual Origins of Islamic Resurgence in the Modern Arab World* (Albany: State University of New York Press, 1996), 66–9.
107. Lia, *The Society of the Muslim Brothers in Egypt*, 38.
108. Ibid., 116.
109. Wendell, *Five Tracts*, "Our Mission", 46.
110. al-Banna, "Bayna al-Ams wa al-Yawm," *Majmuʿat Rasaʾil al-Imam* (Beirut: Dar al-Andalus,1965), 144–64; Wendell, *Five Tracts*, "Between Yesterday and Today," 13–39.
111. Ibid., 163; 36.
112. Hasan al-Banna, "Nahwa al-Nur," in ibid., 162–99; Wendell, "Toward the Light," Five Tracts, 103–32; reproduced in part in al-Banna's *Mudhakkirat*, 236–41.
113. Mitchell, *The Society of the Muslim Brothers*, 27.
114. Ibid., 33.
115. Ibid., 326.
116. Martin Marty and Scott Appleby, "Forward", in James Piscatori (ed.), *Islamic Fundamentalisms and the Gulf Crisis* (Chicago: The American Academy of Arts and Sciences, 1999), xii.
117. The most complete study of Young Egypt remains James Jankowski's *Egypt's Young Rebels* (Stanford, CA: Hoover Institution Press, 1975). See also P.J. Vatikiotis, *Nasser and His Generation* (New York: St. Martin's Press, 1978), 67–84, and Israel Gershoni and James Jankowski, *Redefining the Egyptian Nation*, 98–115. Ahmad Husayn's formative years are charted in his autobiographical *Imani* (Cairo, n.p., 1936).
118. Jankowski, *Egypt's Young Rebels*, 64.
119. Quoted in Heyworth-Dunne, *Religious and Political Trends in Modern Egypt*, 104.

120. Jankowski, *Egypt's Young Rebels*, 40–1.
121. See Quintin Hoare and Geoffrey Nowell Smith (eds), *Selections from the Prison Notebooks of Antonio Gramsci* (New York: International Publishers, 1971), 5–23.
122. A point made by Haifa Khalafallah, "Abbas al-'Aqqad: The Historian," *Arab Studies Journal*, 3 (Spring 1995), 80–93.
123. See *al-Risala* 206 (14 June 1937), 961.
124. Sayyid Qutb, "al-Ghina' al-Marid," *al-Risala*, 374 (2 September 1940), 1382.
125. Sayyid Qutb, "Dariba al-Tatawwur," 44.
126. Sayyid Qutb, "Fi Mustaqbal Amal wa Furas: Muhayya'a li–Istiqlal," *Majallat al-Shu'un al-Ijtima'iyya*, 4 (January 1943), 32; and "Mashru'at al-Islah," *Majallat al-Shu'un al-Ijtima'iyya*, 10 (October 1941), 29. I am indebted to Professor William Shepard for providing me with copies of Qutb's articles from *Majallat al-Shu'un al-Ijtima'iyya*.
127. Sayyid Qutb, "Fi Mustaqbal Amal," 30.
128. Sayyid Qutb, "Dariba al-Tatawwur," 43.
129. Sayyid Qutb, "Mashru'at al-Islah," 28–9.
130. Sayyid Qutb, "al-Alam Yajri,!!" *al-Risala*, 17 (15 September 1933), 13.
131. Sayyid Qutb, "al-Taqlid fi al-Fanun," *al-Risala*, 401 (1941), 300–1.
132. Sayyid Qutb, "Dariba al-Tatawwur," 32.
133. Sayyid Qutb, "al-Alam Yajri!!," 13.
134. Sayyid Qutb, "Fi Mustaqbal Amal," 31; Alexis Carrel, *Man the Unknown* (New York and London: Harper and Brothers, 1935).
135. Sayyid Qutb, "Fi Mustaqbal Amal," 30–1.
136. Charles Taylor, *Hegel and Modern Society* (Cambridge University Press, 1979), 1.
137. Roxanne L. Euben, *Enemy in the Mirror: Islamic Fundamentalism and the Limits of Modern Rationalism* (Princeton University Press, 1999) notes how Qutb critiques post-Enlightenment rationalism in the manner of Western critics.
138. Roger Griffin, "The Reclamation of Fascist Culture," *European History Quarterly*, 31–4 (2001), 610.
139. Sayyid Qutb, *Al-Mustaqbal li–Hadha al-Din* (Cairo: Dar al-Shuruq, 1991), 59 ff., 76; translated as *Islam: The Religion of the Future* (Delhi: Markazi Maktaba Islami, n.d.), 85 ff., 105.
140. Quoted in François Burgat, *The Islamic Movement in North Africa*, translated by William Dowell, new edition (Austin: The Center for Middle Eastern Studies at the University of Texas, 1997), 60.
141. For Qutb's "Mustaqbal Thaqafa fi Misr," see above note 22. Husayn's book was translated by Sidney Glazer as *The Future of Culture in Egypt* (Washington: The American Council of Learned Societies, 1954). Original title *Mustaqbal al-Thaqafa fi Misr* (Cairo: Dar al-Kutub 1937).
142. The main sources for Taha Husayn's life is his three-part autobiography; see chapter 1, note 45 for publication details. See also Pierre Cachia,

Taha Husayn: His Place in the Egyptian Literary Renaissance (Piscataway, NJ: Gorgias Press, 2005; originally published 1956), and Albert Hourani, *Arabic Thought in the Liberal Age*, 324–40.

143. Reid, *Cairo University and the Making of Modern Egypt*, 129.

144. The conceptualization of Egyptian territorial nationalism is treated in Israel Gershoni and James Jankowski, *Egypt, Islam, and the Arabs*.

145. Quoted in Abd al-Fattah Muhammad El-Awaisi, *The Muslim Brothers and the Palestine Question, 1928–1947* (London and New York: Tauris Academic Studies, 1998), 22.

146. Charles D. Smith, *Islam and the Search for Social Order in Egypt: A Biography of Muhammad Husayn Haykal* (Albany: SUNY Press, 1983), 89.

147. Taha Husayn, *The Future of Culture in Egypt*, 106–7.

148. Sayyid Qutb, "Mustaqbal Thaqafa fi Misr," 52.

149. Ibid., 49–51.

150. Ibid., 76–7.

151. Ibid., 31–7

152. Ibid., 37–42.

153. Ibid., 31–46. The Iraqi Sati' al-Husri, writing from an Pan-Arabist perspective, regarded Husayn's *Mustaqbal* as negating Egypt's participation in the *ruh al-'uruba* ("spirit of Arabism"), which, he believed, distinguished Egypt and other Arabic-speaking countries from Europe and other civilizations. See his "Bayn Misr wa al-'Uruba: Kitab Maftuh ila Dr. Taha Husayn," *al-Risala*, 285 (1938).

154. Sayyid Qutb, *Milestones*, revised translation with a forward by Ahmad Zaki Hammad (Indianapolis: American Trust Publications, 1990), 8. Arabic title is *Ma'alim fi al-Tariq*.

155. Gershoni and Jankowski, *Redefining the Egyptian Nation*, 51–2.

156. Sayyid Qutb, "Mustaqbal al-Thaqafa fi Misr," 47. Ahmad Amin, "Bayna al-Gharb wa al-Sharq aw al-Maddiyya wa al-Ruhaniyya," *al-Thaqafa* (10 January 1939), 2–5.

157. See Gershoni and Jankowski, *Redefining the Egyptian Nation*, 52.

158. Rashid El-Enany, "Tawfiq al-Hakim and the West: A New Assessment of the Relationship," *British Journal of Middle Eastern Studies*, 27 (2000), 166. I thank Professor El-Enany for providing me with a copy of his article.

159. Wendell, *Five Tracts*, "Our Mission," 52–6.

160. Adnan A. Musallam, *From Secularism to Jihad: Sayyid Qutb and the Foundations of Radical Islamism* (Westport: Praeger, 2005), 83.

161. Charles D. Smith, "The Intellectual and Modernization: Definitions and Reconsiderations," *Comparative Studies in Society and History*, 22 (1980), 513–33; and *Islam and the Search for Social Order in Modern Egypt: A Biography of Muhammad Husayn Haykal* (Albany: State University of New York Press, 1983), 131–57. Representative works of the "Islamic-liberal" trend include Haykal's *Hayat Muhammad* (Cairo:

Matba'at Dar al-Kutub al-Misriyya, 1356/1937–8); Taha Husayn's *'Ala Hamish al-Sira* (Cairo: al-Matba'at al-Rahmaniyya, 1933); and al-'Aqqad's *'Abqariyat Muhammad* (Cairo: al-Maktaba al-Tijariyya al-Kubra, Matba'at al-Istiqama, 1942).

162. Sayyid Qutb, "Bayt al-Maghrib fi Misr," *al-Risala*, 282 (1937), 1937.
163. Sayyid Qutb, "'Alam Jadid fi Tayyat Hadha al-Jahim," *Majallat al-Shu'un al-Ijtima'iyya*, 8 (August 1941), 54.
164. El-Awaisi, *The Muslim Brothers and the Palestine Question*, 24.
165. Ibid., 31.
166. Lia, *The Society of the Muslim Brothers in Egypt*, 244.
167. Gershoni and Jankowski, *Redefining the Egyptian Nation*, 174–5.
168. Ibid., 167–91.
169. Sayyid Qutb, "Bayt al-Maghrib fi Misr," 1937.
170. Adnan Musallam, "Prelude to Islamic Commitment," 182. Musallam gives the following citation for the poem: *al-Shabab* (5 October 1938), as reprinted in 'Abd al-Latif al-Jada' and Husni Adham Jirar, *Shi'r al-Da'wa al-Islamiyya fi al 'Asr al-Hadith* (Beirut, 1978), 39–40.

3. TURN TO ISLAMISM

1. Sayyid Qutb, *Ma'raka al-Islam wa al-Ra'smaliyya* (Cairo: Dar al-Shuruq, 11th printing, 1990), 6.
2. For an overview of Egypt and the Second World War, see Hoda Gamal Abdel Nasser, *Britain and the Egyptian Nationalist Movement 1936–1952* (Reading: Ithaca Press, 1994), 38–110.
3. Richard P. Mitchell, *The Society of the Muslim Brothers* (New York: Oxford University Press, 1969; 2nd ed. 1993), 22–3.
4. Quoted in Jacques Berque, *Egypt: Imperialism and Revolution*, trans. Jean Steward (New York: Praeger, 1972), 567.
5. 'Abd al-Fatah al-Khalidi, *Sayyid Qutb: Min al-Milad ila al-Istishhad* (Damascus: Dar al-Qalam, 1991), 265–6.
6. Sayyid Qutb, "'Alam Jadid fi Tayyat Hadha al-Jahim," *Majallat al-Shu'un al-Ijtima'iyya*, 8 (Aug. 1941), 52.
7. Sayyid Qutb, "Fi al-Mustabal Amal," *Majallat al-Shu'un al-Ijtima'iyya*, 1 (January1943), 31. Compare this statement with Qutb's later Islamist assertion that "Islam's ultimate aim is to awaken the humanity of man." *Milestones*, revised translation with a foreword by Ahmad Zaki Hammad (Indianapolis: American Trust Publications, 1990), 40; the Arabic title is *Ma'alim fi al-Tariq*. There are many editions; the one available to me is by Dar al-Shuruq, 15th printing, 1992.
8. 'Abd al-Fattah al-Khalidi, *Sayyid Qutb: Min al-Milad Ila al-Istishhad*, 85–92.
9. Ibid., 100.
10. Sayyid Qutb, "Min Laghwi al-Sayf", *al-Risala*, no. 681 (22 July) 1946), 796.

11. Sayyid Qutb, "Kutub wa Shakhsiyyat", *al-Risala*, no. 549 (10 January 1944), 8–10.

12. Sayyid Qutb, "Millim al-Akbar", *al-Risala*, no. 601 (1 January 1945), 43–45; continued idem no. 602 (15 February 1945), 66–8.

13. Sayyid Qutb, "Kifah Tiba li Najib Mahfuz," *al-Risala*, no. 587 (2 October 1944), 889–92.

14. Sayyid Qutb, *al-Risala*, no. 650 (17 December 1945), 1364.

15. Sayyid Qutb, "al-Qahira al-Jadida," *al-Risala*, no. 704 (30 December 1946), 1441.

16. Sayyid Qutb, "Khawatir Mutasawiqa fi al-Naqd wa al-Adab wa Fann," *al-Risala*, no. 597 (27 November 1944), 1044.

17. S. Somekh, *The Changing Rhythm: A Study of Najib Mahfuz' Novels* (Leiden: E.J. Brill, 1973), 50. See also Gamal al-Ghitani, *The Mahfouz Dialogues*, translated by Humphrey Davies (Cairo: The American University in Cairo Press, 2008), 17.

18. Sayyid Qutb, *Kutub wa Shakhsiyyat* (n.p. n.d.[1946]), 84.

19. Sayyid Qutb, *Al-Naqd al-Adabi: Usuluhu wa Manahijuhu* (Cairo: Dar al-Fikr al-'Arabi, 1947), 235.

20. Ibid., 3.

21. Quoted in 'Abd al-Fattah al-Khalidi, *Sayyid Qutb: Min al-Milad Ila al-Istishad.*

22. Sayyid Qutb, *Ashwak* (Cairo: Dar Sa'd Misr, n.d. [1947]).

23. Ibid., 112.

24. Ibid., 119.

25. On this point see Mahdi Fadl Allah, *Ma'a Sayyid Qutb fi Fikrihi al-Siyasi wa al-Dini* (Beirut: Mu'assasat al-Risala, 1989), 44–5.

26. On this point see Leila Ahmed, *Women and Gender in Islam* (New Haven: Yale University Press, 1992), 169–207, and Margot Badran, *Feminists, Islam, and Nation: Gender and the Making of Modern Egypt* (Princeton University Press, 1995).

27. Carolyn Fluehr-Lobban, *Islamic Society in Practice* (Gainsville: University Press of Florida, 1994), 125.

28. Sayyid Qutb, "Thaqifat al-Mar'a al-Misriyya," *Majallat al-Shu'un al-Ijtima'iyya*, no. 4 (April 1940), 34–8.

29. Sayyid Qutb, "Al-Ghina al-Marid," *Al-Risala*, no. 374 (2 September, 1940), 1382–3.

30. Sayyid Qutb, "La Ya Mu'ali al-Wazir," *al-Risala*, no. 631 (4 August 1945), 839–40.

31. Sayyid Qutb, "Afkhadh wa Nuhud", *al-Fikr al-Jadid*, no. 5 (29 January 1948).

32. On the importance of public ethics and collective morals in Islamic society, see Nazih Ayubi, *Political Islam: Religion and Politics in the Arab World* (New York: Routledge, 1991), 35–47.

33. Sayyid Qutb, *Ashwak*, 70.

34. Ibid., 63.

35. 'Abd al-Baqi Muhammad Husayn mentions Qutb's preoccupation with the care of his family in Hulwan as an additional reason for his bachelorhood. *Sayyid Qutb: Hayatuhu wa Adabuhu* (Mansura: Dar al-Wafa', 1986), 28. Nazih Ayubi makes the point that "Marriage is strongly urged upon men in all Islamic treatises, classical and modern, not only for procreation but also for its sheer sexual pleasure." *Political Islam*, 37. Qutb's brother Muhammad and sister Hamida remained unmarried until they were in their fifties.

36. Sayyid Qutb, *In the Shade of the Qur'an*, vol. 1, Surahs 1–2, trans. and ed. M.A. Salahi and A.A. Shamis (Leicester: The Islamic Foundation, 1999), 273.

37. Ibid., 267; referencing Q 2:219–20. See also Lamia Rustum Shehadeh, "Women in the Discourse of Sayyid Qutb," *Arab Studies Quarterly*, vol. 22 no. 3 (Summer 2000), 45–56.

38. Quoted in Israel Gershoni and James Jankowski, *Egypt, Islam and the Arabs: The Search for Egyptian Nationhood, 1900–1930* (New York: Oxford University Press, 1986), 90.

39. Sayyid Qutb, "al-Taswir al-Fanni fi al- Qur'an al-Karim," *al-Muqtataf*, 94, no. 2 (February 1939), 206–22, continued no. 3 (March 1939), 313–18.

40. Sayyid Qutb, *al-Taswir al-Fanni fi al-Qur'an*, ninth printing (Cairo: Daral-Shuruq, 1987). For a discussion of *al-Taswir* within the larger context of the question of the i'jaz, see Issa J. Boullata, "The Rhetorical Interpretation of the Qur'an: I'jaz and Related Topics," in Andrew Rippin (ed.), *Approaches to the History of the Interpretation of the Qur'an* (Oxford: Clarendon Press, 1990), 150–1.

41. Qutb, *al-Taswir al-Fanni*, 7–8.

42. Ibid., 24. This and following is the Author's translation.

43. Ibid., 9–10.

44. Ibid., 135.

45. Ibid., 28–32.

46. Ibid., 36.

47. James Joyce, *A Portrait of the Artist as a Young Man* (London: Penguin, 1968; originally published by Ben Heubsch, 1916), 204–5.

48. Sayyid Qutb, *Al-Taswir al-Fanni*, 11–13.

49. Ibid., 18–24.

50. Sayyid Qutb, *Mashahid al-Qiyama fi al-Qur'an*, 2nd printing (Cairo: Dar al-Ma'arif bi–Misr, 1966).

51. Issa J. Boullata, "Sayyid Qutb's Literary Appreciation of the Qur'an," in Issa J. Boullata (ed.), *Literary Structures of Religious Meaning in the Qur'an* (London: Curzon, 2000), 260–1.

52. Jane Idleman Smith and Yvonne Yazbeck Haddad, *The Islamic Understanding of Death and Resurrection* (Albany: State University of New York Press, 1981), 138–9.

53. Sayyid Qutb, *Al-Taswir al-Fanni*, 10.

54. 'Abdullah 'Azzam, "Muqtatafat min Kitab Imlaq al-Fikr li–Islami al-Shahid Sayyid Qutb." At http://www.khayma.com/alattar/selection/sqotb2.htm. Accessed 9/4/2008.

55. Naguib Mahfouz, *Mirrors*, translated by Roger Allen, illustrated by Seif Wanli (Zeitouna: The American University in Cairo Press, 1999), 119–22.

56. Rasheed El-Enany, *Naguib Mahfouz: The Pursuit of Meaning* (London: Routledge, 1993), 24. I thank Professor El-Enany for drawing my attention to *Mirrors* and the figure of "'Abd al-Wahhab Ismail". According to Mahfouz, "Sayyid Qutb was a talented critic and had it not been for his tendency to extremism, he would have become the most important critic in Egypt." Quoted in Gamal al-Ghitani, *The Mahfouz Dialogues*, 17.

57. To this day, scholars hotly debate the number of Algerians killed at Sétif.

58. Tariq al-Bishri, *al-Haraka al-Siyasiyya fi Misr, 1945–1952*, 233–74.

59. Sayyid Qutb, "Hadhihi Hiya Faransa," *Al-Risala*, no. 624 (18 June 1945), 632.

60. Sayyid Qutb, "Ayna Anta, Ya Mustafa Kamil?" *Al-Risala*, no. 647 (3 December 1945), 1309.

61. Sayyid Qutb, "Min Laghwi al-Sayf: Ha'ula al-Aristuqrat," *Al-Risala*, no. 687 (2 September 1946), 921.

62. Sayyid Qutb, "Ayna Anta, Ya Mustafa Kamil?" 1309.

63. Sayyid Qutb, "Madaris li–al-Sakht," *Al-Risala*, no. 691 (30 September 1946), 1081.

64. Sayyid Qutb, "Ayna Anta, Ya Mustafa Kamil?" 1309.

65. Ibid.

66. Sayyid Qutb, "Mantiq al-Dima' al-Barai'a fi Yawm al-Jala'," *Al-Risala*, no. 661 (4 March 1946), 238.

67. Sayyid Qutb, "Lughat al-'Abidt...", *al-Risala*, no. 709 (3 February 1947), 136.

68. Mitchell, *The Society of the Muslim Brothers* (London: Oxford University Press, 1969), 50.

69. Ibid., 328.

70. Although, as Mitchell notes, evidence from Consultative Assembly listings indicates that the leadership of the society remained overwhelmingly *effendi* in character. See Ibid., 329 and Lia, *The Society of the Muslim Brothers*, 151–4.

71. James Jankowski, *Egypt's Young Rebels* (Stanford, CA: Hoover Institution Press, 1975), 89.

72. Mitchell, *The Society of the Muslim Brothers*, 48.

73. Details of the Brotherhood's secret apparatus surfaced during the famous "Jeep Case" in December 1950, when several Brothers were tried for possession of illegal arms. In the course of the trial it was revealed that only a small number of Muslim Brothers knew of the apparatus' existence. According to Egyptian government sources, membership in the apparatus did not exceed 400. See Mitchell, *Society*, 30–2, 205–6, Christina Phelps Harris, *Nationalism and Revolution in Egypt: The Role of the Muslim Brotherhood* (Stanford CA: Hoover Institution Press, 1964, 191–2, and

I.M. Husayni, *The Muslim Brethren, the Greatest of Modern Islamic Movements*, trans. J.F. Brown and J. Racy (Beirut: Khayat's College Book Cooperative, 1956), 137–43.

74. Sayyid Qutb, "al-Damir al-Amrikani...wa Qadiyat Filastin," *al-Risala*, no. 694 (21 October 1946), 1156.

75. Ibid., 1155. Writing in 1957, Wilfred Cantwell Smith wrote, "Most Westerners have simply no inkling of how deep and fierce is the hate, especially of the West, that has gripped the modernizing Arab." *Islam in Modern History* (Princeton University Press, 1957), 159 n. 203.

76. Sayyid Qutb, "Al-Kalimat al-Yawm li–al-'Arab: Famadha Hum Sana'un?" *al-Risala*, no. 672 (20 May 1946), 549–55.

77. Sayyid Qutb, "Ayuha al-'Arab...," *al-Risala*, no. 647 (26 November 1945), 1281–2.

78. Sayyid Qutb, "Shyluk al-Jadid,, Aw Qidayat Filastin," *Al-Risala*, no. 655 (21 January 1946), 73–4.

79. For a discussion of the Egyptian Communist movement, see Selma Botman, *The Rise of Egyptian Communism, 1939–1970* (Syracuse University Press, 1988).

80. Al-Bishri, *al-Haraka al-Siasiyya fi Misr*, 156–7. The Egyptian Communists followed Moscow's lead in seeing Zionism as a progressive, anti–British, anti–imperialist movement.

81. Ibid., 76–9.

82. Khalid, Khalid M., *From Here We Start* (Washington: American Council of Learned Societies 1953), 95.

83. Vatikiotis, *The History of Egypt*, 367–8.

84. Joel Beinin, "Islamic Responses to the Capitalist Penetration of the Middle East," in Barbara Stowasser (ed.), *The Islamic Impulse* (London: Croom Helm, 1987), 93.

85. Al-Bishri, *al-Haraka al-Siyasiyya fi Misr*, 389–91.

86. Sayyid Qutb, "Adalu Baramijkum," *al-Risala*, no. 627 (9 June 1945), 723.

87. Sayyid Qutb, "al-Mashru'at al-Islah," *Majallat al-Shu'un al-Ijtiima'iyya*, no. 10 (October 1941), 28–33.

88. J. Heyworth-Dunn, *Religious and Political Trends in Modern Egypt* (Washington: Published by author, 1950), 97, n. 63.

89. Sayyid Qutb, "Hadha al-Majalla," *al-Fikr al-Jadid*, no. 1 (1 January 1948). 3.

90. Ibid.

91. Sayyid Qutb, "Antum 'Ayuha al-Mutrafun Tazra'un al-Shuyu'iyya fi Misr," *al-Fikr al-Jadid*, no. 6, (5 February 1948), 3.

92. Sayyid Qutb, "Fa al-Nu'min bi–Anfusina," *al-Fikr al-Jadid*, no. 3, 915 January 1948), 3.

93. Heyworth-Dunn, *Religious and Political Trends in Modern Egypt*, 57.

94. Sayyid Qutb, "Min Laghwi al-Sayf: Ha'ula al-Aristuqrat," 923.

95. Ayubi, referring to the ideology of Islamism generally, in his *Political Islam*, 123.

96. The term "theocentric," as applied to Qutb, is taken from William Shepard, *Sayyid Qutb and Islamic Activism*, xxiv–xxxiv.

97. Here I paraphrase Glifford Geertz's famous definition of religion as found in his *The Interpretation of Cultures* (New York: Basic Books, 1973), 90.

98. I have found Peter G. Stromberg's *Language and Self-Transformation: A Study of the Christian Conversion Narrative* (Cambridge University Press, 1993) useful in explaining Qutb's reorientation to Islamism. Stromberg explains how believers resolve central emotional and other types of conflict by reframing them in terms of the language of Evangelical Christianity.

99. Bruce Lincoln, *Holy Terrors: Thinking about Religion after September 11* (Chicago University Press, 2003), 55.

100. http://www.ghannouchi.net/autobiography.htm. Accessed 5/11/2006. Reproduced in John Calvert, *Islamism: A Documentary and Reference Guide* (Westport, CT: Greenwood Press, 2008), 38–9.

101. Francois Burgat and William Dowell, *The Islamic Movement in North Africa* (new edition) (Austin: The Center for Middle Eastern Studies, 1997), 15–16.

102. Mitchell, *The Society of the Muslim Brothers*, 234–5.

103. Wilfred Cantwell Smith, *The Meaning and End of Religion* (Toronto: The New American Library of Canada Ltd, 1964), 107.

104. Ibid, 303–4, n. 109.

105. A point Vali Nasr communicated to me at Creighton University, 23 Oct. 2009.

106. William Shepard has carefully compared these editions in his *Sayyid Qutb and Islamic Activism: A Translation and Critical Analysis of* Social Justice in Islam (Leiden: E. J. Brill, 1996). Hamid Algar has also translated the book, relying on its fifth edition: *Social Justice in Islam* (Oneonta: Islamic Publications International, 2000). Both Shepard and Algar point to the errors of John Hardie who was the first to translate the book into English (published by the American Council of Learned Society in 1953). The quotes that follow are taken from Shepard's translation of *Social Justice*'s first edition, which reflects Qutb's thought during this period.

107. William Shepard, *Sayyid Qutb and Islamic Activism*, lxi. Qutb says that in the 1954, 2ⁿᵈ edition of the book, he meant "youth" to refer to the Muslim Brothers, whose movement he had by then joined. Al-Khalidi, *Sayyid Qutb*, 317.

108. William Shepard, *Sayyid Qutb and Islamic Activism*, 1–2 .

109. Ibid., 8.

110. Ibid., 9.

111. Ibid., 68 ff.

112. Ibid., 69.

113. Ibid., 39.

114. Ibid., 59.
115. Ibid., 63.
116. Ibid., 59.
117. Ibid., 66.
118. Ibid., 127.
119. Ibid.
120. Ibid., 112.
121. Ibid., 114.
122. Ibid., 108
123. Ibid., 119.
124. Ibid., 111.
125. Ibid., 282.
126. See for example, al-Farabi (d. 950), *The Fusul al-Madani, Aphorisms of the Statesmen*, ed. and trans. D. Dunlop (Cambridge University Press, 1961), 37–9; and Ibn Khaldun (d. 1406), *The Muqaddima*, 3 vols. trans. Franz Rosenthal (Princeton University Press, 1958), who provides the organic model with its classic formulation.
127. Roy P. Mottahedeh, *Loyalty and Leadership in an Early Islamic Society* (Princeton University Press, 1980), 179. For a broad treatment of the subject, see Majid Khadduri, *The Islamic Conception of Justice* (Baltimore: The Johns Hopkins University Press, 1984).
128. Thomas Philipp and Moshe Perlman (eds), *'Abd al-Rahman al-Jabarti's History of Egypt* (Stuttgart: Franz Steiner Verlag, 1994), vol. 1–2, 11–12.
129. See Charles Kurzman, "Recovering the History of Modernist Islam," *ISIM Newsletter*, 12 June 2003, p. 32; and C. Kurzman (ed.), *Modernist Islam, 1840–1940: A Sourcebook* (New York: Oxford University Press, 2002).
130. See, for example, Shepard, *Sayyid Qutb and Islamic Activism*, 119.

4. AMERICAN SOJOURN

1. This section draws heavily on the author's "'The World is an Undutiful Boy!' Sayyid Qutb's American Experience," *Islam and Christian-Muslim Relations*, vol. 11, no. 1, 2000, 87–103.
2. Salah 'Abd al-Fattah al-Khalidi, *Amrika min al-Dakhil bi–Nazar Sayyid Qutb* (Cairo: Dar al-Wafa', 1987), 17–18.
3. Tahir Ahmad Makki, "Sayyid Qutb: Thalath Rasa'il lam Tunshar Qablu," *al-Hilal* (October 1986), 124–6.
4. Al-Khalidi, *Amrika min al-Dakhil*, 19–20.
5. Albert Hourani, *Arabic Thought in the Liberal Age, 1798–1939* (Cambridge University Press, 1983), 69–71.
6. Roger Allen, "The Beginnings of the Arabic Novel," in M.M. Badawi (ed.), *Modern Arabic Literature* (Cambridge University Press, 1992), 184.

7. Hourani, *Arabic Thought in the Liberal Age*, 326.

8. Rasheed El-Enany, "The Promethean Quest in Louis 'Awad's "Memoirs of an Overseas Student," in R. Ostle, E. De Moor and S. Wild (eds), *Writing the Self: Autobiographical Writing in Modern Arabic Literature* (London: Saqi Books, 1998), 64.

9. Ibid.

10. Sayyid Qutb, "Musiqa al-Wujud," *Al-Kitab* (April 1950), 326.

11. Victor Turner, *The Ritual Process: Structure and Anti–Structure* (Ithaca: Cornell University Press, 1969), 95ff.

12. Sayyid Qutb, *Fi Zilal al-Qur'an*, vol. 3 (Cairo: Dar al-Shuruq, 1994), 1786. Author's translation.

13. al-Khalidi, *Sayyid Qutb: Min al-Milad ila al-Istishhad*, 27–8.

14. Letter reproduced in Ibid., 205, and in Makki, "Thalath Rasa'il," 124–6.

15. Qutb had already formulated his view of America in an article he wrote for the newspaper *al-Ahram* in 1934. In the article, Qutb discusses an American youth who believes that "righteousness, honesty, and honour are not essential for success in practical activities, and that the opposites of these virtues can lead to great prosperity and gain. "We are used", Qutb says, "to receiving daily such bizarre ideas and unusual opinions from America." This American youth, Qutb continues "wants to know the market value of virtue and finds that it doesn't have any, or that it is much less than what it costs to maintain it. This approach arises from the economic view of things that dominates the world in general and America in particular." Sayyid Qutb, *al-Ahram* (June 17 1934), 7. I thank Professor William Shepard for bringing this article to my attention.

16. Sayyid Qutb, "Hama'im fi New York," *Al-Kitab* (December 1949), 666–9. Author's translation.

17. Makki, "Thalath Rasa'il," 127–8.

18. Ibid., 128.

19. Al-Khalidi, *Amrika min al-Dakhil*, 30.

20. Al-Khalidi, *Sayyid Qutb: Min al-Milad al-Istishhad*, 197–8.

21. Al-Khalidi, *Amrika min al-Dakhil*, 153–4.

22. As evidenced, for example, in his social satire *Theatre of Society*.

23. Qutb's transcript is Spartan in its details. It indicates that "Sayed Kotb, born 12–10–05", is a resident of "Hilwan, Egypt" and that a copy of the transcript was sent to the Egyptian Embassy in Cairo, which suggests a degree of accountability on Qutb's part. I would like to thank the Registrar's Office at the University of Northern Colorado for its assistance in locating Qutb's records.

24. Al-Khalidi, *Amrika min al-Dakhil*, 31, 158.

25. Malise Ruthven, *A Fury for God* (London: Granta Books, 2002), 81, suggests that Qutb was reticent "to subject himself to appraisal" by instructors he considered less than worthy.

26. Sayyid Qutb, "Hama'im fi NewYork," 663–4.

27. Daniel Brogan, "Al Qaeda's Greeley Roots," *5280 Magazine: Denver's Mile-High Magazine* (June/July 2003), 162–3.

28. Ibid., 163.

29. Sayyid Qutb, "Aduna al-Awal: al-Rijal al-Abid," *al-Risala* (3 November 1952), 1217–19. Author's translation. References to discrimination against "the black man" in America occur in the second and following editions of *Social Justice in Islam*, which appeared after Qutb's return to Egypt; see Shepard, *Sayyid Qutb and Islamic Activism*, 113.

30. Sayyid Qutb, *Ma'raka al-Islam wa al-Ra'smaliyya*, 33.

31. Sayyid Qutb, *Milestones*, 119.

32. Sayed Kotb [Sayyid Qutb], "The World is an Undutiful Boy!" *Fulcrum: The Literary Magazine of Colorado College of Education* vol. 3, no. 1 (Fall 1949), 29.

33. Sayyid Qutb, "Amrika Allati Ra'ayt: Fi Mizan al-Insaniyya," *Al-Risala* no. 959 (19 November 1951), 1303–4.

34. Ibid.

35. Ibid, 1304–6.

36. Al-Khalidi, *Amrika min al-Dakhil*, 31.

37. Ibid., 154–5.

38. For example, Shahrough Akhavi, "Sayyid Qutb," in J. Esposito (ed.), *The Oxford Encyclopedia of the Modern Islamic World* (Oxford University Press, 1995).

39. Sayyid Qutb, "Amrika Allati Ra'ayt: Fi Mizan al-Insaniyya," *Al-Risala* (5 November 1951), no. 957, 1245–6.

40. Sayyid Qutb, "Amrika Allati Ra'ayt: Fi Mizan al-Insaniyya," *Al-Risala*, no. 959 (19 November 1951), 1301–2.

41. Sayyid Qutb, "Amrika Allati Ra'ayt: Fi Mizan al-Insaniyya," *Al-Risala*, no. 961 (3 December 1951), 1358–9.

42. Ibid.

43. Sayyid Qutb, "Amrika Allati Ra'ayt: Fi Mizan al-Insaniyya," *Al-Risala*, no. 957 (5 November 1951), 1245–7.

44. Sadik Jalal al-'Azm, "Orientalism and Orientalism in Reverse," in Alexander Lyon Macfie (ed.), *Orientalism: A Reader* (New York: New York University Press, 2001), 217–38. Originally published in 1981. Also see I. Buruma, and A. Margalit, *Occidentalism: A Short History of Anti–Westernism* (London: Atlantic Books, 2004).

45. It occurs to me that Qutb may well have projected imagery, which he had used in previous writings, onto the scene he witnessed at the infamous church dance. In 1945, several years prior to his American sojourn, Qutb wrote the following concerning nightclubs and dance halls in Cairo: "We all know people who frequent such halls, and we know what goes on inside of them. We know that they spend their time drinking wine in order to release their animal instincts, which are then directed at the cheap flesh found at these places…This cheap flesh is displayed using provocative red

lights, which leads to indecent dancing and lewd gestures..." *Al-Risala* no. 631 (1945), 839–40.

46. Quoted in Olivier Carré, *Mysticism and Politics: A Critical Reading of Fi Zilal al-Qur'an* by Sayyid Qutb, trans. Carol Artigues, revised W. Shepard (Leiden: E.J. Brill, 2003), 293.
47. *Cairo Times*, 27 Sept.-3 Oct. 2001.

5. IN THE ORBIT OF THE MUSLIM BROTHERS

1. 'Abd al-Fattah al-Khalidi, *Amrika min al-Dakhil bi Nizar Sayyid Qutb* (Cairo: Dar al-Wafa', 1987), 38.
2. 'Abd al-Fattah al-Khalidi, *Sayyid Qutb: Min al-Milad ila al-Istishhad* (Damascus: Dar al-Qalam, 1991), 130.
3. Abu al-Hasan al-Nadwi, *Shakhsiyyat wa Kutub* (Damascus: Dar al-Qalam, 1990), 101–6.
4. Translated into English by M.A. Kidwai as *Islam and the World* (Lucknow: Academy of Islamic Research & Publications, 1967). Qutb's introduction is on pp. 1–7. Gustav von Grunebaum treats the book in his *Modern Islam: The Search for Cultural Identity* (New York: Vintage, 1964), 244–57. Of it he writes: "It is difficult not to be impressed with the enthusiasm that permeates Nadwi's presentation...But the admiration aroused by his élan soon shades off into wonderment, and thence to disappointment and a sense of futility, when one realizes that his prescription for the world is simply an injunction to return to, or, as he would say, to resurrect, a golden age that never existed." p. 255.
5. Nadwi, *Islam and the World*, 182–3.
6. William Shepard, "Sayyid Qutb's Doctrine of Jahiliyya," *International Journal of Middle East Studies*, 35 (2003), 533.
7. Sayyid Qutb, *Ma'raka al-Islam wa al-Ra'smaliyya* (Cairo: Dar al-Shuruq, 11th printing, 1990), 8.
8. Ibid., 9.
9. Ibid., 7.
10. Ibid., 17–19.
11. Ibid., 10.
12. Ibid., 21.
13. Ibid., 101–2.
14. Ibid., 114.
15. Ibid.. 6.
16. Ibid., 63, 69, 85.
17. Jakob Skovgaard-Petersen, *Defining Islam for the Egyptian State: Muftis and Fatwas of the Dar al-Ifta* (Leiden: E.J. Brill, 1997), 172.
18. Sayyid Qutb, *Ma'raka al-Islam wa al-Ra'smaliyya*, 99–102.
19. Ibid., 24.
20. Ibid., 19, 23.

21. Ibid., 29.
22. e.g. in his *al-Naqd al-Adabi: Usuluh wa Manahijuhu* (Cairo: Dar al-Fikr al'Arabi, 1947), 26. The Algerian Islamist Malek Bennabi, who was a contemporary of Qutb, also admired Tagore. In his autobiography, Bennabi wrote that Tagore helped "spring the lock of colonialism on my spirit". *Mémoires d'un témoin du siècle: Enfant* (Algiers: Éditions Nationales Algériennes, 1965), 109–10.
23. Sayyid Qutb, *Ma'raka al-Islam wa al-Ra'smaliyya*, 27.
24. Ibid., 59. See also Qutb, "Mujtama' al-'Alami," *Nahwa Mujtama' al-Islami* (Cairo: Dar al-Shuruq [n.d.]), 92 ff; this article was originally written in 1952 or 1953. See Khatab below n. 29.
25. Sayyid Qutb, *Ma'raka al-Islam wa al-Ra'smaliyya*, 35.
26. Wilfred Cantwell Smith, *Islam in Modern History* (Princeton University Press, 1957), 49. Smith writes, "Moreover he [Afghani] seems to have been the first Muslim revivalist to use concepts "Islam" and "the West" as connoting correlative—and of course antagonistic—historical phenomena."
27. Alexandre A. Bennigsen and S. Enders Wimbush, *Muslim National Communism in the Soviet Union: A Revolutionary Strategy for the Colonial World* (University of Chicago Press, 1979).
28. Mark Berger, "After the Third World? History, Destiny and the Fate of Third Worldism," *Third World Quarterly*, vol. 25 no. 1, (2004), 9–39. Robert Malley usefully focuses on newly independent Algeria's role in the formation of Third Worldism. See his *The Call from Algeria: Third Worldism, Revolution and the Turn to Islam* (Berkeley: University of California Press, 1996).
29. Quoted in Sayed Khatab (slightly modified), "Arabism and Islamism in Sayyid Qutb's Thought on Nationalism," *Muslim World*, vol. 94, no. 2 (April 2004), 225.
30. Sayyid Qutb, *Ma'raka al-Islam wa al-Ra'smaliyya*, 40–7.
31. Ibid., 122.
32. Al-Bahi al-Khuli, *Al-Islam...la Shuyu'iyya wa la Ra'smaliyya* (Cairo: n.p. 1951); Muhammad al-Ghazali, *Al-Islam wa Manahij al-Ishtirakiyya* (Cairo: Dar al-Kutub al-Haditha, 2nd ed. 1951).
33. A translation of Siba'i's concept of "mutual social responsibility," taken from his *Ishtirakiyyat al-Islam*, is found in Sami A. Hanna and George H. Gardner, *Arab Socialism: A Documentary Survey* (Salt Lake City, UT: University of Utah Press, 1969), 149–53.
34. Hamid Algar in introduction to his revision of John Hardie's translation of Sayyid Qutb, *Social Justice in Islam* (Oneonta, NY: Islamic Publications International, 2000), 12–13.
35. Sayyid Qutb, "Islam Amrikani," *al-Risala*, no. 991 (1952), 713–15.
36. Albert Memmi, *The Colonizer and the Colonized*, intro. Sean Paul Sartre, afterword by Susan Miller (New York: Beacon Press, 1991; originally published 1965).

37. Abdelrashid Mahmoudi, *Taha Husain's Education: From the Azhar to the Sorbonne* (London: Curzon, 1998), 52.

38. William Shepard, *Sayyid Qutb and Islamic Activism*, 326.

39. See for example Qutb's comments in *The Battle of Islam and Capitalism*, 99.

40. Ibid., 98.

41. William Shepard, *Sayyid Qutb and Islamic Activism*, 287.

42. Ibid., 335.

43. Ibid., 287. Qutb was not alone in referring to an enduring "Crusader spirit". W.C. Smith makes note of the introduction to the 1952 edition of 'Abdullah 'Inan's *Mawaqif Hasima fi Ta'rikh al-Islam* (*Decisive Moments in the History of Islam*), in which the author writes: "The reader will see how the Crusading idea has remained for centuries the axis of this struggle [between East and West], and how it has blazed the more vigorously whenever a new Islamic outburst of power or revival has appeared." *Islam in Modern History*, 101 n. 8. Al Qaeda incorporated into its discourse this identification of Crusaderism and recent US incursions into the Middle East. See for example, Bruce Lawrence (ed.), *Messages to the World: The Statements of Osama Bin Laden* (London and New York: Verso, 2005), 88, 126–7, 133–8, 218.

44. See Mark Cohen, *Under Cross and Crescent: The Jews in the Middle Ages* (Princeton University Press, 1994), 52–74; and Bernard Lewis, *The Jews of Islam* (Princeton University Press, 1987), 21–44.

45. Cohen, *Cross and Crescent*, 6. Antonius was the author of the classic study on the origins of Arab nationalism, *The Arab Awakening* (Philadelphia: J.B. Lippencott, 1939).

46. Sayyid Qutb, *Ma'rakatna ma'a al-Yahud*, 8th printing (Cairo: Dar al-Shuruq, 1987); translated by Ronald Nettler in *Past Trials and Present Tribulations: A Muslim Fundamentalist's View of the Jews* (Oxford: Pergamon Press, 1987), 72–89.

47. *Ma'rakatna*, 20–1.

48. Ibid.

49. Ibid., 22.

50. Ibid., 23.

51. Ibid., 34.

52. Ibid., 27.

53. Ervand Abrahamian, *Khomeinism: Essays on the Islamic Republic* (Berkeley: University of California Press, 1993), 111–31. Another useful study of the "paranoid style" is Paul Silverstein, "An Excess of Truth: Violence, Conspiracy Theorizing and the Algerian Civil War," *Anthropological Quarterly*, vol. 75 no. 4 (October 2002), 643–74.

54. Ervand Abrahamian, *Khomeinism*, 117.

55. Ibid., 111.

56. Ibid.

57. Richard Hofstadter, "The Paranoid Style in American Politics," *Harper's Magazine* (November 1961), 82.

58. "[the colonized] will be nationalist and not, understandably, internationalist. Of course, this being the case, he risks slipping into exclusivism and chauvinism, to hold himself more upright, to oppose national solidarity to human solidarity, and even ethnic solidarity to national solidarity. But to expect the colonized, who has suffered so much from not existing for and by himself, to be open to the world, humanist and internationalist, appears to be comic foolishness." Albert Memmi, *The Colonizer and the Colonized*, 150.

59. For a lively account of US- directed regime change within the larger context of American interventionism, see Stephen Kinzer, *Overthrow: America's Century of Regime Change from Hawaii to Iraq* (New York: Times Books, 2006). A year after the US-UK overthrow of Mossadegh, Secretary of State John Foster Dulles organized another coup, in Guatemala, where the nationalist government had challenged the economic power of the US United Fruit Company. Later, the United States would have a hand in overthrowing "unsuitable" governments in Congo (1960) and South Vietnam (1963).

60. Terry Eagleton, *Ideology: An Introduction* (London: Verso, 1991), 190.

61. Qutb, "When Comes the Help of God and Victory," translated by Batool Isphany, *At-Tawhid, A Quarterly Journal of Islamic Thought and Culture*, vol. 2, no. 1 (August-October) 1989, 131–4; originally published in *al-Risala*, no. 951 (25 September 1951), 1047–9.

62. Salah 'Abd al-Fattah al-Khalidi, *Sayyid Qutb: Min al-Milad ila al-Istishhad* (Damascus: Dar al-Qalam, 1991), 297.

63. Shepard, *Sayyid Qutb and Islamic Activism*, 46.

64. Al-Khalidi, *Sayyid Qutb*, 240–1.

65. Qutb, "Fi Zilal al-Qur'an," *al-Muslimun*, vol. 1, no. 3 (28 January 1952), 237–40; no. 4 (March 1952), 331–9; no. 5 (27 March 1952), 434–42; no. 6 (November 1952), 534–42; no. 7 (June 1952), 749–54; no. 8 (July 1952), 752–62; vol. 3, no. 1 (February 1954), 357–64; no. 5 (March 1954), 453–60.

66. Hugh Galford, "Sayyid Qutb and the Qur'anic Story of Joseph: A Commentary for Today," in Ronald L. Nettler and Suha Taji–Farouki (eds), *Muslim-Jewish Encounters, Intellectual Traditions and Muslim Politics* (Amsterdam: Harwood Academic Publishers), 42. Differences between mediaeval and modern *tafasir* are examined in Kate Zebiri, *Mahmud Shaltut and Islamic Modernism* (Oxford: Clarendon Press, 1993), 128–49.

67. Sayyid Qutb, *Fi Zilal al-Qur'an*, al-juz al-awwal, 2nd ed (Cairo: Al-Maktab al-Arabiyya, n.d. [1956], 6.

68. The accessible and readable character of Qutb's *tafsir* comes across in this notice by Anwar al-Awlaki, a Salafi scholar of Yemeni origin who was educated in the United States. In 2006 al-Awlaki was detained by the

Yemeni authorities, and while in prison had the opportunity to compare Qutb's commentary with that of Ibn Kathir: "With Ibn Kathir his tafsir is full of Hadiths and statements of scholars and rulings so it must be read slowly. I would limit myself to a maximum of 30 pages per day. But because of the flowing style of Sayyid I would read between 100–150 pages a day...I would be so immersed in the author that I would feel that Sayyid was in my cell speaking to me directly." At: http://www.anwar-alawlaki.com/2008/06/22/book-review-3-in-the-shade-of-the-quran-by-sayyid-qutb/. Accessed 9/9/2008.

69. On the *Manar* commentary see J.J.G. Jansen, *The Interpretation of the Koran in Modern Egypt* (Leiden: E.J. Brill, 1974). Olivier Carré compares Qutb's *tafsir* with that of Abduh's and Rida's throughout his *Mysticism and Politics*.

70. J.J.G. Jensen, *The Interpretation of the Koran in Modern Egypt*, 30.

71. According to a 4 March report sent to the British Foreign Office, only "56% of the total electorate had voted but this percentage was reached only because the polling in the provinces was suspiciously high. 69% of the electorate of Upper Egypt may in fact have voted but if they did it can only have been through 'tribal voting' under the direct pressure of land-owners, officials and others in authority. In Cairo only 15% of the electorate or less than 75,000 persons cast their votes." Such figures indicate the population's disenchantment with establishment politics. FO 371/96874, JE1018/104.

72. Caffery to State Department, 1022, 774.00/10–2451.

73. Sayyid Qutb, "'Abbi'u al-Sha'b li al-Kifah, *al-Da'wa*, no. 38 (30 October 1951), 3.

74. Political officers reporting to the US Embassy had this to say about al-Hudaybi: "The eventual aim of the Brotherhood...is to rule Egypt, but Hudaibi and his followers believe that it should wait until it has majority support before taking any overt actions to put its full programme into effect in order not to compromise itself and avoid possible failure." Report to State Department, 5 February 1953, 774–521/2–553.

75. Mitchell, *The Society of the Muslim Brothers*, 89.

76. Ibid., 92. According to Anouar Abdel-Malek, over 600 Egyptian fighters died in the Canal Zone action. *Egypt: Military Society*, translated Charles Lam Markmann (New York: Vintage Books, 1968), 32.

77. Sayyid Qutb, "'Aqida wa Kifah," *al-Da'wa*, no. 41 (27 November 1951), 3. The article is reprinted in Qutb's *Dirasat Islamiyya* (n.p., n.d. [1953]), 227–9.

78. Sayyid Qutb, *al-Misri* (1 January 1952), as cited in al-Bishri, *al-Haraka al-Siyasiyya*, 376–7. Hudaybi answered the criticisms of Qutb and others in the 5 January 1952 edition of *al-Misri*. His reply is reproduced in Caffery to State Department, FO 774.521/2–553.

79. J. Bowyer Bell, *On Revolt: Strategies of National Liberation* (Harvard University Press, 1976), 112–13.

80. "Revenge! Yell Cairo Mobs," *Daily Mirror* (26 January 1952).
81. The following account is based on the newspaper summary of the official inquiry made by the Egyptian Prosecutor-General: *Egyptian Mail* (8 March 1952).
82. The Prosecutor-General's report gives the following breakdown of establishments destroyed: "92 bars and depots of alcoholic drinks; 73 dancing halls, restaurants and cafes; 40 cinemas; 16 clubs; 10 gunsmiths; 8 motor showrooms; 13 hotels; 30 commercial offices; 300 shops; 117 offices and flats."
83. Bell, *On Revolt*, 112.
84. This was the assessment of the British Embassy in Cairo. See Stevenson to Anthony Eden, FO 371/96872, JE 1018/78.
85. According to Anouar Abdel-Malek, *Egypt: Military Society* the events of 25–26 January marked the beginnings of a "genuine popular revolution" (p. 70). Only the later intervention of the Free Officers prevented it from unfolding according to the Chinese or Soviet models or, alternatively, from assuming a "radical democratic" form. In the early 1950s, Abdel-Malek was a member of the Revolutionary Bloc, a breakaway faction of the Communist DMNL. On this point, see also Mahmoud Hussein, *La lutte de classes en Egypte 1945–1970* (Paris: Maspero, 1971), esp. chapters. 2 and 3.
86. The last days of the liberal order are cogently examined in al-Bishri, *al-Haraka*, 554–81, and Joel Gordon, "The Myth of the Savior: Egypt's Just Tyrants on the Eve of the Revolution, January-July 1952," *Journal of the American Research Center in Egypt*, 26 (1989), 223–37.
87. P.J. Vatikiotis, *Nasser and His Generation* (London: Croom Helm, 1978), 49.
88. A reflection of 'Abd al-Nasser's early nationalist activity is recorded in his 1953 *Philosophy of the Revolution* in *Nasser Speaks: Basic Documents*, trans. and edited by E.S. Farag (London: The Morssett Press, 1972), 19–20.
89. Quoted in Raymond Baker, *Egypt's Uncertain Revolution under Nasser and Sadat* (Cambridge, MA: Harvard University Press, 1978), 21.
90. Farag, *Nasser Speaks*, 18.
91. Vatikiotis, *Nasser and His Generation*, 31–2.
92. See Khalid Muhyi al-Din, *Memories of a Revolution: Egypt 1952* (Cairo: American University in Cairo Press, 1996), 21–40.
93. Baker, *Egypt's Uncertain Revolution*, 32.
94. Al-Khalidi, *Sayyid Qutb*, 299; also *Kalimat al-Haqq*, 1, no. 2 (May 1967), 37–9.
95. Al-Khalidi, *Sayyid Qutb*, 298.
96. Ibid., 300.
97. For overviews of the events of this period, see Mitchell, *The Society of the Muslim Brothers*, 99 ff. and Walid Abdelnasser, *The Islamic Movement in*

Egypt. Perceptions of International Relations 1967–81 (New York: Keegan Paul International, 1994), 38–43.

98. 'Adil Hammuda, *Sayyid Qutb: Min al-Qarya ila al-Mishnaqa* (Cairo: Ruz al-Yusuf, 1987), 112.
99. Al-Khalidi, *Sayyid Qutb*, 302.
100. Ibid., 302–3.
101. Qutb, *Limadha A'damuni?* (Shirkat al-Sa'udiyya li–Abath wa-al-Taswiq, n.d), 13.
102. Al-Khalidi, *Sayyid Qutb*, 299.
103. Sayed Khatab, "Arabism and Islamism in Sayyid Qutb's Thought on Nationalism", 224.
104. Al-Khalidi, *Sayyid Qutb*, 87–8.
105. The relations between the Wafd and Free Officers are treated in a report sent by Stevenson to Churchill, 20 April 1953, FO 371/102704. See also Joel Gordon, *Nasser's Blessed Movement* (Oxford University Press, 1992), 68–78.
106. Gordon, *Nasser's Blessed Movement*, 93–8.
107. Quoted in Kirk Beattie, *Egypt During the Nasser Years* (Boulder, CO: Westview Press, 1994), 85.
108. Gordon, *Nasser's Blessed Movement*, 107.
109. Caffery to State Department, 1022, 774.00/10–2451.
110. Al-Khalidi, *Sayyid Qutb*, 305–6.
111. Qutb, "Hajat al-Bashariyya Kulliha Ilayna," *al-Muslimun*, no. 10 (October 1953), 975.
112. Qutb, *Limadha A'damuni?* 12–15.
113. See Jon B. Alterman, *Egypt and American Foreign Assistance 1952–1956* (New York: Palgrave Macmillan, 2002), 126 ff.
114. Qutb, *Limadha A'damuni?* 11.
115. Ibid.
116. Mitchell, *Society of the Muslim Brothers*, 122–4.
117. Brown to Caffery, 12 March 1954, Desp. 2180.
118. Richard Mitchell, *Society of the Muslim Brothers*, 187–8.
119. Al-Khalidi, *Sayyid Qutb*, 335. Reprinted as "Nizam al-Takaful al-Ijtima'i fi al-Islam," in *Dirasat Islamiyya*, 62–72.
120. Sayyid Qutb, *In the Shade of the Qur'an*, vol. 1, surahs 1–2, translated and edited by Adil Salahi and Ashur Shamis (Leicester: The Islamic Foundation, 1999), 358.
121. Al-Khalidi, *Sayyid Qutb*, 336.
122. Jakob Skovgaard-Petersen, *Defining Islam for the Egyptian State*, 158.
123. Qutb, *Limadha A'damuni?* 65.
124. Mitchell, *Society of the Muslim Brothers*, 126; al-Khalidi, *Sayyid Qutb*, 345.
125. Joel Gordon, *Nasser's Blessed Movement*, 105.
126. Richard Mitchell, *The Society of the Muslim Brothers*, 133.
127. Qutb, *Limadha A'damuni?* 12.

128. Said K. Aburish, *Nasser: The Last Arab* (New York: St. Martin's Press, 2004), 53.
129. *Time Magazine*, 8 Nov. 1954.
130. In *Limadha A'damuni?* Qutb told two visiting Muslim Brothers from Libya that the incident "had been organized by Salah Disuqi", a colonel who had recently passed away. pp. 67–8.
131. "An Interview with the Wife of Yusuf Hawwash." Originally published in *al-Da'wa* no. 109, Muharram 1422 (2001); available at: http://www.islamselect.com/en/mat/65081; and A.B. Mehri, *Milestones* (Special edition) http://www.maktabah.net/
132. 'Abd al-Nasser's silencing of protest is treated in Carrie Rosefsky Wickaham, *Mobilizing Islam: Religion, Activism, and Political Change in Egypt* (New York: Columbia University Press, 2002), 21–35; and John Waterbury, *The Egypt of Nasser and Sadat: The Political Economy of Two Regimes* (Princeton University Press, 1983), 333–42.
133. 11 December 1954, FO 371/108319.
134. Al-Khalidi, *Sayyid Qutb*, 347–8.
135. 11 December 1954, FO 371/108319.
136. Mitchell, *The Society of Muslim Brothers*, 161.
137. Al-Khalidi, *Sayyid Qutb*, 349.
138. Ibid., 349–50.
139. Raymond Baker, *Egypt's Uncertain Revolution*, 43.
140. Said K. Aburish, *Nasser: The Last Arab*, 237.

6. RADICALIZATION

1. 'Abd al-Fattah al-Khalidi, *Sayyid Qutb: Min al-Milad ila al-Istishhad* (Damascus: Dar al-Qalam, 1991), 351.
2. In *Search for Identity: An Autobiography* (New York: Harper and Row, 1978), Anwar Sadat writes the following: "In October 1975 as President I took up a pickaxe to strike the first blow at the wall of Turah prison (thereby beginning its demolition)...The bricks were sodden and easy to break. Even the outer coat of plaster was obviously wet, and, as I removed it, innumerable cockroaches came out—ugly contingents of cockroaches." p. 70. See also the report on Liman Tura by The Human Rights Center for the Assistance of Prisoners. Although dated 2002, it gives some idea about the layout of the prison and the conditions that existed there previously. http://hrcap.org/new/reports2.htm. Accessed 7/24/2005.
3. Al-Khalidi, *Sayyid Qutb*, 362.
4. A number of Brothers revealed their prison experiences in works published after their release. Even if one allows for a degree of exaggeration, the overall picture painted in these writings is harrowing. See for example Jabir Rizq, *Madhabih al-Ikhwan fi Sujun Nasir* (Cairo: Dar al-I'tisam, 1977); and Zainab al-Ghazali, *Return of the Pharaoh: Memoir in Nasir's Prison*,

translated by Mokrane Guezzou (Leicester: The Islamic Foundation, 1994), 146 (original title *Ayyam min al-Hayati*, Cairo: al-Matba'a al-Adabiyya, 1987).

5. Zainab al-Ghazali, *Return of the Pharaoh*, 146.
6. Secondary sources for the life of Zaynab al-Ghazali include Leila Ahmed, *Women and Gender in Islam* (New Haven: Yale University Press, 1992), 197–207; Miriam Cooke, *Women Claim Islam: Creating Islamic Feminism through Literature* (New York: Routledge, 2001), 83–106; Aza M. Karam, *Women, Islamisms and the State: Contemporary Feminisms in Egypt* (London: Macmillan, 1998), 207–15; and Valerie Hoffman, "An Islamic Activist: Zaynab al-Ghazali," in Elizabeth W. Fernea (ed.), *Women and the Family in the Middle East: New Voices of Change* (Austin: University of Texas Press, 1985).
7. Al-Khalidi, *Sayyid Qutb*, 365–6.
8. A brief biography of Mariam Jameelah is found in John L. Esposito and John O. Voll, *Makers of Contemporary Islam* (Oxford University Press, 2001), 54–67.
9. At http://angislam.org/books1/e020.htm, pp. 22–4; accessed 5/21/2007. Original print version: *Correspondences between Maulana Maudoodi and Maryam Jameelah*, 4th ed. (Lahore, 1986).
10. Sayyid Qutb, *Milestones*, revised translation with a forward by Ahmad Zaki Hammad (Indianapolis: American Trust Publications, 1990), 96. Arabic title is *Ma'alim fi al-Tariq*.
11. Sayyid Qutb, *In the Shade of the Qur'an*, vol. 1, surahs 1–2, translated and edited by Adil Salahi and Ashur Shamis (Leicester: The Islamic Foundation, 1999), xvii. Arabic original, Sayyid Qutb, *Fi Zilal al-Qur'an* (Beirut: Dar al-Shuruq, 1994), parts 1–4, vol. 1, 11.
12. Olivier Carré, *Mysticism and Politics: A Critical Reading of the Qur'an by Sayyid Qutb, Radical Muslim Brother*, translated by Carol Artigues and revised by W. Shepard (Leiden: E.J. Brill, 2003), 82.
13. Sayyid Qutb, *Fi Zilal al-Qur'an* parts 8–11, vol. 3, 1484.
14. Al-Khalidi, *Sayyid Qutb*, 371.
15. An observation made by Ronald Nettler, "A Modern Confession of Faith and Conception of Religion: Sayyid Qutb's Introduction to the Tafsir, Fi Zilal al-Qur'an," *British Journal of Middle East Studies*, vol. 21, no. 1 (1994), 140, n. 13.
16. Sayyid Qutb, *In the Shade of the Qur'an*, vol. 1, surahs 1–2, xix; *Fi Zilal al-Qur'an*, 13.
17. David Cook, *Martyrdom in Islam* (Cambridge University Press, 2007), 2.
18. In his *Facing the Extreme: Moral Life in the Concentration Camps* (New York: Metropolitan Books, 1996) Tzvetan Todorov looks at the evidence of the Nazi concentration camps and Soviet Gulag to argue that ethical life can flourish in even the most desperate circumstances. The prevailing view has been that extreme conditions erode moral life. Todorov's thesis

seems to hold true for Qutb and other Muslim Brother prisoners who responded to the harsh prison conditions with a moral argument.

19. Qutb, *Limadha A'damuni?* (*Why Did They Execute Me?*) (Al-Sharka al-Sa'udiyya li–Abath wa al-Taswiq, n.d), 19–25.
20. Jeff Goodwin, James M. Jasper and Francesca Polletta (eds), *Passionate Politics: Emotions and Social Movements* (University of Chicago Press, 2001), 8.
21. See Qutb's detailed gloss on sura 3:121–179. The verses unfold against the backdrop of the battle of Uhud. From them Qutb derives lessons for the current generation of "true Muslims". Sayyid Qutb, *In the Shade of the Qur'an*, vol. 2, surah 3, 185–316; *Fi Zilal al-Qur'an*, parts 1–4, vol. 1, 454–553.
22. Sayyid Qutb, "Bawakir al-Kifah," *al-Kifah al-Islami* (26 July 1957), 5.
23. This is one of the theses of Mansoor Moaddel's *Islamic Modernism, Nationalism, and Fundamentalism: Episode and Discourse* (University of Chicago Press, 2005). Among other points, Moaddel argues that "changes in the structure, policies, and ideology of the state had a determining impact on the discourse of the Muslim Brothers. The state's totalitarianism and extensive political repression produced its counterpart in the rise of an equally totalitarian Islamic movement in Egypt." p. 217.
24. According to Luis Martinez, *The Algerian Civil War 1990–1998*, translated by Jonathan Derrick (CERI Series in Comparative Politics and International Studies, London: C. Hurst & Co., 2000), such considerations helped to drive the Algerian conflict of the 1990s.
25. Qutb, *Limadha A'damuni?* 28.
26. Al-Khalidi, *Sayyid Qutb*, 368.
27. Heyworth-Dunne, *Religious and Political Trends in Modern Egypt* (Washington, n.p., 1950), 97, n. 63.
28. Richard Mitchell, *The Society of the Muslim Brothers* (New York: Oxford University Press, 1969; 2nd ed. 1993), 124.
29. Michael Willis, *The Islamist Challenge in Algeria: A Political History* (New York University Press, 1996), 77, 93–4.
30. Safynaz Kazem, "Hagg Wahba: Reference Work," *Al-Ahram Weekly On-Line*, 21–27 no. 513, (December 2000). At: http://weekly.ahram.org. eg/2000/513/profile.htm. Accessed 3/23/2006.
31. Al-Khalidi, *Sayyid Qutb*, 368.
32. Haifaa Khalafallah, PhD dissertation, Georgetown University (1997), "Rethinking Islamic Law: Genesis and Evolution in the Islamic Legal Methods and Structures. The Case of a 20th Century 'Alim's Journey into His Legal Traditions. Muhammad Al-Ghazali (1917–1996)," 101.
33. According to William Shepard, the greatest changes in *Social Justice* "take place between the fifth and the last editions" [i.e. 1958–64]. The later editions have "increased theocentrism"; an "increased emphasis on Islam as a distinct, stable and inwardly consistent religio-social order"; and a "somewhat revised picture of the course of Islamic history. *Sayyid Qutb*

and Islamic Activism: A Translation and Critical Analysis of Social Justice in Islam (Leiden: E.J. Brill, 1996), xxiv.

34. "An Interview with the Wife of Yusuf Hawwash." Originally published in *al-Da'wa*, no. 109, Muharram 1422 (2001); available at: http://www.islamselect.com/en/mat/65081. Accessed 5/24/2007.

35. Qutb, *Limadha A'damuni?* 27.

36. See, for example, the account of this episode by Lawrence Wright, *The Looming Tower: Al-Qaeda and the Road to 9/11* (New York: Knoph, 2006).

37. *Milestones*, 12; *Ma'alim fi al-Tariq*, 17.

38. Sayed Khatab, "Hakimiyya and Jahiliyya in the Thought of Sayyid Qutb," *Middle Eastern Studies*, vol. 38, no. 3 (July 2002), 163.

39. *Milestones*, 74–8; *Ma'alim, fi al-Tariq*, 108–14.

40. Olivier Carré, *Mysticism and Politics*, 75.

41. Qutb, *The Islamic Concept and its Characteristics*, translated by Mohammed Moinuddin Siddiqui (Indianapolis: American Trust Publications, 1991), 85–107; *Khasa'is al-Tasawwur al-Islami wa Muqawwimatih* Cairo: Dar al-Shuruq, 14th printing, 1997), 95–118.

42. *Islam: The Religion of the Future* (Delhi: Markazi Maktaba Islami, 1974), 21–2; *Al-Mustaqbal li–Hadha al-Din*, 11th printing (Beirut: Dar al-Shuruq, 1991), 15.

43. Qutb, *The Islamic Concept and its Characteristics*, 2–16; *Khasa'is*, 5–22.

44. *Milestones*, 69; *Ma'alim*, 104.

45. Ibid., 38; 27.

46. Qutb's gloss of Surah 2:102–3. Sayyid Qutb, *In the Shade of the Qur'an*, vol. 1, surahs 1–2, 99; *Fi Zilal al-Qur'an*, parts 1–4, vol. 1, 95.

47. Sayyid Qutb, *This Religion of Islam* (Delhi: Markazi Maktaba Islami, 1974); Qutb, *Hadha al-Din* (Beirut: Dar al-Shuruq, 13th printing, 1991).

48. Sayyid Qutb, commenting on 3:177–9, *In the Shade of the Qur'an*, vol. 2, surah 3, 306; *Fi Zilal al-Qur'an*, parts 8–11, vol. 2, 526.

49. Sayyid Qutb, *This Religion of Islam*, 4; *Hadha al-Din*, 7.

50. Ibid., 5; 9.

51. Qutb, *The Islamic Concept and Its Characteristics*, 2; *Khasa'is*, 6.

52. *Ma'alim*, 20; *Milestones*, 13.

53. Quoted in Olivier Carré, *Mysticism and Politics*, 318–19 (passage is translated by William Shepard).

54. Roger Griffin, *The Nature of Fascism* (London: Routledge, 1993), 39.

55. Sayyid Qutb, *In the Shade of the Qur'an*, vol. 4, surah 5, 95–6; *Fi Zilal al-Qur'an*, parts 5–7, vol. 2, 882.

56. On Pareto, see Terry Eagleton, *Ideology: An Introduction* ((London: Verso, 1991), 186; on Schmitt, see Heinrich Meier, *The Lesson of Carl Schmitt*, trans. M. Brainard (University of Chicago Press, 1998). Sorel expresses his ideas fully in *Réflexions sur la violence* (1906), trans. T. E. Hulm and J. Roth as *Reflections on Violence* (London: Collier Books,

1950). See also David Gross, "Myth and Symbol in Georges Sorel," in Seymour Drescher, David Sabean and Allan Sharlin (eds), *Political Symbolism in Modern Europe: Essays in Honor of George L. Mosse* (New Brunswick and London: Transaction Books, 1982), p. 109; and J. L. Talmon, "The Legacy of Georges Sorel," *Encounter*, Feb. 1970, 47–60.

57. Gilles Kepel writes: "Mawdudi's book was written in 1941 and was first published in installments in his review, *Tarjuman ul-Qur'an*, in the same year that he founded the *jama'at i islami* in India. In the context, the book's aim was to clarify the association's doctrine and to specify its attitude toward the ruling parties. In other word's, its objectives were not dissimilar to those of *Signposts* [i.e. *Milestones*]." *Muslim Extremism in Egypt*, 48.

58. Ibrahim M. Abu-Rabi, *Intellectual Origins of Islamic Resurgence in the Modern Arab World* (Albany: State University of New York Press, 1996), 139.

59. Bustami Khir, "Sovereignty," *The Encyclopaedia of the Qur'an*, ed. Jane Dammen McAuliffe, vol. 5 (Leiden: Brill Academic Publishers, 2005), 102.

60. Paul Heck, "Politics and the Qur'an," *The Encyclopaedia of the Qur'an*, ed. Jane Dammen McAuliffe, vol. 4 (Leiden: Brill Academic Publishers, 2005), 128. See also Sayed Khatab, "Hakimiyyah and Jahiliyya in the Thought of Sayyid Qutb," 145–170. Khatab provides evidence for the Qur'anic provenance of *hakimiyya* ("sovereignty").

61. On *al-hukm al-shar'i* see Sherman A. Jackson, *Islamic Law and the State* (Leiden: E.J. Brill, 1997), 116–18.

62. Shahrough Akhavi, "The Dialectic in Contemporary Egyptian Social Thought: The Scripturalist and Modernist Discourses of Sayyid Qutb and Hasan Hanafi," *International Journal of Middle East Studies*, 29 (1997), 396 n. 7.

63. Sayyid Qutb, *In the Shade of the Qur'an*, vol. 4, surah 5, 109; *Fi Zilal al-Qur'an*, parts 5–7, vol. 2, 889.

64. Anthony Giddens, *The Nation-State and Violence* (Berkeley: University of California Press, 1987), 282.

65. Erez Manela cogently analyzes the effect of US President Wilson's rhetoric of the "self-determination of nations" on Zaghlul and the Wafd in his *The Wilsonian Moment: Self-Determination and the International Origins of Anticolonial Nationalism* (Oxford University Press, 2007), 63–75, 141–57.

66. Sayyid Qutb, *In the Shade of the Qur'an*, vol. 1, surahs 1–2, 162; *Fi Zilal al-Qur'an*, parts 1–4, vol. 1, 148.

67. Sayyid Qutb, *In the Shade of the Qur'an*, vol. 4, surah 5, 107; *Fi Zilal al-Qur'an*, parts 5–7, vol. 2, 888.

68. *Milestones*, 20; *Ma'alim*, 29.

69. Sayyid Qutb, *In the Shade of the Qur'an*, vol. 1, surahs 1–2, 132–9; *Fi Zilal al-Qur'an*, parts 1–4, vol. 1, 125 ff.

70. Reuven Firestone, *Jihad: The Origin of Holy War in Islam* (Oxford University Press, 1999), 40–1.
71. According to Qutb, *"Jahiliyyah* does not refer to a particular period of time, but to a certain situation which may come into existence at any time. Whenever it exists, it must be described as *jahiliyyah* which is in contrast to Islam." Sayyid Qutb, *In the Shade of the Qur'an*, vol. 4, surah 5, 133; *Fi Zilal al-Qur'an*, parts 5–7, vol. 2, 904.
72. *Milestones*, 15; *Ma'alim*, 21.
73. Sayyid Qutb, *In the Shade of the Qur'an*, vol. 3, surah 4, translated and edited by Adil Salahi and Ashur Shamis (Leicester: The Islamic Foundation, 2001), 107; *Fi Zilal al-Qur'an*, parts 5–7, vol. 2, 632–3 (Qutb citing Mawdudi).
74. *Milestones*, 83–4; *Ma'alim*, 124.
75. Ibid., 67–8; 101.
76. Ibid., 68; 102–3.
77. Ibid., 13; 17.
78. William Shepard, "Sayyid Qutb's Doctrine of Jahiliyya," 529–30.
79. Shepard, *Sayyid Qutb and Islamic Activism*, 320.
80. Ibid., 325.
81. Sayyid Qutb, *In the Shade of the Qur'an*, vol. 4, surah 5, 133; *Fi Zilal al-Qur'an*, parts 5–7, vol. 2, 904.
82. *Milestones* 68–9; *Ma'alim*, 103.
83. Ibid., 79; 116.
84. William Shepard, "Sayyid Qutb's Doctrine of Jahiliyya", 529.
85. According to Toshihiko Izutsu, *Kufr* ("disbelief") refers semantically to an individual's knowing and deliberate ingratitude for the benevolence of God. See his *Ethico Religious Concepts in the Qur'an* (Kingston: McGill-Queen's University Press, 2002 [first published 1959]), 119 ff.
86. *Milestones* 52; *Ma'alim*, 74–5.
87. Khaled Abou El Fadl, *The Great Theft: Wrestling Islam from the Extremists* (New York: HarperOne 2005), 223.
88. As for instance in *Milestones*, 43; *Ma'alim*, 62.
89. See David Cook, *Understanding Jihad* (Berkeley: University of California Press, 2005), 94–7, and Rudolf Peters, *Jihad in Classical and Modern Islam* (Princeton: Marcus Wienner Publishers, 1996), 6–7.
90. *Milestones*, 50; *Ma'alim*, 72.
91. Ibid., 60; 87.
92. Ibid, 46; 66.
93. *Al-Mustaqbal*, 90–2; *Religion of the Future*, 126–9.
94. *Al-Hasad al-Mur* (*The Bitter Harvest: Sixty Years of the Muslim Brotherhood*). Excerpts published in Gilles Kepel and Jean-Pierre Milelli (eds), *Al Qaeda in its Own Words*, trans. Pascale Ghazaleh (Cambridge: Harvard Belknap, 2008), 171–81.
95. Carré, *Mysticism and Politics*, 320.
96. Qutb, *Milestones*, 47–8; *Ma'alim*, 67–8.

97. Ibid., 9.
98. Youssef Choueiri in his *Islamic Fundamentalism* (London: Pinter, 1990), 140–9, believes that the idea of a vanguard came to Qutb via the writings of Alexis Carrel, the French surgeon with fascist leanings who likewise talked of "a new elite that would restore humanity to the right path". Such a view, however, ignores the more general influence of Qutb's environment.
99. Izutsu, *Ethico-Religious Concepts in the Qur'an*, 45 ff.
100. Qutb, *This Religion of Islam*, 9; *Hadha al-Din*, 10–11.\
101. Franz Fanon, *The Wretched of the Earth* (New York: Grove Press, 1963), 94.
102. François Burgat, *The Islamic Movement in North Africa*, new ed. trans. William Dowell (Austin: University of Texas Center for Middle East Studies, 1997), 69.

7. MARTYRDOM

1. Zainab al-Ghazali, *Return of the Pharaoh: Memoir in Nasir's Prison*, translated by Mokrane Guezzou (Leicester: The Islamic Foundation, 1994), 31.
2. Ibid., 35.
3. Emmanuel Sivan, *Radical Islam: Medieval Theology and Modern Politics* (New Haven: Yale University Press, 1985), 108.
4. Qutb, *Limadha A'damuni?* (*Why Did They Execute Me?*) (Al-Sharka al-Sa'udiyya li–Abath wa al-Taswiq, n.d), 57.
5. Zainab al-Ghazali, *Return of the Pharaoh*, 33–6.
6. The origins of the *tanzim* are traced in Salah 'Abd al-Fatah al-Khalidi, *Sayyid Qutb: Min al-Milad ila al-Istishhad* (Damascus: Dar al-Qalam, 1991), 375 ff. Majdi 'Abd al-'Aziz Mitwalli, and Sabri 'Arfa al-Kawmi were latecomers to the organization's leadership. They replaced the original members Muhammad Fathi Rifa'i and Awad 'Abd al-'Al, who then relocated to Algiers. See 'Ali 'Ashmawi, *Al-Ta'rikh Sirri li–Jama'at al-Ikhwan al-Muslimin: Mudhakkirat 'Ali 'Ashmawi Akhir Qadat al-Tanzim al-Khass* (Cairo: Dar al-Hilal, 1993), 70.
7. Zainab al-Ghazali, *Return of the Pharaoh*, 81.
8. Qutb, *Limadha A'damuni?*, 45.
9. 'Ali 'Ashmawi, *Al-Ta'rikh Sirri li–Jama'at al-Ikhwan al-Muslimin*, 56–7.
10. Zainab al-Ghazali, *Return of the Pharaoh*, 122.
11. 'Ali 'Ashmawi, *Al-Ta'rikh Sirri li–Jama'at al-Ikhwan al-Muslimin*, 66–9; 'Abd al-Fattah al-Khalidi, *Sayyid Qutb*, 379–80.
12. Zainab al-Ghazali, *Return of the Pharaoh* 39–40. However, during his trial, Qutb denied that he deliberately "fed" the group the drafts of *Milestones*. See Mahmud Kamil al-'Arusi, *Muhakamat Sayyid Qutb: Wathiqat Muhakamat al-Shaykh Sayyid Qutb wa-Rifaqih fi al-Fatra min 1959–1965* (Cairo: Matba'at al-Jumhuriyya al-Haditha, 1995), 93–121.

13. This is the belief of al-Khalidi, *Sayyid Qutb*, 392.

14. Sayyid Qutb, *Ma'alim fi al-Tariq* (Dar al-Shuruq, 15th printing, 1992), 12–13; translation here is from Sayyid Qutb, *Milestones*, revised translation with a forward by Ahmad Zaki Hammad (Indianapolis: American Trust Publications, 1990), 10.

15. *Milestones*, 5; *Ma'alim fi al-Tariq*, 5.

16. Ibid., 9; 11.

17. Ibid., 16; 22.

18. Ibid., 30; 42.

19. Ibid., 39; 55.

20. Ibid., 61; 89.

21. Zainab al-Ghazali, *Return of the Pharaoh*, 166.

22. Ibid., 40.

23. Ami Ayalon, "Journalists and the Press: The Vicissitudes of Licensed Pluralism," in Shimon Shamir (ed.), *Egypt from Monarchy to Republic: A Reassessment of Revolution and Change* (Boulder: Westview Press, 1995), 270.

24. *Mysticism and Politics: A Critical Reading of the Qur'an by Sayyid Qutb, Radical Muslim Brother*, translated by Carol Artigues and revised by W. Shepard (Leiden: E.J. Brill, 2003), 8. The regime's initial inaction towards the book may have sprung from its tendency in the early 1960s to allow select Brothers publicly to express aspects of their Islamist ideology, in the hope that such expression would lay the groundwork for eventual cooptation. According to Kirk Beattie, Islam, nationalism and socialism all represented for 'Abd al-Nasser "valuable sources of ideals and legitimizing principles" for the new order. *Egypt During the Nasser Years* (Boulder: Westview Press, 1994), 177. According to Alain Roussillon, it was this policy that explained the regime's willingness to countenance Zaynab al-Ghazali's philanthropic activities, in addition to the regime's creation in 1958 of Dar al-'Uruba, which published works by a number of leading Brotherhood theoreticians, including 'Abd al-Qadir 'Awda. "Republican Egypt Interpreted: Revolution and Beyond," in M.W. Daly (ed.), *The Cambridge History of Egypt*, vol. 2 (Cambridge University Press, 1998), 148–9.

25. 'Ali 'Ashmawi, *Al-Ta'rikh Sirri li–Jama'at al-Ikhwan al-Muslimin*, 59–66.

26. See Sabry Hafez's short review of Egyptian prison memoirs, "Torture, Imprisonment, and Political Assassination in the Arab Novel," *al-Jadid*, vol. 8, no. 38 (winter 2002), at: http://www.aljadid.com/features/0838hafez. html. These accounts include Tahir Abdul Hakim's *Bare Feet* (1980), which recounts the author's five-year bloody ordeal (1959–64) in Al Wahat prison camp.

27. Qutb, *Limadha A'damuni?* 31–5.

28. *Faysal al-Tafriqa bayn al-Islam wa al-Zandaqa* (*The Clear Criterion for Distinguishing between Islam and Godlessness*). It forms Appendix I of

al-Ghazali, *Deliverance from Error: Five Key Texts Including His Spiritual Autobiography, al-Munqidh min al-Dalal*, trans. and annotated by R.J. McCarthy (Louisville, KY: Fons Vitae, 2000), pp. 125–49.

29. Qutb, *Limadha A'damuni?* 36–7.

30. Al-Khalidi, *Sayyid Qutb*, 372–3.

31. Charles Tripp, *A History of Iraq* (Cambridge University Press, 2nd ed. 2002), 173–81.

32. Shaykh Amjad al-Zahawi (1883–1967) is famous in Islamist circles for his saying that found its way into the covenant of the Palestinian Islamist party Hamas: "The Islamic world is on fire. Each of us should pour some water, no matter how little, to extinguish whatever one can without waiting for the others."

33. Qutb, *Limadha A'damuni*, 72.

34. Kirk Beattie, *Egypt During the Nasser Years* (Boulder: Westview Press, 1994).

35. A.B. Mehri, *Milestones: Special Edition* (Maktaba), 12. Available at: http://www.maktabah.net/ This explanation is fleshed out in Mahmud 'Abd al-Halim, *Al-Ikhwan al-Muslimun: Ahdath Sana'at al-Tarikh. Ru'iyya min al-Dakhil* (Alexandria: Dar al-Da'wa, 1986), 399–405.

36. Qutb, *Limadha A'damuni?* 72–4; and al-Khalidi, *Sayyid Qutb*, 372–4.

37. John Waterbury, *Egypt: Burdens of the Past, Options for the Future* (Bloomington: Indiana University Press, 1978), 163.

38. See Joel Gordon, *Revolutionary Melodrama: Popular Film and Civic Identify in Nasser's Egypt* (Chicago: Chicago Studies on the Middle East, 2003). Yusuf Shahin's best known film from the revolutionary period is *Bab al-Hadid* (1958) (English title, "Cairo Station"). Qutb earlier summarized his attitude to the arts in a 1954 article in *al-Muslimun*. In the article, Qutb said that true art derives from the Islamic conception. See Adnan A. Musallam, *From Secularism to Jihad: Sayyid Qutb and the Foundations of Radical Islamism* (Westport, CT: Praeger), 148.

39. An epithet attached to Pharaoh in Qur'an 20:24.

40. 'Ali 'Ashmawi, *Al-Ta'rikh Sirri li–Jama'at al-Ikhwan al-Muslimin*, 122.

41. Qutb, *Limadha A'damuni?* 38–9.

42. Al-Khalidi, *Sayyid Qutb*, 391.

43. Qutb, *Limadha A'damuni?* 75. Qutb mentions that during this period (1965) the Saudi Broadcasting Service wired him 143 Egyptian pounds in payment for the broadcasting of segments of *In the Shade of the Qur'an* during the months of Sha'ban and Ramadan of that year. He then found out that the Saudis had been broadcasting his works "for years".

44. Ibid., 40.

45. Ziad Abu-Amr, *Islamic Fundamentalism in the West Bank and Gaza: Muslim Brotherhood and Islamic Jihad* (Bloomington: Indiana University Press, 1994); and Umar F. Abd-Allah, *The Islamic Struggle in Syria* (Berkeley: Mizan Press, 1983).

46. Ibid., 69–71. The Syrian Muslim Brotherhood began in 1945 as a federation of a numerous Syrian Islamic social welfare societies under the leadership of Mustafa al-Siba'i. Was this unnamed Syrian visitor the Islamist, Marwan Hadid? It is likely. Marwan Hadid studied in Egypt between 1956 and 1965 with side trips to Syria. He admired Qutb and was in contact with his followers among the former political detainees. On Marwan Hadid, see Umar F. Abd-Allah, *The Islamic Struggle in Syria*, 104–7.

47. The 1964 attack was a prelude to the much more severe Ba'thist assault on Muslim Brotherhood strongholds in Hama in February 1982 that cost between 10,000 and 25,000 lives. That assault was directed by Rifa'at al-Asad, who was the younger brother of former Syrian president, Hafiz al-Asad. See the account by Robert Fisk, *Pity the Nation: The Abduction of Lebanon* (New York: Nation Books, 4th ed., 2002), 185–6. The 1964 upheaval is treated briefly in Henry Munson, Jr., *Islam and Revolution in the Middle East* (New Haven: Yale University Press, 1988), 86.

48. Qutb, *Limadha A'damuni*, 64–5. The Jordanian branch of the Muslim Brotherhood was formally declared in 1953 as an offshoot of the Palestinian Muslim Brotherhood following the incorporation of the West Bank into the Hashimite Kingdom. See Marion Boulby, *The Muslim Brotherhood and the Kings of Jordan, 1945–1993* (Atlanta: Scholars Press for the University of South Florida, 1999).

49. Ibid ., 76–7. The origins of Algerian Islamism are traced in Michael Willis, *The Islamist Challenge in Algeria: A Political History* (New York University Press, 1996), 1–67. The Algerian visitor may well have been a member of al-Qiyam ("Values"), an Islamist society founded in 1964 whose head, Hachemi Tijani, was impressed by the incisiveness of Qutb's thought. According to Willis, al-Qiyam aimed to promote the Arabic language in Algeria but for practical reasons the society was dependent on French. Al-Qiyam also included a number of *'ulama* formally attached to the Association des Oulémas Musulmans Algériens of Ben Badis (Willis, 41–4).

50. Qutb, *Limadha A'damuni*, 78–9.

51. Mahmud Kamil al-'Arusi, *Muhakamat Sayyid Qutb*, 95–97; and Qutb, *Limadha A'damuni*, 46.

52. Al-'Arusi, *Muhakamat Sayyid Qutb*, 106; and 'Ali 'Ashmawi, *Al-Ta'rikh Sirri li–Jama'at al-Ikhwan al-Muslimin*, 121.

53. Qutb, *Limadha A'damuni?* 52; and al-'Arusi, *Muhakamat Sayyid Qutb*, 104.

54. Qutb, *Limadha A'damuni*, 49; and al-'Arusi, *Muhakamat Sayyid Qutb*, 105–6.

55. Sayyid Qutb, *In the Shade of the Qur'an*, vol. 3, surah 4, translated and edited by Adil Salahi and Ashur Shamis (Leicester: The Islamic Foundation, 2001), 282; *Fi Zilal al-Qur'an*, parts 5–7, vol. 2, 742.

56. Qutb, *Limadha A'damuni?* 42–3. See also Emmanuel Sivan, *Radical Islam: Medieval Theology and Modern Politics* (New Haven: Yale University Press, 1985), 89–90.

57. Qutb, *Limadha A'damuni?* 46–8.
58. Quoted in Mahmud Kamil al-'Arusi, *Muhakamat Sayyid Qutb*, 64–5.
59. Qutb, *Limadha A'damuni?* 49.
60. Ibid., 53.
61. Ibid., 49.
62. al-'Arusi, *Muhakamat Sayyid Qutb*, 106. Also "Cairo Dooms 7 Found Guilty of Plot to Kill Nasser," *New York Times* (21 August 1966).
63. Qutb, *Limadha A'damuni?* 54–5.
64. Ibid., 53.
65. Sayyid Qutb, *In the Shade of the Qur'an*, vol. 8, surah 9, translated and edited by Adil Salahi (Leicester: The Islamic Foundation, 2003), 312; *Fi Zilal al-Qur'an*, parts 8–11, vol. 3, 1741.
66. Qutb, *Limadha A'damuni?* 50–1; and al-'Arusi, *Muhakamat Sayyid Qutb*, 100–1. Also 'Ali 'Ashmawi, *Al-Ta'rikh Sirri li–Jama'at al-Ikhwan al-Muslimin*, 110–13.
67. Selma Botman, *The Rise of Egyptian Communism, 1939–1970* (Syracuse University Press, 1988), 145–6; Raymond Baker, *Egypt's Uncertain Revolution under Nasser and Sadat* (Cambridge: Harvard University Press, 1978), 99.
68. For a concise treatment of Egyptian leftist historiography on the Muslim Brotherhood, see Brynyar Lia, *The Society of the Muslim Brothers in Egypt: The Rise of an Islamic Mass Movement 1928–1942* (Reading: Ithaca Press, 1998), 6–8.
69. Al-Khalidi, *Sayyid Qutb*, 413.
70. On the history of Ra's al-Barr, see *Al-Ahram Weekly* at: http://weekly.ahram.org.eg/2006/823/tr32.htm. Accessed 10/5/2008.
71. Qutb, *Limadha A'damuni*, 16; and al-Khalidi, *Sayyid Qutb*, 419.
72. Al-Khalidi, *Sayyid Qutb*, 417. But see the short panegyric of Qutb by 'Abdullah 'Azzam who identifies the snake in Qutb's account with the Communists who by this time were cooperating with the 'Abd al-Nasser regime. 'Abdullah 'Azzam, "'Amlaq al-Fikr al-Islami al-Shahid Sayyid Qutb." At: http://www.khayma.com/alattar/selection/sqotb2.htm. Accessed 9/4/2008.
73. Sayyid Qutb, *Milestones*, 129–38; *Ma'alim fi al-Tariq*, 188–202.
74. Sayyid Qutb, *In the Shade of the Qur'an*, vol. 2, surah 3, translated and edited by Adil Salahi and Ashur Shamis (Leicester: The Islamic Foundation, 2000), 293; *Fi Zilal al-Qur'an*, parts 1–4, vol. 1, 517.
75. For a historical account of the concept, see David Cook, *Martyrdom in Islam* (Cambridge University Press, 2007), esp. 31–44.
76. Qutb emphasized that Muhammad knew nothing about the organization; that his claims of ignorance on the matter of the organization during his interrogation were honest and legitimate. Al-Khalidi, *Sayyid Qutb*, 439.
77. 'Ali 'Ashmawi, *Al-Ta'rikh Sirri li–Jama'at al-Ikhwan al-Muslimin*, 121.
78. Ibid., 124, 129.
79. Zaynab al-Ghazali, *Return of the Pharaoh*, 44.

80. Qutb, *Limadha A'damuni?* 59; and 'Ali 'Ashmawi, *Al-Ta'rikh Sirri li-Jama'at al-Ikhwan al-Muslimin,*132.
81. Safynaz Kazem, "Hagg Wahba: Reference Work," *Al-Ahram Weekly On-Line,* 21–27 no. 513, (December 2000). At: http://weekly.ahram.org. eg/2000/513/profile.htm. Accessed 3/23/2006.
82. 'Ali 'Ashmawi, *Al-Ta'rikh Sirri li–Jama'at al-Ikhwan al-Muslimin,* 132–7.
83. Al-Khalidi, *Sayyid Qutb,* 421.
84. On the basis of figures supplied by the Egyptian daily *Akhbar al-Yom* (29 March 1975) Kirk Beattie puts the number of detainees at approximately 27,000. *Egypt During the Nasser Years,* 193. John Waterbury, *The Egypt of Nasser and Sadat: The Political Economy of Two Regimes* (Princeton University Press, 1983), quotes Mustafa Amin concerning the imprisonments of the 'Abd al-Nasser period: "The basic rule in those days was that if you were found guilty, you went to prison; and if you were found innocent, you went to the concentration camp." p. 340.
85. Kepel, *Muslim Extremism in Egypt,* 32–3.
86. "An Interview with the Wife of Yusuf Hawwash." Originally published in *al-Da'wa* no. 109, Muharram 1422 (2001); available at: http://www. islamselect.com/en/mat/65081. Accessed 5/24/2007.
87. John O. Voll, "Fundamentalism in the Sunni Arab World," in Martin E. Marty and R. Scott Appleby (eds), *Fundamenatlisms Observed* (University of Chicago Press, 1991), 379.
88. Zaynab al-Ghazali, *Return of the Pharaoh,* 51.
89. Ibid., 44.
90. Ibid., 48–9.
91. Ibid., 48–56.
92. Quoted in Miriam Cooke, "Ayyam Min Hayati—the Prison Memoirs of a Muslim Sister," *Journal of Arabic Literature,* vol. 26, nos. 1–2 (1995), 121–39.
93. Olivier Carré, *Mysticism and Politics,* 11.
94. Gamal al-Ghitani, *The Mahfouz Dialogues,* translated by Humphrey Davies (Cairo: American University in Cairo Press, 2006), 166.
95. Mohamed Heikal, *The Sphinx and the Commissar: The Rise and Fall of Soviet Influence in the Middle East* (New York: Harper and Row, 1978), 143–7.
96. Jeffery T. Kenny, *Muslim Rebels: Kharijites and the Politics of Extremism in Egypt* (Oxford University Press, 2006), 99.
97. Quoted in Kepel, *Muslim Extremism in Egypt,* 60–1.
98. On the traditional religious authority of the *'ulama,* see Jonathan P. Berkey, *The Formation of Islam: Religion and Society in the Near East 600–1800* (Cambridge University Press, 2003), 224–30.
99. 'Abd al-Rahman al-Jabarti, *'Aja'ib al-Athar fi al-Tarajim wa al-Akhbar,* 7 vols. Eds. 'Abd al-Fattah al-Saranjawi and Sayyid Ibrahim Salim (Cairo: Lajnat al-Bayan al-'Arabi, 1958–60), I: 32–40.

100. Kirk J. Beattie, *Egypt During the Nasser Years: Ideology, Politics, and Civil Society* (Boulder: Westview Press, 1994), 192.

101. Carrie Rosefsky Wickaham, *Mobilizing Islam: Religion, Activism, and Political Change in Egypt* (New York: Columbia University Press, 2002), 32.

102. Zaynab al-Ghazali writes of al-Nahhas's funeral procession that it "had been a call by the righteous, a declaration of their truth. It showed the true colour of Egypt and the suppressed feeling of its sons and daughters." *Return of the Pharaoh*, 68–9.

103. John Waterbury, *The Egypt of Nasser and Sadat: The Political Economy of Two Regimes* (Princeton University Press, 1983), 339. On this point, see also al-Khalidi, *Sayyid Qutb*, 414–5; and Kepel. *Muslim Extremism in Egypt*, 32.

104. On the composition of Egypt's security services under 'Abd al-Nasser and the competition among them, see Hamied Ansari, *Egypt: The Stalled Society* (Cairo: The American University in Cairo Press, 1986), 98–9.

105. Sayyid Qutb, *In the Shade of the Qur'an*, vol. 1, surahs 1–2, translated and edited by Adil Salahi and Ashur Shamis (Leicester: The Islamic Foundation, 1999), 66; *Fi Zilal al-Qur'an*, parts 1–4, vol. 1, 71.

106. Zainab al-Ghazali, *Return of the Pharaoh*, 149.

107. Qutb, *Limadha A'damuni?* 3–8

108. Ibid., 91–4.

109. Sami Jawhar, *al-Mawta Yatakallamun* (Cairo: Maktab al-Misri al-Hadith,1987), 110.

110. For outlines of Kharijite theology and history see Ignaz Goldziher, *Introduction to Islamic Theology and Law*, translated by Andras and Ruth Hamori (Princeton University Press, 1981), 170–4; Julius Welhausen, *The Religio-Political Factions in Early Islam*, translated R.C. Ostle and S.M. Walzer, ed. R.C. Ostle (New York: American Elsevier, 1975); Ann K.S. Lambton, *State and Government in Medieval Islam* (Oxford University Press, 1981), 21–7; and Jeffery T. Kenny, *Muslim Rebels*, 19–53.

111. Sivan, *Radical Islam*, 91.

112. Mahmud Kamil al-'Arusi, *Muhakamat Sayyid Qutb*, 77.

113. Qutb is explicit on this point in *Limadha A'damuni*, 38.

114. Qutb's interrogation is covered in Sami Jawhar, *al-Mawta Yatakallamun*, 110–46; also Mahmud Kamil al-'Arusi, *Muhakamat Sayyid Qutb*, 93–121.

115. *New York Times* (21 August 1966).

116. Zainab al-Ghazali, *Return of the Pharaoh*, 156.

117. Sami Jawhar, *al-Mawta Yatakallamun*, 160.

118. Mahmud Kamil al-'Arusi, *Muhakamat Sayyid Qutb*, 141–6.

119. Al-Khalidi, *Sayyid Qutb*, 463.

120. Translation adapted from Badmas 'Lanre Yusuf, "A History of Fi Zilalil-Qur'an," *Hamdard Islamicus*. Vol. 25, no. 2 (April 2002), 19; also Al-Khalidi, *Sayyid Qutb*, 466.

121. 'Ali 'Ashmawi, *Al-Ta'rikh Sirri li–Jama'at al-Ikhwan al-Muslimin*, 150.

122. Al-Khalidi, *Sayyid Qutb*, 468–9.
123. François Burgat and William Dowell, *The Islamic Movement in North Africa*, new ed. (Austin: University of Texas Press, 1997), 254.
124. Al-Khalidi, *Sayyid Qutb*, 469.
125. Al-Khalidi, *Sayyid Qutb*, 472–4.
126. Zainab al-Ghazali, *Return of the Pharaoh*, 165.
127. Sayyid Qutb, *Milestones*, 40.
128. "An Interview with the Wife of Yusuf Hawwash." Originally published in *al-Da'wa* no. 109, Muharram 1422 (2001); available at: http://www.islamselect.com/en/mat/65081; and A.B. Mehri, *Milestones* (Special edition) http://www.maktabah.net/.
129. Muhammad Abdul Aziz Al-Musnad (Translated by Dr. Muhammad Amin Tawfiq), "Two Witnesses to Sayyid Qutb's Hanging" (n.p., n.d.). At: http://www.makingsenseofjihad.com/2008/05/site-updates.html. Accessed 6/15/2008
130. Sayyid Qutb, *In the Shade of the Qur'an*, vol. 2, surah 3, 259; *Fi Zilal al-Qur'an*, parts 1–4, vol. 1, 499.
131. Sami Jawhar, *al-Mawta Yatakallamun*, 197–99; also al-Khalidi, *Sayyid Qutb*, 477–9.
132. Zainab al-Ghazali, *Return of the Pharaoh*, 165.
133. Al-Khalidi, *Sayyid Qutb*, 471.
134. http://www.ikhwan.net/vb/showthread.php?t=13479. Accessed 3/24/09.
135. "Extracts from Al-Jihad Leader Al-Zawahiri's New Book," Available at http://www.fas.org/irp/world/para/ayman_bk.html, 16. [*Knights under the Prophet's Banner* was serialized in the Saudi–owned newspaper *Al-Sharq al-Awsat* (2 Dec. 2001)].
136. Gilles Dorronsoro, *Revolution Unending: Afghanistan, 1979 to the Present* (New York: Columbia University Press, 2005), 75.
137. Valerie Hoffman, "The Role of Visions in Contemporary Egyptian Life," *Religion*, vol. 27, no. 1 (January 1997), 46.
138. Ibid. See also Amira Mittermaier, "The Book of Visions: Dreams, Poetry and Prophecy in Contemporary Egypt," *International Journal of Middle East Studies*, 39 (2007), 229–47.
139. Jane Idleman Smith and Yvonne Yazbeck Haddad, *The Islamic Understanding of Death and Resurrection* (Albany: State University of New York Press, 1981), 52.
140. Hoffman, "Role of Visions," 46–7.
141. Olivier Carré, *Mysticism and Politics*, 69–70
142. Two Qur'anic appellations for the highest levels of Paradise: "Day, verily the record of the Righteous is (preserved) in 'Illiyin." *Surat al-Mutaffifin*, 83:18.
143. Sayyid Qutb *et al*, *Atyaf al-Arba'a*, 8.
144. Hamida Qutb, *Nida ila al-Diffa al-Ukhra* (Cairo: Dar al-Shuruq, 1969), 132.
145. Ibid.
146. Raymond Baker, *Egypt's Uncertain Revolution*, 116.

147. Zainab al-Ghazali, *Return of the Pharaoh*, 178–9.
148. Sayyid Qutb, *In the Shade of the Qur'an*, vol. 2, surah 3, 287; *Fi Zilal al-Qur'an*, parts 1–4, vol. 1, 513.
149. Sayyid Qutb, *In the Shade of the Qur'an*, vol. 1, surahs 1–2, 56; *Fi Zilal al-Qur'an*, parts 1–4, vol. 1, 63–4.
150. Malika Zaghal, "Religion and Politics in Egypt: The Ulema of al-Azhar, Radical Islam, and the State (1952–94)," *International Journal of Middle East Studies*, vol. 31, no. 3 (1999), 381. It is interesting to note in this context that Shaykh Subki was one of Qutb's harshest critics at his trial. He wrote, "Like the *Kharijites*, Qutb employs the concept of *hakimiyya li–Ilah* to call upon Muslims to oppose any earthly sovereignty." Gilles Kepel, *Muslim Extremism in Egypt*, 60. Also see Muhammad Jalal Kishk's *Al Naksa Wa al Ghazw al Fikri* (The Setback and Cultural Invasion. http://www.fathom.com/feature/122175/index.html
151. "An Interview with the Wife of Yusuf Hawwash." See above n. 128.
152. Francis Johnston, *Zeitoun (1968–1971): When Millions Saw Mary*, 4–5; at http://www.zeitun-eg.org/pg0001.htm. Accessed 12/30/2008.

8. EPILOGUE: THE TRAJECTORY OF 'QUTBISM'

1. Al-Khalidi, *Sayyid Qutb: Min al-Milad ila al-Istishhad* (Damascus: Dar al-Qalam, 1991), 45.
2. Hamida Qutb, *Nida ila al-Diffa al-Ukhra* (Cairo: Dar al-Shuruq, 1969), 179.
3. Muhammad Qutb, *Manhaj al-Fann* (Cairo: Dar al-Shuruq, n.d.), 326.
4. Al-Khalidi, *Sayyid Qutb*, 43. A brief biography of Sananiri ("Kamal al-Din al-Sananiri...al-Da'iyya al-Mujahid") is at: http://www.ikhwanonline.com/Article.asp?ArtID=2951&SecID=455 Accessed 1/6/09.
5. Gilles Kepel, *Muslim Extremism in Egypt* (Berkeley: University of California Press, 1993), 75–6.
6. Ibid., 61.
7. This summary is taken from Barbara Zollner, "Prison Talk: The Muslim Brotherhood's Internal Struggle," *International Journal of Middle East Studies*, vol. 39, no. 3 (August 2007), 411–33; and her more extensive treatment *The Muslim Brotherhood: Hasan al-Hudaybi and Ideology* (London and New York: Routledge, 2009). Zollner argues convincingly that Hudaybi wrote *Preachers, Not Judges* with the aid of an unspecified group of Azharis and senior Brothers who were anxious to confront the emergent radical trend among Qutb's disciples.
8. Gilles Kepel, *Muslim Extremism in Egypt*, 75–6.
9. On the Saudi *Sahwa* see Madawi Al-Rasheed, *Contesting the Saudi State: Islamic Voices from a New Generation* (Cambridge University Press, 2007), esp. 59–101; Mamoun Fandy, *Saudi Arabia and the Politics of Dissent*

(New York: St Martin's Press, 1999); David Commins, *The Wahhabi Mission and Saudi Arabia* (London: I.B. Tauris, 2006), chapters 5 and 6; and Stephane Lacroix, "Fundamentalist Islam at a Crossroads: 9/11, Iraq, and the Saudi Religious Debate," Center for Strategic and International Studies, 29 May 2008, at: http://www.csis.org/component/option,com_csis_events/task,view/id,1671/ accessed 23/3/09. The most thorough treatment of Juhayman al-'Utaybi and his movement is Thomas Hegghammer and Stéphane Lacroix, "Rejectionist Islamism in Saudi Arabia: The Story of Juhayman al-'Utaybi," *International Journal of Middle East Studies*, 39 (2007), 103–22; I borrow the term "rejectionist" from this article. See also the account by the journalist Yaroslav Trofimov, *The Siege of Mecca* (New York: Doubleday, 2007).

10. Gilles Kepel, *The War for Muslim Minds: Islam and the West* (Cambridge: Belknap Harvard, 2004), 174–6.

11. Al-Khalidi, *Sayyid Qutb*, 48.

12. Gilles Kepel and Jean-Pierre Milelli (eds), *Al Qaeda in its own Words*, translated by Pascale Ghazaleh (Cambridge: Belknap Harvard, 2008), 90–1.

13. Al-Sananiri's biographical sketch (see above n. 4) and Ayman al-Zawahiri, "Knights under the Prophet's Banner," at: http://tawhed.11omb.com/books/knights_Under_the_Prophet_Banner_english.pdf

14. The full poem is at http://talk.islamicnetwork.com/archive/index.php/t-1474.html and other Islamic sites on the www. Some web commentators suggest that Amina wrote the poem about her brother, Sayyid.

15. On the Muslim student groups, see Gilles Kepel, *Muslim Extremism in Egypt*, 129–71. The late Ahmed Abdalla placed student politics of the 1970s within a wider historical perspective. See his *The Student Movement and National Politics in Egypt, 1923–1973* (London: Al Saqi Books, 1985).

16. "Shahid Sayyid Qutb: Al-Katib al-Islami min Ajal Zilal al-Qur'an," *al-Da'wa*, 4 (Shawwal 1396/October 1976), 2–3.

17. Qutb, *This Religion of Islam* (Delhi: Markazi Maktaba Islami, 1974), 9; Arabic original *Hadha al-Din* (Cairo: Dar al-Qalam, 1962).

18. Quoted in Gilles Kepel, *Muslim Extremism in Egypt*, 64.

19. John Voll, "Fundamentalism in the Sunni Arab World," in Martin E. Marty and R. Scott Appleby (eds), *Fundamentalisms Observed* (University of Chicago Press, 1991), 381.

20. Salwa Ismail, "Islamist Movements as Social Movements: Contestation and Identity Frames," *Historical Reflections/Réflexions Historiques*, vol. 30, no. 3 (2004), 390.

21. Saad Eddine Ibrahim, "Egypt's Islamic Activism in the 1980s," *Third World Quarterly* (April 1988), 632–57. Saad Eddin Ibrahim's studies remain the starting point for any understanding of Egypt's "Islamic groups" of the 1970s and early 1980s. His research was based on exten-

sive interviews with imprisoned members of the Jama'at and is summa-
rized in his "Anatomy of Egypt's Militant Islamic Groups: Methodological
Notes and Preliminary Findings," *International Journal of Middle East
Studies*, 12:4 (December 1980), 423–53, and his "Egypt's Islamic Militants," *MERIP Reports*, 103 (1982), 5–14. Ellis Goldberg, "Smashing
Idols and the State: The Protestant Ethic and Egyptian Sunni Radicalism,"
Comparative Studies in Society and History, vol. 33, no. 1 (Jan. 1991),
3–35, takes cues from Michael Walzer's study of 16th century Calvinist
politics, *Revolution of the Saints* (Cambridge University Press, 1965), to
argue that the Jama'at represented an egalitarian "puritan" reaction to
Nasserist absolutism. See also Gilles Kepel's treatment in *Muslim Extremism in Egypt*, 70–102, and David Cook, *Understanding Jihad* (Berkeley:
University of California Press), 106–10.

22. On Taqi al-Din Nabahani, see Suha Taji–Farouki, *A Fundamental Quest:
Hizb al-Tahrir and the Search for the Islamic Caliphate* (London: Grey
Seal, 1996).

23. Ayman al-Zawahiri, "Knights under the Prophet's Banner," at: http://
tawhed.11omb.com/books/knights_Under_the_Prophet_Banner_english.
pdf

24. Saad Eddine Ibrahim, *Egypt, Islam and Democracy: Twelve Critical
Essays* (Cairo: The American University in Cairo Press, 1996), 21.

25. Ellis Goldberg, "Smashing Idols and the State," 28.

26. As has been evident in this book, Qutb drew heavily on a variety of classical sources, including the *tafasir* of Tabari, Ibn Qayyim al-Jawziya and
Ibn Kathir, although it is true that he always favoured "the unadorned but
complete Islamic idea" over apologetic theology or rationally oriented
Qur'an commentary. See Olivier Carré, *Mysticism and Politics*, 26–7.

27. 'Umar 'Abd al-Rahman's attraction to Qutb's mature Islamism is explicit
in his *Kalimat al-Haqq: Murafa'at al-Duktur 'Umar 'Abd al-Rahman fi
Qadayit al-Jihad* (Dar al-I'tisam: n.d.), 16.

28. Johannes J.G. Jansen, *The Neglected Duty: The Creed of Sadat's Assassins
and the Islamic Resurgence in the Middle East* (London: Macmillan Publishers, 1986), 193. Jensen provides a full translation of Faraj's document
in addition to an explanatory essay.

29. Ibid., 168.

30. Ibid., 172–6.

31. Ibid., 192.

32. Despite his credentials as an Azhari scholar, 'Abd al-Rahman issued almost
all of his advice to his followers orally, in contrast to Faraj's textual justification for Sadat's killing. As Malika Zeghal notes, the lack of textual
evidence "protected him politically. He was therefore released in 1984"
following his trial and brief imprisonment. "Religion and Politics in Egypt:
The Ulema of al-Azhar, Radical Islam, and the State (1952–94)," *International Journal of Middle East Studies*, vol. 31, no. 3 (August 1999),
392–3.

33. Gilles Kepel, *Muslim Extremism in Egypt*, 193–4. Al-Zawahiri writes of the Jihad Group, "…changing the regime became the central idea that preoccupied the Islamists, who rejected partial reforms, patch-up jobs, and the attempts to beautify the ugly face of the regime with some reformatory measures." "Knights under the Prophet's Banner," http://tawhed. 11omb.com/books/knights_Under_the_Prophet_Banner_english.pdf

34. On the disagreement between these groups, see Fawaz A. Gerges, *The Far Enemy: Why Jihad Went Global* (Cambridge University Press, 2005), 99–101.

35. On the regional dimension of the Islamic Group's dissent, see Ma'mun Fandy, "Egypt's Islamic Group: Regional Revenge?" *Middle East Journal*, 48:4 (Autumn 1994), 607–25. However, the Islamic Group did eventually extend its presence to impoverished areas of Greater Cairo. On the social context of radical Islamism in Cairo, see Salwa Ismail, "The Popular Movement Dimensions of Contemporary Militant Islamism: Socio-Spatial Determinants in Urban Cairo," *Comparative Studies in Society and History*, 42 (2000), 263–93.

36. Yusuf al-Qaradawi's membership in the Muslim Brotherhood earned him several prison sentences. His connection with al-Azhar dates from his time at the Azhar Secondary School in Tanta. In 1973, he earned his doctorate from al-Azhar University on the basis of a thesis on "The Role of Legal Alms [Zakat] in the resolution of social problems." For a biographical study of al-Qaradawi see Ana Belén Soage, "Shaykh Yusuf al-Qaradawi: Portrait of a Leading Islamist Cleric," *Middle East Review of Middle East Affairs (MERIA)*, vol. 12, no. 1 (March 2008), at: http://meria.idc.ac.il/journal/2008/issue1/jv12no1a5.asp. Accessed 3/12/09.

37. Yusuf al-Qaradawi, A.S. Shaikh and M.B. Wasfy (eds), *Islamic Awakening between Rejection and Extremism* (Hendron, Va: International Institute of Islamic Thought, 1995), 36. Original Arabic title, *al-Sahwa al-Islami-yya Bayna al-Juhud wa al-Tatarruf*.

38. Adnan A. Musallam, *From Secularism to Jihad: Sayyid Qutb and the Foundations of Radical Islamism* (Westport, CT: Praeger, 2005), 178–9.

39. Jad al-Haq's *fatwa* is included in *al-Fatawa al-Islamiyya* (Cairo: Dar al-Ifta'a al-Misriyya, 1983), vol. 10, no. 29, 3726–92. See the analysis of the *fatwa* by Rachel Scott, "An 'Official' Islamic Response to the Egyptian al-Jihad Movement," *Journal of Political Ideologies*, 8/1 (2003), 39–61.

40. A compendium of Salafi scholarly responses to Sayyid Qutb is found at: http://www.fatwa1.com/anti–erhab/Qutb/index.html. See also the responses collected by Salafipublicaitons.com (in English): http://www.thenoblequran.com/sps/sp.cfm?subsecID=NDV01&articleID=NDV0100 08&articlePages=1 Accessed 3/25/09. One of Qutb's Arabic biographers, Muhammad Tawfiq Barakat, compiled a list of criticisms directed at Qutb in his book *Sayyid Qutb: Khulasatu Hayatihi* (Beirut: Dar al-Da'wa, n.d.), 176–7.

41. Aziz al-Azmeh, *Islams and Modernities* (London: Verso, 1993), 23–4.

42. 'Abbud al-Zumur, "Minhaj Jama'at al-Jihad al-Islami," in Rifa'at Sayyid Ahmad, *al-Nabi al-Musallah, Al-Rafidun*, vol. 1 (London, Dar Riyad Al-Rayyis Li–al-Kutub Wa-al-Nashr, 1st edition, 1991), p. 110 ("Strategy of the Islamic Jihad Group," in The Armed Prophet: The Rejectionists"). Translated in John Calvert, *Islamism: A Documentary and Reference Guide* (Westport, CT: Greenwood, 2008), 154.

43. Wilfred Cantwell Smith, *Islam in Modern History* (Princeton University Press, 1957), 41.

44. Fergal Keane, "The Mind of the Terrorist," in J. Baxter and M. Downing (eds), *The BBC Reports on America, its Allies and Enemies, and the Counterattack on Terrorism* (Woodstock and New York: Overlook Press, 2001), 56.

45. Here I refer the reader to note 20 in the introduction to this book.

46. Mark Juergensmeyer, *Terror in the Mind of God: The Global Rise of Religious Violence* (Berkeley: University of California Press, 2000), 119–44.

47. See Transcript in *Washington Post*, 13 Dec. 2001.

BIBLIOGRAPHY

GOVERNMENT ARCHIVES, 1947–1954

British Public Records Office (FO) 371 (Egypt):

371/62991, 16 April 1947
371/96874, 4 March 1952
371/96872, 18 February 1952
371/96874, 20 April 1953
371/102704, 20 April 1953
371/108319, 11 December 1954

United States National Archives, 611.74 (US–Egypt Relations):

77.00/10–2451, 24 October 1951
774–521/2–553, 5 February 1953
774.00/6–2353, 23 June 1953
Despatch 2180, 12 March 1954

English language newspapers and journals

New York Times
Daily Mirror
Egyptian Mail
Arab Observer
Times Literary Supplement
Fulcrum: The Literary Magazine of Colorado College of Education
Al-Ahram Weekly

Arabic journals and periodicals

Al-Risala
Sahifat Dar al'Ulum
Majallat al-Shu'un al-Ijtima'iyya
Al-Thaqafa
Al-Muqtataf
Al-Fikr al-Jadid
Al-Kitab

Al-Da'wa
Al-Sharq al-Awsat
Al-Muslimun
Al-'Alam al-'Arabi

Sayyid Qutb's books and anthologies

Al-'Adala al-Ijtima'iyya fi al-Islam (Cairo: Dar Ihy al-Kutub al'Arabiyya, 1954 [1949]); William Shepard as *Sayyid Qutb and Islamic Activism: A Translation and Critical Analysis of* Social Justice in Islam (Leiden: E.J. Brill, 1996).

Ashwak [Thorns] (Cairo: Dar Sa'd Misr, n.d. [1947]).

Al-Atyaf al-Arba'a [The Four Phantoms] (n.p., n. d. [1945]).

Dirasat Islamiyya [Islamic Studies] (Cairo: Maktabat Lajnat al-Shabab al-Muslim, 1953).

Fi al-Ta'rikh: Fikr wa Manhaj [History: Thought and Method] (Cairo: Dar al-Shuruq, seventh printing, 1983).

Fi Zilal al-Qur'an, rev. ed. Vols. 1–6 (Beirut: Dar al-Shuruq, 1994); *In the Shade of the Qur'an*, vols. 1–15 (surahs 1–47), translated and edited by Adil Salahi and Ashur Shamis (Leicester: The Islamic Foundation, 2008).

Hadha al-Din (Beirut: Dar al-Shuruq, 13th printing, 1991); translated *This Religion of Islam* (Delhi: Markazi Maktaba Islami, 1974).

Al-Islam wa Mushkilat al-Hadara [Islam and the Problems of Civilization] (Cario: dar Ihya al-Kutub al'Arabiyya, 1962).

Khasa'is al-Tasawwur al-Islami wa Muqawwimatuhu, second printing (Beirut: Dar al-Shuruq, 14th printing, 1997); translated by Mohammed Moinuddin Siddiqui as *The Islamic Concept and its Characteristics* (Indianapolis: American Trust Publications, 1991).

Kutub wa Shakhsiyyat [Books and Personalities] (Beirut: dar al-Shuruq, n.d.).).

Limadha A'damuni? [Why Did They Execute Me?] (Al-Sharka al-Sa'udiyya li–Abath wa al-Taswiq, n.d).

Ma'alim fi al-Tariq (Dar al-Shuruq, 15th printing, 1992); *Milestones*, revised translation with a forward by Ahmad Zaki Hammad (Indianapolis: American Trust Publications, 1990).

Ma'raka al-Islam wa al-Ra'smaliyya [The Battle of Islam and Capitalism] (Cairo: Dar al-Shuruq, 11th printing, 1990 [1951]).

Ma'rakatna ma'a al-Yahud [Our Battles with the Jews] 8th printing (Cairo: Dar al-Shuruq, 1987 [1951?]); translated by Ronald Nettler in *Past Trials and Present Tribulations: A Muslim Fundamentalist's View of the Jews* (Oxford: Pergamon Press, 1987).

Mashahid al-Qiyama fi al-Qur'an [Scenes of Resurrection in the Qur'an] 2nd printing (Cairo: Dar al-Ma'arif bi–Misr, 1966 [1947]).

Muhimmat al-Sha'ir al-Haya wa Shi'r al-Jil al-Hadir [The Mission of the Poet in Life and the Poetry of the Present Generation], (Beirut: Dar al-Shuruq, n.d. [1932]).

BIBLIOGRAPHY

Al-Mustaqbal li–Hatha al-Din, eleventh printing (Beirut: Dar al-Shuruq, 1991); translated as *Islam: The Religion of the Future* (Delhi: Markazi Maktaba Islami, 1974).

Nahwa Mujtama' al-Islami [Toward an Islamic Society] (Cairo: Dar al-Shuruq [n.d.]).

Al-Naqd al-Adabi: Usuluhu wa Manahijuhu [Literary Criticism: Sources and Methods] (Cairo: Dar al-Fikr al-'Arabi, 1947).

Al-Salam al-'Alami wa al-Islam (Cairo: Dar al-Shuruq, ninth printing, 1989); translated as *Islam and Universal Peace* (Indianapolis: American Trust Publications, 1993).

Al-Shati' al-Majhul [The Unknown Shore] (Cairo: Matba'at Sadiq, n.d. [1935]).

Al-Taswir al-Fanni fi al-Qur'an [Artistic Depiction in the Qur'an], 9th printing (Cairo: Daral-Shuruq, 1987 [1944]).

Tifl min al-Qarya (Beirut: Dar al-Hikma, n.d. [1946]; translated, edited and introduced by John Calvert and William Shepard as *A Child from the Village* (Syracuse University Press, 2004).

General books and articles

'Abd al-Baqi, Muhammad Husayn. *Sayyid Qutb: Hayatuhu wa Adabuhu* (Mansura: Dar al-Wafa', 1986).

'Abd al-Halim. Mahmud. *Al-Ikhwan al-Muslimun: Ahdath Sana'at al-Tarikh. Ru'iyya min al-Dakhil* (Alexandria: Dar al-Da'wa, 1986).

'Abd al-Rahman, 'Umar. *Kalimat al-Haqq: Murafa'at al-Duktur 'Umar 'Abd al-Rahman fi Qadayit al-Jihad* (Dar al-I'tisam: n.d.)

Abd-Allah, Umar F. *The Islamic Struggle in Syria* (Berkeley: Mizan Press, 1983).

Abdalla, Ahmad. *The Student Movement and Nationalist Politics in Egypt* (London: Al Saqi Books, 1985).

Abdel-Malek, Anouar. *Egypt: Military Society*, translated Charles Lam Markmann (New York: Vintage Books, 1968).

Abdel Nasser, Hoda Gamal. *Britain and the Egyptian Nationalist Movement 1936–1952* (Reading: Ithaca Press, 1994).

Abdelnasser, Walid. *The Islamic Movement in Egypt. Perceptions of International Relations 1967–81* (New York: Keegan Paul International, 1994).

Abdoul-Enein, Youssef, MSC, USN. "Sheikh Abdel-Fatah Al-Khalidi Revitalizes Sayid Qutb: Inside the Adversary's Anti–American Ideology from the Cold War to Operation Iraqi Freedom," The Combating Terrorism Center, United States Military Academy, West Point, NY. At: http://www.ctc.usma.edu.

Abou El Fadl, Khaled. *The Great Theft: Wrestling Islam from the Extremists* (New York: HarperOne 2005).

Abrahamian, Ervand. *Khomeinism: Essays on the Islamic Republic* (Berkeley: University of Caliornia Press, 1993).

Abu-Amr, Ziad. *Islamic Fundamentalism in the West Bank and Gaza: Muslim Brotherhood and Islamic Jihad* (Bloomington: Indiana University Press, 1994).

Abu-Lughod, Janet. *Cairo: 1001 Years of the City Victorious* (Princeton University Press, 1971).

—— *Rabat: in Urban Apartheid in Morocco* (Princeton University Press, 1980).

Abu-Rabi, Ibrahim M. *Intellectual Origins of Islamic Resurgence in the Modern Arab World* (Albany: State University of New York Press, 1996).

Aburish, Said K. *Nasser: The Last Arab* (New York: St. Martin's Press, 2004).

Ahmed, Leila. *Women and Gender in Islam* (New Haven: Yale University Press, 1992).

Akhavi, Shahrough. "Sayyid Qutb: The 'Poverty of Philosophy' and the Vindication of Islamic Tradition," in Serif Mardin (ed.), *Cultural Transitions in the Middle East* (Leiden: E.J. Brill, 1994), 130–152.

—— "The Dialectic in Contemporary Egyptian Social Thought: The Scripturalist and Modernist Discourses of Sayyid Qutb and Hasan Hanafi, *The International Journal of Middle East Studies*, 29 (1997), 377–401.

Alterman, Jon B. *Egypt and American Foreign Assistance 1952–1956* (New York: Palgrave Macmillan, 2002).

Amin, Ahmad. *Hayati* (Damascus: Matba'at al-Mufid, 1928), trans. Issa Boullata, *My Life* (Leiden: E.J. Brill, 1978).

Anderson, Benedict. *Imagined Communities: Reflections on the Origin and Spread of Nationalism* (London: Verso, 1983).

Anderson, J.N.D. "Law Reform in Egypt: 1850–1950," in P.M. Holt (ed.), *Political and Social Change in Modern Egypt* (London: Oxford University Press, 1968).

Ansari, Hamied. *Egypt: The Stalled Society* (Cairo: The American University in Cairo Press, 1986).

Arjomand, S.A. *The Turban of the Crown: The Islamic Revolution in Iran* (Oxford University Press, 1988).

Aroian, Lois A. *The Nationalization of Arabic and Islamic Education in Egypt: Dar al-'Ulum and al-Azhar*, Cairo Papers in Social Science, 6 (Cairo: The American University in Cairo Press, 1983).

al-'Arusi, Mahmud Kamil. *Muhakamat Sayyid Qutb: Wathiqat Muhakamat al-Shaykh Sayyid Qutb wa-Rifaqih fi al-Fatra min 1959–1965* (Cairo: Matba'at al-Jumhuriyya al-Haditha, 1995).

Asad, Talal. "Religion, Nation State, Secularism" in Peter van der Veer and Hartmut Lehmann (eds), *Nation and Religion: Perspectives on Europe and Asia*, (Princeton University Press, 1999), pp. 178–96.

'Ashmawi, 'Ali, *Al-Ta'rikh Sirri li-Jama'at al-Ikhwan al-Muslimin: Mudhakkirat 'Ali 'Ashmawi Akhir Qadat al-Tanzim al-Khass* (Cairo: Dar al-Hilal, 1993).

El-Awaisi, Abd al-Fattah Muhammad, *The Muslim Brothers and the Palestine Question, 1928–1947* (London and New York: Tauris Academic Studies, 1998).

Ayalon, Ami. "Journalists and the Press: The Vicissitudes of Licensed Pluralism," in Shimon Shamir (ed.), *Egypt from Monarchy to Republic: A Reassessment of Revolution and Change* (Boulder: Westview Press, 1995), 267–79.

Ayubi, Nazih. *Political Islam: Religion and Politics in the Arab World* (New York: Routledge, 1991).

al-'Azm, Sadik Jalal. "Orientalism and Orientalism in Reverse," in Alexander Lyon Macfie (ed.), *Orientalism: A Reader* (New York: New York University Press, 2001), 217–38.

al-Azmeh, Aziz, *Islams and Modernities* (London: Verso, 1993).

'Azzam, Abdullah. "Muqtatafat min Kitab Imlaq al-Fikr li–Islami al-Shahid Sayyid Qutb." At http://www.khayma.com/alattar/selection/sqotb2.htm

Badawi, M.M. *A Critical Introduction to Modern Arabic Poetry* (Cambridge: Cambridge University Press, 1975).

——— (ed.). *Modern Arabic Literature* (Cambridge University Press, 1992).

Badran, Margot. *Feminists,Islam,and Nation: Gender and the Making of Modern Egypt* (Princeton University Press, 1995).

Badrawi, Malak. *Political Violence in Egypt 1910–1925: Secret Societies, Plots and Assassinations* (Richmond: Curzon Press, 2000).

Baedeker, Karl. *Egypt and the Sudan: Handbook for Travellers*, 8th edition (Leipzig: Karl Baedeker Publisher, 1929).

Baer, Gabriel. *A History of Landownership in Modern Egypt, 1800–1952* (London: Oxford University Press, 1962).

Baker, Raymond. *Egypt's Uncertain Revolution under Nasser and Sadat* (Cambridge: Harvard University Press, 1978),

al-Banna, Hasan. *Mudhakkirat al-Da'wa wa al-Da'iya* (Cairo: Dar al-Tawzi' wa al-Nashr al-Islamiyya, 1986).

al-Banna, Imam Hasan, *Letter to a Muslim Student* (Leicester: The Islamic Foundation, 1999).

Baraka, Magda. *The Egyptian Upper Class Between Revolutions, 1919–1952* (Reading: Ithaca Press, 1998).

Barakat, Muhammad Tawfiq compiled a list of criticisms directed at Qutb in his book *Sayyid Qutb: Khulasatu Hayatihi* (Beirut: Dar al-Da'wa, n.d.).

Beattie, Kirk. *Egypt During the Nasser Years* (Boulder, CO: Westview Press, 1994).

Beetham, David. *Max Weber and the Theory of Modern Politics* (Cambridge: Polity Press, 1985).

Beinin, Joel. "Islamic Responses to the Capitalist Penetration of the Middle East," in Barbara Stowasser (ed.), *The Islamic Impulse* (London: Croom Helm, 1987).

——— "Society and Economy, 1923–1952," in M.M. Daly (ed.), *Cambridge History of Egypt*, vol. 2 (Cambridge University Press, 1998), 323–8.

————— and Zackary Lockman. *Workers on the Nile* (Princeton University Press, 1987).

Bell, Bowyer. *On Revolt: Strategies of National Liberation* (Harvard University Press, 1976),

Bennigsen, Alexandre A. and S. Enders Wimbush. *Muslim National Communism in the Soviet Union: A Revolutionary Strategy for the Colonial World* (University of Chicago Press, 1979).

Bergen, Peter L. *The Osama bin Laden I Know* (New York: Free Press, 2006).

Berger, Mark. "After the Third World? History, Destiny and the Fate of Third Worldism," *Third World Quarterly*, vol. 25 no. 1, (2004), 9–39.

Berkey, Jonathan P. *The Formation of Islam: Religion and Society in the Near East 600–1800* (Cambridge University Press, 2003).

Berque, Jacques, *Egypt: Imperialism and Revolution*, trans. Jean Stewart (London: Faber and Faber, 1972).

Billington, James. *Fire in the Minds of Men: The Origins of the Revolutionary Faith* (New York: Basic Books, 1980).

Binder, Leonard. *Islamic Liberalism: A Critique of Development Ideologies* (University of Chicago Press, 1988).

Al-Bishri, Tariq. *Al-Haraka al-Siyasiyya fi Misr, 1945–1952* (Cairo: Dar al-Shuruq, 2nd edition, 1983).

Blackman, Winifred. *The Fellahin of Upper Egypt* (New York: Frank Cass and Co. Ltd., 1968; first published 1927).

Botman, Selma. *The Rise of Egyptian Communism, 1939–1970* (Syracuse University Press, 1988).

Boullata, Issa J. "The Rhetorical Interpretation of the Qur'an: I'jaz and Related Topics," in Andrew Rippin (ed.), *Approaches to the History of the Interpretation of the Qur'an* (Oxford: Clarendon Press, 1990), 139–57.

————— "Sayyid Qutb's Literary Appreciation of the Qur'an," in Issa J. Boullata (ed.), *Literary Structures of Religious Meaning in the Qur'an* (London: Curzon, 2000), 354–71.

Brogan, Daniel. "Al Qaeda's Greeley Roots," *5280 Magazine: Denver's Mile-High Magazine* (June/July 2003).

Brown, Nathan. *Peasant Politics in Modern Egypt* (New Haven and London: Yale University Press, 1990).

Brugman, J. *An Introduction to the History of Modern Arabic Literature* (Leiden: E.J. Brill, 1984).

Burgat, François. *The Islamic Movement in North Africa*, new ed. trans. William Dowell (Austin: University of Texas Center for Middle East Studies, 1997).

Buruma, I. and A. Margalit. *Occidentalism: A Short History of Anti–Westernism* (London: Atlantic Books, 2004).

Cachia, Pierre. *Taha Husayn: His Place in the Egyptian Literary Renaissance* (Piscataway, NJ: Gorgias Press, 2005; originally published 1956).

BIBLIOGRAPHY

Calvert, John. "'The World is an Undutiful Boy!" Sayyid Qutb's American Experience," *Islam and Christian-Muslim Relations*, vol. 11, no. 1 (2000), 87–103.

Carré, Olivier. *Mysticism and Politics: A Critical Reading of the Qur'an by Sayyid Qutb, Radical Muslim Brother*, translated by Carol Artigues and revised by W. Shepard (Leiden: E.J. Brill, 2003).

The Census of Egypt (Cairo: Government Press, 1921).

Chatterjee, Partha. *The Nation and its Fragments: Colonial and Post Colonial Histories* (Princeton University Press, 1993).

Choueiri, Youssef. *Islamic Fundamentalism* (London: Pinter, 1990).

Cohen, Mark. *Under Cross and Crescent: The Jews in the Middle Ages* (Princeton University Press, 1994).

Cole, Juan. *Colonialism and Revolution in the Middle East: Social and Cultural Origins of Egypt's 'Urabi Movement* (Princeton University Press, 1993).

Cook, David. *Understanding Jihad* (Berkeley: University of California Press, 2005).

——— *Martyrdom in Islam* (Cambridge University Press, 2007).

Cooke, Miriam. "Ayyam Min Hayati—the Prison Memoirs of a Muslim Sister," *Journal of Arabic Literature*, vol. 26, nos. 1–2 (1995), 121–39.

——— *Women Claim Islam: Creating Islamic Feminism through Literature* (New York: Routledge, 2001).

Commins, David. *The Wahhabi Mission and Saudi Arabia* (London: I.B. Tauris, 2006).

Coury, Ralph M. *The Making of an Egyptian Arab Nationalist: The Early Years of Azzam Pasha, 1893–1936* (Reading: Ithaca Press, 1998).

Cuno, Kenneth. *The Pasha's Peasants: Land, Society, and Economy in Lower Egypt, 1740–1858* (Cambridge University Press, 1992).

Cruz Jr., Col. Francisco. "Morojihad and the Islamic Vision of Ustadz Salamt Hashim: Understanding MILF's Politico-Religious Ideology," Philippine Institute for Political Violence and Terrorism, Paper Series (August 2008), 1–15.

Darwin, John. *Britain, Egypt and the Middle East: Imperial Policy in the Aftermath of the War, 1918–1922* (New York: St. Martin's Press, 1981).

al-Dasuqi, 'Abd al-'Aziz, *Jama'at Abullu wa Atharuha fi al-Shi'r al-Hadith* (Cairo: Hay'a al-Misriyya al-'Amma li al-Ta'lif wa al-Nashr, 1971).

Davis, Eric. *Challenging Colonialism: Bank Misr and Egyptian Industrialization, 1920–1941* (Princeton University Press, 1983).

Deeb, Marius. *Party Politics in Egypt: The Wafd and its Rivals* (Reading: Ithaca Press, 1979).

——— "The 1919 Popular Uprising: A Genesis of Egyptian Nationalism," *Canadian Review of Studies in Nationalism*, 1 (1973), 106–19.

Delanoue, Gilbert. *Moralistes et politiques musulmans dans l'Egypte du XIX siècle (1798–1882)*, 2 vols. (Institut Français d'Archéologie Orientale du Caire, 1982).

Diyab, Muhammad Hafiz. *Sayyid Qutb: Al-Khitab was al-Idulujiyya* (Cairo: Dar al-Thaqafa al-Jadida, 1989).

Dorronsoro, Gilles. *Revolution Unending: Afghanistan, 1979 to the Present* (New York: Columbia University Press, 2005).

Eagleton, Terry. *Ideology: An Introduction* (London: Verso, 1991).

Eickelman, Dale. "The Art of Memory: Islamic Education and its Social Reproduction," in Juan Cole (ed.), *Comparing Muslim Societies: Knowledge and the State in a World Civilization* (Ann Arbor: University of Michigan Press, 1992), 97–132.

Eisenstadt, S.N. *Fundamentalism, Sectarianism and Revolution: The Jacobin Dimension of Modernity* (Cambridge, Mass: Cambridge University Press, 1999).

El-Enany, Rasheed. *Naguib Mahfouz: The Pursuit of Meaning* (London: Routledge, 1993).

——— "The Promethean Quest in Louis 'Awad's "Memoirs of an Overseas Student," in R. Ostle, E. De Moor and S. Wild (eds), *Writing the Self: Autobiographical Writing in Modern Arabic Literature* (London: Saqi Books, 1998), 61–71.

——— "Tawfiq al-Hakim and the West: A New Assessment of the Relationship," *British Journal of Middle Eastern Studies*, 27 (2000), 165–75.

Ellis, Matthew. "King Me: The Political Culture of Monarch in Interwar Iraq and Egypt," MPhil Thesis, Exeter College, Oxford University, May 2005. At: http://users.ox.ac.uk/~metheses/EllisThesis.htm#_ftn334

Esposito, John L. and John O. Voll. *Makers of Contemporary Islam* (Oxford University Press, 2001).

Euben, Roxanne L. *Enemy in the Mirror: Islamic Fundamentalism and the Limits of Modern Rationalism* (Princeton University Press, 1999).

Fadl Allah, Mahdi. *Ma'a Sayyid Qutb fi Fikrihi al-Siyasi wa al-Dini* (Beirut: Mu'assasat al-Risala, 1989).

Fahmy, Khaled. *All the Pasha's Men: Mehmed Ali, His Army, and the Making of Modern Egypt* (Cambridge University Press, 1997).

Fandy, Ma'mun. "Egypt's Islamic Group: Regional Revenge?" *Middle East Journal*, 48:4 (Autumn 1994), 607–25.

——— *Saudi Arabia and the Politics of Dissent* (New York: St. Martin's Press, 1999).

Fanon, Frantz. *The Wretched of the Earth* (New York: Grove Press, 1963).

Firestone, Reuven. *Jihad: The Origin of Holy War in Islam* (Oxford University Press, 1999).

Fisk, Robert. *Pity the Nation: The Abduction of Lebanon* (New York: Nation Books, 4th ed., 2002).

Fluehr-Lobban, Carolyn, *Islamic Society in Practice* (Gainsville: University Press of Florida, 1994).

Foucault, Michel. *Discipline and Punish: The Birth of the Prison*, trans. Alan Sheridan (New York: Vintage Books, 1979).

BIBLIOGRAPHY

Galford, Hugh. "Sayyid Qutb and the Qur'anic Story of Joseph: A Commentary for Today," in Ronald L. Nettler and Suha Taji–Farouki (eds), *Muslim-Jewish Encounters, Intellectual Traditions and Muslim Politics* (Amsterdam: Harwood Academic Publishers), 39–64.

Gerges, Fawaz A. *The Far Enemy: Why Jihad Went Global* (Cambridge University Press, 2005).

Gershoni, Israel and James Jankowski. *Egypt, Islam, and the Arabs* (New York: Oxford University Press, 1986).

—— *Defining the Egyptian Nation, 1930–1945* (Cambridge University Press, 1995).

al-Ghazali, Zainab. *Return of the Pharaoh: Memoir in Nasir's Prison*, translated by Mokrane Guezzou (Leister: The Islamic Foundation, 1994).

al-Ghitani, Gamal. *The Mahfouz Dialogues*, translated by Humphrey Davies (Cairo: American University in Cairo Press, 2006),

Giddens, Anthony. *A Contemporary Critique of Historical Materialism*, vol. 1 *Power, Property and the State* (London: Macmillan, 1981).

—— *The Nation-State and Violence* (Berkeley: University of California Press, 1987).

Goldberg, Ellis. "Smashing Idols and the State: The Protestant Ethic and Egyptian Sunni Radicalism," *Comparative Studies in Society and History*, vol. 33, no. 1 (Jan. 1991), 3–35.

—— "Peasants in Revolt—Egypt 1919," *International Journal of Middle East Studies*, 24 (1992), 261–80.

Goldschmidt, Jr., Arthur. "The Egyptian Nationalist Party, 1882–1919," in P.M. Holt (ed.), *Political and Social Change in Modern Egypt* (London: Oxford University Press, 1968).

Goldziher, Ignaz. *Introduction to Islamic Theology and Law*, translated by Andras and Ruth Hamori (Princeton University Press, 1981).

Goodwin, Jeff, James M. Jasper, and Francesca Polletta (eds), *Passionate Politics: Emotions and Social Movements* (University of Chicago Press, 2001).

Gordon, Lady Duff. *Letters from Egypt* (New York: [s.n.], 1903.

Gordon, Joel. "The Myth of the Savior: Egypt's Just Tyrants on the Eve of the Revolution, January-July 1952," *Journal of the American Research Center in Egypt*, 26 (1989), 223–37.

—— *Nasser's Blessed Movement* (Oxford University Press, 1992).

—— *Revolutionary Melodrama: Popular Film and Civic Identify in Nasser's Egypt* (Chicago: Chicago Studies on the Middle East, 2003).

Griffin, Roger. *The Nature of Fascism* (London: Routledge, 1993).

Gross, David. "Myth and Symbol in Georges Sorel," in Seymour Drescher, David Sabean and Allan Sharlin (eds), *Political Symbolism in Modern Europe: Essays in Honor of George L. Mosse* (New Brunswick and London: Transaction Books, 1982).

Haddad, Yvonne. "Sayyid Qutb: Ideologue of Islamic Revival," in John Esposito (ed.), *Voices of Resurgent Islam* (Oxford University Press, 1983), 67–98.

Hafez, Sabry. "Torture, Imprisonment, and Political Assassination in the Arab Novel," *al-Jadid*, vol. 8, no. 38 (winter 2002), at: http://www.aljadid.com/features/0838hafez.html.

Hamuda, 'Adil. *Sayyid Qutb: min al-Qarya ila Mishaqa* (Cairo: Ruz al-Yusuf, 1987).

Hamza, Abdel-Maksud. *The Public Debt of Egypt, 1854–1876* (Cairo: Government Press, 1944).

Harris, Christina Phelps. *Nationalism and Revolution in Egypt: The Role of the Muslim Brotherhood* (Stanford, CA: Hoover Institution Press, 1964).

Heck, Paul. "Politics and the Qur'an," *The Encyclopaedia of the Qur'an*, ed. Jane Dammen McAuliffe, vol. 4 (Leiden: Brill Academic Publishers, 2005).

Hegghammer, Thomas. "The Obstacles to Understanding Radical Islam and the Opportunites to Know it Better," *Times Literary Supplement* (2 April 2008). Available on the www at: http://entertainment.timesonline.co.uk/tol/arts_and_entertainment/the_tls/article3667505.ece.

—— and Stéphane Lacroix, "Rejectionist Islamism in Saudi Arabia: The Story of Juhayman al-'Utaybi," *International Journal of Middle East Studies*, 39 (2007).

Heikal, Mohamed. *The Sphinx and the Commissar: The Rise and Fall of Soviet Influence in the Middle East* (New York: Harper and Row, 1978).

Heyworth-Dunne, J. *An Introduction to the History of Education in Modern Egypt* (London: Luzac and Co., 1938).

—— *Religious and Political Trends in Modern Egypt* (Washington, n.p., 1950).

Hoffman, Valerie. "An Islamic Activist: Zaynab al-Ghazali," in Elizabeth W. Fernea (ed.), *Women and the family in the Middle East: New Voices of Change*(Austin: University of Texas Press, 1985).

—— *Sufism, Mystics, and Saints in Modern Egypt* (Columbia: University of South Carolina Press, 1995).

—— "The Role of Visions in Contemporary Egyptian Life," *Religion*, vol. 27, no. 1 (January 1997), 45–64.

Hofstadter, Richard. "The Paranoid Style in American Politics," *Harper's Magazine* (November 1961), 77–86.

Hopkins, Nicholas. "Clan and Class in Two Arab Villages," in Farhad Kazemi and John Waterbury (eds), *Peasants and Politics in the Modern Middle East* (Miami: Florida International University Press, 1991).

Hourani, Albert. *Arabic Thought in the Liberal Age, 1798–1939* (Cambridge University Press, 1983).

Hunter, F. Robert. *Egypt under the Khedives, 1805–1879: From Household Government to Modern Bureaucracy* (Pittsburgh, PA: University of Pittsburgh Press, 1984).

Husayn, Taha. *Al-Ayyam* (Cairo: Matba'at Amin Abd al-Rahman, 1929).

—— *Mustaqbal al-Thaqafa fi Misr* (Cairo: Dar al-Kutub 1937); translated by Sidney Glazer as *The Future of Culture in Egypt* (Washington: The American Council of Learned Societies, 1954).

Husayni, I. M. *The Muslim Brethern, the Greatest of Modern Islamic Movements*, trans. J. F. Brown and J. Racy (Beirut: Khayat's College Book Cooperative, 1956).

Hussein, Mahmoud. *La lutte de classes en Egypte 1945–1970* (Paris: Maspero, 1971).

Ibrahim, Saad Eddine. "Anatomy of Egypt's Militant Islamic Groups: Methodological Notes and Preliminary Findings," *International Journal of Middle East Studies*, 12:4 (December 1980), 423–53.

——— "Egypt's Islamic Activism in the 1980s," *Third World Quarterly* (April 1988), 632–57.

Ibrahim Ibrahim. "Ahmad Amin and 'Abbad Mahmud al-'Aqqad: Between al-Qadim and al-Jadid: European Challenge and Islamic Response," in George Atiyeh and Ibrahim Oweiss (eds), *Arab Civilization: Challenges and Responses* (Albany: SUNY Press, 1988), 208–30.

Ismail, Salwa. "The Popular Movement Dimensions of Contemporary Militant Islamism: Socio-Spatial Determinants in Urban Cairo," *Comparative Studies in Society and History*, 42 (2000), 263–93.

——— "Islamist Movements as Social Movements: Contestation and Identity Frames," *Historical Reflections/Réflexions Historiques*, vol. 30, no. 3 (2004), 385–402.

Issawi, Charles. *The Economic History of the Middle East 1800–1914: A Book of Readings* (University of Chicago Press, 1991).

Izutsu, Toshihiko. *Ethico Religious Concepts in the Qur'an* (Kingston: McGill-Queen's University Press, 2002 [first published 1959]).

al-Jabarti, 'Abd al-Rahman. *'Aja'ib al-Athar fi al-Tarajim wa al-Akhbar*, 7 vols. Eds. 'Abd al-Fattah al-Saranjawi and Sayyid Ibrahim Salim (Cairo: Lajnat al-Bayan al-'Arabi, 1958–60).

Jackson, Sherman A. *Islamic Law and the State* (Leiden: E.J. Brill, 1997).

Jameelah, Maryam. *Correspondence between Maulana Maudoodi and Maryam Jameelah* (Delhi: Crescent Publishing, 1969). At http://angislam.org/books1/e020.htm

Jankowski, James. *Egypt's Young Rebels* (Stanford, CA: Hoover Institution Press, 1975).

Jawhar, Sami. *al-Mawta Yatakallamun* (Cairo: Maktab al-Misri al-Hadith, 1987).

Jansen, J.J.G. *The Interpretation of the Koran in Modern Egypt* (Leiden: E.J. Brill, 1974).

——— *The Neglected Duty: The Creed of Sadat's Assassins and the Islamic Resurgence in the Middle East* (London: Macmillan Publishers, 1986).

Jayyusi, Salama Khadra. *Trends and Movements in Modern Arabic Poetry*, vol. 1 (Leiden: E.J. Brill, 1977).

Johnston, Francis. *Zeitoun (1968–1971): When Millions Saw Mary*, 4–5; at http://www.zeitun-eg.org/pg0001.htm.

Juergensmeyer, Mark. *Terror in the Mind of God: The Global Rise of Religious Violence* (Berkeley: University of California Press, 2000).

Karam, Aza M. Women. *Islamisms and the State: Contemporary Feminisms in Egypt* (London: Macmillan, 1998)

Kazem, Safynaz. "Hagg Wahba: Reference Work," *Al-Ahram Weekly On-Line*, 21–27 no. 513, (December 2000). At: http://weekly.ahram.org.eg/2000/513/profile.htm.

Keane, Fergal. "The Mind of the Terrorist," in J. Baxter and M. Downing (eds), *The BBC Reports on America, its Allies and Enemies, and the Counterattack on Terrorism* (Woodstock and New York: Overlook Press, 2001), 54–67.

Kemp, Barry. *Ancient Egypt: Anatomy of a Civilization* (London and New York: Routledge, 1991).

Kenny, Jeffery T. *Muslim Rebels: Kharijites and the Politics of Extremism in Egypt* (Oxford University Press, 2006).

Kenny, Lorne. "Ali Mubarak, Nineteenth-Century Egyptian Educator and Administrator," *Middle East Journal*, Winter (1967), 35–51.

Kepel, Gilles. *Muslim Extremism in Egypt* (Berkeley: University of California Press, 1993)

——— *The War for Muslim Minds: Islam and the West* (Cambridge: Belknap Harvard, 2004)

——— and Jean-Pierre Milelli (eds). *Al Qaeda in its own Words*, translated by Pascale Ghazaleh (Cambridge: Belknap Harvard, 2008).

al-Khafif, Mahmud. "Shati' al-Majhul: Nazm al-Sha'ir Sayyid Qutb," *al-Risala* (10 June 1935), 959–60.

Khalafallah, Haifaa. "Rethinking Islamic Law: Genesis and Evolution in the Islamic Legal Methods and Structures. The Case of a 20th Century 'Alim's Journey into His Legal Traditions. Muhammad Al-Ghazali (1917–1996)." PhD Dissertation, Georgetown University (1997).

Khalid, Khalid M., *From Here We Start* (Washington: American Council of Learned Societies 1953).

al-Khalidi, 'Abd al-Fattah. *Sayyid Qutb: Min al-Milad ila al-Istishhad* (Damascus: Dar al-Qalam, 1991).

al-Khalidi, Salah 'Abd al-Fattah. *Amrika min al-Dakhil bi–Nazar Sayyid Qutb* (Cairo: Dar al-Wafa', 1987).

Khatab, Sayed. "Hakimiyya and Jahiliyya in the Thought of Sayyid Qutb," *Middle Eastern Studies*, vol. 38, no. 3 (July 2002), 145–70.

——— "Arabism and Islamism in Sayyid Qutb's Thought on Nationalism," *Muslim World*, vol. 94, no. 2 (April 2004), 217–44.

——— *The Political Thought of Sayyid Qutb: The Theory of Jahiliyyah* (London and New York: Routledge, 2006).

——— *The Power of Sovereignty: The Political and Ideological Philosophy of Sayyid Qutb* (London & New York: Routledge, 2006).

Khir, Bustami. "Sovereignty," *The Encyclopaedia of the Qur'an*, ed. Jane Dammen McAuliffe, vol. 5 (Leiden: Brill Academic Publishers, 2005).

Kupferschmidt, Uri. "Reformist and Militant Islam in Urban and Rural Egypt," *Middle Eastern Studies*, vol. 23, 4 (Oct. 1987), 403–18.

Kurzman, Charles (ed.) *Modernist Islam, 1840–1940: A Sourcebook* (New York: Oxford University Press, 2002).

Lacroix, Stephane. "Fundamentalist Islam at a Crossroads: 9/11, Iraq, and the Saudi Religious Debate," Center for Strategic and International Studies, 29 May 2008, at: http://www.csis.org/component/option,com_csis_events/task,view/id,1671/

Lambton, Ann K.S. *State and Government in Medieval Islam* (Oxford University Press, 1981).

Landes, David. *Bankers and Pashas* (Cambridge, Mass.: Harvard University Press, 1958).

Larrain, Jorge. *Theories of Development* (Cambridge: Polity Press, 1989).

Lia, Brynjar. *The Society of the Muslim Brothers in Egypt: The Rise of an Islamic Mass Movement, 1928–1942* (Reading: Ithaca Press, 1998).

——— *Architect of Global Jihad: The Life of Al-Qaida Strategist Abu Mus'ab al-Suri* (London: C. Hurst & Co., 2008).

Lincoln, Bruce. *Holy Terrors: Thinking about Religion after September 11* (University of Chicago Press, 2003).

Malley, Robert. *The Call from Algeria: Third Worldism, Revolution and the Turn to Islam* (Berkeley: University of California Press, 1996).

Malina, Bruce J. *The New Testament World: Insights from Cultural Anthropology* (Louisville, Kentucky: Westminster/John Knox Press, 1993).

Mahfouz, Naguib. *Mirrors*, translated by Roger Allen, illustrated by Seif Wanli (Zeitouna: The American University in Cairo Press, 1999).

Mahmoudi, Abdelrashid. *Taha Husain's Education: From the Azhar to the Sorbonne* (London: Curzon, 1998).

Makki, Tahir Ahmad. "Sayyid Qutb: Thalath Rasa'il lam Tunshar Qablu," *al-Hilal* (October 1986), 124–6.

Malti–Douglas, Fedwa. *Blindness and Autobiography: Al-Ayyam of Taha Husayn* (Princeton University Press, 1988).

Manela, Erez. *The Wilsonian Moment: Self-Determination and the International Origins of Anticolonial Nationalism* (Oxford University Press, 2007).

al-Maqrizi, Ahmad Ibn 'Ali. *Kitab al-Khitat al-Maqriziyya*, 3 vols. (al-Shiyya, Lebanon: Maktabat Ihya al-Ulum,1959).

Marsot, Afaf Lutfi al-Sayyid. *Egypt in the Reign of Muhammad Ali* (Cambridge University Press, 1984).

——— *Egypt's Liberal Experiment, 1922–1936* (Berkeley: University of California Press, 1977).

Martin, Richard C. *Islamic Studies: A History of Religions Approach* (Upper Saddle River, NJ: Prentice Hall, 1996).

Martinez, Luis. *The Algerian Civil War 1990–1998*, translated by Jonathan Derrick, CERI Series in Comparative Politics and International Studies (London: C. Hurst & Co., 2000).

Meier, Heinrich. *The Lesson of Carl Schmitt*, trans. M. Brainard (University of Chicago Press, 1998).

Memmi, Albert. *The Colonizer and the Colonized*, intro. Sean Paul Sartre, afterword by Susan Miller (New York: Beacon Press, 1991; originally published 1965).

Metcalf, Barbara Daly. *Moral Conduct and Authority: The Place of 'Adab' in South Asian Islam* (Berkeley: University of California Press, 1984).

Mitchell, Richard. *The Society of the Muslim Brothers* (New York: Oxford University Press, 1969; 2nd ed. 1993).

Mitchell, Timothy. *Colonizing Egypt* (Berkeley: University of California Press, 1988).

Mittermaier, Amira. "The Book of Visions: Dreams, Poetry and Prophecy in Contemporary Egypt," *International Journal of Middle East Studies*, 39 (2007), 229–47.

Moaddel, Mansoor. *Islamic Modernism, Nationalism, and Fundamentalism: Episode and Discourse* (University of Chicago Press, 2005).

Mottahedeh, Roy P. *Loyalty and Leadership in an Early Islamic Society* (Princeton University Press, 1980).

Munson, Henry Jr. *Islam and Revolution in the Middle East* (New Haven: Yale University Press, 1988).

Mousalli, Ahmad. *Radical Islamic Fundamentalism: The Ideological and Political Discourse of Sayyid Qutb* (Beirut: American University of Beirut Press, 1992).

Mubarak, 'Ali. *al-Khitat al-Tawfiqiyya al-Jadida li–Misr al-Qahira wa-Munduniha wa-Biladiha al-Qadima wa al-Shahira*, 20 vols. (Bulaq: al-Matba'a al-Kubra al-Amiriyya, 1303–1306/1886–1888).

———— *Alam al-Din*, 4 vols. (Alexandria: Matba'at Jarida al-Mahrusa, 1299/1882).

Musa, Salama. *Tarbiyyat Salama Musa* (Cairo: Salama Musa li–Nashr wa-al-Tawzi, n.d.), trans. L.O. Schuman, *The Education of Salama Musa* (Leiden: E.J. Brill, 1961).

Musallam, Adnan. "Prelude to Islamic Commitment: Sayyid Qutb's Literary and Spiritual Orientation, 1932–1938," *Muslim World*, 80 (July-Oct. 1990), 176–89.

———— *From Secularism to Jihad: Sayyid Qutb and the Foundations of Radical Islamism* (Westport, CT: Praeger, 2005).

Al-Musnad, Muhammad Abdul Aziz (translated by Dr Muhammad Amin Tawfiq). "Two Witnesses to Sayyid Qutb's Hanging," (n.p., n.d.). At: http://www.makingsenseofjihad.com/2008/05/site-updates.html

al-Nadwi, Abu al-Hasan. *Shakhsiyyat wa Kutub* (Damascus: Dar al-Qalam, 1990).

———— *Mukhakkirat Sa'ih fi al-Sharq al-Arabi*, 2nd revised ed. (Beirut: Mu'assasat al-Risala, 1975).

al-Namnam, Hilmi. *Sayyid Qutb wa Thawrat Yulyu* (Cairo: Mirit li al-Nashr wa-al-Ma'lumat, 1999).

Nettler, Ronald. "A Modern Confession of Faith and Conception of Religion: Sayyid Qutb's Introduction to the Tafsir, Fi Zilal al-Qur'an," *British Journal of Middle East Studies*, vol. 21, no. 1 (1994), 102–14.

BIBLIOGRAPHY

Owen, Roger. "The Influence of Lord Cromer's Indian Experience on British Policy in Egypt 1883–1907," *St Antony's Papers*, 7 (1965), 109–39.

———— "Egyptian Cotton and the American Civil War," in Charles Issawi (ed.), *The Economic History of the Middle East* (University of Chicago Press, 1966).

Peters, Rudolf. *Jihad in Classical and Modern Islam* (Princeton: Marcus Wienner Publishers, 1996).

Philipp, Thomas and Moshe Perlman (eds). *'Abd al-Rahman al-Jabarti's History of Egypt* (Stuttgart: Franz Steiner Verlag, 1994), vol. 1–2.

Piscatori, James (ed.). *Islamic Fundamentalisms and the Gulf Crisis* (Chicago: The American Academy of Arts and Sciences, 1999).

Al-Qaradawi, Yusuf, A.S. Shaikh and M.B. Wasfy (eds.). *Islamic Awakening between Rejection and Extremism* (Hendron, Va: International Institute of Islamic Thought, 1995).

Qutb, Hamida. *Nida ila al-Diffa al-Ukhra* (Cairo: Dar al-Shuruq, 1969).

al-Rafi'i, Muhammad. *Thawrat 1919*, 2 vols. (Cairo: Maktabat al-Nahda al-Misriyya, 1946).

Ramadan, Abd al-'Azim Muhammad. *Tatawwur al-Haraka al-Wataniyya fi Misr 1918–1936* (Cairo: Madbuli, 1983).

Raymond, Andre. "Cairo," in Mary Wilson, Philip Khoury, Albert Hourani (eds), *The Modern Middle East* (Berkeley: University of California Press, 1993), 311–37.

Al-Rasheed, Madawi. *Contesting the Saudi State: Islamic Voices from a New Generation* (Cambridge University Press, 2007).

Reid, Donald. *Lawyers and Politics in the Arab World* (Minneapolis: Bibliotheca Islamica, 1981).

———— "Political Assassination in Egypt, 1910–1954," *The International Journal of African Historical Studies*, vol. 15, no. 4 (1982), 625–51.

———— *Cairo University and the Making of Modern Egypt* (Cambridge University Press, 1990),

Rizq, Jabir. *Madhabih al-Ikhwan fi Sujun Nasir* (Cairo: Dar al-I'tisam, 1977).

Rooke, Tetz. *In My Childhood: A Study of Arabic Autobiography* (Stockholm: Almquist and Wiksell, 1997).

Rosenwein, Barbara H. "Worrying about Emotions in History," *American Historical Review*, 107/3 (June 2002), 821–45.

Roussillon, Alain. "Republican Egypt Interpreted: Revolution and Beyond," in M.W. Daly (ed.), *The Cambridge History of Egypt*, vol. 2 (Cambridge University Press, 1998), 334–93.

Rugh, Andrea B. "Reshaping Personal Relations in Egypt," in Martin E. Marty and R. Scott Appleby (eds), *Fundamentalisms and Society: Reclaiming the Sciences, the Family, and Education* (University of Chicago Press, 1993).

Ruthven, Malise. *A Fury for God* (London: Granta Books, 2002).

Ryzova, Lucie. "Egyptianizing Modernity through the 'New Effendiyya,'" in Arthur Goldschmidt, Amy Johnson and Barak Salmoni (eds), *Re-Envision-*

ing Egypt 1919–1952 (Cairo: The American University in Cairo Press, 2005), 124–63.

Sadat, Anwar. *Search for Identity: An Autobiography* (New York: Harper and Row, 1978).

Scholch, Alexander. *Egypt for the Egyptians! The Socio-Political Crisis in Egypt, 1878–82* (St Antony's College: Ithaca University Press, 1981).

Schultz, Reinhard. "Colonization and Resistance: The Egyptian Peasant Rebellion, 1919," in *Peasants and Politics in the Modern Middle East*, 203–10.

Schulze, Reinhard. "Mass Culture and Islamic Cultural Production in 19th Century Middle East," in G. Stauth and Sami Zubaida (eds), *Mass Culture, Popular Culture, and Social Life in the Middle East* (Frankfurt: Campus Verlag, 1987), 195–204.

Scott, Rachel. "An 'Official' Islamic Response to the Egyptian al-Jihad Movement," *Journal of Political Ideologies*, 8/1 (2003), 39–61.

Seikaly, Samir. "Prime Minister and Assassin: Butrus Ghali and Wardani," *Middle Eastern Studies*, 13 (1977), 112–23.

Semah, David. *Four Egyptian Literary Critics* (Leiden: E. J. Brill, 1974).

Shak'a, Mustafa M. *Mustafa Sadiq al-Rafi'i* (Beirut Arab University, 1970).

Shehadeh, Lamia Rustum, "Women in the Discourse of Sayyid Qutb," *Arab Studies Quarterly*vol. 22 no. 3 (Summer 2000), 45–56.

Shepard, William. *Sayyid Qutb and Islamic Activism: A Translation and Critical Analysis of* Social Justice in Islam (Leiden: E. J. Brill, 1996).

―――― "Sayyid Qutb's Doctrine of Jahiliyya," *International Journal of Middle East Studies*, 35 (2003), 521–45.

Sivan, Emmanuel. *Radical Islam: Medieval Theology and Modern Politics* (New Haven: Yale University Press, 1985).

Skcopol, Theda. *States and Social Revolutions* (London and New York: Cambridge University Press, 1979).

Skovgaard-Petersen, Jakob. *Defining Islam for the Egyptian State: Muftis and Fatwas of the Dar al-Ifta* (Leiden: E.J. Brill, 1997).

Smith, Charles. *Islam and the Search for Social Order in Modern Egypt: A Biography of Muhammad Husayn Haykal* (Albany: SUNY Press, 1983).

Smith, Jane Idleman and Yvonne Yazbeck Haddad. *The Islamic Understanding of Death and Resurrection* (Albany: State University of New York Press, 1981).

Smith, Wilfred Cantwell. *Islam in Modern History* (Princeton University Press, 1957).

―――― *The Meaning and End of Religion* (Toronto: The New American Library of Canada Ltd, 1964).

Soage, Ana Belén. "Shaykh Yusuf al-Qaradawi: Portrait of a Leading Islamist Cleric," *Middle East Review of Middle East Affairs (MERIA)*, vol. 12, no. 1 (March 2008), at: http://meria.idc.ac.il/journal/2008/issue1/jv12no1a5.asp.

Somekh, S. *The Changing Rhythm: A Study of Najib Mahfuz' Novels* (Leiden: E.J. Brill, 1973).

Sonbol, Amira. *The New Mamluks* (Syracuse University Press, 2000).

Sorel, Georges, trans. T.E. Hulm and J. Roth as *Reflections on Violence* (London: Collier Books, 1950).

Starrett, Gregory. *Putting Islam to Work: Education, Politics, and Religious Transformation in Egypt* (Berkeley: University of California Press, 1998).

Stromberg, Peter G. *Language and Self-Transformation: A Study of the Christian Conversion Narrative* (Cambridge University Press, 1993).

Taji–Farouki, Suha. *A Fundamental Quest: Hizb al-Tahrir and the Search for the Islamic Caliphate* (London: Grey Seal, 1996).

Talmon, J.L. "The Legacy of Georges Sorel," *Encounter*, Feb. 1970, pp. 47–60.

Taylor, Charles. *Hegel and Modern Society* (Cambridge University Press, 1979).

Tignor, Robert. *Modernization and British Colonial Rule in Egypt, 1882–1914* (Princeton University Press, 1966).

Toledano, Ehud. *State and Society in mid-Nineteenth Century Egypt* (Cambridge University Press, 1990).

Trimingham, J. Spencer. *The Sufi Orders in Islam* (Oxford University Press, 1971).

Todorov, Tzvetan. *Facing the Extreme: Moral Life in the Concentration Camps* (New York: Metropolitan Books, 1996).

Tripp, Charles. *A History of Iraq* (Cambridge University Press, 2nd ed. 2002).

Trofimov, Yaroslav. *The Siege of Mecca* (New York: Doubleday, 2007).

Turner, Victor. *The Ritual Process: Structure and Anti–Structure* (Ithaca: Cornell University Press, 1969).

Vatikiotis, P.J. *Nasser and His Generation* (London: Croom Helm, 1978), 49.

Vitalis, Robert. "On the Theory and Practice of Compradors: The Role of 'Abbud Pasha in the Egyptian Political Economy," *International Journal of Middle East Studies*, 22 (1990), 291–315.

Voll, John O. "Fundamentalism in the Sunni Arab World," in Martin E. Marty and R. Scott Appleby (eds), *Fundamentalisms Observed* (University of Chicago Press, 1991), 345–402.

Waterbury, John. *The Egypt of Nasser and Sadat: The Political Economy of Two Regimes* (Princeton University Press, 1983).

Welhausen,,Julius. *The Religio-Political Factions in Early Islam*, translated R.C. Ostle and S.M. Walzer, ed. R.C. Ostle (New York: American Elsevier, 1975).

Wendell, Charles. *Five Tracts of Hasan al-Banna (1906–1949)* (Berkeley: University of California Press, 1978).

Wickaham, Carrie Rosefsky. *Mobilizing Islam: Religion, Activism, and Political Change in Egypt* (New York: Columbia University Press, 2002).

Willis, Michael. *The Islamist Challenge in Algeria: A Political History* (New York University Press, 1996).

Wright, Lawrence. *The Looming Tower: Al-Qaeda and the Road to 9/11* (New York: Knoph, 2006).

Yadlin, Rivka. "The Seeming Duality: Patterns of Interpersonal Relations in a Changing Environment," in Shimon Shamir (ed.), *Egypt from Monarchy to Republic: A Reassessment of Revolution and Change* (Boulder, CO: Westeview Press, 1995).

Yusuf, Badmas 'Lanre. "A History of Fi Zilalil-Qur'an," *Hamdard Islamicus*, Vol. 25, no. 2 (April 2002), 17–27.

al-Zayyat, Montasser. *The Road to Al-Qaeda: The Story of Bin Laden's Right-Hand Man*, translated by Ahmed Fekry, edited by Sara Nimis (London: Pluto Press, 2004).

Zeghal, Malika. "Religion and Politics in Egypt: The Ulema of Al-Azhar, Radical Islam, and the State (1952–94)," *International Journal of Middle East Studies*, 31 (1999), 371–99.

Zollner, Barbara. "Prison Talk: The Muslim Brotherhood's Internal Struggle," *International Journal of Middle East Studies*, vol. 39, no. 3 (August 2007), 411–33.

—— *The Muslim Brotherhood: Hasan al-Hudaybi and Ideology* (London and New York: Routledge, 2009).

al-Zumur, 'Abbud. "Minhaj Jama'at al-Jihad al-Islami," in Rifa'at Sayyid Ahmad, *al-Nabi al-Musallah, Al-Rafidun*, vol. 1 (London, Dar Riyad Al-Rayyis Li–al-Kutub Wa-al-Nashr, 1st edition, 1991).

INDEX

INDEX

desire to revise, 118; invocation of, 103; perception of, 76, 98; signed by Wafd Party, 76; terms of, 76, 78

Apollo Society: and Mutran, Khalil, 70–1; criticisms of al-'Aqqad, 'Abbas Mahmud, 70–1; founded by Shadi, Ahmad Zaki Abu (1932), 66; works reviewed by *al-Risala*, 88

Arab-Israeli War (1948–49), 117, 150; weapons procured during, 234

Arab League: support for creation of, 99, 105

Arab Socialist Union (ASU): conflict with Sadat, Anwar, 275; founded by al-Nasser, Colonel Gamar 'Abd, 195; vanguard of, 245; Youth Organization of, 237

'Arif, 'Abd al-Salam: admirer of al-Nasser, Colonel Gamar 'Abd, 236; house arrest of, 236; influenced by *In the Shade of the Qur'an*, 236; intervention of, 236; president of Iraq, 236

Artistic Depictions in the Qur'an, 111, 115, 122, 128; aesthetic concerns of, 174, 212; completion of, 114

'Ashmawi, 'Ali, 19, 187, 246, 249; and assassination attempts on al-Nasser, Colonel Gamar 'Abd, 243; arrest of, 249; interrogation of, 250; procurement of weaponry, 244; relocation to USA, 261; sentencing of, 260–1

Ashwak, 107–8; portrayal of women, 109–10

Atatürk, Mustafa Kemal: abolishes Caliphate, 49–50, 75; and creation of Turkey, 17, 49

'Azzam, 'Abdullah: and *Mujahadeen*, 6, 115, 277, 290

Badi'a, Muhammad: current Supreme Guide of Muslim Brotherhood, 229–30

Badran, Shams: cabinet chief to Amir, 'Abd al-Hakim, 255

Baghdad Pact (1955): and al-Nasser, Colonel Gamar 'Abd, 195; British sponsorship of, 195

Bank Misr: collapse of (1939), 77; founded by Harb, Tal'at, 77

Battle of Islam and Capitalism, The, 158–160, 162–3; contrasts to *Social Justice in Islam*, 158, 164; religious overtones of, 164; reprints sponsored by Muslim Brotherhood, 173; themes of, 202

Belhadj, Ali: and (FIS), 2

Belgium: *Société Anonyme des Ciments d'Égypte*, 76

Benkirane, Abdallah: and al-Tawhid wa al-Islah (Unity and Reform), 2

Bey, Tal'at: exile of, 48; leader of Young Turks, 48

bin Laden, Osama, ix; and Afghanistan, 290; and Al Qaeda, 6; and Saudi Arabia, 290–1; condemnation of, 155

Bonaparte, Napoleon: invasion of Egypt, 117

Books and Personalities, 106–7

Brezhnev, Leonid: and al-Nasser, Colonel Gamar 'Abd, 252; ruling triumvirate of, 252

Caffrey, Jefferson: and al-Nasser, Colonel Gamar 'Abd, 279; US Ambassador, 185, 279; view of Muslim Brotherhood, 185, 279

Cairo, 36–7, 42, 53, 55–6, 61–2, 101, 106, 148, 175, 178, 241, 244, 261, 263; *al-Hawadith*, 23; and Muslim Brotherhood, 83; and Pasha, Isma'il, 55, 57; American University, ix; and Dar al-Ulum, 58; civil institutions of,

Egypt, 81–2, 86–7; arrest of
members, 248; blamed for
post-Suez Canal battle violence,
178; connection to, 172; dissolved by al-Nuqrashi, Mahmud
Fahmi, 121; founded by al-
Banna, Hasan, 1, 81–2; Guidance
Council of, 192, 194, 234;
ideology of, 127; imprisonment
and torture of members, 198,
201–2, 206, 227, 234; influence
of, 84, 124; influx of nationalist
support, 104; led by al-Hudaybi,
Husan, 176–7; led by Badi'a,
Muhammad, 229–30; moved to
Cairo, 83; perceived dealings
with regime of al-Nasser, Colonel
Gamar 'Abd, 256; perceived view
by Westerners, 144–5; procurement of weaponry, 233–4;
Propagation of the Call Department, 14, 187–8, 191; re-emergence of, 119, 279; regional
presence of, 238–9, 244; rein-
stated (1951), 121; Rover Scout
units of (Jawwala), 83–4, 86;
"Secret Appartus (al-jihaz)",
119–20; sponsored reprints of
Social Justice in Islam and The
Battle of Islam and Capitalism,
173; student support for, 250;
support for Palestinian Arabs, 99,
120; suppression of, 2, 14, 104,
188–9, 192, 254, 256, 279;
tension with RCC, 189, 191;
view of al-Fikr al-Jadid, 126;
writings of members of, 164–5
Muslims, 2–3, 18, 218; and Musha,
26, 28; earliest conversions to
Islam, 113–15, 203, 211, 225,
232; global population of, x, 4, 8,
15; history of, 136; Sunni, 1;
perceived western influence over,
1–2; scholars of, 111–12;
territory of, 1, 4, 17, 74, 136,
161–3, 172; youth, 3

Mustafa, Shukri: arrest and
sentencing of, 283; ideology of,
282–3; imprisonment of, 282
Mutran, Khalil: patron of Apollo
Society, 70–1

Nadwat al-Ulama: and Nadwi, Abu
al-Hasan, 240; correspondence
with, 240
Nadwi, Sayyid Abu Hassan; and
Hajj, 157–8; and Mawdudi, Abu
l-A'la, 158; What has the World
Lost with the Decline of Mus-
lims? 158, 217
Nallino, Carlo Alfonso; and
Husayn, Taha, 166; taught at
Egyptian University, 166
Nasif, Malak Hifni, 108
Nasr, Salah: and interrogation of
Qutb, Sayyid, 257–8
National Liberation Front (FLN):
communist infiltration of, 240
National Union; aims of, 195
Nationalist Party (Hizb al-Watani):
and Ibrahim, al-Hajj Qutb, 73;
and Wafd, 48, 54; founded by
Kamil, Mustafa, 46; led by Farid,
Muhammad and Jawish, 'Abd
al-'Aziz, 48
Neguib, General Muhammad:
arrest of, 190; correspondence
with al-Nahhas, Mustafa, 190;
president of Egyptian republic,
190
New York, 146; 9/11 attacks, 6,
155, 273, 292; potential terror
attacks, 116; Rockefeller
Institute, 91; visit to (1948),
141–4, 151
Non-Aligned Movement: creation
of, 105; meeting of, 162;
membership of, 162, 195

Ottoman Empire, 98; and Egypt,
47, 56, 97; and Hilmi II, 'Abbas,
47; fall of, 93; Sultan of, 34